Toward a New World Trade Policy: The Maidenhead Papers

Toward a New World Trade Policy: The Maidenhead Papers

Edited by
C. Fred Bergsten
The Brookings Institution

Lexington Books
D.C. Heath and Company
Lexington, Massachusetts
Toronto   London

Library of Congress Cataloging in Publication Data

Main entry under title:

Toward a new world trade policy.

    Papers prepared for a conference held in Apr. 1973 at
Maidenhead, Eng.
    Includes index.
    1. Commercial policy—Congresses. 2. Commerce—Congresses.
3. International business enterprises—Congresses. I. Bergsten, C.
Fred, 1941-   ed.
HF1410.T69   382.1   74-22304
ISBN 0-669-96743-2

Published simultaneously in Canada

Printed in the United States of America

International Standard Book Number: 0-669-96743-2

Library of Congress Catalog Card Number: 74-22304

Contents

List of Figures   ix

List of Tables   xi

Introduction, *C. Fred Bergsten*   3

Part I   *Traditional Trade Theory and the Realities of the 1970s*   17

Chapter 1   **Economic Assumptions of the Case for Liberal Trade,** *Richard N. Cooper*   19

Commentary, *Ryutaro Komiya*   33

Chapter 2   **The Probable Effects of Freer Trade on Individual Countries,** *Harry G. Johnson*   35

Chapter 3   **Freer Trade for Higher Employment and Price Level Stability,** *Herbert Giersch*   49

Commentary I, *George H. Hildebrand*   61
Commentary II, *Ryutaro Komiya*   65
Commentary III, *Harry G. Johnson*   67
Reply to Commentary III, *Herbert Giersch*   71

Part II   *Multinational Corporations and World Trade*   73

Chapter 4   **A Macroeconomic Theory of Foreign Direct Investment,** *Kiyoshi Kojima*   75

Appendix: Japanese Private Investment Abroad   101

Chapter 5   **Imperial Chemical Industries Limited: A Case Study,** *Michael Clapham*   105

Appendix: ICI Foreign Interests   113

Chapter 6   **The Case of Bendix,** *W. Michael Blumenthal*   115

Chapter 7   **The Japanese General Trading Company,** *Morihisa Emori*   127

Chapter 8   A Labor Approach to International Corporations, *Nat Weinberg*   137

Chapter 9   Multinational Companies and Trade Unions: A Japanese View, *Masao Aihara*   159

Part III   *The Role of Governments in International Trade and Investment in the 1970s*   171

Chapter 10   National Industrial Policies and International Trade, *Göran Ohlin*   173

Chapter 11   Japan and the World Economy, *Ryutaro Komiya*   183

Chapter 12   State Enterprises and International Trade, *Michael Clapham*   199

Part IV   *Responses to Disturbances Caused by International Trade*   207

Chapter 13   The Adjustment to Free Trade in the Common Market, *Albrecht Düren*   209

Chapter 14   The Trade Policy of the United Steelworkers of America, *Meyer Bernstein*   229

Chapter 15   On the Non-Equivalence of Import Quotas and Voluntary Export Restraints, *C. Fred Bergsten*   239

             Commentary, *Ryutaro Komiya*   273

Chapter 16   Safeguard Mechanisms, *Anthony M. Solomon*   277

             Commentary, *Ryutaro Komiya*   283

Chapter 17   Economic Adjustment to Liberal Trade: A New Approach, *U.S. Chamber of Commerce Task Force, chaired by C. Fred Bergsten*   285

Chapter 18   International Adjustment Assistance, *David Lea*   307

             Part IV Commentary, *Sidney Golt*   315

Part V	*World Trade Policies for the Future*	319
Chapter 19	**Negotiations in Prospect,** *Eric Wyndham-White*	321
Chapter 20	**Future Directions for U.S. Trade Policy,** *C. Fred Bergsten*	341
	Commentary: Recent U.S. Foreign Economic Policy from a Japanese Point of View, *Ryutaro Komiya*	359
Chapter 21	**Japan and the Future of World Trade Policy,** *Kiyoshi Kojima*	365
Appendix A	**The Maidenhead Communique**	373
Appendix B	**List of Participants**	377
	Index	379
	About the Editor and Contributors	395

List of Figures

3-1   Profit Rates and GNP Under Different Degrees of
Competition   55

4-1   Changes in Comparative Advantage Due to Foreign
Direct Investment   85

15-1   The Economic Effects of Trade Restrictions   246

15-2   The Economic Effects of QRs and VERs   252

List of Tables

4-1   Balance of Japan's Direct Overseas Investments, by Industry   78

4-2   Comparative Costs before Direct Investments   84

4-3   Comparative Costs When Direct Investments are Taking Place in Both Industries   85

4-4   Comparative Profit Rates for Country A   87

4-5   Comparative Costs when Direct Investments are Taking Place only in X-Industry   87

4-6   Comparative Profit Rates for Country P   88

4A-1   Japanese Private Investment Abroad   100

5A-1   ICI Foreign Interests   113

7-1   Total Business Turnover of Ten Leading General Trading Companies   130

13-1   European GNP Growth and Shares, 1949-1969   213

13-2   Business Formation and Failure in Germany, 1964-1967   215

13-3   Business Formation and Business Failures in France, 1962-1967   216

15-1   Major U.S. Imports Subject to Voluntary Export Restraints and Import Quotas, 1971   242

15-2   Steel Mill Products: Shipments, Exports, Imports, Apparent Supply, and Steel Trade Balance   249

Toward a New World Trade Policy: The Maidenhead Papers

Introduction

C. Fred Bergsten

In the early 1970s, it appeared that world trade policy was approaching a crucial crossroads. On the one hand, the steady reduction of barriers to international trade throughout the first postwar generation and the relatively effective role played by the General Agreement on Tariffs and Trade (GATT) in regulating commercial policy among nations were widely regarded as having made a major contribution to the economic prosperity of that period, and to political harmony among the non-communist countries. On the other hand, resort to trade barriers, a number of which took forms far more complex than the simple tariffs and quotas of the past, had been rising since the completion of the Kennedy Round in 1967 and protectionist pressures seemed to be intensifying throughout the world. In addition, many observers believed that the GATT had become obsolete and ineffectual in checking such steps. Compounding the dilemma was the widespread view that trade policy was dynamically unstable: it would inevitably move in either a liberalizing or restricting direction, and no *status quo* was tenable. Secretary of State Henry A. Kissinger crystallized this precarious balance when he testified to the Senate Finance Committee on December 3, 1974 that "The major trading nations stand today poised between liberalized trade and unilateral restrictive actions leading toward autarky." So world trade policy is poised at a point of high uncertainty, and the choice of policies in the next few years could well set its direction for a decade or more.

Underlying this policy dilemma were acute new intellectual problems. Did the free-trade recommendations of traditional economic theory continue to hold in a world increasingly influenced by multinational enterprises and state intervention? Did the achievement of a high measure of affluence throughout the industrialized world counsel a change in the traditional approaches to trade policy, as stability and economic security are accorded higher priority than marginal welfare gains in the minds of many and as the liberalization of the past may have already exploited most of the gains that are available? Or did the increasing importance of inflation throughout the world call for renewed attention to maximizing efficiency and the pressures of external competition? How could world trade policy be managed within the new economic structure in which the European Community and Japan had achieved positions comparable to that of the United States—the driving force behind the liberalization of the first postwar generation—particularly when the direction of the trade policy of the United States itself had become unclear? Scores of specific trade policy issues derived from these fundamental questions.

3

In early 1972, a small group of Americans—C. Fred Bergsten of the Brookings Institution, W. Michael Blumenthal of the Bendix Corporation, Richard N. Cooper of Yale University, and William Diebold of the Council on Foreign Relations—concluded that new ways of looking at these problems might be able to help advance both the intellectual understanding and policy thinking that seemed so important. They decided to focus on industrial trade among the industrialized countries, since that area appeared to present the most urgent policy problems and since trade between the industrialized countries and both the developing and non-market economies could not be adequately handled without greatly extending the agenda.[1] Such an effort required contributions from all of the major industrialized countries and from all of the major functional sectors involved directly in industrial trade issues, although all participants would at the same time have to speak wholly as individuals rather than as institutional representatives of the viewpoints of national or functional organizations. In part, this approach represented an effort to replicate the success of the "Bürgenstock" series of meetings on greater flexibility of exchange rates, in which Japanese, North American, and Western European bankers, businessmen, and economists had made a major contribution to the evolution of thinking about international monetary reform and toward the achievement of a consensus between academics and practitioners in 1968-69.[2]

The two trade policy conferences that resulted were thus attended by a small group of businessmen, economists, and labor leaders from Japan, the United States, and Western Europe. (A list of participants appears in Appendix B.) No government officials were involved, although several participants had served previously in their national governments. The conferences were administered by the Brookings Institution under a grant from the Ford Foundation.

This volume not only contains some of the papers prepared for a four-day conference held in April 1973 at Maidenhead, England (hence "The Maidenhead Papers") on the basis of an agenda developed at a two-day conference held in October 1972 in Bermuda, but also the comments on some of them by other participants. Most of the papers encompass both positive analysis and normative recommendations, as the conferees sought throughout to mesh intellectual progress and policy relevance. All of the papers were written in early 1973, although a few have been subsequently modified to a minor extent.

Part I addresses some of the key conceptual issues underlying trade policy in the 1970s. The basic objective of the chapters in Part I is to confront traditional theory with today's practical realities.

Richard N. Cooper begins Part I by systematically listing the assumptions that underlie traditional trade theory and assessing their validity for the 1970s. He notes that there are several conditions whose existence may in some cases justify exceptions to the free-trade recommendations that otherwise derive from trade theory: (1) inequitable distribution of income between or within countries, (2) unemployment, (3) balance-of-payments disequilibrium, (4) "external" effects such as pollution, (5) overdependence on foreign supplies, (6) imperfect markets that require governmental action to protect "infant industries," and (7) costs of adjustment to trade liberalization that exceed the longer term benefits (properly discounted) of that liberalization.

Cooper's "subjective assessment" of the practical importance of these considerations—which is augmented by the analyses of the impact of multinational enterprises and state intervention in Parts II and III—is that a number of them have existed in recent years. But he concludes that liberal trade coupled with complementary measures—such as a more effective international adjustment process (especially regarding exchange-rate changes) to prevent and correct payments disequilibria, antitrust policies to prevent undue market concentration, and manpower policies to help workers adjust to induced changes in the pattern of production—that would deal directly with the distortions cited is the best policy approach (which is a point echoed by Ryutaro Komiya in his commentary on Cooper's chapter). Moreover, in some cases liberal trade helps directly to reduce market distortions, especially in oligopolistic industries.

Trade theory posits that *world* welfare will be enhanced by free trade, but does not necessarily conclude that each *individual country* participating in such a policy will benefit as well. In Chapter 2, Harry Johnson assesses the impact of freer trade on individual countries. One of his major conclusions is that trade liberalization, though its effect is small relative to total national income for most countries, "probably dominates other *policy change* one could seriously consider" in terms of improving economic welfare. He also notes that contrary to some current thinking, small and poor countries stand to gain the most from a liberal regime of international trade and, with Cooper, that the largest countries have the greatest opportunities for exploiting monopoly or monopsony power by levying restrictions on their trade. However, he concludes that the two major theoretical exceptions to the general case for free trade—the "optimum tariff" approach, and the infant-industry case—"do not stand out as significant empirical possibilities in the modern world."

Johnson does find that two problems of contemporary international economic relations—the international mobility of capital and of technology, both of which are excluded by the assumptions of the classical model—*do* raise the theoretical possibility that individual countries can maximize their welfare, particularly the welfare of their labor forces—through imposing barriers to international transactions. Again, however, he finds the practical possibilities for doing so to be extremely limited. Through his analysis, Johnson begins the analytical integration of trade and investment flows that is an important theme of this volume as well as of the current policy debate.

In one of the most important chapters in this volume, Herbert Giersch argues, in Chapter 3, that free trade raises the level of aggregate employment and can play a significant role in alleviating the conflict between high employment and stable prices. He bases his view on a model of "stagflation" (the combination of high unemployment and inflation that has become a common problem throughout the world) that identifies monopoly as the major source of difficulty. (In Commentary I, George Hildebrand adds that changes in the structure of the labor force are also a major part of the problem in the United States.) Giersch then suggests that the injection of new elements of competition is a far more effective policy response than either incomes policies or cutbacks in domestic demand and that for virtually all countries such injections must derive from global—not solely internal—policies, including freer trade and certain types of foreign investment. (Komiya, in Commentary II, adds that the theory of economic policy suggests that individual policy instruments should under some conditions be assigned to specific policy targets and that trade policy would appear far more suited to help promote efficient allocation of resources than to combat unemployment directly.) Finally, Giersch outlines a variety of ways in which the risks engendered by such increased competition can be shared among entrepreneurs, workers, and governments, which augments the analyses of adjustment problems in Part IV.

Part II turns to the relationship between multinational corporations and world trade. It encompasses chapters on the subject from the academic world, from officials of the firms themselves, and from labor.

Kiyoshi Kojima launches the section, in Chapter 4, by arguing that some types of foreign direct investment promote trade by accelerating the transmission of comparative advantage among countries, while some types instead substitute for trade. He views most Japanese foreign investment as trade-creating, motivated by both economic incentives and conscious policy of the Japanese government to export low-wage (and polluting) industries to (primarily) the developing countries. On the other hand, U.S. firms in precisely these same industries (such as steel and textiles) have *not* invested abroad. Instead, most U.S. foreign investment (aside from raw materials) takes place near the top of the product cycle by firms seeking to preserve their oligopolistic positions in world markets. Kojima characterizes this as "trade-destroying investment"—and hence, in the home country, job-destroying and producing balance-of-payments problems as well—on the grounds that such market positions could be maintained by exports by the same firms from their U.S. base. This thesis runs counter to the product-cycle view that trade and investment are complements in such industries, not substitutes, and will undoubtedly generate efforts to test it empirically. Kojima concludes that investment policy should be subordinated to trade policy: trade policy should remain liberal, and "trade-oriented" investment should be encouraged—subject to a number of guidelines that he enumerates—but "anti-trade-oriented" investment should be subject to restrictions by either home or host countries, or both.

In the next three chapters, the company studies by Michael Clapham (Imperial Chemical Industries), Michael Blumenthal (Bendix), and Morihisa Emori (Mitsubishi) present the history and operations of each firm. The authors re-emphasize the existence of wide divergences among firms, and even among the different divisions of individual firms, as well as the resultant difficulties of intellectual or policy generalization. Clapham and Blumenthal stress the importance, for a variety of reasons, to their companies of being present within each of their major markets. Emori focuses on the wide range of functions of the typical Japanese trading company, how it turns very small profit margins on a huge volume of business, how it will in the future become deeply engaged in both outward and inward foreign investment, and (with Kojima) how Japan will in the future be consciously exporting a number of industries to other countries.

Several interesting implications for policy emerge. All three case studies highlight the fact that much foreign direct investment is motivated by tariff or non-tariff barriers to trade. Blumenthal and Clapham agree that differences in national tax rates are usually subsidiary or inconsequential elements in their investment planning, but Blumenthal cites several cases where such differences have been important. Moreover, he confirms that the tax (and other) concessions that countries employ in an effort to attract investment do work in practice, while a recent U.S. tax incentive to promote exports (the DISC) instead of foreign investment has had little impact. Blumenthal also demonstrates how Bendix has provided intra-firm relocation for workers whose jobs were exported by foreign investment, and he takes a dim view of intra-corporate pricing practices that deviate from arm's-length outcomes because of their negative effects on incentives to managers within the firm and hence to efficient output.

Chapters 8 and 9 present the reactions to multinational firms of labor union officials from the United States and Japan. In Chapter 8, Nat Weinberg rejects some of the assumptions underlying traditional trade theory (particularly the existence of full employment, price competition, and international factor immobility) and calls for a wide array of new policy measures to check multinational firms, by analogy with the legislation adopted in most countries to regulate internal corporate activity—which he feels are generally inadequate to deal with firms at the international level. Weinberg lists a number of abuses that he feels have been perpetuated by such firms and proposes a wide-ranging series of "countermeasures" in response, some of which are to operate at the national level (including requirements that the firms provide adjustment assistance for workers laid off due to foreign investments, as Blumenthal indicates has been done by

Bendix) and others through intergovernmental agreement (including "redemption" of the dollar overhang through foreign purchases of the foreign subsidiaries of the U.S. firms "to reverse the trend toward world oligopoly"). He places heavy emphasis on the behavior of firms toward their workers, particularly in the countries abroad in which they are investing, and recommends the adoption of a code of "international fair labor standards."

In Chapter 9, Masao Aihara points to some "merits" of multinationals and the dangers of economic isolationism, but he echoes Weinberg in calling for steps to eliminate the "demerits" of the firms—their impact on job security, the rights of trade unions, the bargaining power of labor, and social justice in host countries. He places great emphasis on strengthening cooperation among national trade unions to meet the challenges posed by the firms, traces some of the history of that effort to date, and candidly lays out some of the difficulties among labor groups that have precluded further progress of such cooperative efforts.

Part III takes up the other major non-market force in international trade—that is, national governments. The focus is not the traditional governmental role in levying tariffs and quotas, but rather its role in affecting trade indirectly through the whole range of modern "domestic" economic and social policies (Chapters 10 and 11) and directly through state enterprises (Chapter 12).

In Chapter 10, Göran Ohlin first describes the kinds of measures that comprise "national industrial policies" (adjustment assistance, aid to declining industries, regional policies, the pursuit of high technology, defensive moves against foreign investment, export promotion, government procurement and credit) and assesses their impact on international trade. He concludes that many of these policies have developed precisely because the reduction of the traditional barriers to trade and international capital movements prompted governments to look for new instruments to achieve their varied—and growing—goals (which is the view shared by Michael Clapham in Chapter 12). Ohlin thus raises deep questions about the degree of real liberalization of international trade that has actually occurred in the past. For the future, he would add industrial policy to the agenda for international trade negotiations. However, he is not sanguine about achieving far-reaching new agreements, both because of the complexity of the issues and because such agreements would require "the abandonment precisely of the national orientation which is its [industrial policy's] hallmark."

In Chapter 11, Ryutaro Komiya dissects "Japan, Inc.," which many view as the most all-encompassing government enterprise of all. He places the Japanese economy in its historical context, explains the social bases for several key Japanese policies (e.g., agricultural protectionism), and describes in detail the process of Japanese economic decision making with regard both to principal actors (including conflicts among them) and policies used. He argues that the yen was substantially overvalued at least until 1965, which required the import controls and export promotion that developed, but he is unsure that the policies raised the rate of economic growth. He cites numerous instances of erroneous and inconsistent government policies and criticizes the failure of policy to respond to the dramatic changes in Japan's external position after 1965. For Japan in the future, he counsels a flexible exchange rate, free trade and capital movements (with government intervention only in "exceptional cases"), an effort to reach international agreement on import safeguard measures and adjustment assistance, deficiency payments (rather than price supports) to protect existing farmers, and direct subsidies to "technological spearhead industries" such as computers.

Michael Clapham, in Chapter 12, provides an analysis of state interventions that may affect international trade: government ownership and management of monopolies or near-monopolies, government procurement, subsidies to labor, the unrequited provision of capital to particular firms, sectoral (especially agricultural) support schemes, cheap export credits, and investment controls. He stresses the legitimacy of the objectives of many of these policies and writes that whether they actually do affect trade flows is an empirical issue to be determined on a case-by-case basis. To prevent trade distortions from arising, Clapham concludes that "it is absolutely essential that all government intervention measures should be transparent"(i.e., fully disclosed to the public) and calls for codification of the relative acceptability of different types of government subvention (tied to the "gravity" of the problem, in the case of regional policy), compensation when other countries suffer injury, and early liberalization of existing restrictions, such as those on government procurement, wherever possible.

Part IV turns to responses to trade flows by the different economic sectors—mainly workers, but also firms and communities—that have been adversely affected. This issue is critical for both economic and political reasons. Economically, as Cooper pointed out in Chapter 1, the costs of adjustment must be compared with the benefits of freer trade in judging the merits of alternative policies. Politically, the fully understandable distaste for dislocation by those who are dislocated, as the result of a policy adopted to promote the welfare of society as a whole, is usually a significant element in determining whether such policies will be adopted or maintained.

There are two broad approaches for public policy to cope with the dislocations caused by trade flows. Either the trade itself can be checked, or help can be provided to those who are adversely affected—that is, to compensate for the losses they suffer in the short run and to facilitate their adjustment into new endeavors for the long run. Part IV begins with two chapters that assess the actual adjustment problems confronted in two very different circumstances and then proceeds to two chapters on each of these policy approaches.

The first of the adjustment circumstances, the move by the Common Market to internal free trade, is analyzed by Albrecht Düren in Chapter 13. He notes that in practice very few serious adjustment problems resulted from this most far-reaching of all trade liberalizations. Moreover, the massive adjustment that did occur resulted primarily from successful macroeconomic growth policies and adaptation by firms themselves, including some industrial reorganization, in the face of the certain elimination of all tariffs on intra-Community trade. Specific aids to adjustment were available but were used very little in the process as it actually developed. Düren is properly cautious about generalizing from the European experience. But lessons can certainly be drawn from its successful combination of liberalization on a fixed and unswerving timetable, advance notice to all concerned, and the availability of specific adjustment assistance measures—in a milieu of rapid growth, full employment, and few balance-of-payments constraints.

Chapter 14 views the problem of adjustment from the standpoint of a large group of workers in an industry affected by rapidly rising imports —the United Steelworkers of America. The chapter is written in a highly personal style by Meyer Bernstein, the long-time director of the International Affairs Department of that union, and provides fascinating insights into the economics and policies of the U.S. steel industry and union. Bernstein opposed their shift to protectionism, which in the case of the union came later than for the firms and was closely tied to issues wholly unrelated to trade. But he calls for effective programs—both restrictions on trade and help for those who must adjust to it—to deal with the problems of trade-impacted workers. Bernstein provides evidence of the failures of the adjustment assistance program undertaken by the U.S. government since 1962 and thus some of the basis for the changes proposed in that program in Chapter 17.

In Chapter 15, C. Fred Bergsten analyzes "voluntary" export restraint agreements (VERs), the barrier to imports most frequently employed by the industrialized countries in recent years. He systematically compares VERs with import quotas and finds that there are significant differences between them in both economic (particularly effectiveness and allocative) and political terms. Bergsten concludes that the VERs of the recent past have hurt international trade and trade policy more than traditional import quotas, because they have been adopted outside the structures of both national and international trade law, and should be brought strictly within the provisions thereof if they are to be used at all in the future.

In Chapter 16, Anthony M. Solomon addresses the overall question of import safeguards and proposes a new two-track mechanism through which individual countries could provide their industries with temporary relief from import competition. Under the first track, countries could restrain imports only through a series of steps outlined in a new GATT procedure, including both an internal determination based on public hearings of the existence of serious injury and international consultations on the actions that they planned to take. In return for complying with these rules, the restraining country would have no obligation to compensate others for its action (or accept retaliation against its exports). Under the second track, where a country acted outside the new rules, it would be obligated to provide compensation or accept retaliation, which would be determined, if necessary, by a compulsory arbitration panel in the GATT.

Solomon's proposal would in effect amend Article 19 of the GATT and should be seen in the context of the call by Eric Wyndham-White in Chapter 19 for general GATT reform. As part of the proposal, Solomon calls for the possibility of applying the new import safeguards on a discriminatory basis, as opposed to the most-favored-nation requirement of the present GATT rules (but corresponding to the practice that has evolved in the implementation of "voluntary" export restraint agreements). This view, which is shared by Wyndham-White in Chapter 19, is opposed in a comment by Ryutaro Komiya on the grounds that such discrimination could hurt developing countries in the early stages of industrialization.

The last two chapters in Part IV analyze adjustment assistance, the alternative to import relief. Chapter 17, prepared in late 1972 by a Task Force of the U.S. Chamber of Commerce chaired by C. Fred Bergsten, assesses the shortcomings of the U.S. program as it developed under the Trade Expansion Act of 1962 and proposes comprehensive changes to improve it. The proposals focus on the criteria under which workers, firms, and communities should be eligible for assistance; ways to provide early warning that such problems are developing; temporary compensation for import-dislocated workers; promotion of real adjustment; administration of the proposed new program; and the costs of the proposals. The proposals of the Task Force were never formally adopted by the Chamber, but were used by the Ways and Means Committee of the House of Representatives as the basis for the adjustment assistance chapters of what eventually became the Trade Act of 1974.

David Lea broadens the issue, in Chapter 18, by outlining the proposals of the Trades Union Congress of the United Kingdom for international financing for national adjustment assistance programs. He also argues that the industrial countries will need the right institutional framework within which to exercise a degree of mutual surveillance of "adjustment assistance" to ensure that their individual programs do not become permanent subsidies to particular industries, and he believes that the OECD is the right body for this job. Lea focuses on adjustment to imports from the developing countries, and hence links adjustment assistance with the extension of foreign aid. Nevertheless, his proposals could, with modifications, be applied to the financing of programs to promote adjustment to imports from all sources.

In his commentary on several chapters in Part IV, Sidney Golt draws a sharp distinction between the major trade policy problems of 1947, when the GATT was written, and the major trade policy problems of the present. In 1947, the world was "wheel-shaped. . . with the United States at the hub and the rest of us round the rim . . .," and the problem was how the non-U.S. countries could "ration their dollar resources among their own competing claims." It was not, like today, a problem of protecting individual domestic industries in a world of "much more nearly equal giant trading partners." Golt thus paves the way for Part V, which seeks to develop new directions for world trade policy.

Part V presents views and proposals for the future of world trade policy from the vantage point of each of the three major geographical areas: Europe, Japan, and the United States. Eric Wyndham-White, who was one of the founding fathers of the GATT and as Director-General guided its first two decades of existence, launches the section by suggesting that the present trade rules are "inadequate and inappropriate" and calling for a renegotiation of the GATT. He proposes changes in many of the existing GATT rules and institutional arrangements, including those that bar discrimination among countries in the implementation of trade policy, involve quantitative import restrictions, deal with balance-of-payments problems, enable old members to continue to discriminate against new members, and permit sanctions against offenders of the rules. He makes specific proposals for altering the import safeguard provisions of Article 19—including the creation of "an international court of justice for trade matters"—that compare with the Solomon suggestions in Chapter 16. And he calls for sweeping changes in the membership of the GATT—including the elimination of multiple membership for the European Community and of all membership for the developing countries—in order to revive its effectiveness in dealing with trade policy disputes. Wyndham-White lays out a detailed scenario through which such changes and an associated resumption of reductions in trade barriers might be accomplished "to build a trading system which looks forward to the eighties and not back to the forties."

C. Fred Bergsten, in Chapter 20, views the future of world trade policy from the perspective of the United States. He analyzes several issues that will go far to determine U.S. trade policy in the coming years, which will in turn have a major impact on world trade policy: the link between trade and international monetary policy (which is also addressed in Ryutaro Komiya's critical comment on U.S. efforts to wrest unilateral trade concessions from Japan); the related question of whether U.S. trade policy will be seeking the traditional objective of higher levels of trade or rather an improvement in the U.S. trade balance; the definition and implementation of "reciprocity"; internal adjustment to external disturbances (as discussed in Part IV); and the negotiating relationships among the United States and other countries. Bergsten's conclusions from a U.S. standpoint reinforce those of Wyndham-White, from a more global standpoint, that the agenda for world trade policy is quite long and that major progress is not likely in the next few years despite the statements of a number of key governments.

In the final chapter of this volume, Kiyoshi Kojima calls for a completely new approach to world trade policies. He doubts the feasibility of another round of reciprocal reductions of tariff and non-tariff barriers and argues that those remaining are "hard core" and hence not susceptible to such an approach and that there is no way to define reciprocity for non-tariff barriers in any event. He looks instead for unilateral reductions and elimination of barriers by individual countries in pursuit of their own internal interests such as fighting inflation (which is the argument for liberalization made by Giersch in Chapter 3). However, Kojima would also support the achievement of "reciprocity over time," through which countries would completely abolish their industrial duties over ten years by moving unilaterally when each is in balance-of-payments surplus. Kojima views such policies as highly desirable for Japan, especially in view of the "free ride"—far greater expansion of export opportunities than of import liberalization—which his calculations indicate was obtained by Japan in the Kennedy Round.

Based on the papers presented as chapters in this volume, the conferees adopted "The Maidenhead Communique" at the conclusion of their second meeting. No such product was planned by the steering committee. During the course of the four days at Maidenhead, however, it became apparent that despite the diverse geographic and functional interests of the participants, a wide measure of agreement existed on a number of the key analytical and policy issues under discussion. In addition, several conferees expressed the view that a statement of such conclusions might prove helpful both to governments and to non-governmental observers in their own efforts to deal with trade policy problems. The communique was thus drafted and issued on April 12, 1973, and received widespread press attention in Japan, the United States, and Western Europe.

The communique, which is reprinted in Appendix A, calls for immediate efforts by the major countries "to head off the severe risks of further slippage toward protectionism" and to fill "the present trade policy vacuum" with renewed movement toward trade liberalization and reform instead. The primary objectives of such an effort would be to help fight inflation, as outlined by Giersch in Chapter 3, and to remove the artificial incentives that tariffs and other trade barriers provide to multinational enterprises to invest abroad, as revealed in several papers in Part II.

To achieve this goal, the communique departs from the conventional wisdom of seeking a new trade-liberalizing negotiation à la Kennedy Round by focusing instead on " reassessing and reforming the rules which govern international trade'' and looking to the possibility of unilateral steps by individual countries, as they seek to deal with their own inflationary problems, to restore momentum to the reduction of trade barriers. The group was encouraged by the virtual absence of adjustment problems which arose during the postwar trade liberalization—even in cases such as the European Community that eliminated trade barriers altogether—but recognized that such problems could develop and hence proposed a series of measures to help deal with them when necessary.

Events subsequent to the Maidenhead meeting appear to lend support to the proposed approach. Numerous countries have indeed unilaterally reduced their barriers to imports, as inflation has accelerated further throughout the world, and thus promoted a new liberalization of world trade. (Indeed, some countries have moved to the opposite extreme by imposing *export* controls, which is a major issue for contemporary trade policy not foreseen at the Maidenhead meeting and thus not covered in this volume.)[3] At the same time, protectionist pressures have revived as a result of the world economic slowdown and the balance-of-payments problems triggered for some countries by the sharp rise in oil prices. The efforts to launch a major international trade negotiation have stalled on several occasions. Dissatisfaction with the rules and institutions governing world trade has continued to grow. Concerns about international investment, including its impact on trade flows, also continue to grow.

The papers in the volume thus address some of the key issues that will determine the trade relations of the industrialized countries for the coming years, offer judgments as to the most desirable outcomes, and propose possible ways for achieving those outcomes. The Bermuda and Maidenhead meetings, at which they were proposed and discussed, demonstrated that thorough discussions of such issues and proposals could generate a surprising degree of consensus among observers from different continents and from different sectors of society. The arrangers of the sessions, and all participants in them, hope that this volume will contribute to better understanding of the issues and perhaps to such consensus on a broader scale.

Notes

1. Important implications can be drawn from the papers in the volume for the trade policies of the developing countries, however. See especially Chapters 3 and 4. For policy proposals regarding the increasingly important

area of trade between industrialized and developing countries see C. Fred Bergsten, "The Response to the Third World," *Foreign Policy* 17, Winter 1974-75.

2. The results of those conferences were published as *Approaches to Greater Flexibility of Exchange Rates: The Bürgenstock Papers*, arranged by C. Fred Bergsten, George N. Halm, Fritz Machlup, and Robert V. Roosa (Princeton, N.J.: Princeton University Press, 1970).

3. For an analysis of that issue, see C. Fred Bergsten, *Completing the GATT: Toward New International Rules to Govern Export Controls*, British-North American Committee, 1974.

**Part I
Traditional Trade Theory
and the Reality of the 1970s**

1

Economic Assumptions of the Case for Liberal Trade

Richard N. Cooper

This chapter outlines briefly the intellectual case for liberal trade and discusses the economic assumptions on which that case rests. It concludes with a subjective assessment of the relative importance of these assumptions in the real world.

The case for liberal trade is essentially the same as the case for a voluntary exchange economy extended to other countries. The case for an exchange economy—as opposed to individual or familial self-sufficiency—rests on the rise in real income that can be obtained by all individuals when each concentrates his efforts on the marketable activities he is best able to do and exchanges the production in excess of his own needs for goods and services that others can produce with relatively greater efficiency through similar concentration of effort. This basic argument does not stop at national borders. Unless exchange can take place readily between as well as within nations, the benefits from trading with foreigners having special skills or technology or location will be lost, and incomes will be lower as a result.

Foreign trade thus represents a possible extension of the production opportunities of every country. If a country's citizens desire to purchase a particular good (or service), the country can either devote its own resources—labor, capital, natural resources—to production of the good, *or* it can devote its resources to the production of something quite different that can in turn be exchanged for the desired good. The latter alternative often will require far fewer resources than the former. This will be true for a variety of reasons. Strong locational factors (e.g., climate, soil quality, good natural harbors), economies of scale, and substantial differences in land per worker, capital per worker, or worker skills all give rise to substantial gains from trade.

This basic proposition holds for all economies, regardless of their form of organization; it is applicable whether an economy is competitive or monopolistic, whether it is capitalist or socialist or communist.

The case for liberal trade (i.e., trade without impediments to making the best possible exchange) does however rest on the philosophical assumption that production is not an end in itself, but only a means to the goods and services produced to satisfy human wants. It also assumes therefore that economic gains by the citizens of other countries are not losses to the citizens of our country—that is, in matters of trade, the world is engaged in

19

a positive sum game. Economists have always recognized that satisfying human wants in the form of goods and services is not the exclusive aim of mankind. In particular, they have acknowledged that "defense is more important than opulence" (or, as it has been put more recently, "prosperity is not a substitute for security"). They are also conscious of the dignity of honest effort. But by and large, they have assumed that labor is a means to an end, not an end in itself, and that as a means, labor can be applied with equal satisfaction to any of a variety of activities and therefore should be applied to those activities where it yields, through production and exchange, the greatest rewards in terms of satisfying human wants.

Under conditions of a competitive market economy, the case for liberal trade, with two broad classes of exceptions, is really a case for free trade (i.e., for the ability of citizens of one country to trade with those of another without government-imposed impediments or stimulants to trade such as tariffs, import quotas, or export subsidies).

The first broad class of exceptions concerns the distribution of income or, more generally, of welfare among those who are affected by free exchange. The second broad class of exceptions concerns discrepancies between the market prices reached in a market economy and the true social cost of production. Each of these classes of exceptions will be taken up in turn and will be followed by a discussion of the time dimension in trade policies—that is, the fact that costs associated with a given change in trade policy may arise during a different time period from the benefits. Finally, a highly subjective assessment of the practical importance of these possible exceptions to the case for liberal trade will be made.

Distributional Effects

If trade is allowed to take place freely between nations, the distribution of income will generally differ from the distribution under a regime in which trade is not allowed to take place freely. Sometimes the effect is on the distribution of income *between* the trading countries (on the assumption that the residents of each country can be meaningfully aggregated into "countries"). A country that has some monopoly power either as a seller or a buyer can improve its real income by restricting its trade somewhat, by in effect imposing a tax on those foreigners that are willing to pay prices above cost.

Sometimes the effect is on the distribution of income *within* the trading countries. Even when a liberal trade policy benefits the country as a whole—by raising total GNP, for instance, or by permitting greater leisure—it may still reduce the real income of certain residents who, because of their special skills or their location, would benefit by restrictions on imported goods. In general, a policy of liberal trade will favor those elements of the economy whose efforts or resources are used relatively intensively in production for export, especially if they are keyed specifically to those industries and are relatively immobile. Cutting down trade will hurt this group for the benefit of those who compete most intensively with imported goods and services.

The theory of welfare economics suggests that liberal trade is superior to restricted trade in spite of these distributional effects, provided that income is redistributed from the prospective gainers to the prospective losers. Since total income will have been increased, it should be possible, by suitable redistribution, to make everyone better off.

When this issue arises *between* nations, it calls for grants from one nation to another—that is, for "foreign aid." As the world is presently structured—with the United States being the single largest national market and hence having the largest "monopsony power," which gives it the greatest gain from restricting trade—this principle would call anomalously for grants from other countries to the United States.

When the distributional issue arises *within* countries it assumes there is a costless mechanism for achieving the required redistribution. Since virtually all taxes introduce their own distortions, however, the process of redistribution almost always itself entails a cost. It may be, therefore, that restrictions on trade are the most economical (i.e., least inefficient) way to achieve a desired distribution of income. While this is a logical possibility, however, it would be surprising indeed if our social notions about desirable distributions of income generally took the relatively few particular forms that could best be achieved by restrictions on foreign trade, although it may do so in a few countries.

Market Prices not Equal to Social Costs

The second broad class of possible qualifications to the case for liberal trade concerns instances in which market prices convey the wrong signals to producers and consumers from a social point of view. This can happen in a large number of different circumstances, and only the most important of them will be reviewed here. Several of these price distortions can pervade the entire economy; most significant distortions concern the failure to achieve full employment in a national recession and the failure to achieve balance-of-payments equilibrium because a country's exchange rate is held at an inappropriate level. Other discrepancies between market prices and social costs operate in particular industries or in particular locations within a country, as when an industry is monopolized by one firm, or when some firms are unable to borrow adequate capital at competitive rates.

Full Employment

The most important assumption underlying the case for liberal trade is that each country's resources will be fully employed. This does not mean that all resources (productive land, the capital stock, and the labor force) will be fully employed all the time, for that is neither possible nor desirable in a dynamic economy. Capital becomes obsolete, the pattern of demand changes, technology alters costs, and all of these factors will give rise to temporary unemployment associated with adjustment to the new circumstances. But it does mean both that most resources are employed most of the time and that any unemployment of resources that does arise is of short duration. If these conditions do not obtain, then a country may be better off under certain circumstances by restricting imports from abroad and under other circumstances by subsidizing exports. In industrialized countries modern techniques of macroeconomic management through monetary and fiscal policy undercut any need to restrict or stimulate trade artificially on a lasting basis in order to maintain employment. Modern techniques of macroeconomic management have not succeeded in avoiding economic recessions altogether, however, so this particular flaw in the price system does exist, even in advanced economies. But trade policies are sufficiently inertial in their effects that they are particularly inappropriate to deal with it. In periods of high unemployment, it is understandably common to hear calls for protection against imported goods, which are seen to compete wastefully with goods and services that could be produced by unemployed domestic labor and capital and land. But appropriate monetary and fiscal policies can generally deal with that unemployment both faster and at lower cost.

Equilibrium in International Payments

A second key assumption underlying the case for liberal trade is that international payments will remain in balance. In this sense the case pertains to the long run, for it is recognized that in any given short period of time payments may be out of equilibrium. Any disequilibrium, however, is assumed to be corrected within a relatively short period of time. Since in the long run a country's payments must be in equilibrium, the difficult problem arises in the "medium run" of two to ten years, in which a country may be able to finance a payments disequilibrium rather than eliminate it.

Since the case for liberal trade is based on specialization and exchange, it does not encompass the case in which, say, a country maintains an overvalued currency for several years—to the point at which a number of firms that compete with imports during the period of disequilibrium are driven from business—or the case in which a country artificially builds up a substantial export industry that can thrive only so long as the country's exchange rate is undervalued. These transactions involve the exchange of goods and services, not for other goods and services or even for long-term debt that represents claims on future goods and services, but for short-term IOUs or other liquid assets that cannot be considered long-term debt.[1] It is the classic case, for a country in deficit, of living beyond its means or, for a country in surplus, of failing to enjoy the maximum possible standard of living. Under these circumstances, firms and workers may be placed under unwarranted hardship in competition from imports that cannot persist, but can persist long enough to do damage.

An undervalued exchange rate may mistakenly attract capital and labor into an industry because of its medium-term capacity to compete with foreign products, but these resources will have to leave the industry when the exchange rate is altered. Under such circumstances, some restrictions on imports by a country with an overvalued currency may be preferable to completely unimpeded trade until such time as the exchange rate is changed. This willingness of the residents of one country to subsidize consumption in another, even when it is known that the subsidy cannot last, should not, however, be considered an unmitigated bad. The particular case must be examined closely to determine the optimal policy.

Market Distortions

Apart from the total market for labor and capital and the market for foreign exchange, distortions arising in any number of particular markets may also affect the case for liberal trade, at least for the affected products. Traditionally, deviations from competition, where one or several firms influence prices by restricting supply, have been the most commonly discussed form of market distortion. Liberal trade operates directly to weaken this form of distortion, however, by increasing the degree of competition in national markets. (Liberal capital movements, in contrast, may increase the degree of oligopoly in the world economy.)

The kind of market imperfection most commonly discussed today concerns "external effects," such as congestion and pollution, that represent social costs but are not costs of production paid by the firm. A liberal trade policy may stimulate an export industry that is a heavy polluter, for example, and the result is more pollution under a liberal trade policy than under a restrictive one. (Of course, the effect could also go the other way. If import-competing industries are heavier polluters than export industries, liberal trade will reduce pollution; this in reality is probably the case for the United States.) Or a liberal trade policy may lead to the demise of an efficient processor whose domestic source of bulky raw material is subject to monopoly pricing, but whose foreign competitors are not placed at a similar disadvantage. (Again, this effect could also go the other way, if the firm facing a monopolist is in an export industry.)

In each of these cases of market distortion, the most appropriate course of action is to eliminate the distortions directly, so that market prices reflect social costs. If it is infeasible to eliminate the distortion, then we are in a world of what economists have come to call "second best," in which a restrictive trade policy may lead to a higher level of welfare than would a liberal trade policy. Trade restrictions may become a second-best policy for dealing with the distortions. But they may not. The analytical difficulty with a world of market imperfections is that easy generalization becomes impossible. Trade restrictions may alleviate the particular problem, but they may also aggravate it, as when they protect a national oligopoly from foreign competition. Each particular case must be examined on its merits by taking into account the ramifications of actions in one area of the economy on other, even seemingly remote, areas of the economy. For this reason also, it is preferable to attack market distortions directly rather than indirectly.

One important possible source of misunderstanding arises in the realm of market imperfections, particularly as governments engage in increasingly detailed governance of national economies. Complaints have been raised about the trade-distorting effects of "regional" policies adopted by many governments in Europe, and a similar issue has been raised with respect to the controls on pollution urged in the United States. But if these policies are accurately aimed at correcting market imperfections, then while they may influence trade flows, they do not *distort* trade flows; on the contrary, they "undistort" trade flows, and thus strengthen the case for liberal trade. A difficulty and a danger is that policies whose origins are to eliminate distortions or inequities may in the course of time take on a life of their own, and be extended where they are not warranted.

Social Risk Aversion

All the previous conditions may be met and a country still might feel the need to restrict trade artificially to avoid becoming overspecialized. A highly specialized economy is more vulnerable to disturbance (e.g., from weather, or from economic developments abroad) than is a widely diversified economy. The residents of a country may be willing to forego some income for the sake of greater stability in income—a lower vulnerability to cyclical shifts in demand from abroad or to technological changes affecting demand for its products. In technical terms, the residents may have a high degree of risk aversion.

But if they are highly averse to risk, will residents not undertake defensive action on an individual basis? Is there any special reason for *social* action on these grounds? In this area, as in the cases discussed above, social action is required only if there is a "distortion" in the choices that individuals and firms face, a distortion that does not reflect the true social choices. Families and firms do have a variety of ways in which they can diversify against risks. Indeed, it is frequently suggested that risk averse firms take more defensive action than the social situation would warrant, for they are concerned with the risks arising from actions of competing firms as well as risks arising for the industry as a whole, and the total risks they perceive exceed the true social risks.

In the case of overspecialization of an entire economy, however, it is possible that residents perceive less risk than is socially present. Any economy appears quite diverse to the individuals in it; there are countless activities to provide services for the local urban and rural populations. Movement into and out of these service activities is often easy for any small number of workers. This being so, workers may collectively flock to the specialized, high-wage export industries, in the confidence that if they should be laid off, they can find employment in the local service industries. But of course this may not be so; major lay-offs will result in severe competition for the service jobs, and they will also perversely reduce the number of service jobs, since purchasing power arising from the export industry has fallen. Of course, only one experience of this type should be necessary to eliminate the myopic behavior of individual workers; but there may be a collective interest in avoiding that experience. Thus, there may be grounds for social action to discourage undue specialization. Such a justification is sometimes given for the protection of local agriculture, against the contingency of a war or other event that reduces or eliminates imported supplies.

The Time Dimension

The "infant-industry" argument has long been acceptable (in certain forms) as an exception to the case for liberal trade. But this argument is simply one of several examples where the analytical question involves comparing costs to society at one point in time with benefits to society accruing at a different point in time. The infant-industry argument has been based on two different elements: learning by doing and economies of scale. One argument runs that an operation that is inefficient at the outset may through experience become efficient, for more economical ways of doing things are discovered with practice. Another argument runs that economies of scale in production, especially in modern manufacturing, may be such that a firm that seems inefficient at a low level of output may be very efficient at a higher level of output. In both cases, it has been argued, protection from imports in the early stages is necessary to permit the firm or industry to get established, at which point the economies (of learning and of scale) will be such that the investment will have been well justified. If this is expected to be the case, however, it might well be asked why the protection is necessary at all, since if the investment will be justified, some entrepreneur will make the investment even without protection. Moreover, import tariffs or other impediments to imports have the perverse effect of raising the domestic prices of those goods, which thus discourages consumption and prolongs the period at which maximum scale economies are achieved.

Thus to represent good policy the infant-industry argument needs some further assumptions. One might be that capital markets are so imperfect that even a very good investment cannot be financed during the investment period. This may well be the case in many less-developed countries, and moderate protection there may represent a second-best measure to a policy of improving capital markets. Another is that the economies of scale are of such a nature that they cannot be achieved by a single firm—that is, they are external to each firm but internal to an industry. Examples would be the shared system of transportation and communication that develops in any industrial area or the training of a well-disciplined and effective labor force.

Whether a policy of protection—or better, a policy of subsidization of the industry, if low-cost taxes can be found—makes sense in these cases then depends upon how well this particular "investment" will pay off relative to alternative investments, and that in turn involves calculations using some discount rate. Even when the infant-industry argument seems to be applicable, protection may still be poor policy because alternative investments are even better. And of course it is intrinsic in the infant-industry case that protection be only for a limited period of time.

The time dimension also comes up in the reverse case—that is, in moving to liberal trade from a position of protection, rather than to protection from a position of liberal trade, as in the infant-industry case. It is not costless to move resources about. Labor has to be retrained and possibly moved physically, capital has to be scrapped or adapted, buildings have to be altered or built anew, and so forth. The case for liberal trade says (subject to the qualifications that have been discussed above) that the country would be better off in the long run to move its resources out of protected industries into other activities, including the export industry. There will be a long-run gain to the country from making the move. But this long-run gain must be compared with the costs of the move, and the results must be compared with alternative investments. It is possible that the costs of a move—or at least of a rapid move—while less than the cumulative expected gain, are still so high as to exceed the present discounted value of the future gain. Then the adjustment will not be worthwhile, just as an identified infant industry still may not represent a worthwhile investment.

A Subjective Assessment of the Qualifications

Very little empirical work has been done on the practical importance of these possible qualifications to the case for liberal trade. Rather than attempt to review in a systematic way the little empirical work that has been done, I will simply provide a subjective assessment of the practical importance of these various factors.

It is not possible to consider here all of the cases of market distortion. In general market imperfections of all types—in the labor market, in the foreign exchange market, in the capital market, and in specific commodity and factor markets—are far greater in less-developed countries than in developed countries. That, indeed, is one reflection of their degree of underdevelopment. As noted above, this fact does not lead to a general case for protection from imports, but rather to a need for careful, detailed examination of the imperfections and the possible corrections for them. Imperfections arising in the foreign exchange market, for instance, usually arise from ill-conceived government action in pegging the exchange rate at an overvalued rate.

The possibility for raising real national income by taxing foreigners through a tariff on imports—the case for an "optimum tariff"—is far smaller than the importance accorded the optimum tariff in the technical economic literature would lead one to believe. There are very few countries that have enough monopoly power in the long run to result in optimum tariffs very much greater than zero. The United States is of course the major exception. The sheer size of the market, relative to the world economy, means that it can tax foreigners by tariffs on imports. But of course from a world distributional point of view to do so would have the perverse effect of redistributing income from the poor to the rich. Other economically large countries—Germany, Japan, Great Britain—are sufficiently important in the purchase of specific products (tea into Britain comes readily to mind) that they too could extract some monopoly gains from their supplying countries. Once again, the distributional effect does not recommend such a policy. The same applies to the European Community, which has become one large trading unit, even larger than the United States, with respect to the rest of the world.

Of course groups of supplying countries acting together may obtain sufficient monopoly power to tax consumers. This seems to be the case with the petroleum-producing countries in OPEC today. Similar attempts are being made among the less-developed countries producing copper.[2]

One final possibility under this category should be mentioned. Because of its great capacity for innovation, the United States may enjoy *temporary* monopoly power while new products produced in the United States are still new. Higher than normal prices can be charged. This monopoly power for any given product will dissipate in the course of time, and the faster international diffusion of new products through the multinational corporation contributes to this dissipation as far as the United States as a country is concerned. (By the same token it may help to prolong the temporary monopoly for the innovating firm.) Organized American labor is apprehensive about the effect of this rapid diffusion of new technical knowledge on employment (really a matter for macroeconomic policy) and on real wages. It is not clear, however, how import restriction will preserve the advantage; inhibitions on foreign direct investment might do so, but it is probable that international communication of new technology has now reached the point that even this would not help for long.

Too little is known to say much about the internal distributional consequences arising from foreign trade. A lively debate in the professional literature over the "Leontief Paradox" addresses this problem for the United States. Leontief's findings, which have been reconfirmed by Baldwin for a more recent period, show that the direct and indirect labor requirements of a million dollars worth of exports from the United States exceed the labor requirements for a million dollars of production in import-competing industries.[3] This fact suggests that liberal trade will raise American wages relative to rents and profits, in addition to raising American incomes generally. Close scrutiny of the data reveals that it is especially skilled labor that benefits. Liberal trade may hurt low-skilled labor in the short run. The long-run answer to this problem of course is to upgrade further the education and skills of American labor and to move unskilled labor into nontradable services, where wages will be pulled up by the growth of the economy.

While evidence on this question is very imperfect for other countries, the data for Germany and Japan suggest a rough neutrality for the effect of trade on the distribution of income between labor and capital. Liberal trade will of course hurt farmers—more accurately, land rents—in countries with high-cost agriculture. In practice, protective agricultural policies have served to benefit mainly wealthy farmers at the expense of wage earners and have generated surplus production. Assistance to small farmers can be given in a much more efficient way, now that the agricultural population is as small as it is in all industrial countries.

Liberal trade will raise wages and/or employment in less-developed countries that are poor in resources. But in countries that are rich in resources, liberal trade may lower real wages in the absence of policies for redistribution of income. A tax on exports of raw materials may be the least-cost way of achieving this, given the limited fiscal capacity of most of these countries.

Market distortions in developed countries are generally attacked directly, as they should be. They have anti-monopoly policies, anti-pollution policies, regional policies. One market distortion of growing importance, however, is government subventions to particular industries. Governments sometimes defend these practices, without very good evidence, on infant industry grounds.[4] Such subsidies tend to reduce private costs at the expense of the taxpayer, and they give the producing firm a greater competitive advantage in world markets than he would otherwise have. Indeed, the government often gets directly involved in foreign sales of the subsidized products, sometimes even using general foreign policy leverage. These practices encompass agriculture, ship building, shipping, airlines, rolling stock, color television, and most advanced armaments, to mention only the more obvious cases.

As noted above, these subsidies are possibly a blessing to foreign consumers, who get the subsidized goods. But they are no blessing to foreign producers, and in fact, they may be predatory in their effect if prices are raised after foreign producers have been put out of the competition. Generally speaking, the infant-industry argument is invalid in the developed countries. Further economies of scale external to the firm are likely to be small, and capital markets are good.

Much the most important imperfections in developed countries are macroeconomic: occasional recessions and excessive delays in needed adjustments of exchange rates. Calls for import protection rise in economic recessions because the costs of adjustment are higher at such times. People put out of work have greater difficulty finding new jobs than when the economy is booming. It is notable that the major trade liberalization that took place within Europe following formation of the European Common Market led to relatively few problems of adjustment. Except for brief periods, the European economies were booming throughout the sixties, and the elimination of tariffs between members was spread over a decade.

It should be mentioned in this context that even when such a drastic trade liberalization as formation of the European Common Market has occurred, the costs of adjustment to new sources of imports were small relative to the costs required by adjustment to other sources of change in a modern economy.[5] Changes in technology and changes in the pattern of government demand impose far greater burdens of adjustment on labor and capital than does trade liberalization. Think only of the introduction of synthetic fibers into the textile industry and of the boom and bust in the United States space industry.

Even more serious in practice than economic recessions, because of their greater duration in the recent past, has been the maintenance of inappropriate exchange rates. American industries were heavily and un-warrantedly hurt by import competition in the late sixties because of overvaluation of the dollar. The impact of course was especially great after 1969, when the economy cooled off, and several American industries found themselves with the worst of both worlds: slack domestic demand and strong import competition. Germany overextended its production of au-tomobiles and possibly a number of other industries because of undervalua-tion of the mark during the sixties. Japan did not move resources out of its textile industry as rapidly as it should have because of undervaluation of the yen relative to the currencies of other textile exporting countries. Improvements in the balance-of-payments adjustment mechanism, such as are now under extensive international discussion, should greatly reduce this particular source of distortion in the future.

Finally, there is the question of costs of adjustment to a policy of liberal trade in economies that have had protection from imports in the past. As noted above, the costs may well outweigh the discounted gains, since the costs are incurred early and the gains only later. This valid point, however, addresses mainly the pace of any trade liberalization rather than its direc-tion. There is a natural turnover of all factors of production. Capital wears out and must be replaced. Workers age and retire, and new ones must be hired and trained to replace them. Thus the costs of adjustment can be spread out with relatively low impact by a policy of less than full replace-ment. To the extent that these adjustment costs are an important and valid objection to liberalizing trade, therefore, their presence suggests that trade liberalization should be prolonged over a period of time. But liberalization should be perceived to be certain to take place, so that unwarranted replacement of retiring labor and capital does not occur.

Notes

1. There are both semantic and conceptual snares here. Some long-term debt can take the form of short-term claims, continually renewed. And in any short period of time it is impossible in practice to disentangle long-term lending from short-term financing.

2. For a suggestion that this phenomenon is likely to spread into a number of additional commodities see C. Fred Bergsten, "The Threat From the Third World," *Foreign Policy* 11 (Summer 1973), pp. 102-24, and

"The New Era in World Commodity Markets," *Challenge*, Sept./Oct. 1974, pp. 32-39.

3. Robert E. Baldwin, "Determinants of the Commodity Structure of U.S. Trade," *American Economic Review* (March 1971), pp. 126-46.

4. A different rationale is more defensible in the case of basic research or even applied research in highly competitive industries: the benefits of successful research spread so rapidly and costlessly that such research will not be undertaken by private enterprises, for they cannot appropriate any of the benefits.

5. See Albrecht Düren, "The Adjustment to Free Trade in the Common Market," Chapter 13.

Chapter 1
Commentary

Ryutaro Komiya

First, I want to emphasize the following point, although it is perhaps quite clear from Cooper's chapter. A country's policy of freer trade through lowering of tariffs and other trade barriers affects some groups within the country favorably and some others unfavorably. Therefore, unless some compensation for those unfavorably affected is provided, the policy of freer trade cannot be said to be unconditionally desirable. This is elementary, but often forgotten.

In particular, if those adversely affected by freer trade policy are weaker members of the society, sufficient compensation should be given them in addition to a reasonable adjustment mechanism. One should not propose a policy that victimizes those groups that are politically and economically weak. On the other hand, it is no wonder that politically stronger groups vigorously resist the trade policy that affects them adversely. It is, then, the task of social scientists to work out a combination of policy measures that makes free trade policy politically workable.

Second, in economics the infant-industry argument has always been discussed in connection with trade policy, but the essential ingredients of the argument—technological progress, learning by doing, irreversible economies of scale, externality of basic knowledge, and so on—have nothing to do with international trade. There can be a case for infant-industry protection even in a closed economy. Thus, the infant-industry situation is an example of market failures. Viewed in this way, infant-industry protection may be beneficial not only to the country in question but also the world economy as a whole, even when capital market is perfect, especially when the resulting decline in costs gives rise to a large increase in consumers' surplus. Also, as Cooper notes, a policy of subsidization is always better than protection by tariffs or other trade barriers, provided that tax revenues necessary for subsidization can be raised with little market distortion.

Cooper considers that the infant-industry argument is, generally speaking, of no consequence in the developed countries today. While I have often seen the argument used too easily and indiscriminately, I think the market failures connected with the process of introducing new technologies are basic and cannot easily be dismissed as irrelevant to already industrialized economies. There can be a situation in which the government should undertake or subsidize basic as well as applied research, collect and propagate industrial and marketing information, and help industries develop basic know-hows that are difficult to be internalized within individual firms.[1]

Third, almost needless to say, the economic argument constitutes only a part of the case for free trade. There are many other good reasons to maintain and encourage free international exchange of goods and services as well as other things, including ideas and persons. Free and orderly international trade is a vehicle for world peace and prosperity.

Note

1. Also, when the world market of a certain commodity is dominated by a foreign monopolist or oligopolist, it is possible that a country's subsidization policy to develop an indigenous firm may give rise to such a large increase in consumers' surplus not only in the country in question but also in other countries that total surplus after subtraction of subsidies is positive.

2

The Probable Effects of Freer Trade on Individual Countries

Harry G. Johnson

Introduction

The economic gains available to the individual nation and the world economy from a more efficient use of existing resources, which can be provided through freer trade, are probably rather small compared with the gains which are available from the augmentation of resources and particularly (in view of the contemporary identification of economic welfare with per capita income) the stock of resources per capita, including education and technology as well as natural resources and accumulated material capital in those stocks.[1]

Trade policies and changes in them have relatively little lasting influence on national levels of real income and economic welfare. Severe disturbances of trade patterns such as those produced by wars, major depressions or inflation, or nationalistic economic policies may have a significant short-run influence (which may of course extend over a period of years that is long relative to the human life span). But unless a country follows changeable policies that give rise to great uncertainty of economic calculations for citizens and foreigners or keeps applying welfare-adverse policies, its economy will become accustomed to whatever broad commercial policies its government pursues, and the evolution of production will be dominated by the more basic factors of capital accumulation, increasing human skills, and technical progress.

This point is borne out by a number of empirical studies aimed at measuring the welfare costs of restrictive trade policies pursued by various countries. None of the measures show, for reasonably well-developed economies, a welfare cost amounting to a significant proportion of national income—usually well under 5, or even 2.5 percent. The same results follow from aggregative estimates employing plausible magnitudes of the tariff rates and demand and production substitution elasticities involved in standard welfare cost formulae although, as will be noted shortly, these studies may not adequately treat dynamic factors such as economies of scale. Only for some of the less-developed countries, where commercial policies are well known to be extremely and irrationally protectionist, do the estimated welfare costs turn out to be impressively significant, and even then they are nowhere within an order of magnitude of accounting for the low incomes per head of these countries as compared with the developed countries.

These results should not be unexpected. First, one would expect differences in the total quantity of resources available to be more important than differences in the efficiency of utilizing them in accounting for differences in income per head. In fact, one might even expect total quantity of resources and efficiency in resource utilization to be positively correlated, broadly speaking. Second, one would expect the political process to have some awareness of the economic costs entailed by policies involving inter-ferences with economic efficiency and hence to moderate such interfer-ences with a view to those costs, so that measurements of the welfare losses from interferences would show those costs as relatively small in relation to total productive potential.

The fact that the gains from more liberal commercial policy ("freer trade") are likely to be small in relation to national income must, however, be carefully interpreted. First, a gain that is small by comparison with national income may—and probably will—be large in terms of the absolute quantity of resources it represents. Second, comparison with the national income is misleading, whether conducted in terms of a ratio or translated into some such terms as the number of months or years of economic growth it represents. The proper comparison is with the amount of additional output or resources that could be created by some comparable change of economic policy; and in these terms, commercial policy liberalization probably dominates any other policy change one could seriously consider. (The only serious rival would seem to be a drastic reduction in military expenditure, and this alternative raises some far-reaching problems of philosophy and of effects.)

Realization that the static theory of comparative advantage yields ap-parently relatively small prospective gains from trade liberalization has led free-trade theorists increasingly to emphasize the possibility of "dynamic" gains of a kind similar to those long claimed for protectionist policies —particularly infant-industry protection—by their proponents. One such consideration, which has yet to be satisfactorily formulated theoretically and empirically tested, relates to economies of scale, the difficulty being to separate economies of scale as such from economies of specialization and division of labor and to arrive at a causal connection between commercial policy and economies of scale. Another, which has become popular in recent years in connection with the concept of "X-efficiency" as a cost of monopoly in the domestic economy, involves the notion that the cushion of protection allows employers and workers alike to relax into slovenly and inefficient ways of conducting production processes.[2]

The Orthodox Theory of the Gains from Trade and Protection

Contemporary theory on the subject of national gains from liberal international trading arrangements and the potentialities for increasing those gains by interventions in the free flow of international trade and payments has its origins in the writings of the English classical school of economics. It is illuminating of the nature of the theory and also of certain difficulties or appearances of "unrealism" in its application to contemporary circumstances to appreciate certain broad aspects of the social, economic, and historical background of that theory before considering its main propositions and the modifications and extensions that have been introduced to fit certain facts of the contemporary world.

First, the theory was developed in reaction to and as a critique of a body of thought generally described as mercantilism. The key features of mercantilism from the present point of view were its concept of the nation-state as something over and above the citizens and/or residents who comprised the bulk of its population, to be run for the benefit of rulers enjoying their status as such by heredity rather than democratic election, and its concern with using economic policies of various kinds to build the power of the state. From this concern followed an instrumental view of economic activity as providing the foundation of state power, rather than as a means of satisfying the private wants of the citizenry. In the field of international economic policy, this meant increasing domestic employment—increasing the working population, not the shorter-run present-day objective of eliminating idleness of productive resources—and promoting balance-of-payments surpluses as a means of increasing the treasure available to the state for the conduct of diplomacy and the waging of foreign wars.

The essence of the classical case for free trade was the joint demonstration that interventions in trade were both inefficient in themselves and reduced productive efficiency in the allocation of resources and that the attempt to use trade interventions to acquire "treasure" via balance-of-payments surpluses would be self-defeating in the long run as a result of the automatic inflationary consequences of the resulting monetary inflows. These two propositions hang together, and both are long-run propositions deriving ultimately from the private welfare standards of economic efficiency. One of the major difficulties that has always plagued the winning of public understanding of the case for free trade—and sometimes eluded the understanding of the proponents of that case—has been the difficulty of understanding the jointness of the real and monetary aspects of the classical analysis, the long-run nature of the propositions, and their dependence on the private satisfaction standard of economic welfare. This difficulty is especially pervasive in contemporary circumstances, in which the superimposition of two world wars on an incomplete transition from hereditary authoritarian government to democratic government has left a legacy of mixed nationalistic and individualistic concepts of the purposes of government.

Second, the concern of the classical economists with the long run enabled them, on the one hand, to assume mobility within the national economy of factors of production—in disregard of short-run adjustment costs—and a consequent general identity of relative money costs of production with real alternative opportunity costs, and on the other hand, to disregard any disruptive influences of domestic or international monetary disturbances. Much of contemporary impatience with the classical prescription of free trade can be attributed to the belief, whether justified or not, that in the relevant time perspective the money costs and prices to which the competitive market system regards do not reflect real social alternative opportunity costs and the fact that in the same perspective national and international monetary disequilibria (specifically, in recent circumstances, differential domestic inflation rates in the context of rigidities of international exchange rates) falsify the market signals conveyed by money costs and prices.

Third, implicit in the theoretical analysis were certain empirical assumptions about the nature of the economic world and the political world of nation-states, which underlaid the two main theoretical exceptions admitted by the classical economists to the general case for freedom of international trade. One exception was the terms-of-trade or "optimum tariff" argument, according to which a nation might be able to improve its national economic welfare by exploiting its monopoly or monopsony power in relation to its trading partners. The other was the "infant-industry argument" for temporary protection, according to which policy action might be required to correct for a failure of the competitive market system to discern and exploit opportunities for eventually profitable production involving investment in "learning by doing" and growing up to the size of operation required to exploit the economies of scale. The latter, it should be noted, in contrast to the former involved no conflict between national well-being and cosmopolitan well-being correctly conceived.

The first empirical assumption was that differences in comparative advantage stemmed primarily from differences in national endowments of natural resources—which naturally carried the corollary of monopoly power, especially as the typical example of the use of monopoly power at the time was direct or indirect state monopolization of access to rare imported natural products such as salt, sugar, and spices. The second was that nations were few in number and of roughly equal size, which supported the assumption that infant industries could be promoted by protected access to the national market. And the infant-industry argument derived further empirical support from the rudimentary state of development of capital markets and the reliance of enterprise on unlimited liability partnership among small numbers of owners of relatively large amounts of private wealth (limited liability companies being a considerably later invention), which implied an "entrepreneurial gap" with respect to the undertaking of risky new activities requiring and justifying state intervention in the form of the insurance provided by monopoly privileges.

One further point about the classical analysis, which had to be rediscovered relatively recently, provides an example of its continuing relevance. While the general presumption was of nations of roughly comparable economic size, some classical theorists—notably John Stuart Mill—paid attention to the influence of relative country sizes on the distribution of the gains from freedom of trade. The specific proposition is that the smaller the country, the relatively more it will benefit from international exchange, because trade between a large country and a small one will produce little change of the internationally available exchange ratio between commodities away from that which would prevail in the large partner under autarkic conditions but considerable change in that ratio away from what would prevail in the smaller partner under self-sufficiency. The corollary proposition is probably of considerably greater practical importance: it is the large and rich country (since economic size is a function of total national income rather than of area or population) not the small and poor country that enjoys significant possibilities of exploiting optimum tariff possibilities by imposing restrictions on trade with its neighbors. Consequently, it is the small and poor countries that stand to gain the most from a liberal regime of international trade (and by extension of international factor movements). The widespread contrary belief must be attributed partly to wishful thinking and envy on the part of the small and poor; partly to the fact that free trade involves less short-run internal dislocation and long-run change of economic structure for large, rich than for small, poor countries and hence appears to be more in the economic interests of the former than of the latter; and partly to what may be called a "fallacy of decomposition," according to which smaller countries endowed with a relative abundance of natural resources or climatic conditions scarce on a world scale attribute to themselves a degree of monopoly power that they could only exercise by effective monopolistic cooperation with all the other small countries similarly endowed.

However well they may have fitted the contemporary empirical facts of the economic and political environment, the exceptions allowed by classical theory to the general case for freedom of international trade do not stand out as significant empirical possibilities in the modern world. The infant-industry argument, empirically, encounters the basic difficulty that the small scale of the national market in most less-developed countries precludes exploitation of whatever potentialities there are in infant-industry protection, with the result that faith in these potentialities has been directed on the one hand into support for subsidization of exports of the products of "new industries" and on the other into demands for tariff preferences for less-developed-country exports of manufactured products to developed countries. In contemporary conditions, also, the technology required is well beyond the capacity of amateur local capitalists and typically requires foreign enterprise or foreign provision of technology; hence it raises problems concerning the net benefit to the incomes of natives of the country. At the theoretical level, the argument has been reduced to finding some sort of benefit from infant-industry investment that cannot be captured by the private investor in the infant firm or industry. Here, increasing sophistication of economic understanding of the availability and characteristics of markets for knowledge, including the patenting or leasing of production know-how and the use of apprenticeship systems to make the worker and not the employer pay for the acquisition of portable human skills, has reduced this sort of theoretical possibility to empirical negligibility.

As regards the optimum tariff argument, monopoly power based on control of unique and rare natural resources is relatively unimportant in a competitive industrial world as well as being dispersed into ineffectiveness among a large number of small countries and subject to severe limitation almost by an infinite range of substitution possibilities made available by biological and physical science. (The currently alarming case of oil illustrates the extent to which producer interests in monopoly have to be reinforced by consumer country collaboration in the exploitation of their own consumers for monopoly objectives to be successfully implemented.) The availability of monopoly power based on unique advantages in particular types of manufacturing came to be considerably overestimated in the 1930s as a result of the imperfect/monopolistic competition revolution in economic theory and the emphasis on differentiation of industrial products. Subsequently general theory has come to identify "product differentiation" with adaptation of the product to market performance requirements, not necessarily conveying monopoly power, and to emphasize the high degree of flexibility of industrial production in developed manufacturing economies and the consequent high degree of substitutability among the products of different nations. In this context, "international monopoly power" is a wasting asset associated with transitory technological leadership, or a continuing phenomenon only to the extent of sustained capacity to innovate. Probably only the United States enjoys international monopoly power in this sense to any significant degree; and this, which could be exploited efficiently only through export restrictions or restrictions on imports of raw materials and primary products, is exploited only partially and inefficiently by current U.S. international economic policies and in important respects is transferred or given away to other countries.[3]

Contemporary Modifications to Traditional Theory

The circumstances of contemporary international economic relations suggest two problems excluded by the classical assumptions: (1) factors of production—and specifically capital—are internationally immobile and (2) technology is either completely immobile internationally (and hence incorporated in otherwise unexplained differences in comparative cost) or else completely and costlessly internationally mobile (so that differences in comparative cost must be attributable to something else than technology differences, except possibly to the extent that technology involves increasing returns to scale). With respect to both, it is necessary to distinguish between the effects of the export of capital or technology on the income of the immobile factor (labor in both cases, possibly also capital in the case of technological transfer) and its effect on national welfare (i.e., the earnings of labor, capital, and ownership of technology taken together).

The export of capital will tend to lower the rate of earnings of immobile labor by comparison with what they would be with a larger stock of capital per head, though it will result in a larger national income to the extent that the returns on capital invested abroad were higher than at home and all these returns accrued to residents of the investing nation. Qualifications are necessary, however, on five counts. First, foreign investment may not reduce the earnings of domestic labor, but merely result in a reallocation of domestic production towards less capital-intensive activities (as will happen in a Heckscher-Ohlin trade model in the absence of trade barriers and with incomplete specialization in domestic production). Second, if the supply of domestic capital is perfectly elastic at the going rate of return, foreign investment will simply add to the domestically owned stock of capital and the earnings of domestic capitalists without affecting the income of domestic labor. Third, if foreign investment tends to reduce the earnings of capital abroad, there is a case parallel to the optimum tariff argument for imposing a tax or other restriction on foreign investment by domestic capitalists.[4]

Fourth, the standard argument applies to capital in the aggregate, independently of the effects of foreign investment on the terms of trade. Insofar as foreign investment increases foreign production of a country's exportable goods beyond what the same capital investment would have increased such production by at home and so tends to reduce their relative prices, there is a terms-of-trade case for restriction of foreign investment. But, conversely, there is a case for subsidization of foreign investment if its effect is to increase the supply of importables and hence tend to improve the country's terms of trade. Finally, if there is a double-taxation agreement and if a firm's activities impose fewer indirect costs (for infrastructure, services, and so forth) on government than they produce in corporate taxes, there is a case for taxation of foreign investment by the difference between the corporate tax revenue lost under the double-taxation agreement and the government expenditure saved by the capital being invested in foreign rather than domestic activity.[5]

On a very broad rough view, it would seem reasonable to judge that only the United States and Japan—though possibly also the expanded European Community when it becomes fully enough integrated economically to be considered an entity from the viewpoint of foreign investment—are likely to be able to influence their terms of trade favorably by investment in foreign sources of supply of raw materials and energy. In addition, only the United States is preponderant enough in foreign direct investment in manufacturing to have a rate-of-return-on-foreign-investment and a double-taxation-agreement motivation for the restriction of foreign investment by its residents. The rate of return motivation, moreover, is probably transitory, since in the longer run supplies of capital restricted by U.S. foreign investment policy would be likely to be made good by capital accumulation and investment by residents of other countries, to the detriment of U.S. national interests insofar as these are identified on mercantilist grounds with the ownership of wealth regardless of the sacrifices entailed in accumulating it. For the same reason of longer-run foreign accumulation of capital, the other possible arguments for restriction of U.S. foreign investment are likely to be transitory, and to leave standing only the double-taxation-agreement argument for intervention in foreign investment—or, more simply, for ending the encouragement given by double-taxation agreements to nationally unprofitable foreign investment by U.S. residents.

In addition, insofar as existing restrictions on international trade in goods, especially the Common Market external tariff, serve to encourage U.S. foreign investment, freer trade would tend to reduce this source of national loss to the United States. Similarly, insofar as overvaluation of the dollar has tended to promote U.S. investment in undervalued-currency countries unduly, the exchange-rate adjustments of the past two years should have the same effect. In general, insofar as foreign investment is a tariff-and-other-trade-barrier-induced substitute for foreign trade, freer trade should serve to reduce any national losses consequent on it.

Much the same analysis applies to the effects on national welfare of the international transfer of technical knowledge. Technical knowledge transfer tends to reduce the return on the capital investment with which it is usually associated or to operate differentially on the relative prices of the transferring country's export and import goods; or, the profits on the rental value of transferred knowledge are subject to double-taxation agreements, although in this case there is the important possible difference that the application of knowledge abroad may cost no extra resources to the knowledge-supplying country since the knowledge already exists and has the character of a public good so that any net earnings it can fetch from use abroad constitute a net gain.[6]

The foregoing relates to the overall effects on national economic welfare of the international investment of capital and transmission of technical knowledge. Most of the heat of controversy over the desirability of restrictions on the foreign operations of the large nationally domiciled multinational corporations of the United States at present comes—as did the similar controversy over foreign investment by British firms and British capitalists in the later nineteenth century—from narrower concern with the presumptively adverse effects on the earnings of labor, the immobile factor of production. This concern is theoretically well justified: enabling capital, or capital plus technology, to move towards cheaper labor supplies in foreign countries obviously undermines the scarcity vlaue of American labor.[7]

The relevant question, though, is the extent to which the scarcity value of labor can be protected by placing barriers on the export of capital and of technical knowledge, and specifically on the foreign activities of the multinational corporation. The possibilities seem to be extremely limited. Capital as such can be exported in many different forms, and if the return to the capital element in domestic investment by multinational corporations debarred from foreign direct investment sinks low enough as a result of restrictions, other forms of capital export will be resorted to.[8]

More important, probably, productive knowledge can be transferred abroad by many alternative routes. Leasing of the knowledge by itself, without the accompaniment of corporate direct investment, which would be permitted or even encouraged by some proponents of restrictions, would have its commercial drawbacks. This method is suitable for types of knowledge that are not subject to rapid obsolescence and so can be neatly packaged, but not for knowledge that is continually being improved by further research and development expenditure. This approach would probably leave little protection for labor in the form of preferred access to domestic corporate capital.

But foreigners can also acquire knowledge of productive techniques without the need for any payments to the multinational enterprises that initially possess it and therefore without being subject to deprivation of its benefits by restrictions on the knowledge-transferring activities of those multinational corporations. It is not even necessary to import the product incorporating the knowledge, at least in any quantity or at any great expense. A prototype to imitate may be sufficient for the purpose; or the knowledge that the product can be produced, together with a rough idea of the principles and methods employed in producing it such as can be gained from the trade literature (not to mention explicit industrial espionage) may suffice; or engineers and scientists with the requisite experience in production can be hired. All of these methods involve costs to the foreign producer and hence leave some protection for domestic labor in the form of preferential access to knowledge, but the resulting benefit is unlikely to be very substantial.

Some Comments on the Apparent Irrelevance of Orthodox
Theory to Practical Reality

As already mentioned, the orthodox case for freedom of trade chronically appears to be irrelevant to practical concerns with commercial policy. One consequence is that movements toward unilateral freeing of trade have been rare and generally (as is the case of Britain in the early nineteenth century) based on an ideological drive covering the suppression of protected vested interests by the active self-interest of burgeoning exporting interests.

Instead, movements towards the freeing of trade have generally been accomplished by reciprocal negotiation, in which the visible losses to protected producers can be presented as outweighed by visible gains to exporting interests.[9] The reason has little or nothing to do with the traditional national-self-interest qualifications to the cosmopolitan case for freedom of trade, though these qualifications are invariably pleaded in support of protectionist policies recommended for other reasons. Instead, the main reasons are, as suggested earlier, to be found in the difference between the assumptions and time perspective of the theory and the actual context of commercial policy making. First, the theory assumes the preservation of domestic and international monetary equilibrium, so that monetary disequilibrium is characteristic of international economic relations—and has been so especially during the past decade or so—and in these circumstances there is a "second-best" case for interventions in international trade and payments. Second, the process of government lends itself readily to the protection of short-run producer interests rather than the service of long-run consumer interests. Pressures in this direction have been accentuated in modern industrial society by the fact that the achievement of high incomes and living standards entails the commitment of substantial human capital to the acquisition of specialized skills, while the acceleration of technical progress and changes in competitive positions in the market subjects this capital to increasing and unpredictable risks of obsolescence and capital loss.

Third, contemporary governments retain a heavy supercargo of the monarchical nation-states' view of the state as an entity over and above its servant citizens, but with much diminished capacity to choose among longer-range policies and enforce these decisions with the public. Hence the concept of the national interest merges more readily with the private interests of the more vocal and economically powerful sectors of the economy and tends to be identified with protection of those sectors. Finally, the concept of protection has become much more sophisticated, and the means of providing it more subtle, as the activities of government have expanded and industrial activity become more complex. The tariff is an extremely crude, as well as highly visible, instrument for intervention in the pattern and direction of economic activity, as compared with such instruments as tax incentives, credit subsidies, government purchasing policies, public support for research and development expenditures, support of "basic research" through "science policy," and the like.[10]

Indeed, the postwar success efforts to liberalize international trade that culminated in the Kennedy Round may be attributable in large part to recognition by governments of the crudity of the traditional tariff and quota instruments of protection and their consequent willingness to abandon these instruments in favor of more subtle ones. An assault on the more subtle instruments, generically lumped into the miscellaneous category of "non-tariff barriers to trade," will be difficult to develop within the framework of traditional methods of negotiating the liberalization of international trade. This—together with the question of whether the European Community countries are interested in attempting the exercise —constitutes the fundamental obstacle in the way of another effort at multilateral liberalization of world trade.

Notes

1. Two points should be noted about the "production per head" measure of economic welfare commonly accepted as a standard of reference. First, earlier economists were well aware that increasing affluence could be used either to raise the standard of living or to increase the population. Indeed, one aim of mercantilist policies was to increase the population and therefore the military strength of the state. Materialism and individualism have since virtually eradicated any argument for expending increasing potential affluence on raising numbers, however, though numbers remain a relevant consideration in the practical politics of many countries or regions of countries. The existence of population as an alternative to prosperity needs to be borne in mind in certain contexts of international trade analysis, however, for the standard complaint of spokesmen for the less-developed countries that liberal trading arrangements in the nineteenth century generally failed to promote economic development in the backward regions of the world ignores the fact that such arrangements provided the basis for a vast expansion of their populations.

Second, in recent years there has been an upsurge of criticism of and disillusionment with the identification of increasing output per head with increasing welfare. One facet of this criticism is expressed currently in terms of concern about "the quality of life" and typically leads to the recommendation that economic growth should be halted forthwith or at least slowed down drastically. It is patently too undemocratic, too unhumanitarian, and too self-centered to be taken seriously. The other criticism concentrates on the inadequacy of national income statistics in capturing and deducting various negative effects on human welfare of the process of production, notably the pollution of the environment. This criticism has substance, but one may reasonably assume (in most cases) that human society is not unaware of the problem and, as it waxes in affluence, will devote increasing amounts of resources to remedification.

2. This line of argument, whatever else may be said about its plausibility, contains a theoretical pitfall for the unwary. Employers or workers who choose more leisure or more comfort on the job at the expense of a reduction of measured output presumably maximize utility by so doing, and if they were forced instead to maximize measured output would lose utility thereby. (This is one aspect of the shortcomings of measured income as an indicator of economic welfare referred to earlier.) Moreover, since consumption of "leisure" (in the two senses mentioned) as contrasted with the alternative of consumption of goods and services is presumably a luxury good, a reduction of the former relative to the latter induced by trade liberalization would presumably reflect a reduction of potential real income rather than an increase.

3. As in the case of oil previously mentioned, or partially through sugar quotas and P.L. 480 transfers of agricultural surpluses created by support of domestic farm prices.

4. If there is inward investment by foreigners and the supply of foreign capital is not perfectly elastic, there is an analogous case for taxation of inward foreign investment.

5. Where particular industries have a high rate of by-production of pollution, it may be socially advantageous to subsidize foreign investment by those industries.

6. With regard to knowledge as a "public good," the complication arises that its use may or may not be charged for. If it is fully charged for, in the sense that its owner fully extracts any saving in costs of production that its use abroad makes possible, there must be a net gain to the country of residence of the owner, since by assumption the earnings of other factors will be unaffected (except indirectly as a result of the increase in total income made possible by the application of knowledge). Otherwise, the effects depend on the impact of the transmission of paid-for knowledge on the prices of products and the earnings of the paid-for factors of production.

7. A distinction must be made, however, between high U.S. wages associated with high levels of acquired skills by comparison with other countries, and high U.S. wages resulting from the scarcity of relatively unskilled labor in the U.S. associated with inward immobility of foreign labor and outward past immobility of U.S. capital and technology. Unfortunately this distinction cannot be clear cut because the scarcity value of unskilled labor raises the cost of acquisition of skills and hence the returns they must command.

8. It is always possible for corporations to pay out their profits to shareholders or to holding companies that are free to invest the funds abroad by these alternative routes.

9. The orthodox case for free trade rests on benefits to consumers as a whole, not to particular producing groups.

10. See Chapter 10.

3

Freer Trade for Higher Employment and Price Level Stability

Herbert Giersch

The theorem advanced in this chapter is that free trade helps to raise the level of employment and to alleviate the conflict between the objectives of high employment and price level stability.

This theorem seems to be contrary to popular thinking and good short-term economic judgment. Do economists not usually assume full employment of domestic resources in their arguments for free trade, and do they not implicitly or openly admit therefore that lapses from full employment and conditions of lasting underemployment constitute arguments for deviations from free trade? How then can it be shown that free trade should help to bring about a higher level of resource utilization?

Moreover, every layman and most politicians would probably argue that one must protect domestic industries and employment if they are severely affected by import competition. The economist may support him in pointing out that there is a grain of truth in such arguments, if and when the resources set free under the pressure of import competition do not have alternative uses. Such a case may quite often arise in the very short and perhaps even in the medium run. Without alternative uses, the argument usually runs, there are no social opportunity costs for the protected domestic commodity, and with zero opportunity costs, it may even pay to grow bananas in Alaska or dig holes in the earth, if only for employment's sake.

The employment-protection argument, however, does not distinguish between the different causes of unemployment. It is derived from the special case of an enduring underemployment of available resources that Keynes established for explaining the Great Depression of the Thirties. However, protection even in this case is only a second-best remedy as compared to expanding effective demand by monetary-fiscal policies. It may even be doubted whether overall protection, as it were needed in this case, would help as quickly as a courageous expansionary demand management. Furthermore, overall protection is only half of the solution on the trade side to improve the competitive position of domestic producers; the other half would be an overall export subsidy. If both sides were properly considered in the context of a general equilibrium analysis, the whole operation on the foreign trade front might amount to nothing less than a flat currency devaluation, which is something that would be needed anyhow in cases where the removal of underemployment by demand expansion would lead to a balance of payments deficit (i.e., in cases where underemployment could be considered as a consequence of currency overvaluation). One immediately thinks of Britain before and of Germany after 1931. Protection by discriminating between different products is an inferior substitute for overall demand expansion *cum* overall devaluation. Nevertheless, the Great Depression gave rise to worldwide protection and international economic disintegration as a politically plausible cure to widespread unemployment. The arguments behind such policies are still popular.

Postwar development in the world economy and in economic thought seem to suggest that the Great Depression of the Thirties was due to mistakes in demand management that are unlikely to be repeated in our lifetimes. Instead, we suffer from inflation, defined as an upward deviation from price level stability. Why we have inflation is a matter of long debate. The explanation that strikes me most is based on the following propositions: (a) people want a level of employment and resource utilization that is higher than we actually have had in most countries, and governments should assume responsibility for providing that level; and (b) according to a widespread belief in public and government quarters, the insufficient level of employment is due to an inadequacy of effective demand, and the remedy, therefore, has to be the same as the remedy that proved successful in fighting the Great Depression.

I largely agree with the ethics of proposition (a): governments should continue to assume responsibility for a higher level of employment. However, I suggest a substantial qualification of proposition (b). Governments must realize that under existing conditions on the supply side, they are unable to raise the level of employment for more than a period of two or three years and that they are bound to suffer a setback afterwards, if they limit themselves to measures of expanding demand. The reason why they are bound to fail in the medium run is that under existing conditions on the supply side, they are unable to control effective (or real)—in contrast to nominal—demand for more than a limited period without having to revert to wage and price controls. By raising nominal demand, they can raise real demand only as long as suppliers do not react by pushing up wages and prices. The interval, during which real demand and employment rises, is determined by the length of the wage lag and of the price lag. These lags are due to stickiness and money illusion.

Public wage and price controls, if effective, work on both components of the wage and price lag. However, as a rule they are not effective in the absence of a strong bureaucratic control machinery. If effective, price controls are bound to impair the entrepreneurial spirit of maximizing profits through reducing the cost level; they rather produce costs or at least permissiveness vis-a-vis cost increases. As regard wage controls, they tend to prevent trade unions from pushing firms into a fight for higher productivity. Price and wage controls thus reduce both the allocative efficiency and the so-called X-efficiency of the market system. By introducing slack into the economy they transform open unemployment into lower productivity or into disguised unemployment, including the unemployment on the job that is bound to arise when wages are kept artificially low (labor hoarding). This is sufficient reason to discard them as a means of raising the level of employment.

One alternative to controls is accelerating inflation. By increasing nominal demand more than necessary to compensate for the rise in prices that can be expected on the basis of recent price inflation, the government can give a lift to effective demand. However, inflation these days does not accelerate without an intermittent period during which effective demand falls under the impact of a wage and price push that follows the wage and price lag. This is why we have less employment than we want, but also an inflation that accelerates with interruptions. "Stagflation" is the name for the period when employment falls and the rate of inflation decelerates to create a new expansion of nominal demand, an expansion that does not fully dissipate in higher prices and wages and thus brings a new upswing in effective demand.

The fundamental cause of the dilemma between full employment and price level stability is monopoly.

1. Under conditions of a stationary equilibrium, we should expect monopoly in goods and factor markets to lead to a less than optimum degree of resource utilization. Monopoly in goods markets alone would imply a situation where marginal revenue equalled marginal costs at a price distinctly above marginal costs and at an output distinctly below competitive output.

2. Similarly, monopoly in factor markets alone would imply that the price of the factor was higher and the absorption of the factor lower than under competitive conditions. If monopoly in factor markets is added to monopoly in goods markets, the degree of resource utilization falls below what it would have been under monopoly in goods markets alone.

3. It is true that monopsony power works in the opposite direction, if supply is negatively elastic; this implies that labor monopoly may be necessary to prevent competitive capitalism, combined with monopsony on the labor market, from leading to an excessive use of labor in production and hence from exploitation. But if labor monopoly is stronger than employers' monopsony, the net effect even in this case must be a reduction in employment to below the optimum.

4. If monopoly prevails over monopsony power in the aggregate, actual resource utilization must be below the optimum under equilibrium conditions. In a dynamic setting, goods and factor prices may lag behind demand conditions for a while, thus approaching competitive prices, at which point resource utilization is equally close to what would prevail under competi-

tive conditions. This situation of "as if competition" is what we call prosperity or boom. It is, however, combined with unexpected inflation. The period afterwards, when wages and prices catch up with nominal demand, is characterized by falling employment. These ups and downs may produce a higher average level of employment than would prevail under equilibrium conditions. What we gain, however, we gain by using up and restoring money illusion. The net effect on employment is probably positive, for the simple reason that there is always some loss of knowledge about inflation, since experienced people who die are replaced by inexperienced people entering the active population. Moreover, people's memories are less than perfect as a store of relevant information. And finally, the hope for stability never ends. It is thus not wholly non-rational to use money illusion to compensate for the bad employment effects of monopoly, provided one is prepared to pay the price of (slowly and unevenly) accelerating inflation.

Such inflation is not produced when underemployment and monopoly are directly attacked (e.g., by injecting new elements of competition). If the above analysis is correct, a rollback of monopoly capitalism towards competitive capitalism should be a means of raising employment without inflation, or of fighting inflation without a substantial decline in employment, or of resolving the conflict between full employment and price level stability. This solution may be unrealistic in the context of a national economy, but it is much less so if use can be made of import competition as well as of internal competition. And there are positive rather than negative side effects resulting from such a radical approach in a worldwide context.

Imported competition in this sense means free trade or a process of freeing trade from quantitative import restrictions and import duties, from export restrictions and export duties on the side of the supplying country, and from all sorts of other impediments to trade, including excessively high transportation costs. It also includes the freeing of factor movements that are a complement to rather than a substitute for trade, such as foreign investments in sales organizations and in facilities for servicing imported goods, or investments abroad that are designed to shift production for domestic use in manufacturing and consumption to foreign locations with lower costs. Imported competition in a wide sense may be conceived to include the import of foreign capital, of foreign management and know-how, and of workers from less-developed countries. Finally, additional elements or doses of competition from abroad can be introduced into the domestic economy by pursuing an exchange rate policy that worsens the competitive position of domestic vis-a-vis foreign producers. The scope for such increased competition goes beyond freedom of trade and factor movements among developed countries. It appears almost unlimited—in spite of the high degree of concentration "achieved" in the industrialized parts of the world—if one thinks of possible competition from less-developed countries with their vast supply of low-wage labor that can be trained to produce the same goods and services for which producers in developed countries still seem to have a monopoly. Looked at it in this way the sources of imported competition have up to now hardly been tapped.

The medicine of imported competition against sellers' inflation is not of a compensatory or allopathic nature. It is homeopathic and hence politically less attractive than the seductive medicine of inflation. Suppliers of all markets and producers at all production stages detest it or reject it. The only political support it can obtain is from savers' organizations and from consumers. These groups, however, have widely dispersed interests, so that their voice in the economic policy debate is weak. The only support they can enlist comes from professional economists who happen to take the long rather than the short view and who happen to believe at the same time that competitive capitalism still has a future.

The medicine of imported competition was, therefore, applied accidentally rather than on purpose. As a by-product of developments with more appeal or political momentum, imported competition played a role in

The postwar liberalization of trade;

The formation of the European Common Market;

The tariff reductions following the Kennedy Round;

The upward floating of the Deutschmark in 1971.

The upward float of the D-Mark showed perhaps most clearly what the strategy amounts to. Like a tariff reduction, it permitted an easier access of foreign competitors to West German markets, but as it was not accompanied by reciprocal concessions, German producers were not compensated by improved export possibilities; on the contrary, exporters received less domestic currency for given dollar earnings and found themselves in worse competitive positions compared with exporters from countries who prevented the dollar rate from falling (or from falling freely). The characteristic feature was thus a decline in profits. But unlike a cyclical decline in profits that hits domestic producers similarly, the float had a differentiated impact. Parallel action (e.g., in cutting investments) was, therefore, not likely to come about. On the contrary, since foreign competitors were the beneficiaries of the float, it appeared to be a matter of survival to maintain rather than cut the volume of cost reducing investments. A comparative reading of German newspapers in 1971, on the one hand, and during the 1967 recession, on the other, clearly reveals the difference. In 1967, there were hardly any severe complaints about the decline in business profits and much applause for the healthy "structural change," although capacity utilization and cyclical employment reached a postwar low. In 1971, however, a very smooth cyclical downturn with very little fall in employment and investment was accompanied by an outcry from the business community expressing deep anxiety. The difference between a decline in profits, which is cyclical, and a decline, which is due to more intense competition, lies in the ratio between profits and investment. Under an increase in competition that is not due to a fall in aggregate demand, investments will hardly be cut. They have to be maintained—and even increased—in spite of lower profits. Such a change cuts deeper into the behavior of what Galbraith calls the "techno-structure." It seems to make past managerial experience and behavioral standards obsolete, as it requires a change in pricing behavior and in financing methods.

Figure 3-1 shows the relationship between the rate of profit on the one hand (Y-axis) and the volume of investment—and GNP—on the other hand (X-axis), under different degrees of competition (Z_1,Z_2,Z_3). A cyclical downturn, which reduces the rate of profit, leaves entrepreneurs on the same Z-line. If they are on Z_1, a fall in profits from P_0 to P_1 induces entrepreneurs to cut investments from Y_0 to Y_1. This intensifies the downturn that becomes a normal recession that leaves most entrepreneurs quite happy. If, on the other hand, the decline in profits is the result of an increase in competition, as described in the previous paragraph, entrepreneurs may fall right through from A to B, without being able to adjust investments. Entrepreneurs may feel depressed, but the economy remains on a high level of employment and capacity utilization, simply because the increase in competition from Z_1 to Z_2 keeps them running as fast as before, although profits are lower.

The diagram is not supposed to illustrate more than can be said to follow from the observation that during a period of increased competition, investments were cut less than one should have expected from a similar decline in profits during a cyclical downturn. Since a downturn can also be described as a period of more intense competition, we need a new name to identify the increase in competition that raises investment (at a given rate of profit) as opposed to the increase in competition that lowers it (through a lower rate of profit). For lack of another name, we call the former type of increase in competition Z-competition. Z-competition is exactly what is needed to raise the level of employment without inflation or to remove the conflict between the objectives of full employment and price level stability. Examples of Z-competition have been given. What is necessary now is to say something about the required doses of the medicine on product markets and on the labor market.

Casual observation suggests that the moves towards free trade in the postwar period brought Z-competition without harm. Economists had pleaded for a speeding up of intra-European trade liberalization, and predictions that the process of tariff reductions within the European Community need not take as long a time as originally envisaged in the Treaty of

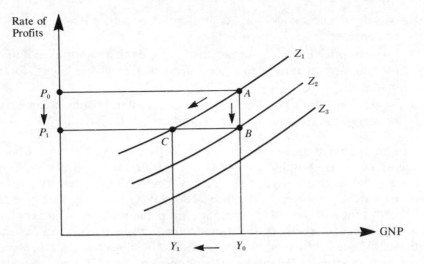

Figure 3-1. Profit Rates and GNP under Different Degrees of Competition.

Rome were borne out by events. It is interesting to note in this context that there were several unilateral steps to speed up the process, each time, incidentally, with a view toward cheapening imports in the context of an anti-inflationary program.

The upward float of the D-Mark in 1971, on the other hand, would hardly have been sustainable for a longer period without a collapse, except if it had resulted in a quick stabilization of costs and prices in West Germany that would have softened the impact on the real exchange rate (which is what matters in this context).

This example teaches an interesting lesson about competition. The final outcome of Z-competition need not necessarily be a fall in profits—unless profits are very high at the beginning. What matters is that firms defend their profits by competitive counteraction and that they remain strong enough to do so. Firms must be willing and able and feel that the following measures are worthwhile:

1. To locate and to remove unnecessary costs in the process of production, in the purchase and sales organizations, in the managerial set-up, and in external activities;

2. To concentrate production on those goods where they are most competitive (have their greatest comparative advantage), even if such concentration, which often leads to economies of scale, means an increase in total entrepreneurial risk;

3. To finance cost saving investments, even if this means more reliance on

outside finance and more control by lenders and new groups of shareholders;

4. To resist price increases for raw material and other inputs even if this is only possible by turning to other sources of supply—perhaps in foreign markets;

5. To resist inflationary wage increases in the interest of maintaining and possibly enlarging the number of workers on the payroll.

The last point shows the difference between the effects of a fall in aggregate demand and Z-competition most clearly. If in a downswing widespread wage pressures emerge, they meet with relatively little resistance from the employers' side since all employers sit in the same boat and know that they all will put up prices in some parallel action. Whatever their organizational strength, their determination to resist must be smaller than that of a single firm that acts under conditions of subjective uncertainty in a competitive struggle for survival. No employers' organization can imitate and can transmit across the bargaining table a genuine feeling of competitive anxiety. The union on the other side of the table, not knowing whether or not employment and survival are at stake, must often go to the extreme of a strike to find out the truth. Under competition, plus uncertainty about whether or not a cost increase can be shifted onto higher prices, however, trade unions may be more prepared to participate in the employment risk.

Such participation can take various forms. The traditional form would be to be more careful in pressing for higher nominal wages, since competitive uncertainty implies that a given increase in nominal wages will amount to a higher increase in real wages, if and when and to the extent that cost increases can no longer be shifted onto higher product prices. Moreover, the structural change that imported Z-competition may entail must make employees aware that they are likely to have better employment opportunities in growth and export industries, but a higher employment risk in industries and firms that have to meet more intense competition. In the latter firms, workers will realize that they have a choice between higher real wages—with dismissals—and lower wage increases—with safer employment. The advice to be given to them would be "lower wage increases," because the alternative means unemployment for those who are dismissed and not immediately able to find employment in expanding industries. Such advice would be equally relevant for the working class as a whole. The reason is simple: if real wages are on the low rather than high side, there will be excess demand for labor rather than unemployment. The excess demand will arise from a stronger demand pull of expanding firms and a smaller rate of dismissals by firms subjected to imported competition. Moreover, there is one important additional consideration: if a change in the structure of employment is brought about through demand pull rather than through dismissals, frictional and structural unemployment will be distinctly lower. The reason is this: when a worker follows a demand pull, he leaves his job because he has found an alternative use for his labor; a worker who is compelled to leave because his firm finds itself in difficulties has been chosen for dismissal because he is of least use for his employer, and there is little regard for whether he will find an alternative job before he reaches retirement age. A small concession in real wages, which transforms a structural change of the cost-push or dismissal type into a demand-pull type, is thus likely to reduce the number of vacancies and the number of job seekers at the same time. More older people and other workers with no alternative employment opportunities will remain employed. This is in addition to the simple employment effect of real wage concessions that consists of an increase in the number of vacancies *in relation* to the number of unemployed persons.

A second and less traditional form by which workers can participate in the risk connected with imported competition is through splitting wages into a contractual part and a residual part. The contractual part would be somewhat lower, and it would be the real wage for which the firm would guarantee employment over the period of the contract. The residual part would be proportional to profits and would be calculated and paid out at the end of the contractual period. Where profit sharing has been tried out already, it may find wider application, once imported competition puts firms under additional pressure. The advantage of this form is that the real wage concession, which may be needed to safeguard employment under conditions of Z-competition, is granted ex ante but not necessarily made ex post. This fits the macroeconomic characteristics of Z-competition very well: by accepting and inviting more competition from abroad and more structural adjustment, the national economy is faced with an additional employment risk ex ante, but as a whole and ex post, the economy is certain to gain in terms of productivity and real incomes.

A third form of redistributing the risk due to Z-competition would be government assistance. The case, however, can hardly be based on the existence or emergence of external economies or nonpecuniary spillover effects, since no such effects seem to be involved. Instead, there is a case for government support to those who are unduly hit by the change for freer trade because they were unable or could not be expected to adjust quickly enough. This case covers the hardship inflicted upon workers who lose their jobs and must change their occupations or their locations—and possibly both. How far it covers entrepreneurs and capital owners is much more debatable, since it is their profession to cope with risks. The only clearcut case would be a compensation for losses that proved to be unavoidable because the change in policy could not be foreseen. To protect the taxpayer and itself against unnecessary claims on these grounds, the government should announce sufficiently well in advance that it is going toward free trade and firms would be well advised to take this into full account in any private planning decisions. Apart from this, the government can create or subsidize institutions that try to assess trends in world markets and that may concentrate on identifying those particular changes likely to arise under the new policy. Private decision makers may thus receive subsidized or free (and refutable) advice that can help to minimize the risks of imported competition.

On the basis of existing knowledge, the following hypotheses can be put forward with good reason.

1. Free trade among industrialized countries does not lead to a clearcut pattern of production. This is because the location of raw material deposits and transportation costs tend to become less important, while the footloose industries that rely on R & D and a highly skilled labor force tend to play an increasing role in the development of the modern industrial state. In terms of locational and regional developments, this will benefit the areas with a preferred climate and a superior leusure value, since labor and capital can be taken as spatially mobile in the medium run. A removal of impediments to trade and factor movements will accelerate this process. If factors are not allowed to move from country to country, free trade will mainly benefit countries where people are more prepared to spend on R & D and the formation of human capital and skill. It will, of course, also benefit more than proportionally those countries that have a sufficiently vigorous class of entrepreneurs who are prepared to meet the challenge of imported competition.

2. To meet the challenge of competition from low-wage countries, entrepreneurs of firms are faced with three options to reduce costs per unit value of output:

First, they can introduce labor-saving machinery and thus substitute capital costs for wage costs in the production of the same products for, of course, only as long as this lowers average total costs.

Second, they can change their product mix so that they are less vulnerable to competition from low-wage countries. The new product mix must, of course, consist of more goods with a high income elasticity of demand and as little as possible of those goods that will increasingly be supplied by producers from low-wage countries.

Third, they themselves can take advantage of the existence of low-wage locations abroad by shifting labor-intense parts of the production process or whole lines of production nearer to their competitors from LDCs. While they are familiar with the peculiarities of demand in the industrialized countries, their competitors have a better knowledge of supply conditions. Joint ventures may save information costs.

3. We can thus envisage a process of world economic growth that has the following characteristics: the industrialized countries concentrate more and more on skill-intensive and research-intensive products; the semi-industrialized countries assume more and more the role of suppliers of manufactured goods; and the least developed of the less-developed countries take up more and more activities that are related to the processing of tropical fruit, the supply of sun-intensive tourist services, and the early stages of processing the indigenous raw materials. Speaking in a very broad sense, it appears that there is and that there will be from the equator northwards up to London, New York, and Tokyo a tendency for the GNP to have

a decreasing content of natural resources, raw materials and labor, and

an increasing content of physical and human capital and of research and development.

This broad view helps to answer such questions as to what kind of employment should be created in the advanced countries, if and when labor is set free due to imported competition from low-wage countries. Such competition and such replacement of labor in advanced countries is indispensible if the latter are to enjoy a higher standard of living including more leisure and a better quality of life.

Chapter 3
Commentary I

George H. Hildebrand

Giersch sees two special virtues in a free trade policy that supplement the more general one of enlarged consumers' welfare. Free trade promotes higher employment and at the same time it contributes to stability of prices. In providing these additional benefits, the policy offers a way of escape from stop-and-go expansions. It does not wrongly presume that unemployment today arises from deficiency of total demand. For the same reason, the policy offers a superior alternative to the standard Keynesian remedies.

The predicament of those who would cure unemployment by increasing total demand is that they get caught in an unsustainable expansion. If they avoid direct controls, they have to rely upon money illusion and sticky prices to increase real demand. But these lags cannot last; the price level shoots up, money demand has to be cut back, and unemployment is left disappointingly high. Alternatively, direct controls may stretch these lags, but they also promote inefficiency. Here the unemployment is disguised through an induced decline in labor productivity: too many employees are required to do the same amount of work.

In Giersch's view, monopoly in both product and factor markets is the basic cause of the conflict between full employment and stable prices. Put differently, with full competition the level of maximum non-inflationary employment would be higher than when monopoly elements are present. If a frontal attack on monopoly is politically impossible, then "imported competition" offers a milder alternative: introduce free international movements of both goods and factors, and when appropriate, manipulate the exchange rate to intensify competition against domestic producers. In consequence, the firms so exposed will be forced to seek cost economies, while their unions will be induced to take it easier on wage increases. If this wage policy becomes more general, it will lower both job vacancies and unemployment together.

For illustration, Giersch cites the appreciation of the mark in 1971. The effect was to squeeze the profits of the export sector and, presumably, of the import-competing industries as well. This compelled higher investments to cut costs, while a cyclical downturn was avoided. At the same time, both output and employment were increased.

On the same logic, I would suggest, devaluation of a currency would work in the wrong direction, because it reduces foreign competition against import-competing industries while simultaneously providing the export sector with price reductions abroad that do not derive from lower domestic costs. Far from stimulating efficiency, devaluation provides added shelter for the inefficient and thereby reduces incentive for cost-cutting investments. It also creates additional "space" for wage increases, which is obviously undesirable where a wage-push movement is already under way. This is not to say that some form of downward revision in the external value of a currency is never needed; rather it is to emphasize that when fixed parities prevail—in other words, when the value of a currency is treated as an administered price—then a one-step devaluation can serve as a means for buying time to check inflation and to introduce greater productive efficiency. But at the same time it supplies false signals to both firms and labor unions, which possibly defeats the official purposes of the devaluation itself.

Two other observations are in order. First, Giersch's appreciation case and the contrasting one of devaluation just considered both presume discrete revaluations of fixed parities. By contrast, with a policy of floating rates, the increasing domestic competitive pressures deriving from an appreciating currency would be continuously applied, rather than coming as a sudden shock. Conversely, with a depreciating currency, the temporary relief to domestic producers would not be concentrated in a single dramatic event, but instead would become incrementally available. This would permit greater attention to be paid to policies for stopping inflation.

Second, Giersch rightly emphasizes that besides appreciation of the external value of a currency, even at stable rates, whether fixed of flexible, free international flows of goods, services, capital, and people all operate to stimulate more efficient uses of scarce resources all around. Trade itself, of course, promotes specialization, which is a major source of higher efficiency. Finding an appropriate system of external values for a currency is essentially a matter of uncovering those activities that a nation can perform better for itself and, *pari passu*, those that it can do better for the rest of the world. This search, of course, requires that barriers to trade and factor flows do not obstruct this endless process of discovery. Equally important, if the external valuation of a currency is left to the market itself, then both the process of search and discovery and its concomitant resource allocation and reallocation are made continuous and automatic. Accordingly, official expertise can be economized as a scarce resource, to be devoted to the tasks of monetary and fiscal management, in place of detailed regulation of trade and capital flows and of efforts to administer fixed parities.

I want now to consider Giersch's view of the linkage between inflation and full employment. If I interpret him correctly, his reason for the link is monopoly in factor and product markets. Freedom of international trade thus follows as a way to check monopoly power to some extent, and through this to raise the level of non-inflationary "full" employment.

I do not disagree in principle, but I do not believe that monopoly in itself is either necessary or sufficient as an explanation of the inflation problem. In labor markets, what monopoly does is to lower the threshold at which the relationship between the total number of job vacancies and the total number of unemployed leads to inflation—such that with a desired further cut in the unemployed there must be introduced a disproportionate increase in vacancies, which in turn will invite the trade unions to accelerate their wage claims. Absent collective bargaining, unemployment (and the unemployment rate) could be reduced further before this critical threshold is reached. Government interventions that raise labor costs work in the same direction. If both unionism and government intervention were not present and the labor supply itself were homogeneous and fully mobile, then the point of balance between total vacancies and total unemployment would be non-inflationary. Structural factors displace this relationship to the right: the point of zero inflation now requires some net excess supply of labor relative to the number of vacancies. Collective bargaining and government intervention increase this displacement still further. Net excess of labor supply must be still larger to permit zero inflation. In a sense, then, we are talking about Friedman's valuable distinction between nominal and natural rates of unemployment.

The inflationary potential of "full" employment depends, of course, on how one defines "full." When Keynes precipitated the issue nearly forty years ago, he offered no quantitative rule. By utilizing a simple aggregative production function with homogeneous labor, in which the marginal and average physical productivity of labor are falling (given capital stock and money wage level), Keynes concluded that prices necessarily begin to rise relative to money wages at some point of total employment.

But these relationships are not very interesting today. However, what can be called the scarce factors theory does attract attention. It recognizes correctly that the unemployed are heterogeneous in skills, efficiency, spatial distribution, and other characteristics. As total demand expands and the general unemployment rate comes down, the supplies of skilled and unusually proficient workers dry up first. As firms now begin to substitute less productive types of labor, their unit labor costs rise. This forces up prices. Thus the general rate of unemployment can reach a floor below which inflation will be encountered, not because of wage raising by unions and the government, but through a special type of non-proportional returns. Collective bargaining and government intervention, of course, can make this situation still worse.

On the scarce factors view, the persistence of an undesirably high general rate of unemployment in the United States, coupled with an equally persistent inflation problem, is not to be attributed to general deficiency of demand or to a growth gap; rather, the root of the problem is structural: the supply of unemployed labor is strongly dominated by youngsters and by adults with unusually low personal productivity because of poor vocational preparation. It takes too long for young job seekers to find their first job. Too many of these starting jobs lead nowhere because of their poor design; accordingly, the voluntary quit rate for youngsters is too high. Together these factors play a major role in bringing about a minimum non-inflationary general unemployment rate that is too high—between 4.5 and 5.0 percent. Demographic shifts under way since 1958 will lower this burden of youth unemployment before long. But they will not remove it entirely.

The cure? Clearly it is not more rapid expansion, which only would inflate costs and prices and drive up interest rates. At this point the authorities either have to accelerate monetary expansion or to slow it down. Thus the system is locked into the dreary sequence of stop-and-go. Rather the solution will have to come from a revised minimum wage tapered downward for ages below 21 years; strengthening of job design and of the links between the school and work; perhaps special work projects for the long-term adult unemployed; and an improved system of labor market information.

There is reason to believe that this problem is peculiarly American. For the European case, Giersch's stress on monopoly factors is probably more appropriate. I conclude then that, as Giersch contends, a liberal trade policy can serve as a check on domestic inefficiency and monopoloid tendencies. However, it will not help to overcome the peculiar structural problems that underlie the high general unemployment rates that have been associated with recent inflation in the United States. Indeed, a liberal international trade policy makes these problems somewhat worse, by allowing disruption of certain vulnerable domestic industries through rapid import penetration. If, then, such a policy is to be pushed anyway, as Giersch and I both think should be done, it has to be accompanied by an effective program on behalf of the losers. In my judgment, such a program ought to combine some system of safeguards with provision of adjustment assistance to induce adaptation or movement of labor and capital, according to the case. Only with an adequate program of this sort can the right kind of trade policy be made politically acceptable in the United States.

Chapter 3
Commentary II

Ryutaro Komiya

The main theme of Giersch's chapter as I understand it is twofold. First, through the process of freeing trade from tariffs and quantitative restrictions on imports as well as exports and of freeing factor movements—such as foreign investments accompanying international marketing or seeking lower costs of production—the degree of competition in each participating country is enhanced and, second, intensified competition through free international trade and investment alleviates the conflict between full employment and price stability, by curbing monopolistic price- and wage-push by oligopolists and trade unions. The policy of freer trade and freer factor movements expands the geographical and economic size of markets, and if at the same time the participating countries' governments cooperate with each other in attacking international cartels and mergers leading to monopoly or oligopoly, the market competitiveness is almost necessarily intensified. This will be a very important force in stabilizing the price level.

Since I agree fully with Giersch on the above theme, my comment on his chapter is concerned with relatively minor points. First, Giersch writes as though economists consider lasting unemployment a reason for deviations from free trade. I think responsible economists don't. The problem here is related to what is called the "assignment problem" in the contemporary theory of economic policy. When there are a number of policy objectives—such as full employment, balance of payments equilibrium, efficient utilization of resources, and so on—all the policy objectives cannot be successfully achieved simultaneously unless there are at least as many policy instruments as there are policy objectives. Moreover, in view of the dynamic process of implementation, one must assign to each policy objective a policy instrument that has the most direct influence on it. For example, adjustment of effective demand through fiscal-monetary policy should be assigned to the objective of full employment, the exchange rate should be assigned to the balance of payments, and so on. I think most economists agree that efficient utilization of resources is one of the most important policy objectives and that assigning protective trade policy to the objective of full employment is obviously a "wrong" assignment.

Second, Giersch argues that wage controls prevent trade unions from pushing firms into a fight for higher productivity and that under what he calls Z-competition, firms are forced and willing to remove unnecessary costs, to finance cost-saving investment through outside funds, to resist inflationary wage increases, and so forth, all of which firms may not do in the absence of Z-competition. I do not question whether these statements were true or not in the special case of Germany in recent years. I point out, however, that these arguments are not based upon economic logic.

According to economic theory, firms always try to maximize profits by fighting for higher productivity, by cutting costs, by undertaking cost-saving investment, and so forth. Whether the market in which they operate is monopolistic, oligopolistic, or competitive is irrelevant.

Apart from a certain inertia, the degree of which is difficult to explain, both monopolistic and competitive firms always pursue cost-reducing and profit-increasing possibilities. The difference between competitive and/or oligopolistic markets is not whether firms pursue such possibilities or not, but whether higher productivity and cost reduction results in lower prices or higher profits (and wages).

Third, the nature of profit in Giersch's discussion is not clear to me. Actual profits in the financial statements of corporations, contain various elements, of which at least the following three conceptually different kinds of profits must be distinguished here: (1) static, monopoly profits, (2) returns on capital funds, and (3) entrepreneurial profits as remuneration for risk-taking activities. Profits in the second and third senses are essential for dynamic economic growth. It is unrealistic that a certain level of investment can be maintained for the long-run, even when the rate of profit is reduced successively from point A towards Yo as shown in Giersch's graph in Figure 3-1.

Chapter 3
Commentary III

Harry G. Johnson

Contrary to what seems a natural interpretation of its message in the light of recent Anglo-American debates over cost-push versus demand-pull inflation, Giersch's chapter does not rest on a naive cost-push theory of inflation and a consequent recommendation of trade liberalization as a means of disciplining cost-push forces. (Such a theory would be open to the objection that monopoly seeks to maximize real profits and will only raise *money* prices continually in an environment of continuing inflation generated by some other mechanism.) Instead, Giersch's chapter is in line with the more sophisticated cost-push theory, according to which the root of the problem is the willingness of government—as a result of commitment to the objective of full employment—to use fiscal and monetary policy to sanction inflationary upward wage and price movements initiated for whatever reason. That particular theory, however, is subject to the critical objection that it leaves undetermined the magnitude of the inflationary wage-price movements that are likely to occur at any time, and therefore the rate of inflation that will result. Carried to its extreme, this criticism points out that if it is well known to wage and price fixers that the government will always bail them out of any adverse employment effects of their actions, there will be no limit to the rate of inflation they will produce.

This logical proposition, however, is itself subject to the objection that employers and unions, as well as the important non-organized sector of the economy, including the service sector and government employment, act as a collectivity in wage and price bargaining. If they do not do so, the rate of inflation will be limited by uncertainty about the actions of other sectors and the reactions of government and the consequential effects of excessive wage and price increases on sectoral employment and sales. If they did do so, they would presumably arrive eventually at some sort of voluntary income policy, since it is easier to calculate real bargains in terms of money of stable purchasing power than in terms of money of depreciating purchasing power.

Giersch's basic model is one in which monopoly prevails over monopsony—the latter in the specific context of a backward-sloping supply curve of labor, a specialization of the case whose significance needs more emphasis in his exposition; monopoly results in a level of unemployment higher than the labor force "wants" or considers desirable in the aggregate and at the level of political decision. Government therefore comes under political pressure to try to raise employment above its "natural" (monopoly-constrained) equilibrium level by demand expansion. It can succeed in this temporarily because of money illusion that enables real monopoly price-fixing to be eroded by inflation; but money illusion fades out with experience, and the employment level regresses towards the natural equilibrium level. This process is generally anticipated and accelerated by a reversal of demand expansion policies prompted by government alarm at the resulting inflation or its concern with its adverse balance-of-payments consequences. Giersch recommends liberal trade policies as a way of breaking the monopoly influence and raising the sustainable equilibrium level of employment.

Giersch's argument, however, seems weak or at least incomplete on one point. How does the employment-reducing effect of monopoly register itself in political pressures for demand-expansionary policies? There are two possibilities of accommodating the labor debarred by monopoly from employment in the monopolized industries. One obvious way suggested by orthodox labor-market theory is the alternative of "leisure," which concept may be extended to include employment in non-monopolized activities. But it is difficult to see in this case a mechanism generating political pressures for demand expansion, except in the case where monopoly is exercised by unions extracting a differential wage over non-union employment or the value of leisure, so that workers in the non-union employment or at leisure can see direct advantages from governmentally induced expansion of demand for the products of unionized industries (or of output in general, which would enable them to shift into the higher-wage unionized industries). Employer monopoly, and monopsony in relation to an upward-sloping labor supply curve, would leave wages equal as between monopolized and competitive industries and/or leisure. The other alternative is that a pool of unemployed labor, registered as such, is attracted to the monopolized industries by the prospect of finding high-paid employment there; again, this assumes union and not employer monopoly, with the exception that employer monopolies may pay wages above the alternative opportunity of labor in order to get a better selection of labor and to obtain disciplinary power over the labor it hires. (Note that in these cases the employers will not end up by paying wages above the marginal product of labor, if the latter is defined properly to include quality and reliability of performance, and indeed if non-monopolized markets were also efficient in labor-market search, the alternative opportunity cost of superior-quality or superior-disciplined labor to monopolized industries will be proportionately higher than that of less attractive types of labor.)

In short, it would appear that to make a bridge from the monopolization hypotheses to the inflationary stop-go policies Giersch assumes it produces, one must concentrate on the particular case of labor monopoly (unionization)—which includes minimum wage laws—and within the context of that case, rely either on conditions that create pools of unemployed labor created by the prospect of part-time or part-year employment at high wages, or on social recognition that demand expansion will create more demand for high-paid labor. The conventional theory of economic policy objectives, which assumes that government policy responds to the relation of the actual unemployment percentage to a target minimum level of unemployment, would make the Giersch analysis depend on the main hypothesis that monopoly is union monopoly and the supplementary hypothesis that such monopoly leads to the creation of a pool of unemployed labor living on the chance of a high-wage job opportunity. (A possible exception must be recognized here too, in the sense that the target unemployment percentage may be pitched far lower than the level ever realized or realizable, in implicit response to the desire of those confined to "leisure" activities in the broad sense by labor monopoly to have the number of high-paid job opportunities expanded.)

In summary, the Giersch analysis as presented does not provide a convincing route from monopoly effects on wages to political pressures for demand expansion.

A final comment is that Giersch looks to trade liberalization and increased international competition to make employers (and workers) work harder for lower real returns; one may question whether this would raise the economic welfare of those concerned, or even of society as a whole on some basis of aggregation.

Reply to Commentary III

Herbert Giersch

Harry Johnson observes that the model in my chapter produces a rate of inflation without limit, unless there is uncertainty. I agree. Moreover, I should have mentioned frictions and intermittent restrictions in the money supply as limits to the rate of inflation.

Johnson also wonders, however, how "the employment-reducing effect of monopoly registers itself in political pressures for demand expansionary policies." My answer is that governments are under an often self-imposed constraint to maintain as high a level of employment, job security, and capacity utilization as the population observes during boom periods. They feel obliged to pursue expansionary policies long before the non-unionized sector has had time to absorb a substantial part of the unused resources. Moreover, there are countries where the non-unionized sector is insignificantly small. While Johnson adopts a long-run approach, I am thinking in terms of a cyclical model.

In addition, I have difficulty in accepting Johnson's broad definition of leisure that embraces what many people, including governments, would regard as involuntary unemployment. Even if those who lose their jobs during a recession considered themselves to be voluntarily unemployed, society, and compcting political forces within, may persuade them that they would be better off if they could find work at prevailing wages. This seems to be the case mentioned by Johnson himself "where monopoly is exercised by unions extracting a differential wage over . . . the value of leisure."

Finally, Johnson questions whether a higher level of employment through increased international competition represents a gain in economic welfare. My answer is that the involuntarily unemployed who are offered jobs and take them are certainly better off. On the other hand, monopoly profits will be reduced, which generates a redistribution of income that even those who do not benefit directly may consider desirable on several grounds, including increased consumer sovereignty and social stability.

Part II
Multinational Corporations and World Trade

4

A Macroeconomic Theory of Foreign Direct Investment

Kiyoshi Kojima

Introduction

One of the most serious omissions in the study of foreign direct investment or the operation of multinational corporations to date is in the area of macroeconomic theory. For an individual firm, the objective of maximizing its profits and/or enlarging its market share through widening territorial horizons towards global logistics is well justified from a microeconomic point of view. However, foreign direct investment has produced a conflict of interests with national objectives of both investing and host countries alike, since national (macro) economic objectives remain paramount under circumstances where national populations—by and large laborers — cannot, practically and institutionally, move internationally with ease. Resolution of this conflict, so that foreign direct investment may contribute harmoniously both to investing and recipient country development, requires a new macroeconomic approach to the problem.[1]

In this chapter, an attempt is made in the second section to identify the characteristics of two different types of foreign direct investment: trade-oriented, which I will argue is the Japanese type, and anti-trade-oriented, which I will argue is the American type.

It will be shown in the third section that comparative profitabilities in trade-oriented, foreign direct investment conform to the direction of potential comparative costs and, therefore, complement each other. In other words, foreign direct investment going from a comparatively disadvantageous industry in the investing country (which is a potentially comparatively advantageous industry in the host country) will harmoniously promote an upgrading of industrial structure on both sides and thus accelerate trade between the two countries.

In comparison, American-type foreign direct investment does not conform to this comparative profitabilities formula, mainly due to the dualistic structure of the American economy—the dichotomy between the new, oligopolistic industries and the traditional, price competitive industries. This type of foreign direct investment is anti-trade oriented and results in balance-of-payments difficulties, the export of jobs, the prevention of structural adjustment, and trade protectionism.

Thus, in the last section of this chapter, a new approach to foreign direct investment policy is formulated and its relationship to trade policy made clear.

75

Trade-Oriented versus Anti-Trade-Oriented Foreign Direct Investment

It is usual to classify the motives for foreign direct investment into resource-oriented, labor-oriented, and market-oriented investment. First, *natural-resource-oriented* investment is obviously trade-oriented or trade-generating for it results from the investing country's desire to increase imports of its comparatively disadvantageously produced or domestically unavailable commodities and it causes growth in vertical specialization between producers of manufactures and primary products. However, there is the problem that integrated production and marketing are often monopolized or oligopolized by big multinationals , which leaves smaller benefits for those countries endowed with natural resources.

Second, the *labor-oriented* investment is also trade-oriented or trade-reorganizing. As wages in the advanced investing country become dearer year by year relative to capital and as new products that are usually more capital- and knowledge-intensive than traditional goods are created one after another, it becomes profitable and rational for the advanced country to contract its own traditional, labor-intensive industries and transfer the location of production to low-wage countries where cheaper labor costs prevail. Thus, corresponding to a dynamic change in comparative advantage, such foreign investment assists the reorganization of the international division of labor and harmonious trade growth between labor-scarce and labor-abundant countries. It should be noted, however, that such foreign direct investment may transfer either traditional labor-intensive industries that are well standardized or new goods that utilize cheap labor intensively from the advanced to the low-wage country. It should also be noted that the labor-oriented investment aims at establishing an export base, rather than import substitution, and the development of exports to the investing country as well as third markets.

Third, *market-oriented* investment can be subdivided into two categories. Foreign direct investment induced by trade barriers in the host country is mostly trade-oriented but in a different way from the trade-oriented investment mentioned above. In this case, heavier tariffs on final products, for example, lead to the substitution for exports of final products of the export of parts and components, intermediate materials, machinery, equipment, and technology necessary to the production of final goods in the investing country. This type of foreign direct investment meets the recipient country's interest in promoting import-substituting activity, not necessarily intended to be competitive in the international market, and therefore results in some waste of resources because of the degree of protection provided to the final goods production. But, if import-substitution industry grows successfully towards export-orientation, then foreign direct investment of this type turns out to be labor-oriented investment. Therefore, there is no essential difference between labor-oriented and *trade-barrier-induced* investment except insofar as one aims at worldwide markets and one is confined to protected domestic markets.

Fourth, there is another type of market-oriented investment that may be called *oligopolistic* foreign direct investment. This is typically found in American investment in new manufacturing product industries in recent decades, as will be seen presently, and is anti-trade-oriented.

Finally, it is probably better to add a fifth type of foreign direct investment—that is, the *internationalization of production and marketing* through vertical and horizontal integration of big multinational enterprises. Whether this is anti-trade-oriented or not depends upon whether the main activity comprises oligopolistic investment or not.

Japanese Foreign Direct Investment

Although there are commitments to a substantial increase in the "official" component in Japan's total aid, foreign investment will play a more significant role in assisting the economic development of developing countries. At the end of 1969, Japan's total foreign investments abroad (including advanced countries) amounted to $2,690 million (see Table 4-1). It is projected that total investments will rise to $11,500 million by 1975 and $27,000 million by 1980[2] and that the outflow in those years will be around $2,000 million and $3,500 million, respectively. Of this, $1,900 million will be directed to Asia and will account for 20 percent of the total foreign investment flow to this area. By 1980, there will be an accumulated Japanese investment in Asia of around $7,000 million. These rapid increases in Japan's investments may well arouse Asian nationalism against Japanese domination.

Direct foreign investment—that is, the transmission to the host country of a package of capital, managerial skill, and technical knowledge—is a potent agent of economic transformation and development. A large increase in Japanese direct investment in developing countries, insofar as it is welcomed by them, will contribute significantly to the development of their natural resources, their agricultural production, and their processing industries, on the one hand, and on the other, to transferring from Japan to developing countries those manufacturing industries suitable to each developing country.

Japan has endeavored to invest in developing countries with the object of securing increased imports of primary products that are vitally important for her economy. This is called "development assistance for import." It was first directed (and is still being directed in increasing amounts) towards

Table 4-1
Balance of Japan's Direct Overseas Investments, by Industry ($U.S. Million and Percent)

| | Balance of Investments | | Percent of Total | |
	1969	1980	1969	1980
Resource- Oriented[a]	1,092	13,881	40.7	50.8
Labor- and Market-Oriented[b]	620	7,148	23.1	26.2
Finance and Services[c]	969	6,280	36.2	23.0
Total	2,683	27,309	100.0	100.0

[a]Agriculture, fishery, forestry.
[b]Foodstuffs, textiles, chemicals iron, non-ferrous, machinery, electrical machinery, transport machinery, construction.
[c]Commerce, finance, insurance.
Source: Japan Economic Research Center, *Japan's Economy in 1980 in the Global Context* (March 1972), p. 50.

natural resource development projects such as oil, natural gas, iron ore, coal, copper, bauxite, and other metals. Wood and timber also have high priority. The benefits of such development assistance are limited, however, to those countries where abundant natural resources are available and the employment and training effects are small insofar as the goods are exported in the form of raw materials. If we can extend our development investment for import to agricultural products, benefits will be spread more widely in developing areas. Thailand's successful development of exports to Japan of maize is a good example. Since February 1970, the Asian Trade Development Corporation has been providing subsidies to development assistance for import, with regard to various agricultural products produced in the wider Asian area. The government is also considering whether to provide low-interest foreign exchange loans to those enterprises that venture to develop new natural resource deposits.

Japan's direct investment for creating manufacturing capacity in developing countries is important and plays a harmonious role for both sides provided appropriate manufacturing industries are selected. The industries to be chosen should be those in which Japan is losing comparative advantage while developing countries are gaining it (or are expected to gain it). Such industries should preferably be export-oriented and should not merely serve the benefit of the economically privileged classes in recipient countries.

Thus, Japanese foreign investment has to date been "trade-oriented." It has been aimed at complementing Japan's comparative advantage position. The major part of investment has been directed towards natural resource development in which the Japanese economy is comparatively disadvantaged.[3] Even investment in manufacturing has been confined either to such traditional industries as textiles, clothing, and processing of steel, in which Japan has been losing its comparative advantage, or the assembly of motor vehicles and the production of parts and components of radios and other electronic machines, in which cheaper labor costs in Southeast Asian countries are achieved and Japanese firms can increase exports,[4] by substituting for exports of final products, exports of machinery and equipment for the factory and technological know-how.[5] In this sense, Japanese foreign direct investment is quite complementary to changes in its comparative advantage position.

A substantial proportion of Japanese foreign direct investments in manufacturing is undertaken by small- and medium-sized firms and on a smaller scale than by American firms[6] that transferred technology suitable to local factor proportions with larger employment and training effects than those characteristic of "enclave" investments. Joint ventures have been preferred to wholly-owned subsidiaries.

Suppose that a textile industry, which is losing comparative advantage in Japan, moves away from Japan through increased direct investment in developing countries. This will promote structural adjustment in Japan and open wider markets for developing-country products. If other advanced countries do the same, markets for developing-country products will become very large. The Japanese textile industry has a long experience of excellent management and technology that is more suitable to developing countries than that of America or Europe. When abundant, relatively cheap labor is combined with this in developing countries, the joint venture products will certainly succeed in international competition.

It is better for Japan to transfer out of those industries in which she is losing her comparative advantage, as she has done, and to invest in developing countries that are gaining a comparative advantage in the same industries. In other words, foreign direct investment to developing countries should be, as Japan's has been, "trade-oriented," and aimed at complementing and strengthening comparative advantage in investing and receiving countries respectively.

In Asia, the success of free trade and investment zones is impressive in Kaoshiung, Taiwan, as is the development of a similar area at the Jurong Industrial Estate, Singapore, as well as the successful industrialization in Korea and Hong Kong. These demonstrate the need for step-by-step transfer of manufacturing industries from advanced to developing countries.

Foreign direct investment, in harmony with changes in comparative advantage, will accelerate structural adjustment in Japan and lead to a contraction of traditional industries of the labor-intensive type. It is in the mother company's interests to make investment activity prosperous by opening markets both in Japan and other advanced countries, even through taking advantage of general preferences provided only for developing-country products. The mother company's market facilities are indispensable for the new entry of developing-country products to advanced-country markets. Foreign direct investments for Japanese small- and medium-scale firms, which played a major part of past manufacturing investments, are a promising outlet for their survival and a great accelerator to internal structural adjustment.

In contrast to Japan, it seems to me that the United States has transferred abroad those industries that ranked in the top of her comparative advantage and has thus brought about balance-of-payments difficulties, unemployment, and then need for protection of her remaining industries.

Typical American-type foreign direct investment is well characterized by Raymond Vernon and Stephen Hymer. The concern of Vernon and others[7] was to explain how a new product is invented and manufactured on a large scale in leading industrial countries. Exports of this product grow insofar as a "technological gap" exists between the product-developing country and foreign countries. Foreign producers imitate the new technology and follow suit. Then exports slow down and through direct investment an attempt is made to secure foreign markets. When the technology is standardized and widely disseminated and the limit of scale economies is reached, trade based on wage costs—or factor proportions—starts, and the country turns to import this product from abroad.

According to Vernon, "the U.S. trade position in manufactured goods is based heavily on a comparative advantage in the generation of innovations, rather than on the more conventional notion of relatively cheap capital," and "the big postwar increase in U.S. overseas investment in manufacturing subsidiaries has come about mainly in the kind of industry that would be expected to have participated in such a process: industries associated with innovation and with oligopoly. It is explained why so much of the investment is found in the chemical industries, the machinery industries, the transportation industries, and the scientific instrument industries."[8] They are "highly innovative and strongly oligopolistic," and "multinational enterprises are found principally in industries that devote a relatively high proportion of their resources to research and advertising and that tend to be dominated by very large firms."[9]

It should be noted that the product cycle or industrial organization approach to foreign direct investment is essentially microeconomic and deals with one commodity. It is partial equilibrium analysis. The approach suggests that once low labor costs become beneficial to the firm, the whole industry had better invest in the lower-wage country. According to comparative advantage theory à la Heckscher-Ohlin, only less capital and knowledge intensive industry profitably invests abroad. There must be some special reason why new industries of the more capital- and knowledge-intensive type move abroad through foreign direct investment from America.

A similar view is seen by Stephen Hymer. After noting the association of multinational corporations with a few large firms, in oligopolistic industries—industries with special characteristics (characterized by large firms, high capital intensity, advanced technology, differentiated products, and so forth)—Hymer points out three factors that determine whether an industry invests abroad or not:

First, there must be some kind of barrier to entry in the industry (technological, economies of scale, differentiated products) so that local firms cannot compete with profits below a level which compensates the multinational corporation for the extra costs of operating in a foreign country and integrating geographically dispersed operation; second, it must be advantageous to produce locally rather than export from a single production center (this depends upon tariffs, the size of the narket, and the threat of local competition); and, third, the firm must find it more profitable to exploit the foreign advantage through direct investment rather than licensing. Hence a technological lead is not a sufficient explanation of foreign investnent. One must also explain why the technology is not sold like other commodities. The answer usually lies in the marketing characteristics of the advantage, that is, the difficulty of extracting full and quasi-rent where markets are imperfect.[10]

Hymer comes to the striking conclusion that "on the assumption that the internationalized sector grows at 8 percent and the non-internationalized sector at 4 percent, international production will account for 50 percent of the total world production by the year 2005 and 80 percent by the year 2040."[11]

Thus, the American economy is split into a dualistic structure: (a) innovative and oligopolistic industries or, in brief, new industries, and (b) traditional industries (textiles and so on) that are price-competitive and relatively stagnant. The genuine product cycles and foreign direct investments take place successively only within the innovative and oligopolistic industry group. Foreign direct investments from these few industries that ranked at the top of American comparative advantage are "anti-trade-oriented" or involve foreign direct investments that work against the structure of comparative advantage. Those new industries should strengthen exports of their final products if they were conscious of national economic interests, but actually they set up foreign subsidiaries, thereby cutting off their own comparative advantage and inducing increased imports of those products from abroad where they invest. Both the loss of foreign markets and reverse imports later on result in balance-of-payments difficulties and the "export of job opportunities."

It may be true, as many researchers[12] claim, that the new industry sector contributes on balance to foreign exchange earnings, due to increased exports of intermediate goods and equipment, the return flow of earnings from past investment, and the like. It should be stressed, however, that if they had been conscious of national economic interests, by refraining from foreign investment and strengthening export promotion, those new industries would have earned greater export surpluses and covered import surpluses in other sectors.

If American foreign manufacturing investment was "trade-oriented," rather than new-industries-oriented it would be welcomed by developing countries and accelerate the reorganization of North-South trade, as in the case of Japan's investment.[13]

Moreover, since innovation and foreign direct investment cycles are confined to the new oligopolistic industry sector, the inflow of resources from the traditional sector is restricted and structural adjustment hindered. An increased labor force was available for employment in traditional industries, but traditional industries have been losing their comparative advantage. In consequence, there has been a rise in protectionist attitudes. Thus the American economy has fallen into a vicious circle due to foreign direct investment of the anti-trade-oriented type.

A Model of Comparative Investment Profitabilities

Comparative advantage changes mainly due to differential rates of growth in factor endowments, as the Heckscher-Ohlin theorem and the Rybczinski theorem show. Foreign direct investment is trade-oriented, or more exactly trade-reorganization-oriented, if it transfers a package of capital, technology, and managerial skill from an industry that has a comparative disadvantage in the investing country to the recipient country in which it develops a comparative advantage. This helps the reorganization of the international division of labor and trade between them by upgrading the industrial structure of both countries. The point is that foreign direct investment must work in a complementary fashion with changes in the pattern of comparative advantage. On the other hand, if foreign direct investment moves out of an industry in which there is a comparative advantage in the investing country, it prevents mutual upgrading of the industrial structure and blocks the reorganization of international trade. This is foreign direct investment of anti-trade-reorganization-oriented type.

In order to make clear the difference of the two types of foreign investment, let us first construct a model of comparative investment profitabilities for trade-oriented or Japanese-type foreign direct investment.

It should be noted that trade-oriented foreign direct investment works only in a competitive world in which standardized commodities are produced and traded and competitiveness is determined by traditional comparative advantage theory à la Ricardian theory or Heckscher-Ohlin theory. In other words, it is not a problem of "technological-gap trade" but in "low-wage trade" in the product cycle.

To understand the determinants of direct investment, it may be useful to set out the following production function:

$$Q = f(L, K, T, M),$$

where Q denotes the output produced, L and K labor and capital, T technology used and M managerial skills or organizational technique.[14] Foreign direct investments transfer the package of K, T and M, but it is assumed that endowment of K, besides L, is *marginal* to total capital formation both in the investing and receiving countries. Technology and management used in country A (advanced industrialized country or Japan) are supposed to be superior to those in country D (developing country) before the foreign direct investment from country A to D takes place, but the foreign direct investment makes it possible for country D to use the same superior technology and management. This is possible because the technology and management are not specific but general factors that we assume are transferable, either in a package or separately between countries on a competitive basis.

Thus, the comparative advantage structure before the foreign direct investment takes place is like that represented in Table 4-2 in which the costs of the two countries are shown in a common monetary unity (say, the dollar). Country D produces more expensively than country A both X-goods (traditional labor-intensive goods, say, textiles) and Y-goods (new capital-knowledge-intensive goods, say, computers) because of its inferior technology and management as compared with country A.[15] However, country A has a comparative advantage in Y-industry while country D its (potential) comparative advantage in X-industry; or

$$\frac{P_{XA}}{P_{YA}} \Big/ \frac{P_{XD}}{P_{YD}} = \frac{100}{100} \Big/ \frac{150}{300} = 2 > 1,$$

where P denotes production cost or price. This comparative advantage pattern results from the assumption that country A has a larger amount of K compared to country D—that is, $K_D/L_A > K_D/L_D$—while X-goods are more labor intensive than Y-goods in both countries alike—that is, $K_{XA}/L_{XA} < K_{YA}/L_{YA}$ and $K_{XD}/L_{XD} < K_{YD}/L_{YD}$—according to the Heckscher-Ohlin theorem.

The situation may be illustrated well by Figure 4-1, where XX and YY are the isoquants for the two sectors in country A and $X'X'$ and $Y'Y'$ those in country D, before foreign direct investment takes place. In country A,

Table 4-2
Comparative Costs Before Direct Investments

	Country A	Country D
X-goods	$100	$150
Y-goods	$100	$300

the factor endowment ratio, K_A/L_A, is shown by PA, the factor price ratio by MN, the equilibrium production points at A and B, and the costs of the two goods are 1:1. In country D, before the foreign direct investment, the factor endowment ratio, K_D/L_D, is shown by P_D, the factor price ratio by α's, the equilibrium production points at a' and b', and the cost of X-goods is lower than Y-goods.

Now, if direct investments take place and T and M are transferred from country A to D, the production function in country D becomes the same as in country A, which is shown by the isoquant XX and YY. However, due to the lower capital endowment and higher capital price ratio in country D, the equilibrium production points would be at a and b, which leaves the product price ratio higher for Y-goods. The new conparative costs when direct investment takes place in both industries may be shown as Table 4-3, in which production costs of both goods in country D are reduced by 40 percent as compared with Table 4-2 (although the degree of cost reduction may vary somewhat in the two industries, the variation must not be so big as to make the new comparative advantage pattern reverse so far as to make the X-industry more labor intensive than the Y-industry) and the cost of X-goods in country D is lowered so that country D's X-goods industry becomes competitive in international market. To reach that situation takes some time for learning the production process, training labor, and realizing economies of scale as Akamatsu's catching-up product cycle theory clearly shows.[16]

In a developing or catching-up country, the product cycle starts from the importation of the new product with some superior quality. "Imports reconnoiter and map out the country's demand," and once increased demand approaches the domestic production threshold, domestic production can be started economically.[17] A learning process follows and is assisted by the importation of technological know-how and/or foreign direct investment. The expansion of production then leads to the exploitation of economies of scale, increases in productivity, improvements in quality, and reductions in costs. This involves an import-substitution process. But as domestic costs reach the international competitive cost threshold, foreign markets are developed, the scale of production is extended further, and costs are reduced again. Thus, the expansion of exports that is originally made possible by the growth of domestic demand, in its

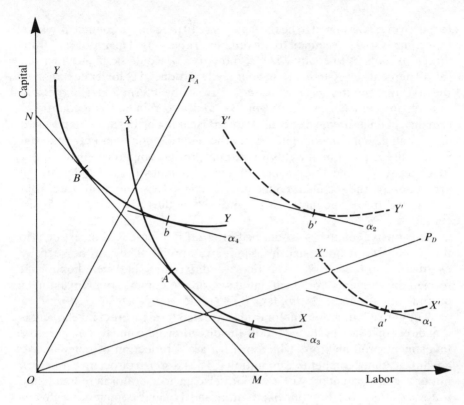

Figure 4-1 Changes in Comparative Advantage Due to Foreign Direct Investment

Table 4-3
Comparative Costs When Direct Investments Are Taking Place in Both Industries

	Country A	Country D
X-goods	$100	$ 90
Y-goods	$100	$180

turn, provides a stimulus to industrial development. In sum, it may be appropriate to call such successive development of imports-domestic production-exports the catching-up product cycle. It should be noted that such a product cycle takes place only for standardized, not new, products and in developing, not leading, industrial countries.

Now, what would be expected profit rates for the investing country A? The profit rate from domestic investment for X- and Y-industries, x_d and y_d

respectively, is assumed to be the same, say 10 percent, in country A where free competition is assumed to prevail (see Table 4-4). The profit rate from direct investment to country D's X-industry, x_f, would be higher than x_d, say 12 percent, for X-industry in country D, produced at lower cost than in the investing country, becomes competitive in the international market and thus retains a greater profit margin. By contrast, Y-industry in country D remains, even if foreign direct investment is taking place, at a comparative disadvantage and uncompetitive in the international market, and the foreign direct investment yields no or small profits compared with domestic investment, y_d, and foreign investment in X-industry, x_f, under strong protection by the recipient country. In Table 4-4, y_f, the profit rate from direct investment in country D's Y-industry is thus assumed to be 5 percent.

Obviously, country A would be better off if it increased investment in the Y-industry at home and in X-industry abroad. This can be seen by examining (a) the absolute profit rate differential between home and foreign investments for each industry or (b) comparative investment profitabilities—that is, $(x_f/y_f)/(x_d/y_d) = (12/15)/(10/10) = 2.4 > 1.$[18]

The core of our argument for trade-oriented foreign direct investment is that direct investment should follow the direction indicated by comparative investment profitabilities, which in turn are a reflection of comparative advantage under competitive conditions. Thus, foreign direct investment is not only complementary with trade but also an accelerator in reorganizing trade patterns in the direction of potential and dynamic comparative advantage. This harmonious potential of foreign direct investment is revealed in the fact that because of comparative investment profitabilities, direct investment from country A actually takes place only in X-industry in country D, and results in the new comparative cost pattern shown in Table 4-5. Table 4-5 reflects the fact that the comparative cost differential is widened due to foreign direct investment as compared with Table 4-2, thereby transforming the X-industry in country D from a potentially advantageous to a strongly competitive exportable industry. Due to such dynamic change in the pattern of comparative advantage, country A is forced and willing to promote structural adjustment to contract investment in and the production of X-goods, which becomes an import industry, and to shift its resources towards foreign direct investment and domestic investment in the Y-industry as well, the comparative advantage of which is strengthened as shown in Table 4-5. Thus, this type of trade-oriented direct investment will bring about an upgrading of industrial structure both in recipient and investing countries alike.

Let us now examine foreign direct investments of the American or anti-trade-oriented type. It is supposed that the pattern of comparative advantage between country P (say a pioneer country like the United States)

Table 4-4
Comparative Profit Rates for Country A

	Domestic Investment		Foreign Direct Investment	
X-industry	x_d	10%	x_f	12%
Y-industry	y_d	10%	y_f	5%

Table 4-5
Comparative Costs When Direct Investments Are Taking Place Only in X-Industry

	Country A	Country D
X-goods	$100	$ 90
Y-goods	$100	$300

and country D is the same as in Table 4-2. Even with such a pattern of comparative advantage, comparative profit rates for country P would be like Table 4-6. First, this is that due to the dualistic structure of the economy separating the new oligopolistic sector, Y, from the traditional competitive sector, X, where the profit rate from domestic investment is not the same in the two sectors but low in the latter, say 5 percent, and high in the former, say 10 percent. Second, since the X-industry is assumed to operate under conpetitive conditions not only in the domestic market but throughout the world, its foreign direct investment, if it takes place, is able to obtain the same profit rate, X_f being 12 percent, as country A's foreign direct investment. Third, the profit rate from foreign direct investment in the Y-industry—that is, Y_f,—ought to be lower (or even negative) than in domestic investment if the industry were under competitive system, but it is assumed to be 15 percent higher than in domestic investment and highest in the comparative profitabilities without any relationship to comparative advantages. This results from such entirely different causes as technological advantage, production differentiation, superior marketing, and so forth, any of which represent some monopolistic element as explained in the previous section.[19] In this case, the package of capital, technology and managerial skill transferred from country P to country D is not a general factor but a factor specific to that monopolistic firm.

Now, in the anti-trade-oriented type, foreign direct investment takes place in Y-industry, the new oligopolistic industry that is top in the rank of comparative advantage, in order to realize the higher profit rate, 15 percent, than that in domestic investment, 10 percent, for the sake of the

Table 4-6
Comparative Profit Rates for Country P

	Domestic Investment		Foreign Direct Investment	
X-industry	X_d	5%	X_f	12%
Y-industry	Y_d	10%	Y_f	15%

company's profit maximization ahead of oligopolistic competitors. This has its rationale from a microeconomic point of view but not from a macroeconomic point of view.

First, though it is interesting but inessential to our argument, in terms of comparative profitabilities—that is, $(Y_f/X_f)/(Y_d/Y_d) = (15/12)/(10/5) = 5/8 > 1$—foreign direct investment in Y-industry is *comparatively* less advantageous than that in X-industry. Thus, the latter is more advantageous for the national economy as a whole, since foreign direct investment in X-industry increases the profit rate by 7 percent (i.e., X_f-X_d), which is larger than 5 percent (i.e., Y_f-Y_d) in Y-industry.

Second, if foreign direct investment takes place in the Y-industry and it is successful from the point of view of the firm, production abroad becomes competitive and cheaper than in the investing country, which results in reverse imports. This means that foreign direct investment of this type reverses the investing country's comparative advantage.

Third, it is true that new products are successively created and new product cycles take place one after the other in America. Multinational corporations grow bigger and maintain monopolistic or oligopolistic gains. But, it is also true that the creation of new products becomes smaller, while the spread of new technology is fast and is accelerated by foreign direct investment.[20] Thus, the American economy will lose its comparative advantage in new products (the Y-industry in our model) sooner or later and has lost it in traditional manufacturing industry (X-industry in our model) for a different reason. In the long run, this brings about difficulties in exporting and thus the balance of payments for the United States. Where are laborers to be employed? They should be employed in the new industry sector. However, the new industry sector does not offer many job opportunities, because of foreign direct investment. Therefore, the labor force has to be absorbed in traditional, comparatively disadvantaged industries and the service sector, which require strong protection. This blocks needed structural adjustments in the economy.

What the American economy needs most is to have its dualistic structure broken into an entirely competitive system in order to allow the traditional sector's resources to move freely into new growth sectors and the reorganization of industrial structure with equal profitability between industries. From the point of view of world resource utilization and welfare, foreign direct investment by monopolistic or oligopolistic multinational firms involves distortions and is not desirable.

It would be even better if the United States invested abroad in such traditional manufacturing industries as textiles, steel, shipbuilding, and so forth, that represent her comparatively disadvantaged industries. It is not understandable that many economists took it for granted that those industries are not suitable for foreign direct investment[21] for they are a promising line of foreign direct investment for Japan and, perhaps a few decades ago, were for the United Kingdom.[22] Thus, not all the foreign direct investment results in the "export of jobs",[23] but the anti-trade-oriented type does.

Trade Policy versus Direct Investment Policy

Should free trade policy be a basic rule to follow and the role of foreign direct investment be subordinate to it, or should it be the reverse? This may be the most important question to be decided in considering the relationship between trade and foreign direct investment policy. It seems to me that the former should be taken as a basic policy attitude.

The decisions and performance of U.S.-based multinationals may be rational and, perhaps wise, in terms of the firm for its profit-maximization. But investment of an anti-trade-oriented type is in conflict with national-economic development as explained above. Labor is still immobile internationally and, therefore, economic development and welfare should be considered in terms of national economy.

Foreign direct investment should be trade-oriented and since this is most beneficial for both sides, this type of investment should be encouraged so as to accelerate the reorganization of North-South trade.

International trade theory aims at clarifying rational national economic development and mutual prosperity of trading nations when international factor movements are absent. The Heckscher-Ohlin-Samuelson theorem proves the possibility of international factor-price equalization, although under strict assumptions, without international factor movements. The international movement of capital, technological and managerial knowledge, with which some country is lacking or lagging, is desirable to complement and facilitate the process of international factor-price equalization and thus national economic development. It should be subordinate to, but not master of, international trade and trade policy.

Unfortunately, however, recent developments in the actual world seem to have been quite the reverse. Stephen Hymer warns:

Multinational corporations, because of their favorable position (large size, wide horizons and proximity to new technology) and the favorable environment (the initial large gold reserves of the United States, the formation of the Common Market, the small size of foreign investment), were in the vanguard of the revolution in world economic structure. The next round is likely to be characterized by increased emphasis on politics rather than economics and a much less free hand for business. The conflict is not so much between nationalism and internationalism, as the supporters of the multinational corporations like to put it; or between corporations and nation-states, as others prefer; but between groups of people within corporations and nation-states struggling over who decides what and who gets what—that is, between large corporations over their share of the world market, between big business which is internationally mobile and small business and labor which are not, between the middle classes of different countries over managerial positions, between high-wage labor in one country and low-wage labor in another, and between excluded groups in each country and their elites in that country.[24]

"During the next ten years, the challenge of European and Japanese firms to American corporations will increase the maneuverability of the third world. But increasingly as firms interpenetrate each other's markets and develop global outlooks, competition will turn to collusion as dominant firms of the center present a united front."[25]

These mean the spread of the dualistic structure of the American economy between the traditional, price competitive sector and the new, oligopolistic sector into the entire world economy. International prices are eroded and twisted by the cost of reducing advantages of economies of scale, marginal costing, product differentiation, intra-corporation pricing, tax-havens, oligopolistic competition, and so forth, all of which belongs to major characteristics of big multinationals, and, therefore, there is considerable disillusionment with the relevance of free trade theory and policy, requiring "the political economy of the second best."[26]

How can foreign direct investment or the activities of multinationals be subordinated to and what kind of contribution can it make to international trade growth? There are three aspects of foreign direct investment of the activities of multinational corporations to be evaluated: (1) the complementation of capital, technological and managerial knowledge that are in shortage in the recipient economy; (2) the monopolistic element, and (3) the internalization of production and marketing for utilizing various kinds of economies of scale.

To complement capital, technological, and managerial knowledge that are short in the recipient economy is a genuine function of foreign direct investment and "a potent agent of economic transformation and development, not only in the more laggard 'developed' countries but also in developing countries of the world."[27] However, it usually involves monopolistic elements since it is undertaken by big, monopolistic or oligopolistic multinational corporations particularly in the case of American type investments.[28]

The monopolistic or oligopolistic nature of multinationals, internal as well as global, should be rectified, for it results in a wastage of world resources. Therefore, a major object of investment policy should be to promote the genuine role of foreign direct investment but to reduce and/or eliminate the monopolistic element. This conforms to free trade policy. A new role for, and form of, foreign direct investment policy should be encouraged[29] in order to maximize its benefits, especially with respect to investment in developing countries.

1. The most important policy is what kind of industry should be gradually transferred from advanced countries to developing countries, appropriate to the stage of the latters' economic development. Foreign companies invest according to private profitability without any consideration of the entire range of (potential) comparative costs, national economic development plans, and priorities in the recipient country.

Hence, there are many accusations against anti-trade-oriented or American type investment but few in principle against the trade-oriented or Japanese type investment, although there are complaints about the performance and behavior of Japanese firms abroad. Therefore, investors should ensure in consultation with the competent authorities that the investment fits satisfactorily into the economic and social development plans and priorities of the host country.[30] It is not necessary for the United States to control and reduce the direct investment outflow in general but to select appropriate industries in each recipient economy. Unless this is done by the United States, a selective control of direct investment inflow by the host country is inevitable and reasonable from the viewpoint of national economic development.

2. Instead of a package of capital, technology, and managerial skill, the transfer of only parts of the package may be considered, if the recipient country desires, through loan-cum-management contracts or by transfer of technology through licensing arrangements rather than direct investment. This may be desired because the package deal is the source of extra monopolistic profits, and because wider spillover effects for genuine national economic development are derived from an unpackaged transfer even if it takes a somewhat longer time and is less efficient than a package transfer.

Technological know-how should genuinely be a public good, provided that there is enough incentive for innovation[31] and should not be the source of monopolistic or oligopolistic gains.

Agricultural technology is improved by public institutions and made available to developing countries' farmers free of charge and even with training help. Why should not the same be done in manufacturing industry? Some special consideration should be given for technology transfer to developing countries.

3. From the same reasoning, joint ventures with local capital are preferable to wholly-owned subsidiaries. It may be most desirable to establish multinational joint ventures in which each advanced country provides either capital or different technology and managerial knowledge according to its advantage.

4. It is also better to transplant technology suitable to local factor proportions rather than sophisticated technology. Small- and medium-scale enterprises are better than the big "enclave-type" enterprises that are usual. In this sense, Japanese type investment is more suitable to developing countries.

5. Priority should be put on investment in industries that have wide spillover effects in technology transfer, labor training, employment, and external economies, and on industries that benefit mass consumption by ordinary people rather than by privileged classes.

6. In the field of natural resource developments, developing countries have strong nationalistic fears against foreign extraction, and they sometimes nationalize such enterprises. Therefore, new forms and new codes of behavior should be devised particularly for this type of foreign investment. Import-linked investments and production-sharing methods, as have been adopted by Japan, may be recommended.

The development of natural resources, including timber, in developing countries is not only highly risky but also expensive for private enterprise since it has to provide infrastructure—such as roads, railways, harbors, and towns—usually provided by the host government in advanced countries. A close combination of private investment and official development assistance should be considered so that the latter accommodates needed infrastructure by making private investment more attractive. Otherwise, natural resource development in advanced countries will go ahead and that in developing countries may be delayed. Also, a risk-insurance system should be introduced by some international organization.

The establishment of facilities for the processing of natural resources within the developing countries where they are extracted is desirable from the point of view of both developing countries and Japan. But it is not necessarily economical. Careful case by case study is required.

7. A progressive transfer of ownership may be necessary if the genuine objective of foreign direct investment is not a permanent source of nonopolistic profit but the complementation of deficient factors in the recipient country. Equity may be gradually transformed into loan capital. Precontracted nationalization, phasing-out, and other divestment methods should be examined seriously.[32]

8. One aim of the above is to make foreign investment more suitable and less expensive for the national economic development of developing countries. The other aim should be to promote the reorganization and

growth of North-South trade. Here, all the policies of advanced countries for increasing the exports of manufactured goods from developing countries should be so accommodated as to promote structural change on both sides and the harmonious development of North-South trade. Thus, an integrated aid, investment *cum* preference, structural adjustment policy is required.[33]

From the point of view of international trade policy in relation to investment policy, it is most essential to liberalize all the tariff and non-tariff barriers to trade so that potential comparative costs will be available in practice. Because of the existence of trade barriers, much foreign direct investment has as its motive the objective of getting behind trade barriers and obtaining extra profits from protection. To put it more generally, because of market imperfections accelerated by trade barriers, there is a stimulus to anti-trade-oriented direct investment, and the desire of multinationals dominates and twists trade policy. In addition, because of the trade barriers in advanced countries against exports from developing countries, true comparative costs are hidden, which lowers profits and thus hinders needed trade-oriented direct investment, and blocks the reorganization of North-South trade as well.

This leads to a comment on present American foreign economic policy. Many economists recognize that American comparative advantages lie only in agriculture and some of the new products that rapidly lose their comparative advantage, however, due to hasty foreign direct investment. America has to live on the return flow from past investment, and therefore increased foreign investment is not only justifiable but most essential to the American balance of payments.[34] This seems to be a logical result of the American-type foreign direct investment, and its admission is a defeatism. The United States seeks trade liberalization by foreign countries but has to increase her own protection for traditional industries. Why does the United States not increase domestic, instead of foreign, investment in order to strengthen the competitiveness of some of her traditional industries and to create new products that are retained for export purposes?

It is also a dilemma for the American economy that it welcomes foreign direct investment from Europe and Japan in order to increase employment. Japanese investment is only profitable in America in such industries as textiles, which are heavily protected except in minor specialities. This further blocks the reorganization of North-South trade.

Finally, how should the so-called internationalization of production and marketing, which consists of the fifth category of foreign direct investment[35] be evaluated? The global logistics of big multinationals are a rational means of maximizing economies of scale in production, in the case of the vertical integration of the firm, and pecuniary economies in the case of horizontal integration or conglomerates. This is a technical rationality that should be encouraged as far as it does not accompany monopolistic behavior, although "the multinational corporation reveals the power of size and the danger of leaving it uncontrolled."[36]

International trade theory has been mainly concerned with the division of labor between firms, coordinated by markets, while multinationals realize the division of labor within firms, coordinated by entrepreneurs.[37] The latter is particularly useful and efficient to promote horizontal trade between parts and components each of which is produced in a different country with the economies of scale greater than minimum optimum.[38] The trouble with this kind of horizontal trade is the difficulty of reaching agreement on specialization between countries.[39] This difficulty is easily overcome in the multinational corporation since agreed specialization is made by the central decision making of the firm. However, a rational specialization program is made possible only in a free-trade area where there are no trade barriers and no fear of increased barriers exists. Certainly, monopolistic behavior should be strictly controlled. This may be feasible if the integrated market is so wide that many enterprises in each industry have to compete with each other.

Alternatively, as far as new manufactured goods are concerned, horizontal trade mainly among advanced countries should be promoted instead of direct investment. Innovation of new goods is required for the reorganization of and new dynamism in the international division of labor, while innovative human resources are relatively scarce in the world as a whole. It might be desirable for advanced countries to arrange an agreement for specialization in the line of innovation in which each country concentrates its effort. Assurance of specialization and accompanying economies of scale will promote liberalization of trade in these commodities. They might also be able to spare innovative human resources to create technology that is more suitable to developing countries.

If all advanced countries liberalize imports of new goods and exporting countries make serious efforts at exporting, mutual trade in these goods among advanced countries will certainly expand and there is no need to undertake foreign direct investment. If firms still dare to undertake direct investment, it is because monopolistic profits are anticipated; such investment should not be allowed.

Such agreed international specialization in the innovative activities may be the only solution for avoiding the vicious circle resulting from Anerican-type foreign direct investment.

In conclusion, it is worth stressing that foreign direct investment and the activities of multinationals should be trade-oriented and subordinated to free trade policy, so as to contribute to the reorganization of the international division of labor and the growth of trade between advanced and developing countries and among industrialized countries alike. A code of behavior of international investments[40] should be thought out along this line.

Notes

1. The following remarks by Harry Johnson are suggestive: "the essence of direct foreign investment is the transmission to the 'host' country of a 'package' of capital, managerial skill, and technical knowledge. The major issues posed for theory are the reasons why the transmission of such a 'package' of capital and knowledge is more profitable than the alternative of transmitting either the capital or the knowledge or both separately, and what the welfare implications are for the 'home' and the 'host' countries respectively. Along with the first issue goes the important empirical question of which industries are likely to be characterized by direct foreign investment and which are not. Economic theory offers two approaches to these questions—that of the theory of industrial organization and that of traditional trade theory. These approaches must be used as complements, since the former is microeconomic in character whereas the latter stresses the requirements of general macroeconomic equilibrium." Harry Johnson, "Survey of the Issues," in Peter Drysdale (ed.), *Direct Foreign Investment in Asia and the Pacific* (Canberra: Australian National University Press, 1972), p. 2.

2. Japan Economic Research Center, *Japan's Economy in 1980 in the Global Context* (Tokyo, March 1972), pp. 45-51.

3. See an excellent explanation of Japan's direct foreign investment in Koichi Hamada, "Japanese Investment Abroad," in Peter Drysdale (ed.), *Direct Foreign Investment in Asia and the Pacific* (Australian National University, 1972). According to a MITI report, in an accumulated total foreign investment of $3,596 million between 1951-70, mining accounts for 31.4 percent, or $963 million; commerce accounts for 10.3 percent, or $370 million; and others (agriculture and forestry, fisheries, construction, finance and insurance) account for 31.4 percent, or $1,126 million (see Table 4-1).

4. Again according to the same MITI report, in a total accumulated foreign investment in manufacturing of $963 million industries between 1951 and 1970, pulp and wood (this belongs rather to natural-resource-oriented) accounts for 22.1 percent; textiles 19.7 percent; steel and metals 14.3 percent; transport machinery 10.6 percent; electric appliances 7.4 percent; other machinery 7.0 percent; foodstuffs 6.3 percent; chemicals 6.2 percent; and others 6.4 percent (see Table 4-1).

5. According to the Second Questionnaire Survey undertaken by the Export-Import Bank of Japan, 90 percent of manufacturing firms abroad

with Japanese direct investment use Japanese technology, 86 percent of them import Japanese machinery and equipment, and Japanese raw materials and intermediate goods account for 58 percent of their imports.

6. As regards Japanese accumulated foreign direct investment by the end of 1969, the four largest investment projects were Arabian Oil in the neutral zone between Kuwait and Saudi Arabia, Minus Steel in Brazil, Pulp industry in Alaska, and oil extracting in North Sumatra. If these are taken separately, the average amount of investment per union is $1.7 to 1.8 million in mining, $0.5 to 0.6 million in manufacturing, and $0.32 nillion in commerce and others.

7. For exanple, Raymond Vernon, "International Investment and International Trade in the Product Cycle," *Quarterly Journal of Economics* (May 1966); G.E. Hufbauer, *Synthetic Materials and the Theory of International Trade* (London: Duckworth, 1966).

8. Raymond Vernon, "The Economic Consequence of U.S. Foreign Direct Investment," *United States International Economic Policy in an Interdependent World, Papers 1* (Washington, D.C., July 1971).

9. Raymond Vernon, ibid., p. 930.

10. Stephen Hymer, "United States Investment Abroad," in Peter Drysdale (ed.), *Direct Investment in Asia and the Pacific* (ANU, 1972), p. 41.

11. Ibid., p. 29.

12. For example, see, Emergency Committee for American Trade, *The Role of the Multinational Corporation in the United States and World Economies* (February 1972).

13. An American labor union researcher states that "U.S.-based multinational operations may adversely affect host countries as well as the United States. The balanced economic and social development of developing economies, for example, is not necessarily promoted by the establishment of electronic subsidiary plants, with high productivity and low wage—with production for export from countries that urgently require educational, health and housing facilities, as well as balanced growth of domestic investment and consumer markets." Nat Goldfinger, "A Labor View of Foreign Investment and Trade Issues," *United States International Economic Policy in an Interdependent World, Papers I* (Washington, D.C.: July 1971), p. 927.

14. Cf. Bo Söndersten, *International Economics* (Macmillan, 1970), pp. 454-55.

15. It is implicitly assumed that there is, besides X and Y industries, a third sector in which country D has comparative advantage.

16. Recently Professor Vernon's "product cycle" theory has become well known, but in Japan, Dr. Akamatsu, Professor Emeritus of Hitotsubashi University, propounded a *"catching-up product cycle"* theory as

early as the mid-1930s. He originally called it "the wild flying geese pattern" (*Ganko Keitai*) of industrial development in developing countries since the time-series curve for imports of a particular product is followed by that of domestic production and later by that of exports, and they form a pattern like "flying wild geese in orderly ranks forming an inverse V, just as airplanes fly in formation." Kaname Akamatsu, "A Historical Pattern of Economic Growth in Developing Countries," *The Developing Economies* (Tokyo: The Institute of Asian Economic Affairs, March-August 1962). See also Kaname Akamatsu, "A Theory of Unbalanced Growth in the World Economy," *Weltwirtschaftliches Archiv* (Band 86 Heft 2, 1961). This theory is widely recognized by now, for example, Benjamin Higgins, in *Economic Development: Problems, Principles, and Policies* (rev. ed., Norton, 1969), pp. 623-24; Miyohei Shinohara, *Growth and Cycles in the Japanese Economic Development* (Tokyo: Kinokuniya, 1962), pp. 57-58.

17. Albert O. Hirschman, *The Strategy of Economic Development* (Yale University Press, 1958), p. 121.

18. The comparative formula is useful in the same way as comparative advantage is, since the decision as to whether home or foreign investment should be undertaken takes place without considering such overall adjustments as changes in the exchange rate, inflation and deflation, and so forth in both countries.

If the investing country revalues its currency and the recipient country devalues its currency both in terms of a common unit, (the dollar), both X- and Y-goods become dearer in country A and cheaper in country D than shown in Table 4-3, which makes the profit rate from domestic investment in both industries proportionately smaller and that from foreign direct investment larger than shown in Table 4-4; but this will not change at all the comparative investment profitabilities. The above illustrates the fact that an overvalued exchange rate stimulates foreign direct investment in general, while an undervalued exchange rate promotes domestic investment and exports.

19. "American direct investment cannot be explained simply in terms of better access to capital, better entrepreneurship, better technology or higher profits abroad ... Analysis of oligopolistic bargaining strategy is however helpful; it is not unusual for leading oligopolists to establish inroads into their competitor's home territory to strengthen their position." Hymer, ibid., p. 41. Such global oligopolistic strategy is the main reason why U.S. multinationals have a strong preference for the wholly-owned subsidiary. (See ibid., p. 44.)

20. "Its [the United States] great strength in innovation and organization cannot be denied. But a striking feature of recent decades is the narrowing of lead-times and the shortening of the product cycle. Direct foreign investment provides one way of meeting this challenge." Hymer,

ibid., p. 44. Also see, Raymond Vernon, "Future of the Multinational Enterprise," in Charles P. Kindleberger (ed.), *The International Corporation* (MIT Press, 1970), pp. 386-7.

21. "Their (multinational enterprises') prominence will be more evident in the advanced technological sectors and in the industries that are reliant on raw materials that are subject to oligopoly control. Multinational enterprises will be less evident with respect to the more mature and standardized products. Indeed, mature industries that are now dominated by multinational enterprises, such as consumer electronics and cigarettes, could very well become more nationally oriented in their ownership and structure." Vernon, ibid., p. 389.

22. Dunning's studies, for example, show that the foreign direct investment of the United Kingdom has long been the trade-oriented type. He makes an interesting comment on British investments: "there is probably too much U.K. investment overseas in traditional-type industries and not enough investment at home in the newer technologically based industries." John H. Dunning, *Studies in International Investment* (London: George Allen & Unwin, 1970), p. 91. Perhaps a proportionate increase in investment of both types is desirable.

23. "The decisions of executives of the U.S.-based multinationals to transfer American technology, for example, or to export American job opportunities may be rational and, perhaps, wise decisions, in terms of the firm. But the interests of the United States, as a nation and of the American people are not identical with the interests of the multinational firm. The responsibility of the U.S. government is to the American people—and not to the U.S.-based multinational companies, without regard to the possibly adverse impacts of their decisions on American workers and communities." Nat Goldfinger, "A Labor View of Foreign Investment and Trade Issues," p. 927.

24. Stephen Hymer, "United States Investment Abroad," pp. 30-31.

25. Stephen Hymer, "The United States Multinational Corporations and Japanese Competition in the Pacific," paper presented for *Conferencia del Pacifica*, Vina del Mar, Chile, September 27 to October 3, 1970. Also see, Louis Turner, *Invisible Empire: Multinational Companies and the Modern World* (London, 1970).

26. Helen Hughes, "Trade and Industrialization Policies: the Political Economy of the Second Best," paper presented for the Fifth Pacific Trade and Development Conference, January 9-13, 1973, at the Japan Economic Research Center.

27. Harry G. Johnson, "The Multinational Corporation as a Development Agent," *Columbia Journal of World Business* (May-June 1970), p. 1.

28. The multinational producing enterprise has been acclaimed as an agent of development and has been condemned as a weapon of exploitation."

"Conflict between the multinational enterprise and the host government may derive from four sources: from the fact that it is *private* and hence may clash with the social and national goals; that it is *large* and oligopolistic and hence possesses market and bargaining power which may be used against the interest of the host country; that it is *foreign*, particularly if it is American, and hence may be serving the national interests of a foreign nation; and that it is *'Western'* and hence may transfer inappropriate knowhow, technology or management practices, or products, designed with characteristics not needed in less-developed countries." Paul Streeten, "Costs and Benefits of Multinational Enterprises in Less-Developed Countries," in John Dunning (ed.), *The Multinational Enterprises* (George Allen & Unwin, 1971), pp.240 and 251.

29. This was discussed intensively at the Chile Conference. See, H.W. Arndt, "Economic Cooperation in the Pacific: A Summing Up," paper presented to Conferencia del Pacifico, Vina del Mar, Chile, from September 27 to October 3, 1970. Also, in Paul Streeten, ibid., pp. 251-4.

30. International Chamber of Commerce, *Guidelines for International Investments* (November 1972).

31. Harry G. Johnson, "The Efficiency and Welfare Implications of the International Corporation," in Charles P. Kindleberger (ed.), *International Corporation*, p. 36.

32. Albert O. Hirschman, *How to Divest in Latin America and Why?* Essays in International Finance, No. 76 (Princeton University, November 1969).

33. See Kiyoshi Kojima, "Reorganization of North-South Trade: Japan's Foreign Econonic Policy for the 1970s," *Hitotsubashi Journal of Economics* (February 1973).

34. See, for example, Lawrence B. Krause, "The U.S. Economy and International Trade," paper presented for the Fifth Pacific Trade and Development Conference, January 9-13, 1973, at the Japan Economic Research Center.

35. Even Vernon points out a need to build another model besides his product cycle sequence. Raymond Vernon, *Sovereignty at Bay, The Multinational Spread of U.S. Enterprises* (Basic Books Inc., 1971), pp. 107-12.

36. Stephen Hymer, "The Efficiency (Contradictions) of Multinational Corporations," *American Economic Review* (May 1970), p. 448.

37. Stephen Hymer, ibid., p. 41.

38. I have in mind such logistical structures as "Ford was making fender steel in Holland for car production in the rest of Europe and tractor components in Germany and motors for compact models in Britain to be used in U.S. assembly plants." Raymond Vernon, ibid., pp. 107-8. This kind of specialization is applicable and beneficial to developing countries.

39. See Kiyoshi Kojima, "Towards a Theory of Agreed Specialization: The Economics of Integration," in W.A. Eltis, M. FG. Scott, and N.N.

Wolfe (eds.), Essays in Honour of Sir Roy Harrod (Oxford, 1970). Reprinted in *Japan and a Pacific Free Trade Area* (London: Macmillan, 1971), Chapter 2.

40. Cf. *The Pacific Basin Charter on International Investments*, PBEC (May 19, 1972) and *Guidelines for International Investment*, International Chamber of Commerce (November 29, 1972). The Japan Chamber of Commerce has also issued independently a similar charter.

Chapter 4
Appendix

Table 4A-1
Japanese Private Investment Abroad
Industrial Classification

Fiscal year Industries	'51-'57 No.	Acct.	'58 No.	Acct.	'59 No.	Acct.	'60 No.	Acct.	'61 No.	Acct.	'62 No.	Acct.	'63 No.	Acct.	'64 No.	Acct.
Food Stuffs	5	712	1	83	10	4,339	12	1,562	13	2,988	4	2,619	10	6,706	2	3,568
Textile	11	10,698	3	1,873	5	3,422	9	10,980	7	6,317	9	2,803	16	7,655	19	13,504
Pulp & Wooden	3	15,556	1	22,693	0	10,598	1	1,397	0	300	0	300	2	9,037	2	10,347
Chemical	4	157	3	95	3	122	8	736	2	298	7	927	16	3,330	5	631
Iron & Metal	2	1,878	0	2,133	3	3,787	3	2,571	4	27,157	3	616	11	2,897	8	15,494
Machinery	6	6,423	1	991	4	2,220	4	1,176	3	642	3	1,045	8	10,241	6	1,142
Electric Appliances	1	24	4	117	3	189	3	495	8	1,308	9	2,235	5	294	7	1,862
Transport Machinery	—	—	4	13,288	1	15	1	2,405	3	3,052	5	8,838	2	3,810	7	5,858
Others	10	1,311	8	1,154	5	654	7	6,555	2	2,119	7	1,368	14	3,141	8	3,529
Subtotal	42	36,759	23	42,427	34	25,346	48	27,877	42	44,181	47	20,756	84	47,111	64	55,933
Agriculture-Forestry	7	1,319	0	250	0	538	3	1,149	0	300	6	1,633	3	1,919	2	670
Fisheries	12	1,463	2	234	5	429	7	2,130	6	1,082	5	961	2	484	3	659
Mining	25	17,176	5	13,148	4	11,510	10	44,630	5	104,086	12	34,366	3	25,534	4	20,916
Subtotal	44	19,958	7	13,632	9	12,477	20	47,908	11	105,468	23	36,961	8	27,937	9	22,245
Construction	—	—	—	—	—	—	—	—	1	12	3	938	4	4,497	3	3,797
Commerce	231	13,120	25	4,216	51	10,930	59	11,716	45	5,142	66	14,148	88	13,505	79	11,206
Finance-Insurance	10	4,289	4	1,843	5	1,769	2	2,654	3	3,438	6	4,517	8	6,651	7	14,513
Others	40	4,428	19	2,520	24	2,535	22	2,570	31	6,546	34	22,106	31	26,275	31	12,591
Subtotal	281	21,837	48	8,579	80	15,234	83	16,940	80	15,158	109	41,709	131	50,929	120	42,107
Total	367	78,554	78	64,640	123	53,062	151	92,729	133	164,811	179	99,425	223	125,977	193	120,291

Fiscal year / Industries	'65 No.	'65 Acct.	'66 No.	'66 Acct.	'67 No.	'67 Acct.	'68 No.	'68 Acct.	'69 No.	'69 Acct.	'70 No.	'70 Acct.	Cumulative total No.	Cumulative total Acct.
Food Stuffs	10	3,583	5	1,618	12	6,877	7	6,233	14	4,167	30	15,785	135	60,841
Textile	16	5,549	15	11,270	20	16,664	31	15,120	52	34,040	46	49,898	259	189,798
Pulp & Wooden	1	3,937	5	36,419	4	2,360	5	17,280	6	3,315	14	78,815	44	212,354
Chemical	20	4,178	12	9,104	16	3,345	17	4,956	24	6,286	40	25,467	175	59632
Iron & Metal	5	4,432	6	6,013	9	19,724	9	3,878	23	38,241	13	9,110	99	137,926
Machinery	3	3,185	6	3,074	19	6,954	19	5,141	19	9,373	37	15,629	138	67,236
Electric Appliances	14	2,744	20	5,102	21	6,096	29	6,579	39	21,960	43	21,885	206	70,890
Transport Machinery	3	20,571	5	14,106	5	11,996	1	4,311	2	11,430	4	2,850	43	102,530
Others	9	1,378	23	2,978	19	3,484	53	5,175	50	6,892	77	21,754	292	61,492
Subtotal	81	49,557	97	89,684	125	77,500	171	68,668	229	135,705	304	241,193	1,391	926,699
Agriculture-Forestry	6	7,216	2	4,834	8	5,665	16	10,625	23	12,009	18	9,566	94	57,693
Fisheries	4	1,317	10	1,050	10	2,518	6	1,533	8	4,904	16	8,453	96	27,218
Mining	12	33,664	17	72,147	14	58,625	15	158,681	31	297,301	38	234,955	195	1,126,743
Subtotal	22	42,197	29	78,032	32	66,809	37	170,840	62	314,216	72	252,974	385	1,211,684
Construction	1	8,228	2	6,269	2	1,330	1	725	5	7,004	10	5,003	32	37,805
Commerce	68	23,050	88	19,559	115	48,018	124	119,358	200	54,995	253	54,141	1,492	403,103
Finance-Insurance	6	29,596	9	20,865	3	46,045	13	49,769	9	43,821	30	92,099	115	321,889
Others	31	4,112	28	12,598	29	35,166	38	147,813	63	111,840	99	268,038	520	659,137
Subtotal	106	64,986	127	59,292	149	130,561	176	317,663	277	217,659	392	419,281	2,159	1,421,935
Total	209	156,739	253	227,008	306	274,867	384	557,174	568	667,579	768	913,449	3,935	3,596,306

Table 4A-1 (continued)
Regional Classification

Fiscal year / Regions	'51-'57 No.	'51-'57 Acct.	'58 No.	'58 Acct.	'59 No.	'59 Acct.	'60 No.	'60 Acct.	'61 No.	'61 Acct.	'62 No.	'62 Acct.	'63 No.	'63 Acct.	'64 No.	'64 Acct.
North America	101	26,681	9	27,503	34	20,354	36	13,236	27	13,822	39	16,370	50	51,227	34	27,360
Latin America	77	26,034	35	23,204	31	12,802	31	22,383	28	39,218	33	29,016	41	21,192	47	44,213
Asia	132	23,771	23	2,879	45	9,277	64	18,855	48	28,384	75	24,047	83	26,284	79	30,358
Middle East	6	242	3	10,818	1	9,125	1	36,015	3	77,889	1	23,896	1	14,671	0	11,530
Europe	40	1,310	5	159	6	925	11	1,005	20	5,171	19	3,340	33	4,335	20	3,862
Africa		515			1	95	2	434	5	287	3	392	9	5,997	10	2,004
Oceania	11	515	3	77	5	484	6	801	2	39	9	2,364	6	1,671	3	954
Total	367	78,552	78	64,640	123	53,063	150	92,729	133	164,811	179	99,425	223	125,977	113	120,291

Fiscal year / Regions	'65 No.	'65 Acct.	'66 No.	'66 Acct.	'67 No.	'67 Acct.	'68 No.	'68 Acct.	'69 No.	'69 Acct.	'70 No.	'70 Acct.	Cumulative total No.	Cumulative total Acct.
North America	53	44,119	70	108,610	65	56,867	82	184,992	139	129,283	173	191,552	912	911,976
Latin America	48	58,932	32	54,414	34	40,671	39	39,950	53	100,523	56	46,121	585	558,673
Asia	74	35,346	108	28,912	165	97,075	197	79,716	286	199,119	367	175,725	1,746	779,745
Middle East	0	11,420	4	24,836	2	19,866	2	28,137	3	37,868	6	27,790	33	334,113
Europe	18	4,656	17	2,066	21	30,814	39	151,148	42	93,506	107	335,537	398	638,434
Africa	10	1,799	8	4,099	5	2,237	6	42,663	16	18,473	23	13,877	98	92,447
Oceania	6	466	14	4,072	14	27,248	19	30,570	29	88,808	36	122,848	163	280,918
Total	209	156,739	253	227,008	306	274,867	384	557,174	568	667,579	768	913,449	3,935	3,596,306

Source: *Japanese Private Investments Abroad: The Summary of Third Questionnaire Survey*, The Export—Import Bank of Japan, October 1972.

5

Imperial Chemical Industries Limited: A Case Study

Michael Clapham

ICI was conceived as multinational. It arose from the merger of four British chemical companies, Brunner Mond, Nobel Industries, United Alkali, and British Dyestuffs. Of these, the first was connected by shareholding and licensing agreements with Solvay of Belgium and, directly or through Solvay, with soda ash manufacturers in several other countries. Nobel Industries was a product of the initiative of that most international of entrepreneurs, Alfred Nobel—a man who exploited his invention of dynamite in virtually every country where there was a major demand for it within ten years of its invention. Between these two companies, there existed a number of factories outside the United Kingdom at the time when ICI was formed by merger in 1926.

Both companies were inheritors of typical nineteenth century methods of operating and consequently saw what was then described as the British Empire as their main field of operations, but each also had ambitions in overseas markets not dominated by their major competitors and occasional collaborators. The letter sent out to shareholders of the merging companies in 1926 stated:

It will be the avowed intention of the new Company . . . to extend the development and importance of the chemical industry throughout the Empire.

It was thus a multinational operation in 1926, and by 1933 it owned or controlled manufacturing companies in Africa, Argentina, Australia, Canada, and Chile and owned merchanting companies in Argentina, Brazil, Chile, China, India, Japan, the Levant, Malaya, and Peru. It is difficult to reconstruct a coherent philosophy for a period forty years back, but I think it probable that the Board of ICI at that time would have taken it for granted that their policy was to manufacture in other countries only those products that enjoyed some natural protection through transport costs or the availability of local raw materials and to base their operations mainly in countries where Imperial Preference gave them an inherent advantage, or where long established connections or partnerships gave them special strength. They would probably have added in private that they would on no account attempt to manufacture in the United States in compeititon with E.I. Du Pont de Nemours, or in Continental Western Europe, dominated by I.G. Farbenindustrie. There was in the early 1930s an explicit agreement for some products and a tacit understanding for others that divided influence between these three groups, while partnerships between Du Pont and ICI shared Canada and Latin America.

History and changing attitudes broke up the cozy world of the 1930s. As the United Kingdom and Germany moved towards war in 1938, the research sharing agreement with I.G. Farbenindustrie was cancelled and the territorial understandings went with it. The U.S. Department of Justice attacked the ICI/Du Pont research agreement soon after the war and finally obtained a judgment terminating it and the territorial understandings that went with it in 1952. At this date, then, there were no limitations on what manufacturing investment ICI could make in the world. The fact that there was no very immediate change in investment was caused by three factors: the enormous effort in staff and resources required just after the war in the United Kingdom, not only to reorient a business that had been turned over to the specialized demands of war but also to exploit two of ICI's own major inventions—polyethylene and polymethylmethacrylate—one other British invention—polyester fibre—that it had acquired in the laboratory stage —and one invention—polyamide fibre (nylon)—acquired from Du Pont under the research-sharing agreement. Outside the United Kingdom the existing overseas subsidiaries were developing on new lines to which they had turned during wartime interruption of supplies, while in the Americas the companies that had been owned jointly with Du Pont were going through a trauma of division and reorganization. Not surprisingly, by the middle 1950s the company was more than 75 percent based in the United Kingdom for investment, though nearly half of its sales went elsewhere.

The 1956 pattern was as follows

	Sales	Assets
United Kingdom	56%	77%
Commonwealth	24%	15%
Rest of the World	20%	8%

By this time, however, thinking about the future activities of the ICI Group was becoming more sophisticated, and the newer generation at the top were thinking in terms of exploiting all major new inventions worldwide. The first formal recognition of this philosophy came in the late 1950s when a small group of senior executives was instructed to prepare a plan for ICI's manufacturing development in Continental Western Europe. From their work and the subsequent formation of a company to organize ICI's Continental development there developed during the 1960s not only a series of manufacturing companies on the Continent but also a philosophy of stepwise development of major manufacturing units in those areas where scale is economically significant. Thus, the first polyethylene plant built in

Holland to serve the northern parts of the EEC drew their ethylene supplies by tanker from a water-side factory in N.E. England where a new ethylene plant could thus be built on a larger and more economic scale.

In 1962, the Board of ICI formally accepted a paper by the then overseas director on investment policy. The basis of this policy was that the greatest continuing advantage from ICI's inventions would arise if it were possible to make use of them by manufacturing investment in every major market where the product could be used, and it set the objective of having a manufacturing base, effectively under the control of the parent company, in each of the major sophisticated markets of the world and also of having the basic organization, and thus the ability to grow, in every populous area of the non-communist world in which a market for the products of the ICI group might be expected to develop.

Two other points about the then accepted policy should be mentioned. First, it was recognized that national aspirations and habits of mind made the total ownership of major manufacturing industries by foreigners un-popular except in the most sophisticated areas of the world. It was, there-fore, decided that excepting Continental Western Europe and the United States, it would be the company's policy to have substantial minorities of local shareholders as a guarantee that the companies would have a local identity and pay regard to local interests. Secondly, it was accepted that in a science-based company, rapid access to new thinking and new develop-ments led to quicker exploitation of inventions and greater synergy, since ready access by all members of the group to the research and development work of the others—at the important stage before effective patent protec-tion is available—is only practicable if there is some assurance that the valuable knowledge thus acquired will be retained within the group. It was therefore laid down that ICI would, so far as possible, retain a controlling interest in its worldwide group of companies, thus keeping the area of idea-sharing as wide as possible. In short, the concept was that a multina-tional company had as its most important asset a collective capability for taking action to utilize invention at any point where that invention served a market, to the benefit of the national company making the invention as well as of the group as a whole. The policy also recognized that while 90 percent of the research was at that time being done in the United Kingdom, the pattern of development would have to be towards developing centers of research and development, as well as of general management skills, in every territory of operation, since no one nation has a surplus of money or brain power sufficient to serve the world.

The implementation of this policy has proceeded steadily, although the problem of breaking into major new markets has limited the speed attain-able. By the end of 1972 the European base had been substantially de-veloped; the acquisition of Atlas Chemical Industries in the United States had greatly increased the size of operations there, and two or three joint companies in Japan were helping to prepare the way for the period when Japan would permit the freedom of investment by foreign companies that she enjoys in their territories. The general pattern of the company's business in 1972—for comparison with 1956—was as follows:

	Sales	Assets
United Kingdom	46%	66%
Commonwealth	27%	16%
Rest of the World	27%	18%

How Important are Exchange-Rate Changes and Regimes?

We are now in the field of tactics rather than strategy. The stable currency of today is not always the one that was most highly regarded ten years ago, and in an industry where the interval between invention and significant profit making is about ten years, a long view has to be taken. Obviously a country suffering from runaway inflation and a corrupt or capricious regime is not regarded as a place for immediate investment, but so far as possible, a base is retained there for future opportunities. For example, in 1961, as the overseas director concerned, I dismissed the possibility of investing in Indonesia under the Sukarno regime but retained a selling company there. Now, eleven years later, with a change in regime and in currency stability, there are three small ICI factories operating in Indonesia, which thus form an operating base for what may one day be a great market. There are other countries in which investment is not being made at present, but which in ten years might be regarded as suitable.

How Important are Trade Barriers—and Which?

Trade barriers surrounding a worthwhile market are a strong incentive to invest within that market, under the following conditions:

1. They are high enough to make up for any diseconomies of scale through investment in plant below the normal world size.
2. They are regarded as likely to be fairly permanent. Australia is a good case in point: it has long been the Australian government's policy to encourage secondary industry, which is regarded as a major economic and political need, by tariffs high enough to offset the disadvantages of a market of only 12 million people. This has resulted in ICI investment there in products that would otherwise only be made in a much larger

manufacturing center. Other trade barriers, such as import controls, have been influential in causing ICI to increase investment in, for example, India and New Zealand. It is difficult to say which trade barriers are most effective in this direction. What is important is their expected duration.

How Important are Capital Controls?

Again it is difficult to be precise. Controls on the export of capital from the United Kingdom have undoubtedly delayed certain developments by ICI in other countries. The ability to borrow internationally has, however, largely offset this disadvantage. Controls on the repatriation of capital from various countries have also, but to a minor extent, influenced investment in them, since it is better to get a return via dividends than to leave the funds unrewarded. This has not, in general, been an important influence.

What Factors Determine the Choice Between Exporting and Investing Abroad?

Ultimately the decision rests simply on the economics of supplying the available market. For example, if a product is of high value and has low transport costs, like dyestuffs and pharmaceuticals, then a single manufacturing center could economically serve the whole world, and the only factor determining its location would be the availability of high-grade scientific manpower for research, development, and production. On the other hand, a commodity type of product, in whose total cost transport would form a large part, must be so located as to serve a radius that may be as low as 100 miles.

Economics, however, may be governed by consideration of tariff or import controls. For example, the United States and India could both be supplied with dyestuffs economically from the United Kingdom (or Germany or Switzerland), but such exports to the United States are prevented by a penal level of tariffs almost equivalent to import prohibition, which is what prevents exports to India. In both these countries, therefore, a U.K.-based company finds it economic to manufacture. The word "ultimately" at the beginning of this section was used advisedly. Suppose that market A is developing twice as fast as market B and that it is currently cheaper to manufacture in market B. If the growth of market A is such that within, say, five years it will be possible through economies of scale to manufacture more cheaply than in market B, then market A will be chosen for the next investment. The scale of expected advantage and disadvantage is clearly infinitely variable, and decisions will sometimes be taken on a close balance. There are other possible exceptions to the rule: an opportunity may arise to manufacture a certain product in a country where it is desired to have a manufacturing base for other and more profitable products, which thus makes it worthwhile to accept a short-term diseconomy. Again, it will sometimes be worthwhile investing at a modest diseconomy in a highly sophisticated market in order to acquire knowledge of technical or commercial development that can be applied more profitably elsewhere.

The Choice of Location for Foreign Investment

The previous section deals basically with the fact that investment is placed at the point from which a market can most economically be served. There are, however, certain limitations on theory, of which the most important is risk, which has been dealt with under an earlier heading. A serious risk of loss of capital through expropriation, war, or other causes clearly inhibits investment in certain territories, and given the desire to control access to valuable technology, so do legal limitations on the ownership or management of companies by foreigners.

The Choice of Production Techniques Used in Foreign Plants

These must always be the most advanced that are economically viable. In a scale-sensitive industry the techniques are normally those appropriate to the expected size of the market. The only major limitation on this rule is if in remote areas, or in countries where skilled labor is short, it is necessary to minimize the risks of breakdown by doubling up on less economic production lines, rather than risking breakdown on a single but more efficient one.

How Important Are Differences in National Tax Policies and Rates?

The life of the average industrial investment is longer than that of the average government in democratic countries. Short-term advantages or disadvantages of tax within the ranges that are normal in developed countries are rarely significant. If a country pursues an abnormally high tax policy for a long period without compensating development allowances or grants, then that country becomes unattractive as an area for investment, since ultimately it is the return to the shareholders of the parent company that is significant. However, a country with a very large market in which growth is to be expected may be thought a suitable recipient for investment if the ability to plough back funds there for future development is not unduly constrained by taxation. In general, however, the average level of tax on corporations over a decade is remarkably similar in most developed countries, and if it is less in some developing countries, the advantage is only such as to balance the risk. On the whole, then, the normal tax variations are not very significant in investment decisions.

Special Requirements by Host Countries

It is difficult to generalize about these. The one that most inhibits investment is generally a requirement to export, since those countries that find it necessary to impose this condition are often those that would be unable to export otherwise, because of some natural disadvantage or one imposed by government policy. Given the policy of manufacturing at the point from which the available market can most economically be served, it follows that exporting to this market from an area less well placed is disadvantageous. Thus, the normal effect of a requirement to export uneconomically is to make the rate of return required from the investment concerned higher.

A requirement to contribute to domestic employment is a disincentive only if it involves a level of employment higher than would normally be required. It is ICI's policy, as far as possible, to use to the maximum both management and labor drawn from the countries in which it operates, so that new investments automatically produce local employment. If the requirement means using uneconomic types of plant, the requirement has to be judged in the light of the protection given to any product that without it would be unable to compete against imports.

The requirement to bring in the latest technology is hardly ever an inhibition, the latest technology being the most economic. It would only prevent investment in a country where the risk of expropriation or loss of control meant that the cost of acquiring the technology would not be required.

Conclusion

ICI has moved over the past 25 years from being a company oriented towards its home market and its home manufacturing base to being a multinational group of companies consciously operating as an entity. It looks on the whole world not just as its market but as its sphere of operations and as the source of its funds for investment and of its managerial and inventive talents, even though national attitudes may at any time limit the extent to which either the funds or the people possessed of these talents can move from country to country. It regards the pooling of ideas and managerial techniques across national frontiers as the means by which the wealth-creating capacity of the world can be most rapidly increased, and it sees this concept as specially valuable to developing countries whose gain in the rapid acquisition of new industrial potential—and above all, of managerial and technical skills enhanced to world standards—far outweighs the cost of rewarding the capital investment from outside the host country. In thus diffusing the capability for economic growth, the multinational company not only increases the global rate of this growth but tends to equalize its benefits between the nations of the world.

Chapter 5
Appendix

Table 5A-1
ICI Foreign Interests

	Over £50 m. Assets	Over £25 m. Assets	Over £5 m. Assets
ICI Manufacturing Investments Overseas	Australasia Canada Germany Holland South Africa United States	Argentina India	France Malaysia Spain

	Under £5 m. Assets	
ICI Minor Manufacturing and Selling Organizations	Austria Bangladesh Belgium Brazil Colombia[a] Denmark Finland Greece[b] Hong Kong[a] Indonesia Iran[a] Ireland Israel[a] Italy Japan Kenya	Mexico Morocco[a] Nigeria Norway Pakistan Peru Portugal Singapore Sri Lanka Sweden Tanzania Thailand[b] Turkey Trinidad[b] Uruguay Zambia

[a]Selling only.

[b]Manufacturing only.

Via subsidiaries, there are also minor interests in Angola, Fiji, Jamaica, Liberia, Malawi, New Guinea, Nicaragua, the Philippines, and Taiwan.

6

The Case of Bendix

W. Michael Blumenthal

Diversity Among Multinational Corporations

To understand the motivations, behavior, and impact of multinational corporations (MCs) it is important to be aware of the many fundamental differences between different companies. Motivations, behavior, and impact on the world economy vary substantially according to these differences. Indeed, one suspects that they are so great and fundamental as to render generalizations about the behavior of the MC almost suspect and often meaningless.

One major difference relates to the industry or industries in which an MC is active. At one extreme, there are raw-materials-oriented companies in the extractive industries with relatively homogenous products. Frequently, such MCs are integrated vertically all the way from raw material exploitation in one or more producing countries to distribution of end products in various consuming countries. Oil companies are a case in point. At the other extreme are MCs producing advanced manufactured products with high technological content of a proprietary nature (i.e., with broad patent protection).

In between, there are MCs operating in one or several manufacturing industries, that produce more or less sophisticated manufactured goods. In some instances, these products may be rather homogenous and similar and relatively easily transportable over extended distances. In other cases, the products—while generically the same—may be particularized to conform to the tastes or technical requirements of individual country markets. They may also be bulky enough to make shipment over large distances impractical. The difference between an MC operating in a few rather similar industries as against a highly diverse MC operating in a wide range of industries involving different product characteristics is also of significance.

There are yet other distinctions between MCs that make generalizations about their motivations and behavior difficult. For example, some MCs have been operating on a worldwide basis for many decades. Their positions in major world markets have therefore evolved over a long historical span. More often than not, such companies today operate through 100-percent-owned affiliates in almost all cases. Many other MCs have entered the world scene in the more recent post-World War II period. Often the problem for such MCs was one of breaking into an already existing market with a number of competitors in place. This has frequently been possible only through the forming of partnerships or via partial acquisitions. As a result, the degree of ownership of their foreign subsidiaries is often less than 100 percent and may vary widely from country to country.

While the above is not intended to be an all-inclusive list of major differences between MCs, it suffices to show the difficulty of generalization about the MC, in general.

The freedom of action of an MC with 100-percent-owned affiliates is quite different from one that operates through less than 100-percent-owned affiliates, or under fifty-fifty partnerships, or with minority-owned operations. The ease of moving production and profits from one country to another is vitally affected by this one factor alone (even if it would be advisable and feasible on other grounds). Again, planning a worldwide strategy for a homogenous product is quite a different matter than the situation faced by the MC with a range of products that have different characteristics in each major market. Investment, marketing, and other business decisions for products that are highly proprietary can be made in quite a different framework than for those sold typically under conditions of more perfect competition, and so on.

The case of Bendix can be used to illustrate the implications of these differences in a more concrete way. Bendix operates in five distinct, though related, product fields:

1. *Automotive Parts* for original equipment manufacturers, as well as for the repair and overhaul market;
2. *Aerospace-Electronics Products* for commercial and government markets;
3. *Industrial Technology Products* for factory automation, precise measuring and instrumentation, and machine tool electronics;
4. *Building Materials,* both lumber and non-lumber, for housing, construction, and home repair;
5. *Recreation Vehicles,* such as caravans, travel trailers, motor homes, and mobile homes.

Bendix' historical experience as an MC in each of these fields is different. For example, the company's overseas investments are heavily concentrated in the automotive parts industry. This involves several hundred million dollars in sales and more than 20,000 employees in a dozen or more countries. Many of these investments originated in the postwar period, but one or two of the most important ones have their origin in the 1920s and 1930s. In this industry, Bendix business is heavily concentrated in the design and production of brakes and braking systems for automobiles and trucks. The market structure is typically oligopolistic, the products involve medium to high level of technology and are fairly proprietary in nature.

But brake and braking systems, while generically the same from one country to the other, are different and distinct depending on the type of automobile or truck for which they are intended. In other words, a brake for a VW is quite different in design and in its major characteristics from the brake for an American car, including the American compact. Brakes for Japanese vehicles are substantially different, and so on. Moreover, brakes and braking systems are heavy in weight, and labor costs constitute only a modest proportion of total costs. Transportation of this product over long distances is generally impractical. Moreover, technical characteristics differ substantially between markets so that brakes produced in Germany as compared to the United States as against those in most other countries are really quite distinct products. Moreover, the major customers generally insist that suppliers for this key product are located "within reach."

In the aerospace-electronics field, Bendix is faced with an entirely different set of circumstances. Here the products involve a very high degree of technology. They are highly unique and proprietary. In many instances there are only three or four producers in the world who have the entire range of capabilities and experience required to design, produce, and service efficiently.

Automatic pilots, flight guidance systems, or complex, computer-guided test equipment for aircraft electronic systems are highly specialized products. Production in subsidiaries abroad generally occurs only if a foreign government insists on it—and is prepared to pay the price of subsidizing the high costs as well as the royalties involved. Where the military is involved, complex government-to-government production-sharing arrangements, for security and balance-of-payments reasons, may be a factor. Unlike the situation in automotive parts, the typical method of serving international markets in this field remains exports or foreign licensing arrangements.

The case of mobile homes and recreational vehicles is entirely different again. Here the product is so bulky as to virtually preclude shipments over anything but short distances. Mobile home shipments are only practical, for example, over a maximum range of 500 miles. Moreover, consumer tastes and market requirements vary substantially. There is little or no proprietary element in the product. Typically, country markets are much less oligopolistic and are often characterized by a fairly large number of producers catering to regional tastes and requirements. A French "caravan," for example, is quite a different product from an American travel trailer. The large American motor home, suitable for driving long distances on relatively empty freeways, is quite different from a VW camper bus. Since there is no technology or proprietary aspect, licensing and export possibilities are quite limited. Here international operations must involve local production affiliates.

To sum up, Bendix operates in some industries where production for a local market must take place in that market and where exports into the market are, generally speaking, precluded (automotive parts). Coordination of the various automotive parts businesses throughout the world is complicated because of the less than 100 percent ownership of many of the subsidiaries. Technology is a factor but the characteristics of the product vary from market to market.

In other Bendix industries, such as aerospace-electronics, production in one country is quite possible and indeed generally preferable, the product requirements are identical from one market to the other, and the high level of technology and proprietary content of the products provides Bendix with a very different bargaining position than in its automotive parts business. Finally, in the third product group discussed, consumer tastes vary substantially from country to country, there is little or no homogeneity of the product, and shipment across national boundaries is practically out of the question. At the same time, there is little proprietary or patent protection making Bendix products unique, and the company can hope to gain a market share in each country only in competition with a relatively large number of more or less equally placed competitors.

Let us now proceed to look briefly at Bendix' basic objectives and major motivations in its worldwide decision making.

The Basic Business Objective of Bendix

The basic business objective of Bendix, common to the entire range of the company's activities, is to secure a maximum profitable share of the world demand for our products in each major world market. We look upon each of our five industry groupings as worldwide businesses and determine for each group the means, or combination of means, by which we expect to achieve this goal, with the highest returns on the total resources employed. It is this worldwide *market* objective that underlies everything we do.

Because the situation is so different in each of the product areas, the methods used and the opportunities open to us necessarily differ substantially. The three major means available for competing throughout the world, which are employed singly or in combination, are *exports, local production,* or *licensing.*

Motivating Factors

Essentially, our Corporate Planning Department, in collaboration with their counterparts in the five worldwide operating units, seeks to determine the best combination of techniques as between exports, local production, and licensing to accomplish the above objective. The external limits on the choices open to us differ for each product group, in accordance with the differences in circumstances briefly described above.

The following sections comment briefly on each of the major motivating factors which are, or are not, at times involved in Bendix' international business planning and decision making.

Market Opportunities

This is without question the single most important factor guiding Bendix' plans and policies. In our major fields, the name of Bendix has a certain worldwide significance. Hence, our main objective in developing our multinational business is to be present as a significant factor in each market area large enough to be interesting to us. We seek a significant share of each significant world market for our major products.

In some of the industries in which we operate, this is necessary because our customers (the U.S. automobile manufacturers as well as the German, British, French, Italian, and Japanese) operate in most major markets. To provide complete services, we must be where they are.

In our other industries, such as recreational vehicles for example, our desire to "be present" worldwide is not dictated by customer requirements as much as by market opportunity, pure and simple. We look upon this industry as "our kind of business," we want to compete for a share of each market in which we recognize an opportunity. Frequently, these are markets that are growing at a faster rate than the corporation as a whole, and this makes it particularly attractive.

In sum, it is market considerations that are the main motivating factor that stimulate us to be multinational in our various activities.

Taxes

Effective tax rates vary considerably between different countries. However, they are relatively equal between the major developed countries in the world. As far as Bendix operations are concerned, it is only in Brazil, Spain, Mexico, and Taiwan that our tax rate is more than a few percentage points lower than in the United States or Europe.

The effective tax rate paid in the United States by Bendix last year was roughly 48 percent. The effective tax rate paid abroad, including the low-tax countries, was roughly 44 percent. Given these relatively minor differences and given our primary motivation in terms of a worldwide presence in all markets, tax considerations are, in practice, a rather subsidiary consideration in making investment decisions. We take the tax rate in a particular country as a given. Since our local competitors have to pay it, we expect equally to pay it and to be no worse off for it. Moreover, we know that the profit opportunity as well as the risk of entering a new market are far more important factors to us than tax considerations. I do not recall a single case in which the tax rate has been a significant factor in determining whether or not to enter a market or whether to enter it via direct production, exports, or licensing.

There are, however, some exceptions to this. Frequently, countries provide one-time subsidies and initial tax breaks for a limited period of time to attract local investment. This is true in many areas in the United States, in most of the European countries, and in many less-developed countries as well. These types of benefits are more of a consideration in our thinking. We study them carefully and accept them as a welcome reduction in the total cost of breaking into a market. However, I do not recall a single case in which they *determined* whether or not to go into a market or by what means to enter the market. They have been a factor in determining precisely where in the country to locate our facilities.

Looking at the other side of the ledger, tax incentives to promote exports, such as the DISC arrangements in the United States, have equally had little or no impact on Bendix' choice as between exports, licensing, and direct investments. For one thing, we know that what the government gives, it can also take away. Therefore, a temporary tax break does not weigh nearly as much in our thinking as the pros and cons of a permanent presence in another country. Secondly, the tax advantages involved—in the case of the DISC essentially a deferral of taxes—are not really important enough to affect our decision making in a fundamental way. These arrangements do have the effect, however, of making us somewhat more competitive in exports. To that limited extent, therefore, we derive some positive benefits by increasing our export volume modestly or by increasing our profit margins.

Export incentives provided by some of the less-developed countries similarly affect our thinking in a somewhat different way. Such incentives can be quite substantial, and there have been cases where they made the difference enabling us to export to third country markets or even, in a more limited way, back to the United States. Such "incentives" can be particularly important when they are coupled with permission to manufacture in the country in the first place, or where domestic production quotas are determined by the percentage of exports achieved. Mexico has a number of programs of this kind, including in the automotive parts industry. The pressure to find export outlets for Mexican-produced products, even though these may be only marginally economic, in order to achieve a higher production quota for the domestic Mexican market can be powerful.

Exchange-Rates Changes and Regimes

Until recently at least, not many Bendix executives would have felt very strongly about the question of flexible versus fixed exchange rates. What we require are reasonably stable and predictable exchange-rate relationships and regimes, and any technique that achieves this is acceptable. In that context, the particular system of exchange rates and adjustment mechanism in effect has had very little impact on Bendix' international business planning and decision making.

Like most other large international companies, sharp, sudden, and unpredictable disturbances in international exchanges are, of course, difficult for us to handle. The events of early 1973 have no doubt made us more cognizant of the perils in such a situation.

Exchange and Capital Controls

While exchange-rate regimes have not heretofore been a serious factor in our thinking, exchange controls and capital restrictions can and have been very important influences on our international business decisions. Even though the market may be enticing, we would choose to license or attempt to export rather than to invest in a particular country if we do not feel secure enough about our freedom to transfer dividends freely out of the country or if local exchange controls make capital transactions too complicated. This is clearly true for some of the Latin American countries. Even within Europe, the greater restrictions in countries such as the United Kingdom and France as compared to say Germany and Holland have at times influenced our thinking.

Finally, a word needs to be said about the effect of U.S. capital exports controls of recent years. In the case of Bendix, these controls did not affect any basic decisions regarding overseas investments or business strategy. However, they did complicate our life considerably. In fact, they necessitated extensive foreign borrowing, frequently at relatively high cost, when other arrangements would have been economic.

Labor Costs

Before launching operations in a particular market, Bendix makes a careful analysis of all relevant factors, beginning with an analysis of the size of the market and the characteristics of the products demanded, plus a careful analysis of all cost factors involved. Labor costs are just one cost element with which we are concerned.

As indicated above, our major international direct investments are in the automotive and in the recreational vehicle fields. The alternative of shipping products over long distances is precluded for reasons explained above. Also, mere licensing of our technology is an uncertain and inadequate way to achieve and protect a significant Bendix market share. Hence, while we carefully consider labor costs as one of the several elements to be analyzed, this is virtually never a factor in determining whether or not to enter into direct production in a particular market. Frequently, it's the only way to get in. Since most of our competitors in that market are faced with the same costs, we take them essentially as given. Moreover, we consider Bendix' advantage to lie in our name, in our management skills, and in our capabilities to organize and employ all factors of production efficiently. We rely on these factors, and our broader technological skills and experience worldwide to give us a competitive edge.

In the case of Bendix, there are two exceptions to the above situation. These involve, in one case, the production of bicycle brakes and certain small automotive electrical parts in Mexico for re-export to the United States. In the other case, it involves an operation in Taiwan, originally for the purpose of manufacturing automotive radios and related products destined for a fairly large number of consuming markets in Europe, Canada, and (soon probably) Japan. These two situations represent about 3 percent of our total foreign sales and a fraction of our total worldwide sales and thus are the exception rather than the rule.

In both instances, labor for assembly and testing constitutes a very high proportion of total cost and relatively limited technology is involved. Moreover, in the case of the Taiwanese operation, the components utilized are available at low cost in Taiwan or Japan, so that assembly on the spot is more efficient than at the consuming point in the United States or in Europe.

Here, the lesser labor cost and the lower capital requirements in Mexico and Taiwan were a definite factor in our thinking and our limited direct investment in these two areas did, in the first instance, constitute a shifting of some jobs from the United States to a foreign area. On a net basis, however, we estimate that we added as many or more jobs in the United States as were lost. For one thing, had we not shifted the production abroad, we would have lost the business totally. Under the alternative we adopted, the design, engineering, distribution, and servicing for these products expanded Bendix' employment in the United States, for we were able to increase our total sales volume in the United States and worldwide. Similarly, because we were able to use our Taiwanese operation to sell to other countries as well, profits, royalties and supporting services generated by this expanded activity create yet additional jobs at home. Parenthetically, it should be noted that some portion of the 300 or 400 workers displaced initially in the United States were directly absorbed by Bendix in other business areas.

Trade Barriers

Given the particulars of the Bendix situation and the limited opportunity for exports, except in the aerospace field, tariff barriers are not a vital factor. Certain non-tariff barrier problems, however, can and have been of real significance. This has been particularly true in the aerospace-electronics field. Here, logic would have frequently dictated not only design and development but also production in one facility in the United States. Yet, because of national security considerations, or the desire to develop a technological base in their own country, or simply for general protective reasons (in Japan for example), the requirements to share production through licensing, sometimes in combination with joint ventures, has affected the means open to us of penetrating individual country markets.

It may be more economic to build all autopilots in one place, or to have only one facility producing numerical controls, or complex gyros for tanks. But frequently individual governments, for reasons mentioned above, created barriers and insisted on regulations that precluded our using the most economic means of serving their market and that shifted production to new areas.

Location of R&D

In Bendix, R&D is carried on by central research laboratories in the United States. These labs serve all divisions of the corporation in the United States and are funded by the divisions on the basis of an assessment as well as through individually negotiated contracts. The central labs supplement this in-house activity for Bendix by accepting certain outside paid research contracts from non-Bendix sources.

As regards our overseas affiliates, the situation is somewhat different for the few that are 100 percent owned, as compared to the others in which Bendix is only a partial owner.

As regards the latter, Bendix could not and would not dictate when, how, and whether research is to be undertaken by them. Bendix, of course, gets involved in approving the budget for research, but has never objected to their independent research activities as long as the projects are reasonable and appropriate, the earmarked funds are sound in relation to other corporate requirements, and the total funds flow. Indeed, we have encouraged them to promote their own R&D, even where this has been at the cost of creating some duplication of effort. The result is that most of our large affiliates overseas have their own research facilities, and these often take substantially different approaches to solving analogous problems. At the same time, our overseas affiliates can and do contract to the United States Bendix labs certain research assignments that are too complex or too expensive to be carried out on their own.

In 100-percent-owned affiliates, we have greater freedom of action but even here we would consider it bad policy to prevent these companies from allocating a normal portion of their resources to local R&D. Moreover, the question of motivating the executives of our 100-percent-owned affiliates to operate efficiently and effectively in running their own business is no different than it is in partly-owned affiliates. We find that it is important to keep each affiliate pursuing its own R&D ideas in order to keep motivation high.

It may be worth noting that the results of this policy of permitting individual R&D activities to be pursued around the world have been very good for Bendix. We are seeing an increasing flow of licenses taken out by Bendix from its overseas affiliates. Some of the technology used today in the U.S. parent was developed by overseas affiliates, and royalties are now being paid to them. To some extent, this involves shifting money "from one pocket to the other." We do this for the simple reason that we think it gives us the best results.

Final Comments

The above brief description of why we do what we do is intended to underline the fact that the overriding notion motivating us relates to market considerations around the world. Secondly, I wanted to show that simple notions about the MC greatly oversimplify reality. There is a third factor that anyone who understands how a bureaucracy operates must bear in mind. Even if we had one product and owned all affiliates 100 percent, shifting production and profits at will would give us serious problems of morale and motivation. The incentives we pay, and the responsibility we assign to senior members in individual operations, make each of them fight for best results in their operation. No company can easily shift profits or production without taking into account the negative impact on the overall organization and on the executives involved.

The fact is that we negotiate between different parts of the company almost on an arm's length basis. We think that, from this competitive internal effort, the best results develop for Bendix as a whole. Moreover, I wanted to make the point that where there are many units that are less than 100 percent owned, the differences in interest are particularly clear, and shifting around at will is totally impossible, even in majority-controlled subsidiaries.

Finally, a word about the end result as far as Bendix is concerned. Foreign sales of Bendix products this year will be in excess of $600 million. Of this amount, a little more than $100 million is direct exports from the United States. Imports into the United States are about one-tenth of that. Our income from foreign royalties received is about $10 million. That is about 20 times as much as we pay out in foreign royalties to others. Our employment in the United States has risen steadily, at the same time as our foreign involvement has had a positive impact on the U.S. balance of payments and trade, on the number of work places in the United States, and on the development of foreign economies throughout the world.

7 The Japanese General Trading Company

Morishisa Emori

Nature and History

The so-called general trading companies are business organizations unique to Japan. They have no counterparts elsewhere in the world that can claim to be similar in all respects.

In other advanced countries, there are, of course, large scale enterprises whose main activity is based on business and commerce. But they are to be classified roughly into four categories: (1) the sales divisions or international divisions of giant industrial organizations; (2) trading firms that deal internationally in specific items such as raw cotton, sugar and grains; (3) merchant houses of the British style whose main lines are trade and shipping with former colonial areas; and (4) enterprises engaged in chain-store or mail-order operations aimed at the consumer markets. Some Afro-Asian countries have also extensive business systems run by Chinese and Indian merchants and engage in international trade.

However, these are no comparison with the Japanese general trading companies that are multi-purpose business institutions with both traditional and new facets. Those in the top class employ more than 10,000 well-educated staff, locate more than 120 overseas and 60 domestic offices, record $14 to 15 billion worth of annual sales, and hold virtually the same amount of outstanding commitments on short and long terms at the turn of each six-month fiscal period, basically through their performance of intermediary services.

Due to their mammoth business scope and very flexible nature, even the Japanese have no exact idea as to what these trading companies are doing, particularly when they have to adjust themselves quickly to the highly changeable economic and political situations of the world as well as of Japan today. It is, therefore, only natural for those coming from overseas to wonder what they are, and how useful they are in facilitating distribution. It is often questioned why such mysterious and apparently old-fashioned organizations of primarily commercial capital should still be needed in Japan, when she claims to be the number two or three industrially productive nation in the Free World, and how they could manage to survive in the future when priority is bound to be placed on speedy and direct communications and contacts between producers and users.

To explain the built-in raison d'etre of such trading companies in the

127

Japanese economy, it may be necessary to refer to history. Indeed, the general trading company is a product of a long history. When Japan awoke a century ago from the 250 years of peaceful isolation under the Tokugawa Regency, she found herself far behind other nations in respect to industrialization and development of a capitalist economy.

As those peaceful days had developed a fairly educated and intelligent population as well as an accumulation of local capital, it was not very difficult for young leaders of the new Meiji era, after traveling abroad, to import into Japan some of the industries and the economic systems then existing in the Western world. Those early industries were introduced and operated mostly by the government itself, but they were gradually transferred to the private sector in order to attain more efficient and progressive management.

But because these industries were still in primitive stages, entrepreneurs and technicians were kept busy for many years in the area of production by learning and mastering what seemed to be advanced technologies for them. As a result, the marketing and shipping side of business had to be taken care of by the language-trained commercial experts, who were also commissioned to introduce new technical and market information from abroad.

With the gradual build-up of a capitalist economic structure in Japan, there were formed a number of the so-called *Zaibatsu* or family-owned holding companies that might be deemed as forerunners of today's "conglomerates." Each controlled a variety of industrial and financial enterprises as well as a marketing and information division, which was sooner or later made independent and called a trading company. As time went on and the nation's economic power expanded, it grew more extensively engaged in international trade with commodities needed or produced not only by the associated industries but also by outsiders, and extended its activities to all parts of the world. As a trading company became larger and more diversified, it was called a *soogoo-shoosha* or "general trading company."

Functions and Roles

In view of this historic background, it may become clearer why the Japanese manufacturers still considered it convenient and advantageous for them to employ the services of trading companies even after the Second World War and the complete dissolution of *Zaibatsu,* or holding company systems, with their respective enterprises each developing into an independent corporation owned by the public shareholders.

Since Japan has no mentionable supply of natural resources, within its four small islands totalling 370 thousand km² with a bare 16 percent as arable land, the only way to achieve economic growth is to import, first of all, voluminous quantities of energy sources and various industrial materials; and after processing them into manufactured goods and satisfying the demand of the 100 million people at home, export 20 to 30 percent of production in order to earn foreign exchange to import again. Japan's basic structure of industry and foreign trade should thus be termed "processing-oriented," apart from a 75 to 80 percent self-sufficiency in foods and feeds.

It is in these theatres that the general trading companies are traditionally capable of performing commercial functions and providing worldwide information that meets the requirements of time and market. With the support of financial houses, they are also in a position to advance credits to the industrialists for plant and equipment necessary for capacity expansion, import raw materials with a few months' grace for payment, and advance payment for manufactures even before actual sales to internal or external markets. Furthermore, they act as agents for insurance, transportation, and warehousing, as well as takers of the risks in exchange rate and commodity price fluctuations through their extensive operations.

Today, fourteen general trading companies are members of the "Trading Firms' Presidents Club," which would often exercise an influence on not only Japan's external trade policy but also nationwide economic progress. Table 7-1 indicates the total business turnover of the ten leading general trading companies for the fiscal years 1969-71 (April to March next year), divided by trade types (i.e., export from Japan; import into Japan; domestic trade; and trade outside of Japan).

It is shown that the sales of these firms accounted for nearly 50 percent of the country's total exports, and more than 60 percent of its entire imports, while their domestic transactions tended to grow to more than half of their total sales, thanks to the continued steady growth of Japan's economy during the four or five years until 1970 inclusive, and particularly the 23 percent annual growth rate of private fixed capital formation for plant and equipment. Their overall sales used to grow faster than Japan's GNP (in nominal terms), which Table 7-1 also indicates, although the picture had to undergo a considerable change during fiscal 1971 as will be referred to later.

The top-class companies of these "Big Ten" handle 9 to 10 percent of Japan's total exports and over 13 percent of the nation's imports. These deals, together with domestic transactions, keep their staff members quite busy in conducting pre-contract surveys and negotiations, fixing terms and conditions for sales and purchases, and effecting physical deliveries of commodities valued at 12 to 13 billion yen or about $45 million on an average day throughout the year, including Sundays and holidays.

Viewed from another angle, the general trading companies daily deal in

Table 7-1
Total Business Turnover of Ten Leading General Trading Companies
(By Fiscal Years[a]*)*

	(Millions of U.S. Dollars)			
	1969	*1970*	*1971*	
Export from Japan:				
10's Total (A)	$7,935	$9,746	$12,809	
Annual Growth Rate (%)	20.1	22.8	31.4	
Share by Trade Type (%)	17.1	17.1	19.3	
Japan's Total (B)	$16,812	$20,250	$25,134	
(Customs Clearance Basis)[b]				
Annual Growth Rate (%)	23.0	20.6	24.1	
A/B (%)	47.2	48.1	51.0	
Import to Japan:				
10's Total (A)	$9,996	$12,125	$12,220	
Annual Growth Rate (%)	19.2	21.3	0.8	
Share by Trade Type (%)	21.5	21.2	18.4	
Japan's Total (B)				
(Customs Clearance Basis)[b]	$16,005	$19,353	$20,256	
Annual Growth Rate (%)	20.4	20.9	4.7	
A/B (%)	62.5	62.3	60.3	
Domestic Trade:				
10's Total	$26,683	$32,553	$37,487	
Annual Growth Rate (%)	28.6	22.0	15.2	
Share by Trade Type	57.5	57.0	56.4	
Trade Outside of Japan:				
10's Total	$1,792	$2,700	$3,977	
Annual Growth Rate (%)	28.6	50.7	47.3	
Share by Trade Type (%)	3.9	4.7	6.0	
Total Sales				*Yen basis*
10's Total	$46,406	$57,125	$66,494	
Annual Growth Rate (X)(%)	24.9	23.1	16.4	9.28(X)
Share by Trade Type (%)	100	100	100	
Japan's GNP Nominal	$173,426	$203,371	$240,065	
Annual Growth Rate (Y)(%)	18.3	17.3	18.0	10.8(Y)
X/Y	1.4	1.3	0.9	
	Ex at $1= y360	Ex at $1= y360	Ex at $1= y338	

[a]Japanese fiscal year 1969 runs from April 1969 through March 1970, and so forth.
[b]Exports f.o.b., imports c.i.f.

about 7,000 different commodities, ranging from turn-key industrial plants and 300,000-ton mammoth tankers to small packages of raisins and instant coffee or noodles. It should be pointed out, however, that all these operations are done each on a surprisingly small margin. The trading companies, collecting such small margins, can only please their shareholders through large-scale turnover.

These margins basically originate from the manufacturers to whom the trading companies offer their services. However, since producers' margins are gradually dwindling, traders must take measures to warrant their profits, in addition to the said mass transactions. Here enters the strong financial power possessed by the general trading companies, whose historical credibility and reputation enables them to utilize the funds provided by various financing agencies at home and abroad. While trading companies act as buffers by taking credit risks for regular financing institutions, there arise possibilities of supplementing their operational margins by means of arbitrage, not to speak of the possibility that such colossal financing strength will contribute to the overall expansion of their activities in traditional and new fields. The total floating amount of long- and short-term funds by each of the largest houses would now reach $2 billion or more.

Circumstantial Changes

In this world today, both political and economic circumstances are subject to rapid changes. Peoples' ways of living are also changing in many countries. And Japan is no exception, as has been stated.

During the years from 1966 to 1970, Japan could achieve considerable expansion in its economy, industry, and trade thanks to the worldwide, strong, inflationary demands for industrial products mainly accruing from the Vietnam escalation. Average annual growth rates were 17 percent for GNP in nominal or 12 percent in real terms; 18 percent for both exports and imports; and, as said, 23 percent for private domestic investment for plant and equipment. Operations of the trading companies at home and abroad became much broader and freer as Japan emerged to score annual surpluses in its trade account and gradual increases in its international reserves.

At the same time, manufacturers of such "sophisticated," durable consumer goods as motorcars, ball-bearings, electronics, electrical equipment, watches, cameras, and so forth, which would require extensive and highly technical after services, strengthened their own exports. Including shipbuilding and mass-production capital goods, such as construction and agricultural machines, producers' direct sales to overseas are now likely to amount approximately to 30 percent of Japan's total, although trading companies are still involved occasionally as marketing pioneers, financial aides, and negotiating collaborators wherever needed.

The same applies to importing as well. Some large chain and department stores, more au courant with consumers' taste and changes in fashion (though trading companies do sometimes introduce or even create new fashions), try to buy finished goods direct from foreign manufacturers, although those are yet negligible in value.

President Nixon's announcement of his New Economic Policy in August, the inevitable floating of the yen, and finally the Smithsonian Agreement in December, as well as the sharp decline in all indices of Japan's domestic economy, were indeed big changes during 1971. The spirit of "invest as you like," prevalent among the Japanese entrepreneurs during the 1960s, sank deeply in the face of colossal, excessive production capacities against actual demand (or so-called "deflation gaps") in major industries.

At the same time, a set of serious socioeconomic problems came to the front. Strong civic resistance against air and water pollution, and also extreme urban density, would hereafter tend to decelerate further expansion of hitherto prosperous processing industries. While emphasis is being placed on people's welfare and better living, industries should develop themselves into more technology-intensive or knowledge-intensive areas by working out diversification and multi-polarization of their principal business.

There are now signs that Japan's national economy itself is going to have structural changes, however slowly. Instead of allocating its economic resources to a large extent to private domestic investment for industrial capacity and eventual exports, weight will be shifted more to both personal consumption and government expenditures that are related to the quality of the national life. Those industries found to be less competitive internationally will gradually be discarded, and more overseas direct investment will be promoted by Japanese entrepreneurs, in both developed and developing areas, in order to establish larger-scale factories for manufacturing and/or resources processing. Japan's imports of industrial raw materials that, combined with fuel, still make up nearly 70 percent of the total will gradually be slowed down; and more quality foods and consumer goods, both durable and non-durable, will flow in.

The general trading companies, which are always alert and apt at adjusting themselves to any circumstantial change and progress of time, are trying to find ways and means to remain profitable enterprises. What are some of the possible new activities?

New Activities

The answer may differ according to their individual history and character. But one thing that is commonly true is that in addition to their traditional marketing functions and financial roles as middlemen, they should undertake to develop their business in more long-range and highly systematized fields with wider scopes and spheres. They should also try to establish closer and stronger ties with the production, consumption, and recreation sectors of the economy.

To put it more pragmatically, the subsequent activities that are now being taken up, both at home and abroad, by the general trading companies of Japan include the following.

1. *To organize group activity.* It is quite natural in the present-day world that there is a trend to integration of enterprises, or group-forming, in view of ever-magnifying, ever-diversifying, and highly competitive economies. The so-called multinational companies and conglomerates are examples.

In addition to the daily business tie-ups, the group members, whether within the old *Zaibatsu* companies or among the new associates, try to help each other by undertaking jointly new and large-scale investment projects, exchanging up-to-date information, and holding management consultations. It is in this area that the general trading companies can ensure future business, acting as co-ordinators and organizers for the group but not necessarily as conglomerate leader.

2. *To assist in the development of resources abroad for Japanese industries.* Steel mills, non-ferrous smelters, oil refineries, chemical producers, power and gas companies, paper mills and food and feed processors are constantly in need of larger volumes of imported materials and fuel to maintain the growth of the Japanese economy. It is the general trading companies that are actively engaged in promoting exploration and exploitation of the needed resources as well as arranging for investment and financing.

It may be required hereafter to carry out processing of those resources into semi-finished or finished goods and leave added value at the place of production. The trading companies will study the possibilities according to the kinds of resources and the requirements of owner countries, as well as methods to minimize possible pollution. As need may be, products will be sold not only to Japan and home markets but also to third countries.

3. *To help promote various ventures overseas for Japanese, or in Japan for foreign entrepreneurs.* It is one of the activities required of the general trading companies that they should achieve competence in carrying out feasibility studies through systems engineering for any kind of ventures, manufacturing or non-manufacturing. Not only are they expected to be conversant with aspects and prospects of the market concerned, but they should also master the techniques to organize the whole project on an economically sound basis. Particularly in the case of new and larger-scale ventures, emphasis will be placed on making them more export-oriented and capable of providing jobs to the growing generations in host countries.

4. *To promote business wholly outside Japan.* Each general trading company has a vision to be a world enterprise. Although it has been long engaged in international trade, its business has been bound to center on Japan with meager sales being recorded as "Trade outside Japan" in Table 7-1. (However, the records have failed to include transactions between the locally incorporated overseas offices due to their independent bookkeeping.)

The time is now due for Japan's general trading companies to promote new systems whereby they should be engaged more actively and widely in business wholly outside Japan. Trade between third countries and business within a third country should be increased up to, say, 20 percent of their total sales by letting each overseas office operate more freely and extensively for the people and by the people of the host country. We do not mean that we are aiming at multinationalism, but we would like to contribute to the promotion of total welfare of each nation and the world.

Turning now to the domestic front, the following tasks can now be undertaken by the general trading companies.

1. *To strengthen ties with consumer markets at home.* The general trading companies have recently commenced taking up the mass sales systems of consumer goods by being heavily involved in supermarket, chain-store, and shopping-center ventures, financially and commercially. Through this new undertaking, it is hoped that the sector of retail business, which is deemed to be one of the most backward and unproductive areas of the Japanese economy, may be somewhat rationalized so as to contribute to slowing down the ever-soaring consumer price indices.

They have started being also engaged in the import of consumer goods from various countries with different designs and ideas, particularly from those countries that have trade deficits with Japan. Japanese consumers are thus becoming familiar with foreign-made articles and even to prefer them to home-made in view of their originality, personality, and ingenuity.

2. *To launch into new knowledge industry and systems engineering.* The mass communication of today tells us that there are many potential fields of business that can be undertaken by private enterprise. There is mention of post-industrial economic community, where the present key industries will play only a secondary role. Although such a possibility seems yet very remote, a new age of the three Ss (Software technology, Systems engineering, and Specialized knowledge) is bound to come. And these techniques would apply to new industrial or area development projects, including those for pleasure purposes.

The general trading companies have started paying attention to, or making themselves involved in, megalopolis/housing projects; anti-pollution or environmental works; oceanography or underseas developments; purchases and sales of knowledge and technology; industries concerned with educational, recreational, and medical systems.

How far the general trading companies can be successful in performing these new activities remains to be seen. But, in order to survive, they should be constantly on their guard for maintaining good, efficient, and flexible management and carrying out strict control over sales and profits so that increasing expenses may not exceed earnings in this day and age when borders between expenses and earnings are inevitably narrowing.

8

A Labor Approach to International Corporations

Nat Weinberg

The Problem of the International Corporation[1]

The crux of the matter can be summed up in three propositions:

1. The ICs command enormous and rapidly growing power.
2. The use of that power is motivated not by socially determined purposes but by the selfish interests of those who wield it (and, to a lesser degree, of the stockholders to whom they are theoretically responsible) that are often in conflict with the public interest.
3. No effective means presently exist either to prevent abuse of that power or to channel its use into socially desirable directions.

The significance of the first of the above propositions has been forcefully stated by Professor Raymond Vernon in the book he appropriately titled *Sovereignty at Bay:*

> I personally am mistrustful of any large concentration of economic power, on the grounds that Lord Acton so aptly summarized: Power corrupts. Men with power have an extraordinary capacity to convince themselves that what they want to do happens to coincide with what society needs done for its good. This comfortable illusion is shared as much by strong leaders of enterprise as by strong leaders of government.[2]

In support of the second proposition, it is not necessary to attribute evil intent to the wielders of corporate power. One need not follow Adam Smith in generalizing about "the mean rapacity" of merchants and manufacturers.[3] Executives of ICs are probably no better and no worse than the general run of human beings. But they are encouraged—indeed enjoined—to believe that by satisfying their own acquisitive instincts they serve society. The combination of socially sanctioned avarice, enormous power, and the "comfortable illusion" bred by power is a hazardous mixture with which to fuel an economy. It is that mixture, rather than malice, that makes it possible to say that nothing essential has changed —except for a quantum jump in the magnitude of the danger—since Adam Smith described businessmen as follows:

> . . . an order to men, whose interest is never exactly the same with that of the public, who have generally an interest to deceive and even to oppress the public, and who accordingly have, upon many occasions, both deceived and oppressed it.[4]

The stock counter-argument, in recent years, is that we are amply protected by the growing sense of public responsibility on the part of corporate executives. According to Professor Adolf Berle, for example:

. . . the corporation, almost against its will, has been compelled to assume in appreciable part the role of conscience-carrier of twentieth-century American society.[5]

To this, the best reply I know was given by Professor Ben Lewis who wrote:

A succinct comment would be: It is not going to happen; if it did happen it would not work; and if it did work it would still be intolerable to free men. I am willing to dream, perhaps selfishly, of a society of selfless men. Certainly if those who direct our corporate concentrates are to be free from regulation either by competition or government, I can only hope that they will be conscientious, responsible, and kindly men; and I am prepared to be grateful if this proves to be the case. But I shall still be uneasy and a little ashamed, with others who are ashamed, to be living my economic life within the limits set by the gracious bounty of the precious few. If we are to have rulers, let them be men of good will; but above all, let us join in choosing our rulers—and in ruling them.[6]

[The corporate conscience] may assure us that the men who make the decisions will be well intentioned and good, but it tells neither them nor us anything about the shape of goodness; it tells no one what society wants done and, hence, what to do.[7]

Ponder the plight of the management of a giant firm producing a basic commodity, employing thousands of workers at good wages, making splendid profits, and presently facing a crippling strike unless it accedes to a demand for a wage increase. The increase can easily be passed along in higher prices. Workers want higher wages and no interruption in employment; consumers want continued output at an increasing rate and so do stockholders. The public does not want further inflation, and large numbers of small firms do not want further increases in wages. The White House, which wants high production, full employment, healthy wages, abundant profits, and low prices, now admonishes industrial statesmen to recognize their public responsibility and to adopt measures appropriate to the maintenance of equity, full employment, stability, and progress. The management—as allocator, distributor, stabilizer, trustee, conservator, prophet, and chaplain, as well as manager—consults its conscience. The diagnosis of the attending psychiatrist will be 'multiple schizophrenia': The management's personality will not be split. It will be shredded and powdered![18]

Professor Lewis was, in effect, providing a graphic example of why, in Adam Smith's words, "merchants and manufacturers . . . neither are, nor ought to be, the rulers of mankind. . . ."[9]

The third proposition listed above is self-evident—although spokesmen for the ICs frequently attempt to deny it. Today's ICs are a far cry from Adam Smith's ideal of the small entrepreneur whose selfishness could be made to serve the public interest by the "invisible hand" of competition. Smith advocated that even within nations, the corporate form of business be limited to banking, insurance, canals and waterworks—activities requiring large amounts of capital capable of being amassed only by corporations—because he feared that corporations established in other fields would grow powerful enough to break free from the grip of the invisible hand, as they have done.

As a result, all advanced countries have found it necessary to enact elaborate regulatory legislation dealing in intimate detail with a wide range of corporate activities in order to protect the public interest against the anti-social consequences of unbridled pursuit of profits.

The ICs argue that national legislation is sufficient to regulate or control their activities. They claim they are bound by the laws of the countries in which they operate and that they comply with those laws. This defense overlooks several vital points. First, powerful corporations have great influence in molding the laws to suit their purposes in home and host countries alike. Their influence is particulary great in host countries competing for their favors. Second, the ICs are frequently able to obtain change in or exemptions from the laws—often induced by threats to withhold or relocate investments or by bribery. Third, with rare exceptions (largely confined to the extractive industries), they can escape any national law they find irksome by locating in or moving operations to a country that does not have such legislation. Fourth, national laws, with few exceptions, are written on the assumption that the operations of the corporations they cover are confined within national boundaries and therefore do not come to grips with the special problems created by ICs. Fifth, ICs have means available, in addition to relocation of operations, to escape or evade national legislation. For example, through manipulation of transfer prices, they can evade (or minimize) taxes on their profits, tariffs, and foreign exchange controls. Sixth, outright violation of laws by corporations is certainly not a completely unknown phenomenon—even in advanced, industrialized countries with well-developed law enforcement machinery—and ICs are among the violators in their home countries. It is not difficult to imagine what goes on in host countries where law enforcement is inefficient or polluted by corruption or inhibited by fears of scaring off foreign investment. Seventh, when all else fails, ICs, not infrequently, are able to enlist pressure from their home country governments to bend or break host country laws. In Chile, ITT tried to enlist CIA and other U.S. help to nullify the results of a democratic election.[10]

All this is not to say that national legislation can accomplish nothing in curbing abuse of the power of the ICs. But here one must distinguish between home and host countries, particularly when the hosts are LDCs. Host countries are at a severe disadvantage in attempting to regulate ICs operating within their boundaries because they are in competition with each other for foreign capital, managerial skills, and technology—to say nothing of employment opportunities that the LDCs, in particular, need desperately. Home countries, generally, may be in a somewhat better position to control ICs headquartered inside their borders, but such countries also may be hesitant to make full use of their powers for fear of putting "their" corporations at a disadvantage relative to corporations based in other countries or even (as will be illustrated below) for fear of losing the headquarters.

The essence of the problem created by the growth and spread of the ICs is thus the familiar one of power without accountability. As Professor Vernon has written:

. . . the multinational enterprise as a unit, though capable of wielding substantial economic power, is not accountable to any public authority that matches it in geographical reach and that represents the aggregate interests of all the countries the enterprise affects.[11]

In other words, meaningful accountability requires creation of international machinery to regulate the ICs.

The very existence of power without accountability calls for regulation. It should not be necessary to prove that the power in question has been abused so long as the way is open for abuse. The potentials for abuse are evident in the "Guidelines for International Investment" adopted by the Council of the International Chamber of Commerce (ICC) in November 1972. Separate sets of guidelines are set forth, respectively, for investors (i.e., ICs), home governments, and host governments. A glance through those applicable to the ICs—32 in number—provides a frightening, even though incomplete, catalogue of the wide and varied range of abuses that they are capable of perpetrating. (As might be expected, the ICC's guidelines for the ICs are so hedged with qualifications as to leave the way open to serious abuse even if they were respected in practice.) Many of the guidelines for home and host governments, guardedly worded though they are, suggest additional abuses that the ICs would like to remain free to commit and questionable privileges that they seek to obtain and, in many cases, have obtained.

While the ICC publication, predictably, makes no confessions of guilt, it seems reasonable to suppose that its guidelines were not drawn out of thin air but rather grew out of actual practices by ICs that gave rise to complaints of improper behavior.

A Bill of Particulars

There is no need to rely on conjecture, however. Through many years of contacts with trade unionists from other countries, including LDCs, and based upon what was reported to me by responsible people (including government officials and U.S. and other foreign development advisors) during eight months I spent in Asia, I am in a position to list some of the actual abuses committed by ICs against LDCs—and, in some cases, against developed countries as well.

The ICs pillage natural resources that often represent the only significant capital possessed by the LDCs, while resisting or evading commitments for local processing of those resources that could create desperately needed employment opportunities, useful spread effects, and viable export industries for the host countries. In manufacturing, as well as in the extractive industries, they create enclaves without backward or forward linkages that could be helpful in fostering development. They distort the direction of development and divert host-country development resources to suboptimal uses. They push the sale of products harmful to the people, the environment, or the social and political stability of the LDCs. They import technologies intact from their home bases and refuse to adapt them so as to create the additional employment that is increasingly recognized as the most urgent need of most LDCs. Their insistence upon exorbitant rates of return tends to make the host countries net exporters of capital, which undermines their foreign exchange positions.

As noted, they evade profits taxes and exchange controls by manipulation of transfer prices. In many cases, they use the host countries solely as sources of "cheap labor" to carry on simple manual assembly operations (which require no significant investment and provide no useful training of the local labor force) or to produce parts and components for products made and sold elsewhere. Whether it be assembly or parts manufacture, no viable industry is established that can be continued without the cooperation of the IC. The latter is likely either to pull up stakes when it finds even "cheaper" labor elsewhere, or to use the threat to do so as a means to blackmail the host country into granting additional concessions. ICs engage in unfair and repressive labor relations practices and racial discrimination that would not be tolerated, and in some cases are outlawed, in their home countries. They often resist training of host country personnel for managerial and technical positions in order to keep the LDCs in a dependent position. Despite predictable disavowals, the ICs do engage in corruption of host government officials. The ICs tend to form alliances with the most reactionary elements in the host countries—sometimes displaying a particular compatibility with dictatorships—which thus helps to stifle democratic elements, to block urgently needed reforms, and to pave the way for political turmoil. They intervene overtly or covertly in the political life of the LDCs. They persuade their home governments to bring economic and other pressures to bear against LDC governments taking actions that they find distasteful.

The ICs gain the opportunity to operate in the irresponsible fashion illustrated above by playing off nation against nation—and not only the LDCs—in the "investment climate" game. In the United States, to our sorrow, we are all too familiar with the practical meaning of that phrase as it is used by corporations in their lobbying activities in state capitals and city halls.

The investment climate is deemed best in states and cities where business taxes are lightest (and public services, consequently, most substandard); where labor laws are most restrictive, unions weakest, and wages lowest; where toleration of environmental pollution is greatest; and, in general, where legislatures and city councils are most easily intimidated to do the bidding of the corporations.

On the international scene, similarly, "investment climate," backed up by threats to withhold or relocate investments, is used to blackmail nations into mutually damaging competition that enables the ICs to extort concessions, subsidies, and special privileges that largely nullify whatever public benefits might otherwise flow from their investments. A kind of Gresham's law operates under which bad social standards drive out good standards.

The depredations of ICs are greatest among the LDCs, whose urgent needs for investment place them in weak bargaining positions in relation to ICs. (Exceptions are possible only for countries, such as those in the Organization of Petroleum Exporting Countries, that control a scarce resource and are able to maintain a rare degree of solidarity.) But even advanced industrial countries of Western Europe debase themselves in competition for new plants proposed to be built by U.S.-based ICs.

Among the concessions sought and all too often obtained are tax holidays or other forms of tax abatement, exceptions to foreign exchange regulations, costly infra-structure investment by the host country, and various other types of subsidies, tariff protection, monopoly privileges, restrictions on the export markets that local IC branches or subsidiaries are permitted to serve, restrictive labor legislation, and other measures to assure "cheap labor."

As might be expected, the investment climate gambit is also used against unions. One well-known example is Mr. Henry Ford II's threat to striking British Ford workers that his company would make no further investments in their country unless they came to heel. In addition, major U.S.-based ICs have approached union leaders in separate countries of Western Europe in attempts to entice them into competitive degradation of collective agreement standards as a means to gain or preserve employment opportunities.

The international allocation of private investment based upon extorted concessions and special privileges bears, at best, only coincidental resemblance to the allocation that would result from comparative advantage in the usual meaning of the phrase. The allocation is further deflected from genuine comparative advantage when ICs are induced to invest in countries other than those in which they are headquartered by tax preferences for foreign investment provided by their home countries (e.g., tax deferral for unrepatriated profits of foreign subsidiaries provided under U.S. law) or by tariff or non-tariff trade barriers erected by host countries.

Countermeasures: National Action

What can be done to alleviate the problems created by the rise of the ICs and who should do it?

The international labor movement was the first major institution to react to the dangers inherent in unchecked exercise of power by ICs. Unions have taken important steps toward coordinated international action to cope more effectively with the ICs. But the process of achieving adequate coordination is slow and difficult for a variety of reasons too numerous to detail here. Unionists are well aware, moreover, that collective bargaining is limited in its scope, that unions alone cannot mobilize sufficient countervailing power to offset that of the ICs and that the latter endanger workers not only as employees but also in their roles as citizens and consumers.

The labor movement has always turned to governments for help in solving problems that it is unable to solve itself either for lack of sufficient power or because the matters involved were outside the scope of collective bargaining. The growth and spread of the ICs has given rise to calls by unions for governmental and intergovernmental intervention into new fields.

As noted, host countries, acting individually, are at a serious disadvantage in attempting to regulate the ICs operating within their boundaries. Home countries, within limits, might be somewhat more effective in curbing abuses by their own ICs both inside and outside their borders. With respect to the latter, there is precedent in the U.S. government's application of its antitrust laws and its Trading with the Enemy Act to foreign subsidiaries of U.S.-based ICs.

One form that home country regulation might take was outlined in a resolution adopted by the UAW's International Executive Board in June 1971. The resolution proposed that government licenses be required for foreign investments proposed to be made by U.S. corporations, including reinvestment of profits made in foreign operations.

The applicant for a license would be required to show that the proposed investment would serve the interests of the United States economically with certain qualifications favoring LDCs) and would be free from harmful political consequences. Licenses would be conditioned on a guarantee that the applicant will compensate in full for loss of wages, fringe benefits, seniority rights, and so forth any U.S. workers adversely affected by the investment, whether because of imports or because of loss of export sales resulting from the investment. The licensee would be required, further, to conform to a comprehensive code of good behavior in relation to workers employed in the foreign operation.[12]

Application of such a code of good behavior, in effect, would make the ICs transmission belts for good labor standards as they now claim to be for good managerial practices and so forth. One consequence would be refusal of licenses for investments in countries that, for example, deny the right of free collective bargaining to their workers or enforce racial discrimination. Refusal of licenses on those grounds would not represent improper interference in the internal affairs of such countries any more than would insistence by an IC, as a condition for making an investment, that it be given an exemption from the potential host country's foreign exchange controls in order to be free to remit dividends to the parent corporation. In either case, the country involved remains free to refuse to meet the prerequisite for obtaining the investment.

The license requirement could be extended, of course, to cover a wide variety of other matters of concern to non-workers as well as to labor (e.g., adherence by the IC in host countries to home country environmental standards).

The guarantees for displaced U.S. workers proposed in the UAW licensing proposal would simply give practical expression to the universally accepted principle that an action is economically sound only if its benefits outweigh its costs. If a proposed foreign investment cannot meet the social as well as the private costs involved, the investment is economically unsound and should not be permitted to be made. In economic jargon, such a guarantee would "internalize the externalities."

Considerations of economic soundness also dictate that, in the United States and possibly in other countries as well, tax laws that distort the international allocation of private investment be eliminated. (I would, however, favor measures that would tend to redirect private foreign investment—provided it was not exploitative—away from the developed countries, where most of it now goes, to the LDCs.)[13] This would require, for example, that the provision of the U.S. Internal Revenue Code that presently permits "deferral" of taxes on unrepatriated profits of foreign subsidiaries be repealed. Where such profits are reinvested in other countries instead of being paid as dividends to the U.S. parent corporation, tax deferral, in effect, becomes tax exemption. At the very least, the U.S. taxes involved represent an interest-free government loan until the profits are repatriated.

Independently of the licensing proposal (although it could be made one of the conditions for a license), national legislation could impose financial disclosure requirements on ICs that would be valuable for various purposes to home and host countries alike as well as to the various national unions bargaining with them. Host countries, despite the competitive (with other countries) disadvantages they suffer in relation to the ICs, in some cases, have required the disclosure of certain data by IC subsidiaries within their respective jurisdictions. But such requirements are of limited use if the IC varies its accounting practices from country to country. Combined with the transfer pricing problem, lack of international consistency in accounting makes it well-nigh impossible for both governments and unions to determine how much of the IC's total profit properly is attributable to its operation in any single country. Home countries (e.g., the United States through amendment of SEC regulations or, if necessary, new legislation could require their ICs to publish financial data calculated on a uniform basis for each national subsidiary, including the formula for determining and the amount of the corporation-wide costs (e.g., research costs) allocated to each subsidiary.

Countermeasures: International Action

In the current situation, with reform of the international monetary system a crucial issue, the United States has a unique opportunity to take national action to combat a major threat created by the ICs the trend toward international oligopoly that threatens not only workers but the world's consumers as well. Richard J. Barber has written: "A good guess is that by 1980 three hundred large corporations will control 75 percent of all the world's manufacturing assets."[14] Others have made similar projections.

While international oligopoly grows apace, moves toward monetary reform are seriously impeded by the "dollar overhang"—the problem of how to dispose of the variously estimated 60 to 80 billion U.S. dollars in the hands of foreign governments, central banks, and private organizations and individuals around the world. Those dollars emigrated largely as a result of foreign investment by U.S.-based ICs. They obviously cannot be redeemed out of the nation's limited gold holdings, and it is almost certain that their holders will demand something more tangible than SDRs for their dollars.

Two problems could be alleviated simultaneously if the U.S. government would encourage foreign owners of dollars to use them to acquire the assets of the subsidiaries of U.S.-based ICs operating within their respective national boundaries. Those subsidiaries could then become independent national competitors of their present parent ICs, which would thus reverse—at least temporarily—the trend toward world oligopoly. At the same time, a substantial part of the dollar overhang would be removed as an obstacle to reform of the international monetary system. While the Nixon Administration was unlikely to advance such a proposal, it might have been compelled to accept it under pressure from other governments, some of which are deeply disturbed by the power exerted within their boundaries by U.S.-based ICs.

An alternative that has been proposed—investment of foreign-held dollars in U.S. enterprises, old or new—would contribute to solution of the monetary problem, but through the strengthening of existing non-U.S.-based ICs and the creation of new ones, it might aggravate the oligopoly problem.

National action by the ICs' headquarters governments could also be effective, at least to some degree, in curbing speculation by the ICs in international monetary markets—which, from all indications, was a major factor tending to aggravate if not, indeed, to cause recent monetary crises. A requirement for immediate publication by the ICs of all currency transactions exceeding a specified amount and the reason for each such transaction would be likely, in itself, to discourage speculation. The drafting of legislation designed to assure that all significant currency transactions and their timing were in response to legitimate business requirements would be somewhat more complex but certainly not impossible.

As previously noted, unilateral action by individual governments is severely limited in its ability to curb abuses by the ICs. The latter can escape attempts at national regulation through the cracks represented by national boundaries, and the ICs are adept at finding and devising escape hatches. It is most unlikely that corporations would refrain from taking advantage of international boundaries when they take the fullest possible advantage of state boundaries within the United States. For example, the *Wall Street Journal* for July 17, 1972, carried a rather detailed article headed, in part: "Many Companies Work to Avoid Local Taxes—With Great Success," and "They Transfer Funds, Goods Around the U.S. to Avert Levies of Various States,"[15] Some of the devices the *Journal* reported were technically legal (e.g., an annual, temporary withdrawal of deposits from Illinois banks for shipment to other states or for purchase of tax-exempt government securities to avoid Illinois' personal property tax that is assessed on cash on deposit within the state as of April 1. The article also noted that corporations allocated costs and profits among the states to minimize or avoid profits taxes and established shadow offices (in one case consisting of two file drawers on the premises of a law firm) to avoid certain other taxes. Some of the methods used are not even technically legal, as indicated by the following from the *Journal's* report:

. . . some companies have found the simplest way to avoid state taxes is to tell different stories to different officials. 'In coping with state B, the company may attribute income to state A, but when they are dealing with state A they may attribute that very same income to state B,' Mr. Corrigan says. 'So the income may wind up not being taxed at all.'[16]

(The Mr. Corrigan quoted is associated with the Multistate Tax Commission which is attempting, over company opposition, to develop means to minimize corporate evasion of state tax laws.)

Needless to say, ICs have far greater opportunities for evading separate national laws than U.S. corporations have for evading or undermining the laws of the separate states. For example, an IC that seeks to escape national environmental controls in order to reduce costs may relocate (or threaten to relocate) its plants in countries more tolerant of pollution. In that case, the country with strict controls is faced with the choice of relaxing them and thus permitting environmental damage or maintaining them at the cost either of making its remaining domestic producers of the project involved non-competitive or of seeing them relocate also. (I am moved to ask whether such relocation can be considered a response to comparative advantage.)

The limitations of purely national legislation affecting ICs currently are being demonstrated in striking fashion in Canada. According to the March 17, 1973, issue of *Business Week*,[17] Massey-Ferguson, Ltd., is threatening to move its world headquarters out of Canada in order to escape new legislation that would tax certain forms of its overseas income previously free from Canadian taxes. The same magazine article reports that in recent months, a dozen smaller ICs actually did move their headquarters out of Canada and cited the tax change as a major reason.

It is inconceivable that governments will remain supine indefinitely in the fact of such challenges to their sovereignty repeatedly thrown in their faces by the ICs. As former U.S. Under-Secretary of State George Ball has written: ". . . multi-national corporations and nation-states are on a collision course."[18]

Mr. Ball's proposal for avoiding the collision would require the governments, in effect, to yield the right-of-way to the ICs. His solution is as follows:

. . . the establishment by treaty of an international companies law, administered by a supranational body, including representatives drawn from various countries, who would not only exercise normal domiciliary supervision but would also enforce antimonopoly laws and administer guarantees with regard to uncompensated expropriation. *An international companies law could place limitations, for example, on the restrictions nation-states might be permitted to impose on companies established under its sanction.* [emphasis added][19]

That would be worse than no solution at all. The essence of the problem is that the power of the ICs is already approaching the point where they are able to free themselves, even without the assistance Mr. Ball proposes to give them, from restrictions that the nation-states have felt compelled to impose in order to protect the public interest.

The obvious need is for replacement of decreasingly effective national restrictions by effective international machinery. An international companies law could be a means to that end, but it would have to take a form quite different from that envisioned by Mr. Ball. The ultimate goal must be a comprehensive and enforceable code of good behavior applicable to all the operations of all ICs, where located. As will be indicated below, certain small steps pointing in that direction are already being taken. Meanwhile there are a number of less ambitious goals that are worth pursuing in the short run in order to minimize certain IC abuses.

1. *International Fair Labor Standards*. As long ago as 1948, the representatives of some fifty nations who signed the Havana charter for an International Trade Organization recognized the need for elimination of unfair labor standards in international trade. Article 7 of the Charter, headed "Fair Labour Standards," therefore provided in part:

The Members recognize that measures relating to employment must take fully into account the rights of workers under intergovernmental declarations, conventions and agreements. They recognize that all countries have a common interest in the achievement and maintenance of fair labor standards related to productivity, and thus in the improvement of wages and working conditions as productivity may permit. The Members recognize that unfair labor conditions, particularly in production for export, create difficulties in international trade, and, accordingly, each Member shall take whatever action may be appropriate and feasible to eliminate such conditions within its territory.[20]

With the rise of the ICs effectuation of the purposes of that Article has taken on far greater importance because unfair labor standards now distort international investment as well as trade patterns.

Although the Havana Charter never came into effect, maintenance of fair labor standards is, nevertheless, at least a moral obligation of the parties to the GATT agreement, Article 29 of which provides:

The contracting parties undertake to observe to the fullest extent of their executive authority the general principles . . . of the Havana Charter pending their acceptance of it in accordance with their constitutional procedures.[21]

The U.S. government has raised the issue of fair labor standards in GATT negotiations from time to time but, apparently, has never given it the emphasis it deserves. The Report to the President submitted by the Special Representative for Trade Negotiations, entitled "Future United States Foreign Trade Policy" (Roth Report), issued in 1969, spoke out strongly on the matter and concluded:

The United States should . . . seek, through the Gatt and the ILO and possibly other international organizations, to develop international agreement upon a workable definition of fair labor standards and upon realistic means for their enforcement.[22]

More recently, the Report to the President submitted by the Commission on International Trade and Investment Policy, entitled "United States International Economic Policy in an Interdependent World" (Williams Commission Report), a majority of whose members were bankers and industrialists, said:

The Commission therefore recommends that the United States actively support a multilateral effort to gain international acceptance of a code of fair labor standards which would include a workable definition of the concept and realistic means for enforcing the code.[23]

Present circumstances—growing protectionism in the United States; Europe's fears of the increasing penetration of its markets by Japanese goods; Japan's fear of increasing restrictions on its exports and growing concern internationally with the "cheap labor" abuses of the ICs—may provide a unique opportunity to make the international fair labor standards principle a practical as well as a moral obligation.

There is a great deal more to be said on the subject of international fair labor standards, particularly as it pertains to the LDCs. It must be stressed, in that connection, that the Havana Charter refers to "fair labor standards related to productivity." Thus, where technology or other causes resulted in low productivity, *commensurately* low wages would create no problem. However, on the principle previously stated that labor is not a commodity, implementation of international fair labor standards would compel ICs to determine the geographical allocation of their investments on the basis of factors other than the relative degrees to which workers in various countries could be exploited (i.e., denied a reasonable share of the wealth they helped to produce).

The Havana Charter provided for consultation and cooperation with the International Labor Organization in connection with international fair labor standards. A proposal that the ILO immediately take the initiative with respect to the ICs and certain labor standards (not including wages) was made at a "Meeting on the Relationship between Multinational Corporations and Social Policy" convened by that organization in the fall of 1972. The worker participants urged unsuccessfully that the meeting call upon the governing body of the ILO to consider adoption of a convention under which governments of countries in which ICs are headquartered would obligate themselves to require such ICs to adhere to existing ILO standards in all their operations, regardless of the countries in which they are located. The effect would be similar, in part, to that of the code of good behavior contemplated by the UAW's proposal for licensing capital exports.

Such an ILO convention would be binding only upon those governments that ratified it (and, even then, only after there had been specified minimum number of ratifications). Nevertheless, the adoption of such a convention by the ILO would provide a useful rallying point for the mobilization of union and other pressure upon governments as well as a vehicle to bring to the attention of the general public the need for international action to curb abuses by IC .

Although the proposal was not adopted it undoubtedly will be raised again in the future.

2. *Restrictions on Concessions to ICs*. Governments of LDCs and developed host countries alike are coming increasingly to recognize that competition in concessions and subsidies offered to ICs is a losing game for all of them. It may be possible, therefore, to work out intergovernmental agreements that at least would set limits to the kinds and amounts of concessions offered.

Canada, apparently, has taken a unilateral step in that direction. According to the same *Business Week* [24] article previously cited, Alcan, Ltd., recently withdrew from a possible fluorite mining venture in Tunisia because new legislation bars Canadian corporations from taking advantage of tax incentives offered by developing countries.[25] (The law also covers similar concessions offered by industrialized countries.) If the Tunisian mining operation would have been unprofitable in the absence of the tax incentive, it obviously would have represented a misallocation of world resources.

3. *Relieving Pressures on LDCs*. The LDCs are forced into self-defeating competition for the favors of the ICs by a desperate need for capital and the failure of most governments of the industrialized world to contribute significantly to meeting that need through grants and soft loans. The record of the United States in this respect is particularly disgraceful for a variety of political reasons.

The political obstacles could be minimized in the United States, and probably in other countries as well, through the so-called "link"—the allocation by the International Monetary Fund of a proportion of newly created SDRs to the LDCs for development purposes. This would avoid the necessity for direct budgetary appropriations for development aid that call for more courage and farsightedness than most politicians seem to possess. Under the present method of allocation of SDRs, the wealthy nations receive the bulk of the claims on real resources created by the international community. That situation should be reversed.

The "link" would provide the additional advantage of multilateral allocation and administration of development aid, thereby reducing, although probably not completely eliminating, the fears of political interference aroused in the LDCs by bilateral aid arrangements.

To the extent that development assistance became available in the form of SDRs, the LDCs would be less vulnerable to the "investment climate" game, which results in ruthless exploitation of their peoples and their resources by the ICs, the undermining of social standards internationally, and frequently, a net outflow of capital on private investment accounts. The link would enable the LDCs to feel freer than many would at present to participate in the type of agreement suggested above to limit concessions to the ICs.

4. *Other Possibilities.* It seems at least possible that governments, in the relatively near future, will come to see the need for concerted action to minimize the damage done by the ICs in certain other areas. It is hard to believe, for example, that discussions of reform of the international monetary system will ignore the need for action to prevent the disturbances to the system resulting from currency speculation by the ICs. The manipulation of transfer prices by the ICs is a matter of grave concern for the tax, customs, and foreign exchange authorities of a growing number of countries. The issue of restrictive business practices, with particular reference to the ICs, has been raised in UNCTAD. A draft of a proposed international agreement on restrictive practices is currently being circulated by a committee of the American Bar Association.

Comprehensive Regulation

The issues mentioned above cover only a part of the broad spectrum of IC abuses, actual and potential, that require international regulation. The proposals outlined represent a piecemeal approach to those abuses that would be helpful but far from sufficient to protect world welfare against the presently largely unrestrained power of the ICs.

As noted earlier, the ultimate goal must be a comprehensive code of enforceable international law. Such a code will have to be almost as wide-ranging and as detailed as the national legislation that in advanced countries attempts—although with something less than full success—to channel private corporate power into service of the public interest. The code should apply not only to international "corporations," narrowly defined, but also to the growing number of Soviet and Soviet-bloc enterprises operating in non-communist countries.

The development of such a code today appears to be a matter for the relatively distant future. It may be hastened, however, by four factors. One is the restiveness of the ICs themselves, reflected in Mr. Ball's writings on the subject, with the complications they face as a result of the multiplicity and variety, to say nothing of the overlapping and contradictions, of the separate national laws applicable to their operations. A second factor is the growing concern of the LDCs with the exploitative nature of IC activities within their respective boundaries, manifested, to cite just one example, by the five-nation Andean Pact. A third factor is the growing fear of many developed countries that control of their economic destinies is slipping out of their hands into those of the ICs. A fourth factor is the increasing pressure of the international labor movement for intergovernmental action with respect to the ICs. The influence of the labor movement, in this matter, although not as great as I would like to see it, should not be underestimated.

A concrete manifestation of that influence is to be found in the proposed European Companies Statute which Mr. Ball has cited as a step in the direction of his goal of an international companies law. The draft for that statute includes provisions that would subject companies covered by it to co-determination (i.e., worker representation on their supervisory boards) and would require them to deal with European-wide Works Councils that would have veto power over management with respect to a wide range of personnel matters and the right to be consulted before decisions are made on others. It also provides for European-wide collective agreements if the unions involved desire them.

As was noted in a resolution on ICs adopted by the 1971 Congress of the International Metalworkers' Federation, which includes unions from sixty countries representing 11 million workers:

Fortunately, unions have close ties with political parties that are, or have been and are likely to be again, the government parties in countries that play a leading role in determining the rules for economic and social relations among the world's nations.[26]

Among the so-called "Group of Ten," which plays the decisive role in world monetary matters, for example, Labor and Social-Democratic parties are or fairly recently have been in the governments of England, Germany, Italy, Sweden, Belgium, and the Netherlands. In France, if the Socialist-Communist coalition formed for the recent elections can be maintained, it might be able to win control of the government in the not-too-distant future. In Canada, where there is widespread concern with domination of the national economy by U.S.-based ICs, the union-supported New Democratic Party holds the balance of power in Parliament. Socialists also play a major political role in Switzerland, which, although technically not a member of the Group of Ten, functions for many purposes as if it were. If some or all of those countries were to propose an international code to govern ICs, they would undoubtedly have the support of many of the LDCs that have expressed themselves in the UN, UNCTAD, ECOSOC, and the ILO as seriously concerned with IC abuses.

The same resolution, therefore, called upon the International Metalworkers' Federation Secretariat:

. . . to take the initiative toward the creation of an international task force, including representatives of other trade union organizations and progressive political forces, to develop a proposal for a comprehensive code of international corporation law.[27]

With official representatives of influential political parties (including some from the LDCs) involved in formulating the proposed code, the likelihood of its being raised and seriously considered at the intergovernmental level would be greatly enhanced.

Under the code contemplated by the resolution of the Metalworkers' Federation: "No firm [would] be permitted to carry on activities in more than one country unless it conforms to the requirements of [the proposed] international laws."[28] The laws would cover not only labor matters but also all others ". . . with respect to which the activities of international corporations endanger the social interest, nationally and internationally."[29]

The international code would come into force by treaty, which would mean that it would supersede national laws in conflict with it. The treaty could pave the way for its universal acceptance by providing that once a sufficient number of countries had ratified it, they would apply certain economic sanctions in concert to countries refusing to accept it, as well as to those accepting but violating it.

The proposed task force was called upon:

. . . to determine among other things, whether admistration and enforcement of its proposed code . . . should be entrusted partly or wholly to existing intergovernmental organizations or whether a new agency should be created for some or all of the purposes involved.[30]

Thus, existing agencies such an GATT, the ILO, the International Monetary Fund, UNCTAD, ECOSOC, and so forth might each carry out certain functions, or a new UN agency might be created either to take on the entire task or to share it with one or more of the existing organizations.

Partly on the initiative of the labor movement, as well as because of the concern of certain governments, particularly LDC governments, the issue of the ICs is already on the agenda of intergovernmental organizations. The United Nations Economic and Social Council (ECOSOC) adopted a resolution on the subject in July 1972. The resolution took note of the statement in the UN's *World Economic Survey, 1971* as follows:

. . . while these corporations [the ICs] are frequently effective agents for the transfer of technology as well as capital to developing countries, their role is sometimes viewed with awe, since their size and power may surpass the host country's entire economy. The international community has yet to formulate a positive policy and establish effective machinery for dealing with the issues raised by the activities of these corporations.[31]

The main operative paragraph of the resolution called for creation of a study group on ICs charged, among other things, ". . . to submit recommendations for appropriate international action."[32]

At the previously mentioned ILO meeting on the ICs and social policy, the government, management, and labor experts participating unanimously recommended that the organization undertake a study that would include the "elements of principles and guidelines" for ICs in the field of social policy.

What has been done thus far at the intergovernmental level amounts to little more than verbal recognition of the fact that the ICs present a problem requiring international action. How soon that recognition will yield meaningful results is a matter for conjecture although, as noted, there are factors tending to accelerate the normally glacial pace of intergovernmental movement from words to deeds. The concern manifested by the ICs themselves—exemplified, among other things, by the need the ICC felt to issue its "Guidelines for International Investment"—provides some basis for optimism that action will not be unduly delayed. Whether it comes soon or later, however, there seems little question but that the ICs inevitably will be brought under the rule of some form of world law. As Professor Vernon has written:

The basic asymmetry between multinational enterprises and national governments may be tolerable up to a point, but beyond that point there is a need to reestablish balance. When this occurs, the response is bound to have some of the elements of the world corporation concept: accountability to some body, charged with weighing the activities of the multinational enterprise against a set of social yardsticks that are multinational in scope. If this does not happen, some of the apocalyptic projections of the future of multinational enterprise will grow more plausible.[33]

Notes

1. With regard to terminology, I consider "international" or "supranational" a better adjective for the corporations under consideration than "multinational." The last assumes (or at least has as a possible connotation of) loyalties to more than one nation. That, in turn, assumes that the interests and goals of all the nations involved are always in harmony. If the latter assumption is invalid, as obviously it is, simultaneous loyalty to all of

them is impossible. The fact is that the corporations under examination are loyal only to their own profit-maximizing objectives and subordinate the interests of home and host countries alike to pursuit of those objectives. Any other course would subject the officers of those corporations to legitimate complaints from stockholders.

The word "enterprise" does not seem to me to be appropriate in discussing corporations that in most cases function as oligopolies—which means that they tend to be unenterprising in terms of price competition and often other matters as well. (Until we can think of a better word, however, "enterprise" does have the merit of comprehending the growing number of Soviet-bloc businesses operating in the non-communist world that seem to behave not much differently in host countries from capitalist corporations.)

When I refer to a "labor" approach, I have in mind the broadly inclusive and internationalist traditions of the labor movement. I am concerned with the impact of international corporations (ICs) not only on American workers or the wage and salary workers of the industrialized world but on all whose livelihoods are obtained by toil, everywhere in the world, including the landless laborers, tenant farmers and poor owners of small farms in the less-developed countries (LDCs).

2. Raymond Vernon, *Sovereignty at Bay* (Basic Books, 1971), p. 272.

3. Smith, *Wealth of Nations,* p. 460.

4. Ibid., p. 250.

5. Adolf Berle, as quoted in Ben W. Lewis, "Economics by Admonition," *Papers and Proceedings of the Seventy-first Annual Meeting, 1958, American Economic Review* Vol. XLIX, May 1959, p. 395.

6. Ibid.

7. Ibid., pp. 395-6.

8. Ibid., p. 396.

9. Smith, *Wealth of Nations,* p. 460.

10. "When $25,000 stood between ITT and Ecuador," *Business Week,* August 11, 1973, pp. 102-3.

11. Vernon, *Sovereignty at Bay,* p. 249.

12. Sweden has already taken the first steps toward imposing such a code on its international corporations. Their investments in certain LDCs are eligible for government guarantees only if they meet specified standards for workers in the host countries covering such matters as collective bargaining rights; benefits for loss of wages during illness, injury and layoff; pensions; a number of other health and welfare matters and racially nondiscriminatory employment policies. I have been told that the Swedish effort has been ineffective because the number of LDCs covered by the investment guarantee was small and because Swedish firms contemplating

investment in those countries prefer to forego the guarantee rather than be bound by the code. The UAW's licensing proposal would avoid the defects of the Swedish approach.

13. I am inclined to agree with Gunnar Myrdal, however, that management contracts are far preferable from the standpoint of the LDCs than direct, foreign, private investment. More generous development aid from the advanced countries and the so-called "link," would supply the LDCs with the capital and foreign exchange required in connection with management contracts. Gunnar Myrdal, *The Challenge of World Poverty* (Pantheon Books, 1970), pp. 330-2.

14. Richard J. Barber, *The American Corporation, Its Power, Its Money, Its Politics* (E.P. Dutton, 1970), p. 264.

25. William M. Carley, "One Step Ahead," *Wall Street Journal*, July 17, 1972, p. 1.

16. Ibid., p. 23.

17. "Canada: A Tax Law That Must Go Too Far," *Business Week*, March 17, 1973, p. 41.

18. George Ball, "Excerpts from Comments by George M. Ball," in "The Probable Impact of U.S. Trade Legislation on the Foreign Operations of U.S. Companies" (New York: The Conference Board, January 18, 1973, processed), p. 1.

19. George W. Ball, "Remarks at the Annual Dinner," speech delivered to the British National Committee, International Chamber of Commerce, London, October 18, 1967, processed, p. 12.

20. *Havana Charter for an International Trade Organization, Final Act and Related Documents,* Department of State Publication 3117, April 1947.

21. General Agreement on Tariffs and Trade (GATT), *Basic Instruments and Selected Documents, Volume IV* (Geneva: GATT, March 1969), p. 49.

22. Special Representative for Trade Negotiations, *Future U.S. Foreign Trade Policy* (Roth Report), Report to the President, January 14, 1969 (Government Printing Office, 1969), p. 44.

23. Commission on International Trade and Investment Policy, *U.S. International Economic Policy in an Interdependent World* (Williams Commission Report), Report to the President, (Government Printing Office, July 1971), p. 65.

24. "Canada: A Tax Law That Must Go Too Far," *Business Week*, March 17, 1973, p. 41.

25. Although the *Business Week* article referred only to developing countries, the law applies equally to developed countries. Unfortunately

the effective date for all parts of the new tax law, including the provisions referred to above that were objected to by Massey-Ferguson, has been postponed for two years.

26. "Resolution on Multinationals," 22d Congress of the International Metalworkers' Federation, Lausanne, Switzerland, October 26-30, 1971, p. 144.

27. Ibid.

28. Ibid.

29. Ibid.

30. Ibid.

31. UN Economic and Social Council Res. 1721 (LIII), August 14, 1972, p. 1.

32. Ibid, p. 2.

33. Vernon, *Sovereignty at Bay,* p. 284.

9 Multinational Companies and Trade Unions: A Japanese View

Masao Aihara

Today, the world map is painted with various colors from one end to the other. But if we take a look at the economic factors, the boundaries of countries are losing their significance.

People are saying that the world economy will be dominated by a handful of companies that will operate completely free from national boundaries, not in the distant future but within less than twenty years. Even now, if we compare the economic power of MNCs with that of medium-sized developed countries, the total sales of General Motors are bigger than the Gross National Products of the Netherlands, Belgium, Norway, and Denmark combined.

What Are MNCs and How Should We Take Up the MNCs from the Trade Union Viewpoint?

First of all, there are a lot of terms for MNCs—for instance, international enterprise, transnational enterprise, world enterprise—and there are also a lot of definitions. We are at a loss to define its real meaning. As trade unionists, we see MNCs as companies that operate production and service business beyond national boundaries.

Causes of Development of MNC

World trade is expanding in quantity and accelerating interdependent relations between states. The world is becoming smaller and smaller, through the development of communication and transportation. This tendency goes beyond the barriers of ideologies and leads respective countries to open their doors to world markets.

There are a number of reasons for the phenomenal rise in direct foreign investments over the last twenty years: the attraction of faster growing foreign markets; the desire to get exemption from tariff barriers; the possibility of reducing production costs with cheaper labor, raw materials, and transport; and the benefits of more lenient taxation systems and exchange control regulations. The net result of those factors has been a radical transformation of the international economy with the multinational company rather than the individual country becoming more and more the basic unit of production, trade, and accounting. The effects of such companies on national economic and social situations, and the consequent reactions of governments and trade unions are examined in the two following sections.

The world market invites business firms to secure and enlarge their shares, increase their desire to be exempt from taxes and trade barriers, and to obtain cheap labor, low-cost materials, and so on. Thus world trade has developed from the free exchange of commodities to that of capital, technology, and personnel. It is no exaggeration to say that economics and the activities of enterprises are greater than politics and the activities of states, and the latter are following the former.

Merits and Demerits of the MNC

Merits of the MNC. We admit the merits of the MNC in the following areas, but we do it only as long as the activities of MNCs are not inconsistent with the welfare of workers.

1. MNCs have contributed to the development of the world economy by providing job opportunities in host countries and elevating their technological standard.
2. MNCs have helped to eliminate the concept of differences based on boundaries and brought about more interdependent and friendly relations between states.
3. The MNC has served world peace through the exchange of personnel and culture and has promoted mutual understandings across national boundaries.

As mentioned above, some of the effects of the activities of multinational companies are positive.

ICFTU pointed out in the statement adopted by its Ninth World Congress that "the international organization of production can play an important role in spreading new technical know-how and in giving an impetus to economic growth and social progress, provided that trade union action in all its aspects is brought to bear upon multinational companies so as to safeguard the interests of the workers and the public as a whole."

Demerits of the MNC. The MNC is nothing but a private enterprise that is supremely oriented to profit making, and MNCs are operating in many countries for their own selfish purposes. They move their investment capital across borders, motivated only by the desire to maximize profits and without regard for the economic and social consequences for the people of either the country in which they are headquartered or of the host country. Pursuit of profits leads them to invest where labor costs are cheapest, exploitation of workers is least restrained, and the degree of social responsibility required of them is in general minimal. They engage in buying human labor in the cheapest markets and selling the products everywhere at the inflated prices of shared monopolies. Thus, they deny to workers and consumers alike the benefits of international trade.

If it is allowed to operate without restraints, there will be a lot of demerits, as in the following areas:

1. Impact on the workers. I will make a detailed explanation of this item in the next section.
2. The MNC is creating the danger of a worldwide polarization between haves and have-nots through the battle for world market shares between the gigantic MNCs and the small national companies.
3. Threats to free world trade. The MNC is changing world trade from free trade to limited private trade between parent companies and their subsidiaries. The MNC is forming economic blocs through its gigantic economic influence and through the absorption of small enterprise and the large-scale integration of economic activities in host countries.
4. Exporting uncontrolled pollution. The development of MNCs is said to be beneficial to the world economy because it accelerates the transfer of technology and capital to less-developed countries. We must keep in mind that new technologies unrelated to the real needs of a particular country may be of little benefit. They may indeed actually be harmful if they have the effect of exporting uncontrolled environmental pollution.

The question to which we must find the answer is how to preserve the merits of international trade while eliminating the demerits. Answers must be found to these problems but we should be aware that easy solutions may bring on even more serious problems. History teaches us that economic isolationism is the wrong answer. The trade wars of the 1930s made a major contribution to bringing on a worldwide depression and the outbreak of World War II.

Impact on Workers

The most accurate statement of the relationship of trade unions to the MNC was made by the ICFTU at its economic conference on free trade unions and multinational companies. Its conclusion says:

[T]he trade union movement has always been alive to the danger which the international operations of capital could represent for the exercise of trade union rights and the earnings and job security of workers. Now, however, it is faced with a far more fundamental challenge in the phenomenal development in the size and power of multinational companies; trade unions which have achieved a recognized place in the industrial relations systems of democratic countries only after long years of struggle are now finding their position in such systems jeopardized by the attitude of these companies.

Owing no allegiance to any particular country, escaping any form of democratic control or social responsibility, and guided primarily by motives of expansion and profit-maximization, the growth of these industrial and commercial giants straddling the five continents has serious implications not only for trade unions but also for national governments.

From this viewpoint, I'd like to touch on the demerits of the MNC on the following items.

1. *Job Security*. The MNC operates on a worldwide scale. It easily transfers its production and research from one country to another, for instance, from a high-wage country to a cheap-labor country or from a country in which trade unions exist to a country in which workers are in a state of oppression. Thus, capital has worldwide mobility but workers have little mobility. They have to stay in their region, and as a result, workers face loss of job security and other serious social effects that MNC activities have caused in capital-exporting countries. That is what has been called "job export" resulting from firms setting up subsidiaries abroad to supply the home market. This has been particularly evident in U.S. industry, which has transferred a number of its labor intensive processes to cheap-labor countries.

2. *Trade Union Rights*. Examples of subsidiaries of multinational companies actually refusing to recognize trade unions are: IBM, Kodak, Gillette, Holokrome, Caterpillar Tractor, Roberts Arundel and, in respect particularly of non-manual labor, Comprehensive Designers (an American firm closely linked with Lockheed), Continental Oil, Nestle, Goodyear, Cummins Engines, Firestone, KLM, Air Canada, and TWA—all in Britain; the United Fruit Company subsidiaries in various Latin American countries; and two German firms-Müller Wipperfürth and Kurt Wokan in Austria. Serious difficulties have been experienced with Monsanto and Du Pont de Nemours in Luxemburg. The reluctance of some multinational firms to establish collective bargaining procedures has caused trouble in Sweden (IBM) and Britain (the American-owned automobile companies, in particular by refusing to join the employers' associations). Problems arising from difficulties in identifying the center of decision making or in finding out the real profitability of multinational companies are reported from many countries.

In many countries, especially developing countries, multinational companies, by playing on the need for foreign investment, have provoked competition between governments offering investment incentives of all kinds (including restrictions on trade union freedom), the cost of which obviously has to be borne by the people concerned. Capital-receiving countries should on the contrary seek to cooperate in regionally coordinated investment-attraction policies.

3. *Changes in the Balance of Power of Bargaining*. Many times MNCs challenge the established system of industrial relations. In extreme cases, they refuse to recognize unions and make collective bargaining harder due to the absence of published information on global profitability or sometimes because of the difficulty in identifying the real center of decision making. Unless faced with a countervailing coordination of trade union power across national frontiers, they can, moreover, with threats of switching production to other countries or in case of a strike moving a plant from one country to another to make up the strike deficit through subsidiaries in various countries, tilt the balance of bargaining power decisively in favor of international capital. The more fundamental trade union anxiety at the growth of international companies arises from the change in the balance of power, both between management and labor.

MNC's attempts to exploit workers and raw materials resources often generate antipathy among the peoples of the host countries. Workers in such countries are dissatisfied with the fact that the branch office of the MNC has no ability to deal with trade unions because decision-making authority belongs to the headquarters of the MNC. This distorts and manages industrial relations and sometimes strikes result.

4. *Challenges to Social Justice*. MNC policy is to fulfill minimum social responsibility in countries and to try to make maximum profits. For instance, they are making use of apartheid in South Africa.

Countermeasures of Trade Unions to Impacts of MNCs

During the 1960s, trade unions began to approach the whole problem of MNCs. The first target was the enforcement of fair labor standards in international trade, and this still remains one of the major objectives.

Now the unprecedented growth of MNCs is posing a much wider, more complex challenge to the pattern of industrial relations, trade union rights, and national independence in respect to economic planning, taxation, and balance of payments. The ICFTU started appealing to all its affiliates to take three major countermeasures against these challenges:

1. Strengthen international trade union cooperation and coordination to meet MNC challenges, and exchange information on MNCs activities;

2. Pressure respective governments to take necessary restrictions;
3. Pressure international organizations to take action on formulating an international code of behavior for MNCs.

ICFTU failed once to obtain the adoption of a resolution on MNCs at the ILO General Convention in 1968 because of the opposition of the employer's group, but in 1969 the conference adopted a report that referred to the significant effect on industrial relations that the rapid expansion of large international corporations might have and suggested that the nature and consequences of such developments for governments, workers, and employers should be studied by the ILO. In April 1970, at Caracas at the 9th ILO America Regional Conference, a resolution was adopted calling for an examination of the effects of policies of multinational companies on working and living conditions in the countries where they operate. The question was also raised with particular reference to trade union rights by workers' delegates at the 14th session of the ILO Asian Advisory Committee (Bandung, September 1970). More recently, the ILO Metal Trades Committee at its 9th session (Geneva, January 1971) adopted a resolution proposed by the workers' group calling on the ILO to prepare a report on the social effects of multinational company activities in the metal trades. Under OECD auspices, a meeting of trade union experts (Paris, November 1969) discussed problems arising from the growth of multinational companies. They recommended to the OECD further study on the size and effects of multinational company activities, for the purpose of locating the site and origin of economic power within these companies, and the collection of comprehensive statistical information on such things as capital flows, export and import contribution, and profit distribution, as well as intergovernmental cooperation through OECD and other international organizations with a view to the adoption of a code of conduct for multinational companies.

At the same time ICFTU called attention to the "moral responsibility of governments of capital-exporting countries to ensure that multinational companies offer satisfactory conditions of employment, including recognition of trade union activities, in their overseas subsidiaries." A pacesetting example of a practical measure for implementing this moral responsibility has been devised in Sweden with the introduction of "social conditions" for those wishing to benefit from an official guarantee scheme for private overseas investment.

The international trade secretariats have played and will undoubtedly continue to play a major and increasing role in coordinating trade union activity in respect of multinational companies. Their traditional functions of collecting information and organizing solidarity action between affiliated unions in the same trade or industry clearly prepared them for dealing with the practical problems arising from MNC operations. It was not therefore surprising that the ITS started to react to the multinational challenge at a comparatively early stage. But the actions taken by trade unions are much behind the time if we compare them with that of MNCs.

Trade union interest in international fair labor standards as one countermeasure to MNCs increased considerably during the 1950s. A special subcommittee was set up by the ICFTU executive board to study the problem. The ultimate objective was usually seen as the enforcement of such standards by intergovernmental bodies—in general by the ILO and in particular by GATT, so far as international trade was concerned. But this period also saw the beginnings of direct trade union action for dealing with the problem. The campaign of the International Transport Workers' Federation to bring up to international standards the wages and working conditions of seamen in "runaway" shipping sailing under "flags of convenience" was a striking example of such direct action and met with considerable success. It was during this decade, too, that the International Metalworkers' Federation (IMF) started organizing international conferences of unions dealing with particular firms in the automotive industry.

International Metalworkers' Federation conferences to deal with particular firms in the world automotive industry began in the mid-1950s. During the 1960s the IMF set up permanent auto workers' councils for the following multinational firms: Ford, General Motors, Chrysler, Volkswagen, Fiat-Citroen, Nissan, Toyota, BLM, Renault-Peugeot. Meeting every four years, these councils exchange information and agree on bargaining tactics. One common objective was recommended for all these councils by the 1968 World Automotive Conference held in Turin: the establishment of common termination dates for collective agreements. The latest such conference (London, March 1971) enlarged this objective to include: higher earnings, ironing out of unfair wage differentials, protection of purchasing power; trade union rights at shop floor level, including a say in safety arrangements, work tempo, training, and protection of youth and women workers; guaranteed annual wages; shorter hours without loss of pay and longer holidays; and adequate pensions with transferable extra-legal pensions. Apart from collective bargaining objectives, the IMF automotive conference took a stand on the wider implications of the growth of multinational companies by calling for pressure on governments and international organizations to take appropriate measures for preventing the misuse of power by these companies.

The IMF has also started organizing similar groups for multinational agricultural implement and electrical engineering firms. IMF activities in Europe have been dealt with in the paragraph on trade union reactions at the regional level.

In 1967 the International Federation of Chemical and General Workers' Unions held a conference on coordinated collective bargaining and subsequently decided to set up councils for unions dealing with the same company. They have been established for the chemical, rubber, petroleum, and paper industries. In connection with internationally coordinated collective bargaining, the best known example is undoubtedly the action taken by the ICF in respect of the glass-making operations of the St. Gobain concern. A committee representing all the unions involved was set up and agreed not to sign any contract without its authorization. In strikes of St. Gobain workers, which took place in the United States and Italy, demands on behalf of workers in the other country were put forward. Wage parity for Canadian workers, it may be recalled, was one of the objectives (which was in fact achieved) of a strike called by the UAW in the United States in 1967. There was also the threat of a fifteen-minute warning strike by Peugeot workers in France in 1969 that helped to persuade the firm to negotiate with its workers on strike in Argentina.

Solidarity action of a less dramatic, but often very effective, kind is of course much commoner. The ICF successfully organized pressure on the parent company in Germany and financial help in the case of a dispute at the Turkish subsidiary of the Germany-based pharmaceutical company Hoechst. Similar action was taken in 1967 by the International Union of Food and Allied Workers' Associations to secure recognition of a union in Pakistan by the British American Tobacco Company and of another in Liberia by Intercontinental Hotels (a Pan-Am subsidiary). The IUF also organized support for one of its US affiliates in a long drawn out strike at the Nabisco (biscuit making) concern in 1969; IUF affiliates in other councils refused to accept switched production or to do extra overtime and thus contributed to the successful outcome of the strike in the United States. To a certain extent, internationally coordinated collective bargaining has been a long-standing practice, too, among the civil aviation unions grouped in the ITF. The International Federation of Commercial, Clerical and Technical Employees (FIET) has been devoting increasing attention to these problems: a conference of trade sections (Oslo, 1970) dealt exclusively with multinational companies and, as a first step towards coordinated collective bargaining, FIET has been compiling fact sheets of information on various companies.

In Japan, many Japanese enterprises are investing their capitals in many countries, especially Southeast Asian countries, and now they are on their way to multinationalization. Japanese trade unions are paying attention to these activities of management and trade unions are called on to take necessary countermeasures. IMF affiliated trade unions in Japan, and the electric workers unions, have decided at their recent convention to strengthen international cooperation and coordination, especially with Asian trade unions, and give necessary assistance to organize trade unions in this region. Japanese autoworkers unions, as a member of IMF automotive councils, are now preparing to form Nissan and Toyota world councils to meet the challenges to worldwide multinational enterprises.

The Problems in Multinational Unions

The workers in the world must overcome the following problems:

1. Workers are divided by the following factors: customs, languages, traditions, ideologies, religions, and political backgrounds.
2. There are conflicts of interest between workers in different countries; there are wide differences of wages levels and working conditions, and it is difficult to harmonize these differences.
3. There are the restrictions of industrial dispute acts. Many countries have restrictions and prohibitions on secondary boycotts in their labor acts.
4. There are difficulties in persuading workers to assist other workers who are in another country because they are not directly faced with their problems.

It is not too much to say that the countermeasures of trade unions are at a preliminary stage and multinational unions have just started, but this movement now is going steadily and overcoming the above-mentioned difficulties step by step through strengthening its educational and other activities. These international cooperation movements go beyond the ICFTU bond, and we see cooperation between ICFTU affiliates and WCL affiliates and even more with communist WFTU affiliate unions in Italy and France. Thus, the multinational movement is growing steadily, and this movement forward will be continued and accelerated with strong steps by the workers of the world.

In conclusion, I would like to quote the conclusion of the ICFTU Conference on MNCs, which points the way toward further collaboration by workers around the world to deal with such firms. First, the conference appeals to ICFTU-affiliated organizations to adopt the following measures at the national level:

1. The promotion of the widest possible research into the activities of multinational firms operating on their territory, the institution of a wide-ranging discussion in the trade union press and elsewhere of the problems involved, the holding where appropriate of seminars and conferences and the adoption of national policies for dealing with the multinational challenges;
2. Such policies would aim at activating and aiding the affiliated unions concerned and encouraging them to cooperate wherever feasible with their appropriate

international trade secretariats in regional or international activities designed to strengthen the international solidarity of workers;

3. National policies would also identify measures which the ICFTU affiliates would seek to have implemented by their governments, including:

(a) the adoption of guidelines for controlling multinational companies in matters such as observance of established industrial relations procedures (ILO standards), manpower planning, industrial concentration and mergers especially conglomerates, intra-company trading and financial practices, and their policies on research, tax liability and dividend remittance, as well as the obligation to publish global balance sheets together with financial accounts for all their individual subsidiaries;

(b) the institution of regular consultation, with trade union participation, between governments and multinational companies in order to ensure that the current and planned operations of the latter conform to national economic and social objectives and that their inward and outward investments and earnings are subject to closer control;

(c) the possibility of local public participation in the capital of multinational subsidiaries as one means of achieving social control;

(d) cooperation between governments of capital-exporting and receiving countries to ensure that private investments in developing countries are in accordance with the real economic and social growth needs of receiving countries in particular that they respect international labor standards and trade union rights (e.g. by conditions attached to overseas investment guarantees):

(e) concertation with other governments to achieve closer supervision of the companies in matters escaping the control of any single national authority or involving undesirable competition, as for example escalating investment incentives instead of agreement among receiving countries on such incentives, together where possible with regional investment attraction policies, and a mutually agreed scheme to be introduced where appropriate for special contributions from multinational companies operating in developing countries, the proceeds being used for socially useful purposes under the joint supervision of the government, employers and trade unions of the host country.

Secondly, the conference appeals at the same time to the free trade union movement at the international level for:

1. Closer cooperation on research into the ramifications of multinational companies, in particular conglomerates operating in more than one sector, and the regular exchange of information which could include the publication of black lists of persistent offenders against accepted standards of conduct and respect for trade union rights;

2. Continuing support for the efforts of the international trade secretariats in working towards coordinated collective bargaining with the companies;

3. Intensified activity in international and regional organizations, in particular UN bodies, GATT, ILO and OECD, to secure the adoption of an international agreement laying down a code of conduct for multinational companies along the lines mentioned above for action by national governments, also making institutional provisions with trade union participation for its enforcement including a complaints procedure, furthermore laying special emphasis on the introduction of democratic

control at each level of decision so as to promote the democratization of multinational companies; and

4. Steps for keeping all these problems under continuing international review.

International Codes of Behavior

The problems that are created by MNCs affect the workers very seriously, and it will be difficult to meet those problems if the workers try to solve them only through the frameworks of trade union activities at the national level.

It is absolutely necessary to formulate international codes of laws and regulations to minimize the impact and effect of MNCs. These international codes and regulations will serve not only trade unions and governments, but also MNCs themselves by smoothing their activities in every corner of the world.

The ICFTU suggests that the formulation of codes of conduct for multinational companies could include the obligation to abide by all relevant ILO conventions and recommendations, to comply with social legislation, and to conform to established national patterns of industrial relations. These codes would be supervised by an independent body set up by the international agencies directly concerned—in the first place the ILO, UNCTAD, GATT, and OECD—and would include provisions for participation of trade union bodies in handling complaints about infringements of the convention.

Such a convention would obviously serve as a model for national legislation and would undoubtedly strengthen the hand of governments in developing countries who might otherwise hesitate to take on singlehandedly some of these huge international giants.

Work for Governments

MNCs are able to escape national laws and regulations, and a single government is not able to control the full range of their international activities. There is no doubt that national governments (in common with the trade unions) need to have fuller information than at present about the finances and plans of multinational companies, not only in order to ensure that they meet their tax liabilities but also to secure greater harmonization of their activities with national economic planning. Governments must have some guide lines for foreign investment, and also they have to take some action to minimize the damage caused their people and the people of the world by MNCs. The Swedish government has shown the way. It will guarantee Swedish investments in developing countries only if the

Sweden-based MNC conforms to a code of good behavior, with respect to workers in such countries, that embraces among other things collective bargaining rights; benefits for loss of wages during illness; injury and layoff; pensions; a number of other health and welfare matters and non-discriminatory employment policies.

Multinational Trade Unionism

Enterprises started at the local level, grew up to regional and national levels, and have now grown up to the international level. The trade union movement, as a counterpart to enterprises, has also grown in this way. Now the enterprises have an international network to protect the wages, working conditions, and job security of all workers.

There is no doubt that there has been a growing awareness in the trade union movement of the implications of the growth of multinational companies and of the need for a coordinated international strategy for dealing with the problems that arise. It is obvious that in the absence of such a strategy, the growing weight and size of these companies would tip the balance of power in favor of international capital against labor. It is also obvious that trade union operations on a purely national basis are no longer appropriate for dealing with these huge international organizations. One of the roles of the international trade union movement is to provide a counter-force to MNCs. There is urgent necessity for integrating and coordinating trade union strategy of collective bargaining with MNCs. For instance, the IMF automotive conference 1967 in Turin adopted the following conclusions:

All member unions taking part in the work of the World Auto Council have agreed on a two-pronged long-range program to meet the challenge of the multinationals:

First, to work toward common contract termination dates within each corporation.

Common contract termination dates within industries in the United States have made it possible for us to make noteworthy progress in collective bargaining.

Another objective in the IMF is to harmonize world auto contracts. Because we recognize that widespread cultural differences are mirrored in contracts, we cannot hope to achieve a single, worldwide model. But we can harmonize many provisions, starting with relief time, work week, overtime pay and so on. Such harmonization is already proving to be an achievable goal in Europe.

Part III
The Role of Governments in International Trade and Investment in the 1970s

10 National Industrial Policies and International Trade

Göran Ohlin

So much has been written and said about industrial policy in the last decade that one might be forgiven for thinking that it has a reasonably clear meaning. This is hardly the case. Looking at official reports on the subject, such as the presentations of the OECD countries' industrial policies, one is struck with a tendency to enumerate any and all types of legislation, regulation, or administrative measures that have any bearing whatever on industrial activity.[1] A 1968 memorandum from the EEC Commission spoke extensively of what in those days was still called the environment of industry and would now, to avoid confusion, have to be called something else, as the term encompassed the whole legal, financial, and fiscal framework of business.[2]

It can be argued that anything governments do that affects industry in any way at all is quite likely also to affect comparative advantage and international trade, inadvertently or not. Yet it is rarely claimed that the provision of superior business education at public expense or a streamlining of patent legislation would constitute objectionable practices. In recent years, however, governments have come to devote a new attention to industry and have intervened more actively and deliberately in industrial affairs. These new measures are of a bewildering variety, and they are also seen very differently by different observers.

Market Improvement or a New Protectionism?

Some of the measures that seek to ease industrial adjustment and structural change aim to raise resource mobility. The training and retraining of manpower and the general streamlining of employment services are meant to improve market performance. The same can be said of some kinds of indicative planning that seek to reduce uncertainty and increase the confidence of investors.

On the other hand, virtually all industrial policy is often regarded as a new and devious policy of protectionism. It is sometimes presented as nothing but a huge complex of non-tariff barriers. The "structural" problems towards which industrial policy is oriented are, in this view, only the symptoms of inadequate overall economic policy.

As the Rey report dryly observed, "the concept of industrial policy is often rather weak, and sometimes no more than a by-product of social, regional or economic growth objectives.''[3] In order to tell whether in this mixed bag there is anything to cause genuine concern from the point of view of international trade policy, one has to make at least a summary inventory of the more conspicuous elements of industrial policy. I shall leave out of the following account such non-tariff barriers as health and safety standards, environmental protection, or rebatable excise and value-added taxes, and concentrate on policies with a high content of discretionary action and a special concern for industrial structure and growth.

Adjustment Policies

One type of industrial policy that not only escapes the charge of protectionism but is usually thought to be part and parcel of trade liberalization is adjustment assistance to producers who will be harmed or have been harmed by increasing imports. It is assumed that the social benefits of freer trade will be large enough to make it indisputably worthwhile to compensate the losers, which in any case is taken to be a political necessity.

This type of assistance, while widely recommended, is rarely found in the real world. Some of the reasons are not difficult to see. A declining industry will usually suffer on many counts, from cost increases, technological displacement, intensified international competition, and so forth. It will be hard to show that a rise in imports is more than a contributory factor in its difficulties. This has been the principal reason why relatively few petitions to the U.S. Tariff Commission under the Trade Expansion Act have been successful.

Secondly, it is not so obvious as often assumed that the social gain from enlarged trade will be so large that no reasonable adjustment assistance can nullify it. It depends chiefly on the speed with which resources—in the first place, labor—can be shifted to new employment. If these shifts are very slow, the social cost of change may well offset even the future gains to consumers if these are appropriately discounted. Unless there are new jobs, there will thus be no net social surplus out of which to compensate injured companies.

Thirdly, it is only too likely that assistance that is meant to ease the phasing-out of an industry will in fact be used in attempts to increase productivity and restore competitiveness. Unless the support is coupled with deliberate steps to liquidate capacity, an effort to revive the industry is particularly likely if the troubles due to tariff reduction are not distinguishable from other troubles besetting ailing industries and are dealt with, not by special adjustment policies, but under comprehensive schemes for aid to industry.

Thus, a well-intentioned liberal policy may easily turn into something of a very different character.

Declining Industries

In conditions of rapid technological change, high levels of capital accumulation, and relatively stable population, it is inevitable, even without trade liberalization, that there will be significant changes in the structure of production and that some industries will decline while others expand.

The irritating tendency of public officials and politicians to use the term "structural problems" as a substitute for thought has led many economists to the opposite exaggeration of denying that structure can be a problem at all. (To economists, market structure has been of far greater interest than the changing composition of output.) But there is a fundamental asymmetry between expansion and contraction. Industrial expansion does not give rise to complaints of structural change. Contraction, on the other hand, is painful both to capital and labor, and in democratic societies such strains will be political realities.

There are different possible responses. One is to help labor move, occupationally and geographically, into expanding sectors. This is meant to cut short the agonies of contraction, improve resource allocations, and so forth.

Even if this is tried, all experience shows that in a modern state, governments will simultaneously promote the opposite objective. By their different aids to the industries in question they will provide artificial respiration, as if they hoped to resuscitate the patient. In some cases such aids will be combined with attempts to regroup and reorganize in order to make at least part of the industry viable. In other cases it will be a matter of ad hoc bailing-out operations.

This illustrates an almost built-in conflict. As Stoleru remarks in his brilliant discussion of French industrial policy, the state gives with one hand and takes away with the other.[4] Before condemning this confusion and compromise, one should consider some of the reasons for it. To rely entirely on manpower policy might by some economists be considered the best policy, but everybody will not or cannot move, and the accelerated contraction of the industry may in the short run—long enough to count in this life—be the cause of greater insecurity and instability. On the other hand, it is often quite reasonable to believe that the industry, once it is pared down, reorganized, and regrouped, may survive. There will also be insistent demands for assistance, and if trade liberalization is too firmly established for any hopes of traditional protection, these demands will be for credit, subsidies, research, and a number of other prizes in the government's giving.

Regional Policies

The same conflicts arise in depressed areas, and with particular force if a declining industry is regionally concentrated, which is often the case. Of all the pressures towards "structural" intervention in the last decade, regional imbalance and the growing impatience with it has undoubtedly been one of the strongest and most universal. Regional economics has been called "the economics of resource immobility,"[5] and some of the efforts devoted to regional development have indeed aimed at moving resources out and depopulating the troubled regions. However, even less than in the case of a declining industry will this be an entirely satisfactory political solution. It is precisely the depopulation that is being objected to, and there will be a strong call for more positive help.

Some of the forms that support has traditionally taken will not give rise to the objection of trade distortion. Improvement of all kinds of infrastructure (the provision of public services beyond what the local tax base can carry, the use of transport subsidies, and so forth) have long been practised without objections. That these measures have also been fairly effective is suggested by the long historical trend towards regional equality in industrialized countries. The new pressure for regional development seems to have its roots in a lower tolerance of inequality, and perhaps greater awareness of it, rather than in an actual worsening of the imbalance.

Whatever the causes, the efforts to create local job opportunities have been stepped up in most countries, and grants and concessional loans to firms in development zones are now found almost everywhere. Such practices were sanctioned in the Treaty of Rome as well as by EFTA and GATT—not because they do not distort trade but because the motive was taken to be a worthy one. Many of the regional aids are of course used as a lure to foreign investors, and it is sometimes argued that if they are available to domestic and foreign investors on a non-discriminatory basis, there can be no problem. But this is not so. These measures seek to twist comparative advantage in directions that are usually not efficient in the long run. It is quite obvious that they have now grown to such proportions that they can no longer be accepted as an incidental problem. The current efforts within the EEC to evoke a mutually acceptable policy of restraint is indicative of this.

The Pursuit of High Technology

Distinctly novel was the sudden alarm about the "technological gap" in European countries in the sixties. One might well ask to what Europeans earlier attributed the well-documented lag between the U.S. and European productivity. "Technology" was not invoked as the main factor in economic growth, and one which might with a little effort be snatched from its privileged processor.

It was a naive conception of technology and its role in growth, but it left its mark on European policies. In the first place, the fact that the U.S. government paid large sums for research led to the belief that similar subsidies were called for elsewhere. Second, the link between bigness and R&D strengthened the conviction that bigger companies held the key to growth. "La grande technologie," especially in the glamor fields of electronics and computors, space and aeronautics, seemed an indispensable attribute of national power. Many European governments were led to commit vast sums to foolish pursuits of "national" solutions and technologies that in the end had to be reluctantly abandoned.

Quite apart from such mistakes, most of the industries said to represent the "commanding heights" in a modern economy are so linked to defence and other government needs that close ties to the state will exist in all countries. In such fields non-economic considerations will count heavily, both in domestic affairs and international trade. It is in this area that the economic nationalism of modern industrial policy is most in evidence.

Foreign Investment and Control

Foreign investors in industries of advanced technology are likely to be found suspect, even when they seem indispensable for the time being. But even investments in more mundane fields have been viewed with great wariness, especially when domestic companies have been bought out. The specter of the multinational company has certainly stalked across Europe.

In the traditional view of international trade policy, trade and investment could be held fairly strictly apart. Most of the theory of international trade was premised on factor immobility. Foreign investment was thought to be exceptional and the international division of labor was primarily achieved through trade. Now, however, there is a trend towards extensive trade in whole companies, and ordinary trade increasingly takes place among the subsidiaries of multinational companies. This is perfectly understandable in view of the tremendous advances in communication that have totally upset the traditional premises for international economic cooperation. It also does, as is so often heard now, leave "sovereignty at bay," and one of the great and difficult tasks of industrial policy has been to seek some guidelines for the treatment of foreign enterprise.

The caution with which it is regarded is not always due to irrational chauvinism. Planners fear that foreign management or owners will be less sensitive to the objectives of national policy or to the gentle hints and pressures by which much domestic policy is effected. But these apprehensions are offset by the scramble to invite foreign companies to invest in depressed regions, to become technical collaborators, or simply to take over. The commission in Brussels has found it irksome that most of these foreign companies have been American and that there has been so little progress towards the formation of large European companies. Its reaction, characteristically, was to suggest the use of Community subsidies for the creation of "transnational" European companies.

At the same time, governments treasure their own multinationals and see in them sources of national strength and pride. To the extent that industrial policy has been relatively tolerant of foreign investment, one suspects that this has been due primarily to a sound fear of retaliation.

Export Promotion

The neo-mercantilist strand in modern economic policies is manifest in the special value attributed to exports. Export promotion is thought to be a natural responsibility of governments. Outright subsidies may have been suppressed by international rules, but the maintenance of extensive commercial representation and the provision of favorable export credits or guarantees are taken for granted in industrialized countries.

It is possible that the fixation on exports is simply a legacy of the postwar experience of dollar shortage and of overvalued and fixed exchange rates. But probably it also stems from the fact that exports to a large extent remain beyond the control of a government. It may be unlikely that exports are in fact more effectively promoted by the policies specifically devoted to it than by an overall economic policy that would enhance competitiveness, but the preoccupation with exports gives a clue to the psychology of economic nationalism.

Public Procurement and Credit

That government procurement will favor domestic suppliers to the virtual exclusion of foreign competitors is so widely accepted that many have given up the hope of changing this practice. It has been one of the concerns of the Brussels Commission that the Common Market has in fact not been opened up very effectively to those industries heavily dependent on government sales. But the solution that is recommended is a liberalization only on a community basis.

The tying of foreign aid has met equally strong objections and been the subject of interminable international talks and noncommittal resolutions. The results have been nil.

While public procurement and aid tying are blatantly and overtly protectionist, the opposite is usually the case with the credit facilities supplied by government through investment banks and development banks, specialized agencies for the financing of housing, regional development, exports, small business, and so forth. When the interest on such loans is squarely below the government bond rate, the element of subsidy would seem to be obvious, but politically speaking it is nevertheless not very conspicuous. When the terms are more nearly commercial, except perhaps that the maturities are longer, the situation is more obscure. In the capital markets of many countries, the borrowers favored with such loans may simply not have access to private credit at all, at any rate not long-term credit. If the subsidy is to be measured by the government's losses on the operation, it will be a long time before they materialize and most probably the situation can never be completely disentangled.

In these cases, some subsidy is very likely to be warranted on grounds that social benefits exceed private ones or that the social risks are lower. The correction of such distortions by subsidies or by taxes is preferable to adjustments at the border, which discriminate and distort. Here, then, as with labor, there is often a case for measures that seek to correct market distortions and improve market performance. Even when this is not so, schemes for public financing will proceed as if this were their object, and it will usually be difficult to demonstrate if and when they have a distorting effect.

Public and Semi-Public Enterprise

The direction of the state-owned industries is in most countries considered part of industrial policy. But the pattern of public enterprise in most industrialized countries is random and accidental, often a legacy of the depression in the 1930s, of foreign occupation, or postwar political upheavals. State industries have rarely been founded or acquired with any clear economic objective. There may be a general notion that the state as an industrialist ought to observe a greater measure of social responsibility than private companies, but it is usually difficult to discern anything that sets public industry sharply apart from private competitors, except superior access to funds and a capacity to sustain losses that the competitors bitterly resent.

In Italy, where public corporations have become exceptionally powerful, this is an expression of the weakness rather than the strength of the state and its capacity for economic policy. In other countries, being a major industrialist may have made the state more attuned to industrial interests and viewpoints. In this way it may well have enhanced the readiness to resort to industrial aids and covert protection. But it would be rash to claim that state enterprises in mixed economies generally give rise to worse distortions than those flowing from the assistance to private industry.

The Triumph of the Ad Hoc

The rise of industrial policy in the sixties has not been due to design. It has been a response to a particular situation, which explains at least some of its fragmented character. The fear of inflation and balance-of-payments deficits restrained most governments from expansionary policies and drove them into a sequence of ad hoc measures. The new policy came to displace national planning rather than to supplement it. Even in France, where indicative planning had been something of a model for so many others, the plan was dethroned by regional development and industrial policy.

The unifying characteristic of ad hoc and structural policy is its unabashed nationalism. The second circumstance to which it has been a response has been precisely the liberalization of trade and capital movements. Deprived of their traditional instruments, governments have looked for others. In some cases this has raised the quality of economic policy, but in others, probably more numerous, it has frustrated liberalization and created a confusing situation.

It was only to be expected that the relationship between state and industry would take on different national styles depending on local circumstances. In countries like France and Japan, government by particularist agreements with individual firms or branches of industry had long been practiced and are not felt to conflict with legal or political tradition. In many other countries, however, the increasing number of discretionary favors or denials of favors have been seen as gravely discriminatory. This easily creates pressure towards the generalization of ad hoc favors—nullifying many of the intended effects but restoring peace.

Is Industrial Policy Negotiable?

Clearly industrial policy is becoming increasingly noxious in the eyes of competing countries. This is enough to include it in the agenda of trade negotiations. But, as in the case of non-tariff barriers generally, industrial policy is more difficult to negotiate about than tariffs.

This is not just because industrial policy is the response to such heavy domestic pressures that it might seem not to be politically negotiable. The same is true of all protection. But industrial policy involves such a variegated and elusive range of government supports that formidable technical obstacles will obstruct any negotiation.

In the past the trade restrictions that have lent themselves to international agreement and restriction have been those where particular dangers of competitive retaliation have prevailed. Although industrial policy has not always had a clearly retaliatory character, it has been competitive in nature. In some cases, a virtual race has developed, as in export credits or in the bidding for foreign investors by means of regional subsidies. In these instances, many suggestions have also been made that it would be to mutual benefit to check the process, and in the case of export credits very specific efforts have been made. Situations like these seem to offer the best hope for negotiated standstills or the acceptance of general rules.

Generally speaking, however, it is the ad hoc character of industrial policy that raises the greatest obstacles to international codification or agreement. In some cases it does not seem to be necessary. Industrial policy cannot always be charged with seriously distorting effects and does not automatically give rise to imitation or competition. However, in regard to its more objectionable aspects it seems clear that as with non-tariff barriers, an effective and acceptable solution is not likely to be reached by intermittent negotiation and agreement. It requires more permanent machinery and more intimate collaboration—in short, the abandonment precisely of the national orientation that is its hallmark.

It is natural to pin great hopes to the greater flexibility of exchange rates and to expect the balance-of-payments preoccupations of the past to fade away and thus reduce at least one of the powerful forces behind the protectionist elements of industrial policy. But such hopes may be illusory. Inside the European Community, the situation is the other way around, as the determination to fix parities must throw a heavier burden on other means of adjustment. Moreover, the industrial policy of the last decade has everywhere been a prolific spawner of new agencies and benefit schemes that are not easily dismantled. One may well wonder if industrial policy is in fact reversible at all.

Notes

1. Organization for Economic Cooperation and Development, *The Industrial Policies of 14 Member Countries* (Paris: OECD, 1971).

2. Commission des Communautés Européenes, *La politique industrielle de la Communauté* (Bruxelles, 1970).

3. Organization for Economic Cooperation and Development, *Policy Perspectives for International Trade and Economic Relations,* Report by the High Level Group on Trade (Paris: OECD, 1972).

4. Lionel G. Stoleru, *L'imperatif industriel* (Paris, 1970).

5. John R. Meyer, "Regional Economics: A Survey," *Surveys of Economic Theory,* Vol. II (New York, 1966), p. 246.

11

Japan and the World Economy

Ryutaro Komiya

Historical and Social Backgroumd

The Japanese government's policies in regard to Japan's economic relations with other countries today may be criticized as inappropriate in various respects. Yet, while it is easy to point out major defects in Japan's international economic policies and institutional arrangements from an economic point of view, it is more difficult to understand political, social, and historical-cultural forces behind them. In the "democratic" environment of postwar Japan, the government could undertake drastic changes in foreign trade, investment, or exchange policies only when a majority of people could be convinced that such changes were beneficial to the country *and* when the interests of each major group were well taken care of.

It is then still more difficult to propose a policy change that will be really workable. Policy proposals that ignore the wishes and fears of those concerned and disregard the interests of those unfavorably affected are not only politically impractical but also economically unsound.

Poverty and Insecurity

Japan has long been a poor country. The country has little natural resources and only a small amount of arable land. The standard of living (especially housing and public facilities) of a large part of its population is still substantially lower than that of other advanced countries. The society is quite egalitarian and income distribution is perhaps more equal in postwar Japan than in most European countries. There are very few people who are really rich according to other countries' standards. Most leaders in various circles come from middle-class families.

Economic philosophy or basic economic principles of the average Japanese have been, and still are, those of the poor or the middle classes striving for survival and improvement: diligence, thrift, and saving. A philosophy of "export or die" and "accumulate or die" has underlined the Japanese government's economic policy and institutional arrangements until recently.[1] It is now slowly changing. It is unrealistic to expect that such a basic attitude or idea can change rapidly.[2]

Another important factor that has a great influence on Japanese gov-

183

ernment international economic policy is a conscious or unconscious feeling of insecurity and isolation among Japanese. Japan is the only industrialized country outside of Western culture. When it was emerging as a modern state in the 1860s, the country was about to be occupied militarily by the Western powers. [3] In the 1930s Japanese goods were boycotted and discriminated against in many countries, mainly because Japanese goods were too cheap. Japan's balance of payments was not in surplus throughout the 1930s.

In postwar years, when Japan joined GATT in 1955, major trading countries including Australia, Austria, Belgium, Brazil, France, India, the Netherlands, New Zealand, and the United Kingdom invoked GATT Article 35 against Japan and refused to establish GATT (MFN) relationships with Japan. Since around 1964 most European countries withdrew invocation of Article 35 against Japan, but about twenty out of the total of eighty member countries of GATT still apply Article 35 against Japan. [4] There are very few other cases in which Article 35 has been invoked.

Most European countries have by now withdrawn the use of Article 35 against Japan, but there remain other forms of discrimination against Japanese exports to European countries. Discrimination against Japanese exports takes various forms, all in violation of GATT. The most serious is quite extensive special QRs applied only to imports from Japan. [5] Another form of discrimination is the request of voluntary export restrictions by the United States, Canada, the United Kingdom, Germany and several other countries. It must be noted that the GATT Article 35 discrimination, discriminatory QRs, and the request of voluntary export restrictions were already serious trade problems for Japan in the 1950s and early 1960s when its balance of payments often turned into deficits.

Today, Japan does not belong to any regional or commonwealth bloc, nor can it be largely self-sufficient like the United States or the Soviet Union. Also, the fact that Japan is now adjacent to two big powers, China and the Soviet Union that have different social systems, tends to promote feelings of insecurity and vulnerability. [6]

Attitude towards Agriculture

Japan's agriculture is very heavily protected today. Agricultural imports are increasing rapidly (they have almost tripled between 1960 and 1970), and now Japan imports about 20 percent of domestic consumption of foodstuffs. The ratio of domestic supply to total consumption is declining. But the domestic prices of foodstuffs are often far higher than the international levels.

The political forces behind agricultural protection in Japan are not much different from those in other countries. Peasants have strong political power. In spite of a recent great exodus of population from rural to urban areas, distribution of the seats in the Diet among constituencies has not changed for many years, so that rural votes count much more than urban votes. The ruling Conservatives lean heavily on rural votes. The Socialists and other non-government parties are stronger in urban than in rural areas, yet they often propose more heavily protectionist policies than the government towards agriculture.

Political explanation, however, is only a part of the story, in my view. First, urban or non-agricultural people have sympathy for peasants. Generally speaking, peasants who benefit from agricultural protection are relatively poor among Japanese. There is justification in the minds of many Japanese for protecting elder and poor peasants in remote villages. In many regions the population exodus has been so severe that only elder people, for whom moving is difficult, remain. They confront difficulties in maintaining their traditional village communities. If the government removes protection, they will face still more serious difficulties. Also, because of the small size of the farms, the benefits of the price support of rice, for example, are much more widely distributed than the benefits of the U.S. agricultural price-support system. Moreover, many city residents are the second generation of peasants. They return to their ancestral country homes twice a year, on the *Bon* festival and New Year Day, to meet their parents and families.

Second, many Japanese vaguely think that it is dangerous to depend heavily on imports as far as foodstuffs are concerned—or that a large part of foodstuffs consumed should be produced domestically—in view of possible cessation of importation in case of an emergency. When such an argument is made, it is often not clear what sort of emergency situations are presumed. It may be pointed out that Japan now depends very heavily on petroleum imports as a vital source of energy supplies and that if the level of import is reduced, say, by 30 percent because of some emergency, Japan will face a very serious situation even when a large proportion of foodstuffs is supplied domestically. Also a systematic stockpiling program may cost much less than agricultural protection to prepare for possible emergencies. Yet, there is a strong popular resistance to the policy of increasing dependence on imported foodstuffs, or at least common people tolerate agricultural protection, in view of vaguely conceived possible emergencies.

The Role of the Government

It is well known that immediately after the Meiji Restoration in 1868, the Japanese government was the main force of modernization and industrialization. The Meiji government was organized by lower-strata *samurais* of a few leading feudal clans that overthrew the Tokugawa Shogunate and won the civil war. Between 1868 and 1890, the Meiji government organized the national army and navy based upon a national conscription system, established the Bank of Japan and a commercial banking system, introduced a compulsory education system, a national postal system, and so on. In other words, the government took all kinds of measures to change a feudal country into a modern nation-state within a very short period. Yet during this period, there was no popularly elected national diet or congress.

The first national Diet was elected in 1890, but only about one percent of the total population was given the right to vote. Thus the Meiji government was an absolutist government. The situation did not change much until World War II. The power of the Diet to check the administration was very weak constitutionally as well as in practice, and the government was omnipotent in prewar Japan.

"Enrich the Nation and [or 'in order to'] strengthen the Army" and "foster industries and promote enterprise" were perhaps the two most popular slogans of the Meiji government. In the early Meiji period the government started many new industries by first building its own plants and then handing them over to private capitalists. Later, the government built the first steel mill in 1897 with a part of the indemnity of the Sino-Japanese war and operated it as a government factory until 1934. The steel mill developed into the New Japan Steel Company, the largest firm in the industry today.

The traditions of free enterprise and liberalism were nearly non-existent in prewar Japan. The big *Zaibatsu* firms that dominated the Japanese economy in prewar years were closely tied with (or subordinated to) the government and the military. The businessmen in the Kansai area, especially those in the cotton textile industry and overseas trading, tended to be more liberal-minded, and in the Taisho period (1912-1926), there was some shift towards liberalism. But the basic tone was that the government was omnipotent in economic as well as in other matters. The businessmen were considered as belonging to a caste lower than that of the government officials and the military.

During World War II and the period immediately after the war, extensive direct controls were a necessity as in many other countries. This led to a further expansion of the basis of government interventions. The decontrol process after the war was much slower in Japan than in other countries. After the democratization measures were enforced by the American Occupation, people were uncertain about where to return through the decontrol process. The democratization measures in the economic field included a very extensive and successful program of land reform,[7] less thoroughgoing but quite effective dissolution of *Zaibatsu,* and introduction of antitrust laws. Also, the constitutional status of the Diet in regard to the government budget and economic policy was raised. However, the extensive involvement of the government in economic affairs and its close relationship with business were not drastically changed by the democratization measures.

Industrial Policy in Postwar Japan

Entities in the Game

I will describe the process of industrial policy making in postwar Japan first by listing principal entities that exert important influences in the process. No one entity is decisive in formulating the policy. The process of policy making is primarily mutual persuasion. If one of them could persuade others concerned that a certain policy measure is desirable for the national economy or for the industry (very often these two are intentionally mixed up), it will succeed in putting the policy measure into effect.

Genkyoku. Perhaps the most important entities in the process are *genkyoku.* A *genkyoku* is a government agency that has jurisdiction (authority) over the industry in question. *Genkyoku* may be literally translated as an "original bureau," but it could mean a ministry, a bureau, or a division within a bureau. For example, the Ministry of Agriculture is the *genkyoku* for agriculture. The Bureau of Heavy Industries, Ministry of Industry and International Trade (MITI), is naturally the *genkyoku* for heavy industries such as iron and steel, all kinds of machinery and automobiles. The Division of Electronic Industries within the Bureau of Heavy Industries is the *genkyoku* for electronic industries. The *genkyoku* is in principle a supervisor for the industry in question, but sometimes it also acts as an advisor, protector, lawyer or deputy for the industry.

MITI is the biggest *genkyoku,* but it is not the only *genkyoku* ministry supervising manufacturing industries. Food processing industries are under the Ministry of Agriculture, the pharmaceutical industry is under the Ministry of Welfare, shipbuilding (but not aircraft) as well as all kinds of transportation is under the Ministry of Transportation. The Ministry of Finance is the *genkyoku* for the liquor industry as well as banking, security, and insurance. Not all the bureaus of MITI are *genkyoku,* which are also called "vertical" divisions. "Horizontal divisions" such as the Bureau of Enterprise, the Bureau of International Trade or the Small Business Agency are also important and influential offices within MITI. These "horizontal divisions" and Minister's Secretariat (*Kanbō*) often have their own policy ideas, and also act as a coordinator and mediator within the ministry.

The Role of the Finance Ministry and Other Agencies. The Ministry of Finance plays a role in the coordinating and mediating body among ministries. Needless to say, the annual budget as well as the "fiscal investment and financing plan" must go through the Bureau of Budget, which is generally considered as having the greatest power within the government. Moreover, the Ministry of Finance has the final responsibility for tariff policy (Bureau of Tariffs), special tax incentive measures (Bureau of Taxes), and the policy on inward and outward direct investment (Bureau of International Finance).

The above are the most important governmental entities in the process of industrial policy making. Less important ones to be mentioned are various advisory councils and boards attached to government ministries, the Economic Planning Agency, and the Fair Trade Commission.

Only a brief mention will be made of the latter two. In the process of economic policy making, the role of EPA is a minor one. It is concerned with (1) "economic planning," which is essentially no more than a long-term forecast with some flavor of wishful thinking of those concerned, (2) short-term forecast and research, and (3) coordination in the sphere of regional allocation of industry. The Fair Trade Commission is responsible for antitrust policy and has often been in conflict with MITI. Its relative strength within the government vis-à-vis *genkyoku* ministries has recently been rising, but its role in the whole process of industrial policy making is still a minor one.[8]

Councils and Boards. Formally, the role of councils and boards is advisory: members are supposed to investigate problems on which the minister consulted them and to make fair and dispassionate judgments. Actually, however, most councils on industrial affairs, to which the discussion here is limited, are the place for exchange of information, mutual persuasion, and negotiation.[9] Main participants of persuasion and negotiation are government officials (who are not members of councils but who speak most of the time during their sessions), some ex-government officials, and representatives of the industries concerned (the latter two are formal members). Usually a few professors and journalists are included as "men of learning and experience," but in most cases the government officials choose those "men of learning and experience" who are convenient from their point of view—that is, those who will support their policy lines or at least will not oppose them while adding to the prestige of the councils. It is rather rare that a council really investigates and deliberates seriously and then presents a report that is worthwhile to read even after, say, two years.

Why then do government officials bother themselves with setting up councils rather than do whatever they like? The answer is that, first, it is a convenient place for mutual persuasion and exchange of information. Second, government officials can partly avoid their responsibility. When a government policy turns out to be a wrong one, officials can say that they followed the advice embodied in the report of a certain council.

Politicians such as influential Diet members (conservatives) or former ministers may play a role in the process of industrial policy making. They may be asked to help some industry association and put pressure on the government agencies. But they have not been too powerful. When a politician acts that way, the public becomes suspicious of bribery.[10] Although their salaries are surprisingly low, they are under the life-time employment scheme, and they can take prestigious and well-paid jobs after retirement from the civil service.

Gyokai and Zaikai. On the side of the private sector, major entities in the policy-making process are each *gyokai* (the industry) and the *Zaikai* (central business circles). A *gyokai* usually has a formal industry association to represent the industry, which collaborates with the *genkyoku* in charge of industry. Often such an association is dominated by a few leading companies, the presidents or chairmen of which alternate as the president of the association.

The *Zaikai* is a vague word referring to a group of leading businessmen who like political activities and act as the representatives or the leading spokesmen of the business world. In my view, the influence of the central *Zaikai* itself is usually a limited one. For one thing, *Zaikai* businessmen are concentrated in a few industries, such as banking, electric power supply, iron and steel, and chemicals. None of the executives of many high-prestige corporations such as Hitachi, Matsushita, Toyota, Ito-Chu are involved in *Zaikai* activities. From their point of view *Zaikai* men are too political, and they like to concentrate upon their own business.

Besides *gyokai* and *Zaikai,* commercial and long-term financing banks, government banks, and *Zaibatsu* or other groups are important entities in the process of mutual persuasion and negotiation behind policy decisions.

The process of policy making involves these entities and none of them have decisive power. All are supposed to contribute towards a policy of advancing the national interests, but since, in fact, each acts according to its own interests, there always arise conflicts and rivalries. The art (or the game) of policy making is how to reach a compromise among those concerned.

It is often said that Japanese government and industries closely collaborate and behave jointly. But the extent of collaboration is often exaggerated. There are often antagonisms between the supervising *genkyoku* and the industries, among government agencies sponsoring different interests, and among industries. The attitude of private businessmen towards the government is often described as *"Menju-fukuhai,"* meaning "superficially following the direction but actually behaving otherwise." The resentment against government officials is deep-seated and pervasive among Japanese businessmen. Moreover, even when the government had powerful "leverage" towards individual companies such as those described below, there were disobedient companies[11] that openly resisted the government instruction at one time or another.

Means of Interventions

In postwar Japan, the principal means of government intervention used for industrial policy include the following.

1. *Subsidies.* Except for the period immediately after the war, direct subsidies have been given to industry only in exceptional cases. Recently, research and development activities in a few areas and certain "large-scale (research) projects" have been subsidized. The total amount of direct subsidies to industries is very small.

2. *Government Financing.* The Japan Development Bank and Japan Export Import Bank have supplied a significant share of long-term funds to industry, especially in the early postwar period. Recently, shipbuilding and marine transportation are the main recipients of the low-interest government funds.

3. *Tax Incentives.* Highly complicated and discriminatory tax measures have been used to promote investment in particular industries. The list of industries, products, machinery, and equipment to which special tax measures are applicable is extremely complicated and has been changed year by year.[12]

4. *Import Quotas.* In the past, this was MITI's most powerful "leverage" not only towards industries but also towards individual countries. Now, however, only a few items remain under import quotas; as a means of industrial (apart from agricultural) policy, import quotas largely belong to the past.[13]

5. *Authorization of Patent and Know-How Contracts and Joint Ventures.* Until recently, important patent and know-how contracts as well as joint ventures between Japanese and foreign companies had to be authorized one by one, essentially by the *genkyoku.*[14] This authority has been another powerful MITI "leverage." It is no wonder that MITI officials resist strongly liberalization of inward direct investment or licensing of technology. This means is also beginning to lose importance as a result of liberalization of direct investment and licensing.

6. *Particular Industry Acts.* For some industries, there are special laws

that give certain powers to the *genkyoku*. Some laws are temporary (for three to five years) and others are permanent. Two extreme cases are shipbuilding and petroleum. Not only a new dock but also each new ship built above a certain size must be individually authorized. Similarly, a new petroleum refining plant must be authorized before being built. The purpose is to avoid excess supplies and, in the latter case, also to limit the share of foreign-owned oil companies. But these are exceptional cases.

While the above methods are the principal means of government intervention, many of them have been losing their significance. Excessive intervention by the government has always been criticized and increasingly so recently.

Industry Pattern and Trends

The extent of government intervention differs by industry and from period to period.

In the period immediately after the war, coal, electric power supply, steel, and shipping were called "the four most important industries," and all possible efforts were made to increase production and services of these industries. Fertilizers and shipbuilding were also favored in this period. Coal and fertilizer dropped from the priority list very early. Later certain machinery, electrical machinery, and chemicals industries were given priority, and especially "new" industries such as automobiles, synthetic fibers, and petrochemicals were given extensive government assistance. More recently, electronics, computers and aircraft are considered as "technological spearhead" industries.

Throughout the whole postwar period, steel, shipbuilding, and marine transportation were among those that received the most extensive government assistance. Coal mining, non-ferrous metals, and sulphur are similar to agriculture. Protective as well as adjustment assistance measures were taken for these industries.

On the other hand, textiles and other light manufactured goods, most industries in machinery, and electrical machinery groups such as machine tools, bearings, electrical household appliances and communication equipment are relatively free from government protection and interventions. Most rapidly rising new Japanese exports, such as motorcycles, bearings (especially miniature bearings), transistor radios, TV sets, tape recorders, stereo sets, pianos and zippers, received little government assistance even in their infancy periods. Essentially, they were able to stand up by themselves.

In paper and pulp, textiles, cement, steel, certain chemicals, and a few other industries, the government industrial policy has laid emphasis on curbing what is called "excessive competition" either in the domestic or export market or in both. In order to curb "excessive competition" the government attempted to reduce excess supplies and excessive capacity by cartelizing and "reorganizing" (merging firms within) the industry.

Generally speaking, government interventions were most extensive in the period immediately after the war. It is perhaps not too much of a simplification to say that their importance has steadily declined throughout the whole postwar years. Since around 1970, the decontrol and liberalization process has been accelerated by two factors. First under the pressure from foreign countries, especially the United States, the government had to pursue a policy of liberalization of import restrictions, licensing agreement, and joint ventures, and *genkyoku* has been losing the principal leverage towards the industry and individual firms.

Second, the government's policy in the last twenty years, which gave the top priority to industrial growth, capital accumulation, and expansion of export, has recently been criticized as neglecting the pollution problem and the welfare of people. An anti-pollution campaign undertaken by leading newspapers, leaders of public opinion, and radical groups since 1970 has had a great impact on the collusive relationships between the government and industry. Nowadays the government agencies that tend to protect industries are often viewed with suspicion and criticism. Also, since a high rate of industrial growth has been sustained for many years and since export surplus has reached an unprecedented figure, public opinion is beginning to think that extensive government interventions aimed at industrial growth are largely unnecessary now.

Trade and Industrial Policy for Japan

Throughout the postwar years, until around 1965, the yen was substantially overvalued and Japan's balance of payments often turned into deficits even with extensive direct and indirect measures to restrict imports and encourage exports. Unless such a substantial degree of currency overvaluation was corrected by appropriate exchange rate adjustment, the government had to resort to all kinds of discriminatory measures of import restriction and export promotion for balance of payments' sake. Such measures, however, are often unfair and wasteful, and obviously interfere with efficiency.[15]

The purpose of the industrial policy of the Japanese government as a whole has been to accelerate technological progress and capital accumulation in export as well as import competing industries. Undoubtedly it has contributed to increasing exports and reducing imports, but whether it has raised the rate of economic growth is still an open question. Since most industries are either export or import competing industries, favorable treatment of individual industries mostly cancel each other out.

One could cite an endless number of examples in which government policy did not make much sense. First, in one period, commercial banks were discouraged from making loans to hotels and inns since they are purely consumption oriented and have nothing to do with technological progress or capital accumulation. Shortly afterwards it was decided that Japan Development Bank make low-interest loans to hotels since they were supposed to attract foreign tourists and earned precious foreign exchange. Second, the government gave a special tax privilege to incomes earned from exports, even when the exports in question were under voluntary export restrictions. Third, in my view, except for the early postwar period, the government's generous assistance in various forms to iron and steel, shipbuilding, and marine transportation is an unwarranted one: a large part of the tremendous amount of subsidies (in indirect forms) that went to these industries was in effect passed over to foreigners. Moreover, the steel industry often ran into a serious excess capacity situation, and MITI had difficulty curbing "excessive competition" in investment among steel makers. Fourth, in the early postwar period, the import quotas for crude oils, raw sugar, and several other raw materials were based upon the existing capacity, so that many small, inefficient refining plants were built even when there was an excess capacity in the industry.[16]

Without all these discriminatory measures, and with a proper exchange rate that reflected the real preciousness of the yen, Japan's rate of growth might have been higher.

On the other hand, the whole process of industrial policy making in postwar Japan was a very effective means of propagating information on industries, individual firms, new technologies, and domestic and overseas market conditions to all those concerned. Probably information related to industrial and business affairs is more abundant and easily obtainable in Japan than in most other countries. Viewed as a system of information collection and dissemination, Japanese industrial policy, apart from the direct or indirect effects of policy measures themselves, may have been among the most important factors in Japan's high rate of industrial growth.

When Japan's balance of payments turned into chronic surpluses around 1965, liquidation of the industrial policy designed for the deficit period was in order, but the process of policy change has been too slow. There have been and still are various vested interests resisting the change, and people's notions or philosophy change slowly.

At the present, in my view, the following are the main areas in which Japan's foreign economic policy should be changed in more constructive directions.

194

Currency Adjustment and Free Trade

The exchange rate for the yen should be near its equilibrium rate—equating demand and supply. One way of achieving this is to maintain "clean" flexible rates or to return to a fixed rate somewhere between 260 and 270 yen per dollar and then start crawling. A 265-yen-per-dollar rate is a very substantial upvaluation from the pre-Smithsonian 360-yen rate, and its impact could be quite costly in terms of domestic unemployment in certain industries. But when a disequilibrium has reached the dimension as large as the present one, there can be no easy way out. In the future one should not allow a disequilibrium to aggravate over a long period to reach such a dimension. One should start correcting disequilibrium as early as possible.

With a proper exchange rate, there is no need for the government to intervene in imports and exports for balance-of-payments reasons. The basic principle of free trade is the best policy for Japan.

Agriculture

It seems to me that the best policy for Japan's agriculture is to abolish all quotas and tariffs on and state trading of agricultural imports, on the one hand, and to establish a general deficiency payment system to protect the existing producers (but not new ones), on the other hand.

When, because of a lack of mobility, existing workers cannot be gainfully employed in other industries or when the subjective value of their staying in the traditional village communities is very high, a policy of keeping them for the time being in their present jobs is not only a fair and equitable policy but also an efficient one. Mobility will be achieved as the generation goes by.

If it is difficult to finance such a deficiency payment system from the general tax revenues, a second- (or third-) best financing method would be to introduce a general, flat-rate tariff on all agricultural (and other) imports, and to use tariff revenues to finance deficiency payments.

Technological Spearhead Industries

From an economic point of view it is desirable that the government help technological progress not by tariffs or import restriction, but by subsidies. Import restrictions of technological spearhead products such as computers should be lifted, but complete laissez-faire may not be the best policy here. The government should subsidize research and development, especially in certain "spearhead" industries where few monopolistic firms dominate the world market.

Safeguards and Adjustment Assistance

Japan has so far not experienced serious adjustment problems caused by imports from other countries. But as trade is liberalized, tariffs lowered, and the wages rise in Japan, it is likely that such a situation will arise in the near future. The Japanese government should therefore be eager to reach a reasonable international agreement on safeguard procedures and the adjustment problem.

Inward Direct Investment

In principle, both "newly establishing a company" and "purchases of (or into) existing companies" should be completely liberalized, and the government should intervene only in exceptional cases in which "national interests are seriously affected." This is a policy similar to the French government's. I discussed the Japanese policy on inward direct investment in my earlier paper [17] and have little to add to it now. I wish, however, to make two additional points.

First, one of the most restrictive aspects within the Japanese government's current policy towards inward direct investment, besides its insistence on the fifty-fifty principle and its screening case-by-case of purchases of existing companies, is the requirement that the Japanese partner in a fifty-fifty joint venture belong to the same industry as the foreign partner. This requirement amounts to virtually suppressing competitive new entries from abroad into the industry and should be removed as soon as possible.

Second, while the Japanese restrictive policy is unwarranted from an economic point of view and should be liberalized as soon as possible, foreigners and especially the U.S. government should understand that the problem of direct investment has non-economic, cultural aspects. It is often related to deep-seated national emotions, not only in Japan but in many other countries including France and Canada.

Direct investment is more a movement of firms than a movement of capital and is similar to immigration (movement of people) in that it arouses social or national uneasiness. The reasons why it is difficult for the Japanese government to liberalize American direct investment into Japan are very similar to the reasons why it was (or still is) difficult for the U.S.

government or the Australian government to accept Japanese immigrants. On problems such as immigration or direct investment, the governments should not press other countries' governments very hard.

Notes

1. To cite just an example, the Center for Promoting Saving, a semi-official organization established during wartime within the Bank of Japan, is still about as active as before.

2. Other examples of such basic, slowly changing principles that are observed not only in Japan but in other countries also are (1) the notion of the balanced budget, (2) asymmetric treatments of export and import, (3) the preference for the gold standard, and (4) the dislike of flexible exchange rates.

3. The recent U.S. request of liberalizing direct investment into Japan was called the "Second Black Ships." The "Black Ships" in Japanese means the American warships under Commodore Mathew Perry that visited Japan at the end of the Tokugawa regime. Perry and the Black Ships came to Japan in 1852 and requested the opening of the country. Japan was then under a national isolation policy. The policy was pursued from about 1630 and lasted until the 1860s. Isolationist mentality is still quite prevalent in Japan.

4. Certain African countries still invoke Article 35 against Japan, in order to restrict certain textile imports from the low-wage country Japan!

5. In some cases, a few other GATT members such as Hong Kong, Korea, and Czechoslovakia are discriminated against together with Japan.

6. For example, if Japan were surrounded by close, friendly neighbor countries that would supply foodstuffs to Japan, the political forces behind agricultural protection would be much weaker.

7. After the land reform large landlords disappeared (except the owners of forests), and the economic conditions of peasants were drastically improved. These small peasants are now the stronghold of agricultural protectionism.

8. In the 1950s, under the direction of MITI, cartels in conflict with the anti-trust law were organized. Firms concerned were exempted from anti-trust prosecution, because they acted under the "administrative guidance" of MITI. Frustration of FTC officials was severe. Recently such a disregard of FTC has become impossible.

9. I do not know the precise total number of councils and boards, but by counting only those belonging to the central government, it is perhaps

somewhere between 100 and 200. Relatively important ones in the sphere of economic affairs may number 30 to 50.

10. There are very few cases in which high government officials in charge of industrial policy were involved in bribery. The reason is that for government officials it does not pay to be involved in a bribery.

11. For example, Kawasaki and Sumitomo Metal, both in steel, Idemitsu in oil, Sanko in shipping.

12. See R. Komiya, "Japan," *Tax Policies and Economic Growth* (Columbia University Press, 1966).

13. See R. Komiya, "Japan's Non-Tariff Barriers to Trade in Manufactured Products," in H.E. English and Keith A. J. Hay (eds.), *Obstacles to Trade in the Pacific Area* (Ottawa: Carleton University, 1972).

14. See R. Komiya, "Direct Foreign Investment in Postwar Japan," in Peter Drysdale (ed.), *Direct Foreign Investment in Asia and the Pacific* (Canberra: Australian National University Press, 1972).

15. The same applies to the current U.S. situation.

16. Under the quota systems, it is possible that the domestic prices of imports or products refined from imported raw materials are so high, that it pays to build an inefficient plant simply for the purpose of receiving a quota.

17. R. Komiya, "Direct Foreign Investment in Postwar Japan," in P. Drysdale (ed.), *Direct Foreign Investment in Asia and the Pacific* (Canberra: Australian National University Press, 1972).

12 State Enterprises and International Trade

Michael Clapham

Introduction

One of the results of the various tariff-cutting negotiations that have taken place in postwar years has been to bring into sharper relief other impediments to trade that were either not apparent or of little consequence when tariff rates were high. Furthermore, it was perhaps inevitable that countries would be tempted to replace tariffs by more subtle non-tariff protection of their industries in order to circumvent some of their new international obligations, thereby threatening to wipe out at least part of the trade liberalization achieved to date. Whatever the reasons, the already long list of recognized non-tariff barriers has been growing in recent years.

Not all of the new barriers arise from government attempts to act directly on trade flows; indeed, many of the traditional instruments for action of this kind—such as quotas, export subsidies, and dumping—are already regulated by international agreement. The additions to the list stem rather from government intervention, which does not have the blocking of imports or the stimulation of exports as its primary aim, but rather from domestic objectives such as the maintenance or creation of employment. In many ways, the new distortions to international trade reflect the growing pressure on governments to accept more direct responsibility for national economic and social welfare.

Definition of the Subject

Governments can and do intervene in the operation of national economies in countless ways that affect international trade flows. For analytical purposes, these numerous measures can be broadly classified into the following categories.

1. *Government Intervention in Specific Industries, Enterprises, or Projects.* This type of intervention is by its nature discriminatory. It is usually adopted for national security reasons and in order to help industries or enterprises in severe commercial difficulties. Most of the following industries have enjoyed such assistance in all developed nations: aerospace, computers, nuclear energy, air transport, railway transport, shipbuilding, shipping, agriculture, textiles, coal, and steel.

2. *Government Measures to Help Particular Regions*. In the sense that any enterprise is potentially eligible for assistance, this type of intervention is non-discriminatory. However, it does discriminate on a geographical basis. Because of a growing concern with the social costs of regional imbalance, this type of intervention has gained in importance over recent years and is now a standard feature of national economic policy.

3. *Government Measures that Affect All Industries and Areas*. This type of intervention includes free depreciation, industrial training, infrastructure provision, indirect taxation, and general credit policy. In principle, these measures are non-discriminatory. They are intended either (a) to make industry as a whole more efficient and competitive by increasing productivity and labor mobility or (b) to regulate the level of economic activity.

These categories are not, of course, mutually exclusive: government intervention in a specific industry may overlap with measures to promote balanced industrial growth by way of regional policies; and more general policy instruments, such as indirect taxation, can be used to discriminate for or against a particular sector even though, in principle, they affect all industries.

Scope of the Chapter

Ideally, any study of the effects of state intervention on international trade should deal comprehensively with all the measures government take to manage their domestic economies. Such a study would, however, constitute a major research effort and is clearly beyond the scope of this chapter. This chapter will therefore confine itself to the measures falling within category 1, although category 2 measures will be briefly considered. The general intervention measures of category 3 will not be examined. Furthermore, the chapter will examine only free market economies; for, although a number of state trading countries are now members of the GATT, the accommodation of these countries in a multilateral system where comparative advantage in principle determines trade flows throws up a whole host of problems. The difficulty of achieving reciprocity in the exchange of trade concessions with these nations and of avoiding the consequences of politically manipulated prices suggests that absolute state control of trade should be counterbalanced by state purchasing by trading partners.

The scope of this chapter has been limited for two reasons. First, the intervention measures that affect specific industries are often considered to have a greater impact on international trade than the measures falling within categories 2 and 3. Government measures that affect all industries equally do not affect the relative costs of individual sectors and hence are not regarded as distorting the allocation of resources and thus the conditions governing international trade. And, in any event, government measures affecting the competitiveness of all industries can be compensated for by parity changes. Regional subsidies, though they often have an effect on trade flows, are not generally considered to be a serious distortion since they are in principle given merely to compensate enterprises for the additional costs of location in second-choice areas; the subsidy-receiving enterprises will not enjoy a greater cost advantage than if they had set up in their first-choice area without assistance.

Secondly, a comprehensive study whose aim was the *complete* harmonization of the conditions of competition would not be politically realistic. Even in the EEC, where its member states are committed to economic and political union, perfect harmonization is not considered a feasible goal in the foreseeable future. Time and effort are likely to be better rewarded if multilateral negotiations in GATT and elsewhere concentrate on the more readily negotiable specific aids to industries or enterprises.

Specific Measures of Government Intervention

In order to determine the impact of specific intervention measures on international trade and to facilitate international negotiation and agreement, specific intervention measures should be examined by broad categories rather than on an industry-by-industry basis.

First, the most obvious form of government intervention in specific industries is government ownership and management of monopolies or near monopolies. This type of intervention, however, is essentially a vehicle for the distribution of government assistance rather than a non-tariff, trade-distorting intervention measure in itself. Government ownership of industries or enterprises has often arisen from historical, defense, or social reasons, as with the production of fissile uranium and munitions in the U.K. and France, the import of alcohol into Finland, and the management of rail and air services in many countries. Ownership then allows governments to implement more easily subsidization policies and other assistance measures. It should be noted, however, that government ownership does not *necessarily* entail assistance to the industry concerned nor hence the certainty of trade distortion, for governments may own large parts of an industry and yet not exercise management control.

Secondly, and in contrast, governments may have no financial stake in an industry and may yet determine its future. For example, one of the most effective measures that governments employ to assist industries is government purchasing. Governments are major purchasers of both goods and services. According to Professor Baldwin, in 1963, for instance, government agencies bought 17 percent of the goods and services produced in the United Kingdom, 13 percent in France, 19 percent in Sweden, and 18 percent in the United States.[1] Furthermore, the share of public authorities' spending in total national expenditures is increasing from year to year. And the proportion of public sector investment in total national investment spending is even more sizeable—over 35 percent in the United Kingdom, 33 percent in France, 30 percent in Italy, and 18 percent in Germany. Public purchasing power is often used discriminately to support a particular industry or to subsidize the research and development base of a company, for example, by the granting of defense contracts. British European Airways have been required on occasions to buy British-produced aircraft; and government purchasing of goods in the United States for domestic use is conditioned by the so-called "Buy American Act" of 1933, which requires that the government purchase domestic products unless this can be shown to be against the public interest, unreasonable from the cost point of view, or not feasible as a result of supply or quality constraints.

Thirdly, trade effects may arise from government subsidizing labor, either to promote exports or compete with imports. In the United Kingdom, for example, under the Selective Employment Payments Act of 1966, manufacturing industries used to benefit from a refund of the Selective Employment Tax plus a premium.

Fourthly, perhaps the most important form of government intervention is government provision of unrequited capital by grants, guarantees, loans, capital write-offs, tax credits, and subsidized interest rates. This area of intervention is vast and takes many forms. At one extreme, governments may control the allocation of capital to industry as a whole, thereby not only increasing the potential level of investment but also aiding investment planning. This is the case in Japan where the structure of company assets—on average 80 percent debt and 20 percent equity in major enterprises—is based on a commercial banking system that is hugely overlent and is therefore dependent on central bank support in the last resort. Then again, governments intervene by providing cheap capital through the medium of state-controlled institutions. The IRI in Italy, for example, supplies industry with low-cost capital by its control of sectoral holding companies, which raise money on the capital market at cheap rates. And the French Economic and Social Fund, by converting short-term private savings into longer-term loans to industry, not only increases the availability of capital but provides it at less than market rates. Again, the methods by which governments intervene directly in particular industries, enterprises, or projects are numerous. The United Kingdom, for example, provides investment grants for new ships; long-term, interest-free loans have been given to the Japanese coal industry. Specific firms and projects may be subsidized, underpinned, or rescued, as were Rolls Royce in the United Kingdom and the Lockheed Tristar project in the United States.

Fifthly, governments give substantial assistance and therefore competitive advantages to specific sectors, by a mixture of aids such as a guaranteed market or subsidies to the factors of production. This is particularly so in the agricultural sector. In the United Kingdom, for example, farmers have benefitted not only from deficiency payments that bridged the gap between guaranteed prices and average prices received from the market, but also from production grants and subsidies for fertilizers, cattle raising, and various other activities. By intervention buying in order to maintain target prices, the EEC's common agricultural policy involves massive, if disguised, production subsidies. Similar devices are to be found in the farm policies of most industrial countries.

Sixthly, governments often stimulate sales by such means as cheap credit and tied aid, which are measures of intervention that have a direct effect on trade flows since they are usually applied to sales in the export market. In the majority of industrialized countries, export financing is currently conducted through official bodies such as the Export-Import Banks of Washington and Japan, which provide facilities that include the financing of long-term export credits and guarantees for privately granted credit. Doubts have been expressed as to the extent, if any, to which such bodies subsidize export financing arrangements; but more overt examples of subsidization can easily be found, like the cost escalation finance cover for contract that is currently operated in France.

And finally, governments may directly affect the industrial structure of countries through controls on investment and through bodies like the now defunct Industrial Reorganization Corporation in the United Kingdom and the IDI in France.

This classification of types of government intervention does not purport to be exhaustive; but it does cover the major areas and also serves to illustrate the magnitude and complexity of the subject.

Motives for Government Intervention

It would be unrealistic to expect intervention measures to be judged solely by their effects on international trade. Unlike tariffs, which are often maintained simply to increase bargaining power, the aim of specific intervention measures is usually the improvement of the health of industries or enterprises vital to the domestic economy. The motives for specific intervention include: the slowing down of a rapid contraction of a declining industry in order that resources can be shifted less painfully into more profitable channels; the improvement of the efficiency and competitiveness of industries or enterprises that make a major contribution to national or regional employment; and the promotion of science-based industries so that the economy in general may benefit from the usual spin-off effects. Any trade effects that do result from intervention measures designed to achieve these aims, although perhaps of great importance to trading partners, are therefore largely residual consequences of measures to stimulate domestic production and employment. Any political solution must recognize the domestic economic and social issues involved.

A second point of significance in the search for solutions is that while intervention measures may affect the relative costs of the industries concerned and hence *may* distort the volume and direction of international trade, it is entirely an empirical matter whether in fact significant trade effects do result. Unlike tariffs and the more obvious non-tariff barriers such as quota restrictions, many government intervention measures cannot be assumed a priori either to curtail imports or promote exports significantly.

Proposals for Solutions to the Problem of Trade Distorting Effects of Governmental Intervention Measures

General Principles

As already noted, it would not be realistic to judge the international acceptability of government measures purely in terms of their effects on international trade. Yet, at the same time, the benefits of free trade through the efficient use of the world's resources, and the costs of trading partners brought about by trade distortions, must be clearly recognized. The way to improvement lies in the acceptance of two principles for the implementation of all government intervention measures. First, any trade distortion effects should be minimized; and secondly, any remaining trade distortion costs should not, in general, be borne indirectly by trading partners.

Specific Proposals

Transparency. In order to minimize the level of trade distortion, it is absolutely essential that all government intervention measures should be transparent. In this respect, state enterprises should declare their rates of return on capital employed in the same way the private sector does. And the value of all subsidies to these enterprises should be openly declared. In principle, only then will the effects of such measures on international trade be calculable.

Codification of "Allowable" Forms of Government Aid. In the present state of international opinion, a purely voluntary scheme of transparency and public declaration of all intervention measures must be considered a rather forlorn hope; it should, however, be retained as a long-term negotiable objective. A somewhat more realistic short-term objective might be for the GATT to codify those types of government aid that, because their propensity to distort trade is low, would be generally accepted as permissible by the international community. Given the variety of measures currently employed that would be unlikely to qualify as permissible under such a codification and the natural reluctance of governments to abandon all these measures overnight, acceptability would be enhanced if the code was introduced gradually and after an initial transitional period.

Compensation and Sanctions. Governments have strong political motives for some of their investment decisions and will not often be prepared to abandon them because they distort trade. But when trade distortion is shown to result, it is reasonable to demand that governments should regard such subsidies as having similar effects to a tariff. Governments that distort trade flows by intervening in industry should therefore be obliged to consult with trading partners at the latter's request; and where the distortion is significant the injured party should have the right to compensation in the form of reductions in the level of protection on other products. This process of consultation and compensation would be assisted by the codification of permissible types of intervention since the employment of aids falling outside the permitted categories would carry with it a presumption of injury to trading partners. Despite the trade-distorting nature of sanctions, realism demands that some form of retaliation by injured trading partners should be allowed. But retaliation should follow only after consultation, and after adequate and just compensation has been refused by the country at fault.

Regional Intervention. Regional policy, as a particular form of government intervention, poses special problems from the point of view of negotiation. It has been suggested that a "code of conduct" is needed to define an acceptable program of regional aids, and international criteria that would determine the level of trade distortion compatible with a "fair" regional policy. This implicit acceptance of a certain degree of trade distortion stems from the realization that, so far as regional aids are concerned, the willingness of governments to negotiate will depend on the seriousness of their regional problem. In order to facilitate negotiation and international agreement, the permissible level of trade distortion could be allowed to vary with the gravity of the regional problem, ''gravity'' being determined according to agreed criteria such as the level of unemployment or the rate of depopulation.

Finally, for those measures of government intervention whose principal function would appear to be discrimination against foreign supplies, like many instances of both public procurement and controls on inward investment, preparations should be made to bring about their early curtailment. Total abolition of these two categories of intervention is not a realistic objective for reasons of national security; but care must be taken to ensure that the importance of national defense is not overexaggerated for protectionist reasons. As for the control of inward investment, governments should operate any necessary restrictions solely by means of a negative list of industries into which foreign enterprises are forbidden entry. Government procurement should be liberalized sector-by-sector on the basis of reciprocity; reciprocity will be determined according to some subsidy-equivalent criterion, the subsidy-equivalent of discriminatory public procurement being the difference between the price the public agency actually paid and the price that it would have paid had there been no discrimination.

Note

1. Robert Baldwin, *Non-Tariff Barriers to International Trade* (Brookings Institution, 1970).

**Part IV
Responses to Disturbances
Caused by International
Trade**

13 The Adjustment to Free Trade in the Common Market

Albrecht Düren

The European Community (EC) and European Free Trade Area (EFTA) are the only recent cases in which countries have virtually eliminated barriers to manufactured trade among them. Adjustment problems were bound to arise, but the success of the endeavors indicates that they were met successfully. Was that due simply to rapid growth? To the fact that much of the new trade was intra-industry? To cartelization? To the staging of tariff reductions over a number of years? To the existence of the European Fund? These cases should thus be valuable in assessing the nature of the problems that would arise if a broader group of countries moved to free (or freer) trade and the likelihood that these problems will be taken care of through market forces without the conscious adoption of new adjustment policies, and in suggesting possible new government policies, at both the national and international levels, to deal with them if necessary.

The European Community's Rules and Results

The Rome Treaty establishing the European Economic Community calls for relations among its member countries that go far beyond the creation of a mere free trade area. The preamble of the treaty speaks of the removal of those existing obstacles that require concerted action in order to guarantee steady expansion, balanced trade, and fair competition; calls for the partners to strengthen the unity of their economies and to ensure their harmonious development by reducing the differences existing between the various regions and by mitigating the backwardness of the less favored; and finally expresses the desire of contributing, by means of a common commercial policy, to the progressive abolition of restrictions on international trade.

The experiment of integrating through competition in a Common Market is to be implemented by an agreement to eliminate gradually the customs duties between member states (Articles 12 to 17) and quantitative restrictions on imports and exports (Articles 30 to 37); to ensure (Articles 48 to 73) the free movement of workers within the community, freedom of establishment of nationals of a member state in the territory of another member state, and free supply of services and free movement of capital belonging to persons resident in member states. Added to this are rules

209

governing competition, including dumping practices (Articles 85 to 91), aids granted by states as far as they distort or threaten to distort competition (Articles 92 to 94), fiscal provisions falling upon the circulation of goods produced within the community (Articles 95 to 99), and such legislative and administrative provisions as have a direct incidence on the establishment or functioning of the Common Market (Articles 100 to 102).

The treaty thus stated that competition was to take over the regulating function in the economy of the Community. In addition, it provides other and farther reaching methods of integration. One is the common regulation of certain policies in which, for decades, every national state has developed individual systems of intervention, namely agriculture (Articles 38 to 47) and transport (Articles 74 to 84). In both of these cases, common organs shall be authorized to take measures that are binding for the member states. As the specific contents of these policies are not fixed in the treaty, its partners are bound to agree upon certain principles under which these spheres of the economy shall be commonly arranged; in these arrangements, competition does not necessarily have to be the critical characteristic.

Coordination of national economic policies is to be considered as another means of integration. The member states are to carry on their economic policies principally autonomously, under their own responsibility. But the autonomy is limited by treaty obligations (Articles 103 to 109), which say that certain measures have to be discontinued, for instance, if they violate the principle of free interchange of goods and services in a Common Market. Other measures may be used only under certain conditions, after previous understanding or with the express consent of the partners and/or the organs of the Community. Continuing debates over central principles, like "planification" against "market economy under conditions of macroeconomic management," demonstrate that the process of integration has not yet found a definitive form. Nevertheless, a resolution of the Council of Ministers, dated March 21, 1971, and reconfirmed on March 22, 1972, states that a common economic policy should be enforced not later than 1980.

Article 226 governs the application of safeguard measures within the Community during the transitional period. Only in cases that may seriously impair the economic situation in any region may a member state ask for authorization to take safeguard measures in order to restore the situation and adapt the sector concerned to the Common Market economy. The Brussels Commission shall, by an expedited procedure, immediately determine the measures that it considers necessary. These may even include derogations from the provisions of the treaty, to the extent and for the periods strictly necessary.

EFTA (founded in 1960 with seven members and Finland as an associate) limited its objective to the removal of duties and QRs on imports from partner countries, except on agricultural and fishery products. It did not set up a common outer tariff and therefore could not renounce clearing of the customs among member countries to avoid distortion of competition. To limit the duty-free circulation of goods to EFTA-products, a strict control of origin had to be installed; goods for which duty-free import was claimed had to show at least 50 percent of manufacturing or finishing in an EFTA-country.

Trade flows responded in the following ways to the creation of the EEC and EFTA, from 1959 to 1969 (1959=100):

1. total exports of EEC countries increased to 300; of EFTA countries to 225; while total world trade increased only to 235.

2. By region, exports increased:

	of EEC countries	of EFTA countries
In member countries	446	333
In third countries	231	201
In the respective other preferential area	245	250

3. As a percentage of world exports:

	1950	1959	1969
EEC	16.9	24.8	27.2
EFTA	17.4	16.4	13.7
EEC without Germany	13.3	15.2	16.8
Great Britain	11.0	9.2	6.2
EFTA without Great Britain	6.4	7.2	7.5

Creating a duty preference area has basic consequences for the foreign trade in that (a) trade is created by the substitution of imports from the preference area for home-made products and (b) trade is diverted by substituting production inside the preference area for imports from third countries. Trade creation leads to an increased division of labor within the preference area and increases productivity in general. Trade diversion reduces the relative share of third countries in imports of the preference area. The incidence of macroeconomic benefits depends on the intensity of competition, above all on the protective effect of the customs duties. Third countries can share the increase of prosperity of the preference area only through spillover effects. This can be achieved if the growth of trade in the preferential area is higher than the average growth rate of world trade, as has been the case in the EEC in several years.

The protective effect of EEC tariffs was quite different from EFTA, because its common outer tariff was based on the arithmetic average of the former four national tariffs. Thus the degree of protection in the individual countries was changed considerably—that is, the average French import duty fell from about 25 percent to 12 percent, the average German charge increased from about 5 percent to 12 percent. (This disregards the linear reductions agreed upon in later international negotiations.) In EFTA, the protection towards third countries remained unchanged. In both cases, all duties were eliminated in the internal relations of the preference areas.

The increase of real GNP in the European countries participating in the integration areas can be seen in Table 13-1. The EEC countries more or less maintained their rate of expansion, and the EFTA countries accelerated their growth. Aggregate GNP, in billions of 1963 dollars, increased as follows (1959=100):

| | Billions of 1963 dollars | | 1959= 100 |
	1959	1969	1969
EEC	201.3	352.9	175.3
EFTA	123.9	178.7	144.2
Great Britain	75.3	100.99	134.2
other EFTA	48.6	77.71	158.6

The mutual dependence of growth and foreign trade can be demonstrated with some examples from EEC countries. The German council of economic advisers, in its 1964-65 report, attributed the surprisingly high rates of economic growth in some countries of the Community in the postwar period mainly to the demand generated by worldwide expansion. It regarded the high rates of growth in countries with restrictive monetary and fiscal policy as export-driven growth.

The German assortment of export goods is comprised largely of commodities that due to worldwide growth, face above-average increases of demand. (The share of investment goods is above 50 percent of total German exports.) After this process of growth has been started, it proceeds to a certain degree automatically. With growing exports, a strong competitive position can be strengthened. Contrary to growth founded on domestic activities, it will not be strangled because of excessive imports, which is the normal symptom of balance-of-payments difficulties. On the contrary, it will continue, have more speed, effect more progress in productivity, and favor further gaps in competitiveness in export markets.

In the 1962-63 cycle, the Federal Republic even became a favored supplier for consumer goods to its EEC partners. In Italy, enlarged demand for consumption led to import increases from Germany in 1962 of 21.3 percent, in 1963 of 33 percent, and still in the first quarter of 1964 by another

Table 13-1
European GNP Growth and Shares, 1949-1969

| | Average Increase Per Year | | 1959 Share in the GNP of | |
	1949-1959	1959-1969	EEC	EFTA
Germany (1950-59)	7.4	5.2	35.9	
Italy	6.1	5.6	19.4	
Austria	5.7	4.6		5.2
Switzerland	5.1	4.6		7.5
Netherlands	4.5	5.3	6.0	
France	4.5	5.9	32.8	
Finland	4.4	6.7 (1959-68)		4.1
Portugal	4.1	6.1 (1959-68)		1.9
Luxemburg	4.1	2.9	0.26	
Denmark	3.5	4.9		5.3
Norway	3.5	4.7		3.9
Sweden	3.4	4.4		11.3
Belgium	3.1	4.7	5.7	
Great Britain	2.5	3.0		60.8

13 percent. In the same period, German exports to France expanded by 13.9 and 16.1 percent, to the Netherlands by 2.7 and 17.1 percent.

The annual report of the German council of economic advisers one year later analyzed the reversal of this trend. An unusually strong growth of German domestic demand, along with an autonomous German reduction of import duties, made German imports jump after mid-1964. In 1965, about 50 percent of the growth of German imports came from the EEC countries whose share in the total of German imports in just that one year increased from 34.7 percent (1964) to 37.8 percent (1965).

The mild recession, which began in Germany in late 1965, caused a stagnation of German imports in the first half of 1966. At about the same time, however, a new cycle was showing up in France and Italy, so German exports could largely compensate for reduced domestic sales. The German balance of trade, passive in mid-1965, thus again showed substantial surpluses. Holland and Belgium, struck later by the downgoing cycle, also found increasing market outlets in France and Italy (and even more in third markets).

From this analysis derives the conclusion that not only the growth of GNP in the member countries favors the interchange of goods and performing of services—especially between the member countries—but that intervals in the cycles of member countries may prove useful. In the beginning of the 1960s, cycles in the EEC countries ran off in equal phases and the conjunctural bursts intensified each other. But the later differentiating of the phases reduced their pressure on individual countries instead. This of course does not exclude the possibility that such effects through foreign trade may also take place outside of the Community. The German automobile industry was, during the general setback of 1966, in an especially difficult situation. In response, it concentrated its export endeavors on the most essential foreign market, the United States, and increased its sales there by 30 percent. Likewise, the export of machines and electrical products to the United States was raised and the German exports into the United States in the first three quarters of 1966 increased by about 25 percent.

Growth and Industrial Reorganization

Steady and suitable growth necessitates changes in economic structures. In periods of growth, the relationships between demand for investment and consumer goods are changing, as are the relationships of demand between the state and private sectors, and between home consumption and exports. But growth also offers a good basis for adjustment to a changing structure of the economy. In the boom years of 1964 and 1965, 159 and 161 new German enterprises were founded. On the other hand, in the recession years of 1966 and 1967, 689 firms with more than 50,000 workers and 757 firms with almost 70,000 workers had to close.[1] (See Table 13-2.)

In France, however, in spite of a considerable number of new foundings, the total figure of enterprises in French manufacturing industries is declining yearly by 2.5 percent.[2] (See Table 13-3.) Branches with numerous small firms (below ten employees) show reductions throughout. Under increasing division of labor, suppliers necessarily have to specialize more and more. In the particularism typical for the European countries, continual change is also necessary for such groups of industry that are on an even technical level with their foreign competitors. Therefore, in the general expansion, the share of investment goods imported has risen steadily in the highly industrialized countries.

	1958	1961	1965
Germany	7.6	11.1	12.0
Belgium-Luxemburg	16.0	21.8	22.2
France	12.4	16.1	19.1
Italy	12.2	16.9	14.7
Netherlands	18.4	22.8	22.2
Great Britain	6.0	8.4	10.6
Sweden	22.2	23.7	25.2
United States	6.1	8.6	11.8

Interrogations of German industry show that two-thirds of the imported investment goods had been bought abroad because comparable products were not produced domestically.

Table 13-2
Business Formation and Failure in Germany, 1964-1967

Industry	Year	New Businesses		Business Failures		Net Business Formation	
		No.	Employees	No.	Employees	No.	Employees
Manufacturing	1964	159	5,191	—	—	—	—
	1965	151	4,731	—	—	—	—
	1966	114	4,624	803	58,372	−589	−53,748
	1967	130	3,959	887	73,431	−757	−69,462
Food	1964	13	649	—	—	—	—
	1965	11	287	—	—	—	—
	1966	7	229	39	2,297	−32	−2,068
	1967	14	432	60	3,161	−46	−2,729
Textiles	1964	10	599	—	—	—	—
	1965	5	132	—	—	—	—
	1966	2	32	73	9,819	−71	−9,787
	1967	6	188	102	7,811	−96	−7,623
Clothing	1964	25	648	—	—	—	—
	1965	31	755	—	—	—	—
	1966	18	1,310	212	10,669	−194	−9,359
	1967	23	688	211	9,666	−188	−8,978
Lumber and Furniture	1964	8	303	—	—	—	—
	1965	4	161	—	—	—	—
	1966	3	74	57	2,608	−54	−2,534
	1967	11	304	53	3,584	−42	−3,280
Leather	1964	5	105	—	—	—	—
	1965	6	292	—	—	—	—
	1966	4	90	66	3,548	−56	−3,458
	1967	4	113	72	4,128	−68	−4,015
Chemicals	1964	22	552	—	—	—	—
	1965	23	534	—	—	—	—
	1966	16	820	36	2,208	−20	−1,388
	1967	22	749	49	5,555	−27	−4,806
Stone and Earth	1964	—	—	—	—	—	—
	1965	1	218	—	—	—	—
	1966	2	178	8	598	−6	−420
	1967	1	10	8	1,029	−7	−1,019
Metals and Machinery	1964	38	813	—	—	—	—
	1965	43	1,169	—	—	—	—
	1966	39	962	161	16,188	−122	−15,226
	1967	29	805	190	24,343	−161	−23,537
Electrical Equipment	1964	8	188	—	—	—	—
	1965	13	265	—	—	—	—
	1966	12	629	44	4,532	−32	−3,903
	1967	8	127	55	7,010	−47	−6,883
Others	1964	30	1,333	—	—	—	—
	1965	24	918	—	—	—	—
	1966	11	300	123	5,005	−102	−5,605
	1967	12	552	87	7,144	−75	−6,592

Note: Business failures in mining in 1966 numbered 31 (33,558 employees) and in 1967, 15 (19,675 employees).

Table 13-3
Business Formation and Business Failures in France, 1962-1967

Industry		1963	1964	1965	1966	1967	
Manufacturing:	formation	18,681	17,759	18,590	19,297	19,085	18,442
	failure	28,827	29,301	27,394	27,660	27,329	27,051
	net formation	−10,145	−11,542	−8,754	−8,353	−8,244	−8,519
Food:	formation	1,619	1,590	1,535	1,740	1,744	2,031
	failure	2,895	2,564	2,868	2,838	2,994	2,769
	net formation	−1,276	−974	−1,333	−1,098	−1,250	−739
Textiles:	formation	709	619	677	649	576	519
	failure	1,504	1,540	1,203	1,513	1,479	1,574
	net formation	−795	−921	−526	−859	−903	−1,055
Clothing:	formation	4,186	3,810	3,511	3,218	3,134	2,934
	failure	9,316	9,095	9,894	8,273	7,518	7,218
	net formation	−5,130	−5,286	−5,383	−5,055	−4,384	−4,284
Lumber and Furniture:	formation	2,152	1,995	2,182	2,284	2,100	2,008
	failure	3,220	3,078	3,070	3,157	3,034	3,202
	net formation	−1,068	−1,083	−838	−873	−934	−1,194
Paper:	formation	151	138	162	143	156	135
	failure	196	198	144	165	192	165
	net formation	−45	−60	−18	−22	−36	−30
Leather:	formation	262	292	232	232	219	132
	failure	793	858	770	751	692	691
	net formation	−531	−566	−538	−519	−473	−509
Rubber and Plastics:	formation	495	427	444	445	471	455
	failure	410	469	347	363	436	450
	net formation	+85	−42	+97	+82	+39	+5
Chemicals:	formation	496	447	418	327	472	452
	failure	578	716	420	434	513	474
	net formation	−82	−269	−2	−107	−41	−12
Petroleum Products:	formation	26	32	62	44	65	28
	failure	26	37	15	30	45	86
	net formation	—	−5	+44	+14	+20	−58
Stone and Earths:	formation	751	738	921	928	853	793
	failure	962	926	750	755	814	926
	net formation	−111	−188	+171	+173	+39	−133
Basic Metals:	formation	102	112	120	112	123	120
	failure	187	189	140	148	195	194
	net formation	−85	−77	−20	−36	−73	−74
Metal Products:	formation	2,522	2,335	2,557	2,670	2,383	2,335
	failure	4,073	4,117	4,230	4,208	4,081	4,035
	net formation	−1,551	−1,781	−1,673	−1,533	−1,698	−1,700
Machinery:	formation	726	627	708	780	748	666
	failure	669	733	557	927	670	697
	net formation	+57	−106	+151	−147	+78	−31
Electrical Equipment	formation	1,013	997	1,103	1,255	1,373	1,286

Table 13-3 (continued)
Business Formation and Business Failures in France, 1962-1967

Industry		1963	1964	1965	1966	1967	
	failure	850	982	765	803	587	1,010
	net formation	+163	+15	+338	+452	+385	+276
Transportation Equipment	formation	2,195	2,182	2,491	2,838	2,922	2,779
	failure	1,998	2,239	2,029	2,117	2,247	2,220
	net formation	+197	−53	+462	+721	+675	+559

Corresponding to the change of structure inside the EEC are changes in its economic relations with third countries. The Community still is the world's greatest importer of raw materials, but their share in its imports decreased between 1958 and 1970 from 30 to 20 percent, and the share of foodstuffs went down from 26 to 16 percent. The import of manufactured goods amounted to almost 50 percent, compared to 27 percent in 1958. In exports, the percentage of finished goods—already 80 percent in 1958—became even larger, 85 percent in 1970. Technical equipment comprises the biggest share. It is therefore not surprising that the importance of the trade partners changed correspondingly.

	Imports				Exports			
	1958		1970		1958		1970	
	Million Dollars	%	Million Dollars	%	Million Dollars	%	Million Dollars	%
Extra EEC of which:	16,156	100	45,621	100	15,911	100	45,198	100
Industrialized Countries	8,526	53	26,411	58	8,638	54	29,836	66
LDCs	6,824	42	16,105	35	6,125	39	11,546	26

Barriers to Entry

At the beginning of the 1960s it was fairly difficult, if possible at all, for a newcomer to enter the market of the industrialized countries of the Community. Many of the markets had an oligopolistic structure, which meant barriers to entry. Even existing firms—within the Community or abroad —that had not developed new products and new marketing systems or had not erected new plants had, and have, no easy chances to cross these barriers. The only successful way seemed to be, and remains so far, buying up at least the majority of an existing enterprise.

Nevertheless, the removal of the main obstacles to free circulation of goods brought more competition into the Common Market. For example, in the mid-1950s, the European motor car market was cut off from foreign supply. In France and Italy, in 1956, the share of imports was about 2 percent; in Germany, it was a little more than 4 percent. The customs duties in Germany were near 17 percent; in Benelux, 24 percent; in France, 30 percent; and in Italy, 40 percent. As demand increased with growing wealth, the capacities of production were enlarged but the wishes of the buyers could not be satisfied without long delivery terms. Each of the large producers in France, Italy, and Germany operated only in parts of the market; the mobility of demand was very limited between the individual parts of the market, large portions of which showed almost monopolistic features. Yet a decade later the market share of foreign suppliers, mostly from elsewhere in the EEC, was 17.6 percent in Germany, 15.3 percent in France, and 12.4 percent in Italy. All classes of buyers have become aware not only of domestic but also of foreign production and consider it to be equivalent. Each of the producers now has competitors with comparable potential, who show unrestrained determination to plan and follow an offensive strategy. The consumer has a real choice, and the growing intensity of competition executes pressure on prices and profits. The process of integration reduced the number of suppliers without making the number too small for efficient competition; the average size of an enterprise increased, so the competitiveness of the whole industry was improved.

It seems justified to call this particular continental market oligopolistic. Nevertheless, its progress cannot be attributed to cartelization, but rather to the opening of the markets and the strengthening of the remaining competitors. This does not of course exclude the danger of falling back into rigidity as soon as more concentration would favor the development of narrow, peaceful oligopolists.

A second example is the refrigerator industry in France.[3] At the end of the 1950s, the French market for household refrigerators was supplied by almost a dozen French producers who manufactured a large variety of types in low numbers. Their production was inefficient, but in 1960 they still served 98 percent of the domestic market. Since integration, their share declined to 76.2 percent by 1965. Demands by the French government to gain Community consent for applying the safeguard clauses of the Rome Treaty were refused by the commission in Brussels. Import pressure grew, particularly from Italy. The French producers had to readjust, and only four remain. Though the general cost of living index increased by 24 percent from 1962 to 1968, the prices for French refrigerators remained almost the same. Since then, exports of the French industry have grown faster than average, and the rate of expansion of imports from Italy and Germany is strongly declining. Their European scale of manufacturing now provides the French with a market position that enables them to pursue an offensive strategy on other markets.

In the European countries, with their traditionally great variety of small and medium firms in many industries, concentration is necessary to achieve competitiveness in a large market, especially on a really international scale. Nevertheless, the process of concentration causes dangers. There is, on the one side, the release of concentrated national groups that retard or bar the integration across the frontiers. On the other hand, the European ambition to equal foreign (i.e., American) firms in areas of highly advanced technology induces extra commercial influence, which as a rule brings in aspects of political prestige. The target of all-European concerns originated in this context.

A high degree of concentration involves the danger of creating structures that are less favorable for efficient competition and the chance of proper adjustment. In the Community, even more than in the individual national markets, the number of suppliers must remain large enough to secure efficient competition. The declarations of the Council of Ministers—to say nothing of the commission—in favor of competition cannot be ignored. But whether the national authorities will give distinct outlines to the intentions and articles of the Rome Treaty—beyond the dilatory and endless discussions of the Council of Ministers and the decisions of the European Court of Justice—cannot be forecast. At least in the case of an efficient control of mergers, action in the integration area is urgent.

The entry of new members, particularly Great Britain, could increase the scope for efficient competition as new suppliers penetrate the area. The number of rivals is now increasing, and the degree of concentration declining. But the dimensions of mergers already achieved in Great Britain could suggest that, similar to the reaction after the great invasion of American-owned international companies, a new wave of mergers could be initiated, motivated either by defensive or preventative purposes.

Market forces have proved their ability to mobilize the necessary energies for the fast adaptation of all participants in economic life to changing conditions. They will have to keep their influence in the expanded Common Market. When strong and interested parties change completely their strictly negative attitude towards the control of mergers, as the German Federation of Industries did in early 1973, a constructive solution for this complicated problem seems feasible.

To deny the existence of, or the tendency to, organize cartels, mainly in some branches of mass production of homogeneous products, would be wrong. To attribute to them an importance worth mentioning for the success of the integration process, or an undisturbed adjustment to the far-reaching changes of economic structure would go too far.

EC Adjustment Aids

The reduction of import duties, QRs, and other trade barriers among the member states excited in many places fear of setbacks, above all in branches that had been pushed forward in times of disintegration of the world economy under the protection of high customs duties and QRs. No government within the EEC was willing to accept unemployment even if, under medium- or long-term prospects, gains in prosperity could be foreseen. There were no supranational institutions to determine emergency cases of adjustment and decree appropriate economic countermeasures, and none could be created in a short time. Therefore, several remedies to avoid or eliminate adjustment difficulties were introduced into the text of the treaty. A transition period of a minimum of twelve and a maximum of fifteen years was agreed upon in order to lessen the number and intensity of adjustment frictions.

The large companies, and the prominent individual firms, prepared their activities almost immediately after the signing and ratification of the Rome Treaty, if not before. In these strategies, most of them anticipated the final stage of the transition period, for instance, in reducing their sales prices by the amounts of tariff reduction that were due later. They built up nets of sales agencies or service stations long before the large market unit was effective. The main problem for the vast number of medium and small firms was to comprehend the change of circumstances in which they had to act and react in the future. Very strong efforts by all types of trade associations in the member countries were necessary to accomplish this immense task of information and instruction. However, when the first phase of transition neared its end, there was no demand to claim the provided prolongation, either from the side of the trade unions or the enterprises, though the latter in 1962 had not overcome at all their apprehension of powerful foreign competitors. The Council of Ministers voted in 1962 unanimously for the immediate entry into the second phase. The passage to the third phase and the end of the transition period were also accepted and carried out according to the treaty. Twelve years were not enough, by far, to fill out the large gaps of the treaty to come to an economic and monetary union—not to mention the political union—but they were more or less sufficient to make the business community alert and acquainted with the new situation.

The first, second and third General Surveys of the commission about the activities of the Community (the third being published in February 1970—after the transitional period expired) report only a few cases of demands for authorization to take safeguard measures. These concerned mainly problems of mining industries in peripheral Italian regions (sulphur, lead, zinc), to a minor extent problems of processed foodstuffs, and two serious cases of industrial goods—products of weaving mills and electrical household equipment. Even in these cases, the commission decided that in an expanding economy that is undergoing a process of integration and considering the progress reached in creating a customs tariff union, the problems of structure and expansion of enterprises should not be approached mainly by import restraints.

According to Article 130, the European Investment Bank is to contribute to the harmonious development of the Common Market in the interest of the Community. By granting loans and giving securities it shall assist projects to promote less-developed areas, projects to convert or modernize enterprises or to create new jobs.'' The bank limits its activities to the transfer of capital within the Community. It acts like a bank (i.e., without giving subsidies). Prior to the end of 1971, it had issued 369 contracts comprised of 2,315.5 million units of account (formerly equal to the United States dollars, but after the changes of parities continuously valued with 0.8887 grams of gold). The distribution among the nations was Italy, 51.7 percent; France, 18.4 percent; Germany, 9.6 percent; Belgium, 2.3 percent; Holland, 1.8 percent; and Luxemburg 0.4. The distribution on projects shows infrastructure, 56.3 percent; industry, 40.6 percent; and trade, 0.5 percent.

The Social Fund likewise does not accord investment aids. Article 123 urges the furthering of the free movement of labor into different professions and regions of the Community. According to the Memorandum Industriepolitik 1970, the accumulated financial contributions amounting to 225 million units of account could be used for 1.5 million cases of job retraining. This is not much in relation to the changes that have taken place in the Community since 1958: from 1958 to 1966, 4.7 million workers have transferred to different jobs within trade and industry in the Common Market. In agriculture, prior to 1970, more than 5 million farmers, peasants and workers were shifted to other branches. According to the last plan of the commission, prior to 1980 another 5 million of the remaining 10.5 million on the farms should migrate from the country areas or from their agricultural jobs.

In an open society, transplanting millions of men into other professions and living circumstances cannot be accomplished without friction. In states with a market economy, democratic government, and a pluralistic society, strong forces can be mobilized to slow down the pace of change if not to bring it to a standstill. National programs to help employees retrain, transfer to new jobs, and so forth are therefore important, particularly in economies with high rates of structural change. In the Federal Republic of Germany, a special ''Arbeitsfoerderungsgesetz'' was passed for this purpose.

The special funds for reshaping coal mining and iron and steel industries

(Articles 54 and 56 of the ECSC) and for improving the structure of agriculture have minor importance for general adjustment assistance, especially as long as the economic policy for heavy industries or agriculture preeminently has the effect of conserving the present structure. Since the resolutions of the Council of Ministers in May 1971, the agrarian fund (partly designated to finance the manipulation of the markets, partly to finance structural measures in agriculture) is intended to contribute 50 million units of account per year to common measures of regional policy. Private investments, which aim at furnishing areas that have fallen behind with new permanent jobs for withdrawing peasants, are to be supported. This is not essential because of the amount of money made available, which is certainly tiny in proportion to the problem, but it is important in principle. The Community will now initiate activities that were not defined in the treaty. In this way, the commission also brings another element of financial compensation into the game between weak and strong members.

The first program of medium-term economic policy of the commission, published in 1966, contained a chapter about regional policy. It was based on the command of the treaty to ensure the harmonious development of the Common Market as a whole, by reducing the differences between the various regions and by mitigating the backwardness of the less favored. Not only the structure of production and of the labor force was to be considered, but also improvement of the regional structure should be begun on a common basis. The numerous national programs and different systems were compared with each other, and the first suggestions made to include them into the policy of the Community. The progress of implementing this conception was very slow.

Only in October 1971 was the necessity of a regional policy under common provisions acknowledged when the Council of Ministers required the national governments to observe certain rules if granting aids for regional purposes. The essence of these resolutions is to limit the government aid for investment cost to a maximum of 20 percent, and granting aid even to this extent is not justified in every backward area. During 1972, all aids are to be made transparent, and at the end of 1973, the subsidies will be examined again. Since October 1971, another common fund to finance regional activities has been under discussion. As regional policies are closely interwoven with economic policy, and as the destiny of the Community to become an economic and monetary union is still somewhat controversial (not so much concerning aims, but certainly concerning ways and means), it is not surprising that the definition of a common regional policy and its financial settlement among the interested parties is still at stake. Nevertheless, the participants at the last summit in Paris agreed upon starting the new fund from the beginning of 1974.

The impressive regional problems introduced by the new members, mainly the United Kingdom, might help the EC to get away from the long discussions of the past that only camouflaged the intentions of securing the "juste retour" of contributions. The material progress of the backward regions will of course not be accelerated by the joining of Ireland and several parts of the United Kingdom; in the Community of the Six it was slow enough, when measured by the contribution of the "basic regions" to the social product:

	Lowest Value	Highest Value	Maximum Difference
1960	25.5	209.7	184.2
1969	33.2	209.6	176.4

Future Adjustment in the EC

Finally, I conclude with some critical remarks about the present state of the Community with reference to the topics of this chapter.

The Community is endowed with sovereign rights that are unparalleled in international organizations or traditional trade arrangements between states. The Brussels Commission, independent from the member states, has the task of applying and carrying through the rules of the treaty. It has to rely on cooperation with the most prominent political organ, the Council of Ministers, which has to find and to make decisions on behalf of and in the name of the Community. In the council, the representatives of the member states have to act for the Community. They create law that supersedes national law. Neither the commission nor the Council of Ministers is controlled by the European Parliament, whose authority is more or less limited to consultative functions.

In distinct divergence from the treaty, the unanimity rule of the Council of Ministers is maintained for all those decisions in which one member claims to have vital interests. This is why, for instance, essential differences still exist in the national systems of taxation and the competence for all fiscal affairs has remained national, and why the existence of state monopolies with their far-reaching privileges is unquestionable, despite the fact that free movement of goods and the uncontrolled crossing of internal frontiers are for reasons of different taxation or monopoly interests impracticable. The unsatisfactory status of negotiations about a control of mergers also hints at the still dominating unanimity rule; likewise the incomplete assimilation of legal standards not only prevents individuals from utilizing their right of free settlement (professional regulations can be very protective for the insiders) but stands in the way of free movement of factors of production, payments, and so forth—in other words, of mutual penetration of markets.

The commission has the right of legislative initiative, but this has been curtailed by the failure of the majority of the ministers' council to support enforcement of the observance of the treaty through majority votes. Wanting no strong supranational authority, and still insisting on having their own national way, the ministers several times have placed the commission in the role of a rejected mover, so diminishing its position and prestige. This has led to weak compromises, in order to avoid the risk of more failures, and induced a policy of always seeking the lowest common denominator for the dissenting national interests. Social policy is a good example. The treaty is fairly vague about it. With economic integration proceeding, this deficiency was felt to be unsatisfactory, not so much since social policy causes factor costs but since the Community was intended to be a very modern structure. In fact, today the Community is far from being a nucleus of modern European social policy. The politicians kept their aims and programs within the national framework; promoting the social welfare and increasing public expenditure for social purposes is now, as before, the most striking appeal in fighting for votes. This has to happen in the national constituent bodies; the European Parliament is not directly elected, it has only delegated deputies.

The endeavors of the commission to improve the unsatisfactory state of a common social policy were weakened by reverses in the disputes with the ministers. It remains to be seen whether the presumptuous declarations at the EEC summit in Paris will bring about progress worth mentioning in this field. The trade unions, heavily engaged in their national problems, restricted themselves to permanently demanding more activity; in fact they supported the pragmatism that kept the financial means at the national disposal.

For these reasons the financial capacity and the applicability of the rules of the Social Fund are insufficient, in proportion to the social consequences of the change of structure in the European economy.

The last question that is interesting for this chapter is whether the policy of the past fifteen years in the economically integrated compound of Europe can give indications for future developments. The resistance to a common economic and monetary policy will probably continue; the existence of efficient and truly supranational authorities will therefore remain unwelcome. On the other hand, the free movement of persons, goods, and services (including transfer of capital) will remain desirable, or else the international competitiveness of the small national entities in Europe might not be secured. Thus different national policies will have to exist for some time side by side. Real integration among them will have to take place step by step; consultation has to be encouraged, the interchange of experiences has to be strengthened, and aims and methods gradually have to be aligned. Wherever common policies can be carried out they should be secured and put on a solid basis in the interest of the firmly growing mutual interdependence of the partners.

If the above-mentioned observations are in line with the development of the leading features in European integration, what deductions are permissible for the problems of adjustment in the industrial states of the Western world in case of achieving freer trade?

There do not exist other agreements as comprehensive as the Rome Treaty, and there are no international institutions that have mandates comparable to the EC and its organs to harmonize economic and trade policies. This will not make any easier the disputes that lie before the negotiators in the next GATT round. Lacking the determination for political aims that prevailed in the Europe of the 1950s, the negotiators in the imminent GATT round should not try to combine the demand for freer trade with the expectation of a degree of integration as it is—in spite of many setbacks—reached at present in Europe. If foreign trade is to cause a favorable effect on the allocation of factors and on the economic growth of all partners, as much competition and free movement of productive factors as possible should be guaranteed. Thus, freer trade could effect a greater division of labor, and more growth, and with it additional structural changes. In this way the problems of adjustment for enterprises could be kept on a tolerable level. But opening up of the markets and securing a high degree of competition cannot be based just upon general sympathizing with theoretical principles. The larger the area of free (or freer) trade will be, the more the differences of structure of enterprises will gain weight. No doubt, under present conditions, a small number of Japanese companies, extremely big and powerful as well as concentrated broadly in horizontal and vertical directions, have obtained disproportionate chances of competition compared with tens of thousands of small and medium firms in Western Europe that are now acting on an international scale and that for their survival largely depend on equal chances in international competition and cooperation. And if more liberal principles could be agreed upon and if, moreover, state-owned companies in communist countries would become participants in very liberal arrangements, the problem of comparability of the competitors would gain special significance. Markets with traditionally free access would be threatened with domination or strong influence by competitors whose preponderance is based mainly on government influence in one way or another. Therefore it is also hard to imagine how to come to a mutual consent about the principles of merger and to keep them under an effective control of partners that belong to different regimes. The necessary removal of NTB's and of direct or indirect export subsidies, as well as the harmonization of standards that eventually have the effect of NTB's, has not yet been accomplished satisfactorily even in the EC, though the Rome Treaty gave much incentive to do so. What developed in decades or a century often needs more than sixteen years to be removed again.

Any removal of existing trade barriers, however, should be announced reasonably early in order to give business time to draw conclusions and to prepare reactions. If the barriers are high, they should be reduced in stages over a number of years with announcement of the time schedule. Governments should try to come to an agreement not to subsidize the conservation, but—if at all—only the adjustment of industries; the agreement should stipulate the kind, volume, and duration of premiums to be granted to those firms that want to convert to other activities. Complementary to such agreements, medium-term projections could be commonly devised on the future of individual industries. The financing of larger programs for converting enterprises will be, in the foreseeable future, purely of national concern. This should not exclude common efforts to break through to accumulating supranational pools of resources.

The social aspect of the adjustment process deserves special attention. For instance, a six-month "early-warning" advance notice of changes in investment plans, or in the general direction of activities in the enterprise, will not be enough. In modern states, workers are used to receiving aid in many respects when great changes lie ahead. Social security systems differ very much among the great industrial nations; for example, the German legislation promoting vocational training, retraining, and so forth (*Arbeitsfoerderungsgesetz*) means spending annually more than 2 billion DM, whereas this problem is given little attention and correspondingly not much financial support in other countries. This distorts social conditions from one country to another and evokes tensions, but no obligation to harmonize these practices and to offer equal chances in all industrial countries exists, or could be within sight. In any event, the growing share of public contributions in the financing of social security systems will involve state-to-state arrangements.

The aim of creating international adjustment mechanisms, in the form of compensation automatically coming into force, appears unrealistic. According to different sociological philosophies, the governments taking part in international negotiations will reserve various measures for adjustment assistance for themselves that fit into their general domestic policy. However, official interventions should only be complementary. When the German council of economic advisers contributed towards the exchange of opinions about the principles of flexibility in a modern economy, in its annual report for 1965-66, it expressed the requirements for action from all parties concerned:

The readiness of the entrepreneurs to make use of technical progress and—by conversion or closing down—to anticipate or at least to respond to the structural changes in demand, stipulated by growth, the willingness of the employees to extend and to revive acquired knowledge and abilities and—if necessary—to change their workbench or the factory, the profession or the place of residence, the open-mindedness of all persons active in the economy to move from traditional prejudices about social grades of certain professions wherever economic progress makes them obsolete, the determination of the negotiating partners to further the training and re-training of the employees, to reduce resistance against technical progress by explanations and to meet halfway the changing prices on the market in the wage agreements, the readiness of the negotiating partners together with the legislator to overhaul old regulations and traditions in social and labor law, and to see whether they can be replaced by modern ways of guaranteeing proper incomes which retard structural changes to a lesser extent, a new orientation of structural policy in federal and Länder-governments which give in less to the pressure of groups which demand conservation subsidies out of self-pity. This would give more room for measures which would make it easier for enterprises and regions to adjust themselves to the structure of tomorrow.

Notes

1. Memorandum of the EEC Commission to the Council of Ministers, "Die Industriepolitik der Gemeinschaft" (Brussels, 1970).
2. Ibid.
3. See Studien, Reihe Industrie, H.3, Auswirkungen des Gem. Marktes auf dem Gebiet der elktrotechn. Gebrauchsgüter, Kommission der EWG (Brussels, 1970).

14

The Trade Policy of the United Steelworkers of America

Meyer Bernstein

The Steelworkers' Union has traditionally supported liberal trade both on the basis of principle and on the basis of its own interest. The freest possible trade, especially under the reciprocal trade laws introduced by Roosevelt in 1934, has traditionally been a part of its thinking. Furthermore, America has traditionally been a steel-exporting country, especially since the beginning of World War II.

For the same reasons of interest, the steel industry supported liberal trade laws until the middle 1950s. About that time, the European and Japanese steel industries began to recover from the effects of World War II. The restrictive policies of the allies with respect to the size of the Japanese and German steel industries changed because of developments in the Cold War. In addition, from time to time, a gray market and shortages arose within the United States, attributable first to the Korean War and then on a smaller scale to steel strikes and an overheated economy. European steel plants then began to capture the American market for certain products such as barbed wire, nails, and the like.

After a while, the steel industry and even the union became alarmed. The industry took up the question with Congress. The union brought up the matter at a meeting of the International Metalworkers' Federation. Both approaches were fruitless.

Steel shortages, generated by an overheated economy, were last evident (until quite recently) in 1957. American steel consumers made efforts to obtain steel abroad, though they generally were not successful. Imports were only slightly above 1 million tons, while exports were in excess of 5 million tons.

While 1958 was a recession year for steel, the American steel industry still raised prices in August. At the same time, the European and Japanese had reached a position to put new capacity into operation, so they could begin to export to the United States. Indeed, imports rose by 50 percent over 1957, and exports dropped by about the same percentage:

	1957	(tons)	1958
Imports	1,155,000		1,707,000
Exports	5,348,000		2,823,000

229

Early 1959 saw the most publicized collective bargaining negotiations in steel history. The union and the companies were so far apart, and so bitterly opposed, that a strike of long duration seemed inevitable. Steel-consuming companies took the warning and built inventories to the greatest possible extent. They pushed domestic production to the limits, and vigorously sought new sources of steel abroad.

True to prediction, the steel strike was bitter and long. It lasted 116 days and, even after the workers returned to their jobs under a Taft-Hartley injunction, there was every indication that they would go out again after the expiration of the eighty-day cooling-off period.

The result was that for the first time there was a substantial increase of steel imports over exports. In fact, almost three times as much steel was imported as exported that year (4,396,000 tons against 1,677,000 tons). From that time on, steel imports exceeded exports in every year.

During the 1959 steel negotiations and strike, the American steel industry made imports a major negotiating issue. It called attention to the lower real wages paid abroad and argued that every increase in the gap between the American scale would, in effect, cause an export of jobs since it would result in an increase in imports.

At first, the American Iron and Steel Institute propaganda was almost completely false. It compared American wages, including fringe benefits, to European wages, excluding fringe benefits. Fringe benefits in Europe are much more extensive than in the United States, so this misrepresentation was great. The Institute failed to take into account the vastly superior American productivity and never mentioned unit labor costs, nor did it call attention to the very substantial advantages that the American steel industry had over the Europeans and Japanese: that our materials costs were considerably below those of out competitors, our financing costs were lower, our profit margins were higher, and so forth.

In any event, "low-wage foreign competition" became a basic part of the American steel industry vocabulary. In addition to using this argument against its employees in collective bargaining matters, the industry also sought some sort of relief—never spelled out in detail—from Congress. It testified before committees of the Congress against the dangers of "low-wage foreign competition" and emphasized hourly wage differentials. However, as the Human Relations Committee, established jointly under the 1960 settlement, became more and more effective and led to wage agreements of smaller and smaller amounts, the industry gradually dropped references to low foreign hourly wages and began to center its attack on foreign competition as such.

Although imports of steel products had exceeded exports of steel products in 1959, and continued to do so in all years thereafter, total steel exports—that is, steel products plus steel in final manufactured goods

—remained greater than total steel imports. This was because our overall exports were higher than our overall imports, and we were exporting a wide range of machinery made of steel, trucks made of steel, and many other kinds of equipment and appliances made of steel. True, steel was also entering the United States in manufactured form such as in small automobiles, but this total was much less than the export total. It was, therefore, still in the interest of the union and the industry to support a liberal trade policy.

The change began in 1965. Negotiations that year were difficult and prolonged because of the Steelworkers' election. They began in December 1964 and were not over until September 1965. This period coincided with a substantial expansion in the American economy. There was, therefore, a substantial demand for imports; in fact, imports jumped by two-thirds in a rise from 6.4 million tons in 1964 to 10.4 million tons in 1965. At the same time, exports dropped by almost one-third, from 3.4 million tons in 1964 to 2.5 million tons in 1965.

At the same time, the overall American trade surplus began to show signs of weakening. Total trade in steel—direct and indirect—now suffered a reversal: more steel was coming in than going out. The steel industry became thoroughly alarmed and changed its policy to outright protectionism. The steel union did not follow suit immediately.

A complicating factor was that at the same time that steel product imports were increasing, iron ore imports were also increasing at a faster pace. Up to about the middle of the 1950s, the United States was largely self-sufficient in iron ore. However, the best quality ores were rapidly being used up and a new pelletizing process was not yet proved. Furthermore, there was a tax advantage in seeking foreign sources, so American steel companies began looking abroad and found them first in South America, then in Canada, and then in Africa.

There is a vast difference between imports of steel products and imports of iron ore. Steel product imports are purchased by steel-consuming companies, in competition with the product of the American steel industry. Iron ore, on the other hand, is mined in foreign operations by foreign subsidiaries of American companies for the purpose of supplying the needs of its steel plants in the United States. In other words, the American steel companies import their own iron ore from abroad. The tax advantage is that they do not have to pay U.S. taxes on the profits of these foreign operations unless such profits are sent to the United States. But the American steel companies do not open up mines abroad for profit on the sales of that iron ore. They do so for the purpose of extracting the iron ore and using it in their American furnaces. So they reinvest the profits abroad to get out more iron ore and thus avoid paying any taxes at all to the American government.

In a normal year, some 45 million long tons of iron ore are imported by

American steel companies from their own mines abroad. There is no tariff on this iron ore, so the advantages double. Imports of iron ore are now over 50 percent of domestic production, while imports of steel products are only about 10 percent of domestic steel production.

Meanwhile, production of iron ore in the United States began declining, unquestionably because of imports. This is different from the situation with respect to steel. As steel imports increased, domestic steel production increased, for both were due to the same factor—an expanding economy. But iron ore was different because foreign ores were generally of higher quality than domestic ones. A number of American mines, particularly underground mines, were closed and blast furnaces they formerly served now got their iron ore from higher quality ores from abroad.

The steel industry was in a dilemma. It was for restrictions on steel imports, but just as strongly for continued duty-free imports of iron ore. The United Steelworkers, representing iron ore miners both in the United States and Canada, continued to support duty-free imports of iron ore and a liberal trade policy with respect to steel products.

The Trade Expansion Act of 1962 was whole-heartedly endorsed by the union but only lukewarmly tolerated by the industry. The union expected to take advantage of the readjustment allowance provision of the new adjustment assistance program, to help tide over steelworkers or miners whose jobs were affected by imports. This program, however, proved to be a dead letter. The U.S. Tariff Commission interpreted it in such a restrictive manner that no readjustment allowances were paid during the first five years of the Trade Expansion Act.

The union filed a petition in 1963 on behalf of the iron ore miners of the U.S. Steel Corporation's mine in Fairfield, Alabama. The U.S. Steel subsidiary was built there because of the existence of iron ore (and coal). Gradually, however, the United States Steel Corporation found it advantageous to supplant low-quality domestic ore with higher-quality waterborne ore from Venezuela. In 1963, they shut down the Fairfield Red Mountain mines entirely. In spite of the clear job loss through substitution of foreign supply, the U.S. Tariff Commission refused the union's petition.[1]

In 1963, the steel industry decided to try the anti-dumping route to stop steel imports. They hired Dean Acheson's law firm to represent them first before the Treasury Department, which must make a determination as to less than fair value sales, and then before the U.S. Tariff Commission, which must make a determination with respect to injury. The industry was successful in part at the Treasury, but failed completely before the Tariff Commission.

The industry then felt that it might get relief if it succeeded in persuading Congress to make an investigation of steel imports. Senator Vance Hartke of Indiana held a series of hearings on a bill calling for a Commerce Department investigation. The union agreed that an investigation would be helpful, but had two main suggestions to make. First, the investigation ought to be carried out in some sort of adversary approach, which could compel answers to significant questions. The union also suggested that iron ore be included in the investigation. The government witnesses all opposed any investigation as did, of course, the representatives of the European and Japanese steel producers. The Senate Finance Committee finally decided to employ a steel expert, Dr. Robert Weidenhemmer of the University of Pittsburgh, as a consultant, and instructed him to carry out the investigation alone. The report has never been published.

Meanwhile, the steel industry had decided upon another course. Beginning in early 1966, steel industry leaders began making speeches denouncing foreign competition. Their main theme was that imported steel caused the loss of either 70,000 or 85,000 jobs—the figure varied with different speakers. They revived the low-wage foreign competition argument and urged that something had to be done about it. On February 8, 1967, the American Iron and Steel Institute invited a large number of senators and representatives to a breakfast meeting. The leaders of the industry repeated their thesis and called for protection in the form of a temporary special steel import levy. Later it became clear that they wanted relief from about 80 percent of some 11 million tons of steel coming in annually, for an initial five-year period.

The industry did not consult with the union, or even advise it, prior to this meeting. It did, however, ask that the union cease its criticism of the steel industry's foreign competition complaints at least until the industry's plan was made public. After the steel industry unfolded its plan for the special temporary import levy, the union issued a statement commenting on the industry's proposal. The newspapers interpreted the statement as generally in support of the steel industry's proposal for a special import levy. The proposal itself, however, was badly received. Most editorials dealing with the subject, including *The Wall Street Journal* and *The Washington Post,* disapproved. There was scarcely any support.

I. W. Abel, President of the Steelworkers, assured me personally that the Steelworkers' Union would not endorse the industry proposal for a special levy. Nevertheless, we still had a problem. The industry had begun a full-scale campaign to convince its employees that imports were the cause of all layoffs. This propaganda was much more successful with our membership than it was with the public generally. The Steelworkers' Union is one of the most democratic in the world; the membership, therefore, can change the union's policy. Their next opportunity to do so would be at the forthcoming convention. If the convention were held during a period of relatively high operations, there would be little danger of an upset. The officers could easily convince the delegates that a liberal trade policy is best for the union. But, if before the convention there should be a build-up of inventories, protracted collective bargaining negotiations, and then the usual cutback once the contract is signed as had happened so often in the past, a convention debate on trade policy might very well turn out differently. The same could be expected if the recession were to affect the steel industry. Something thus had to be done to deal with these contingencies.

After a long series of discussions with union and government experts, I drew up a proposal for establishing a relationship between imports and the level of domestic production. I offered this to the newly created committee established by the executive board to work out a trade policy recommendation for the union. First we had a meeting among ourselves at which I outlined my plan, which was favorably received except for an agreement that Canada could not accept any restriction.

The industry soon learned of the creation of this committee and extended an invitation to the committee members to meet with industry leaders to discuss the problem. Accordingly, the committee gathered in Pittsburgh on August 15, 1967. Several of the industry leaders spoke on the need for some sort of protective action. The union was urged to support the special import levy, but the industry noted that it was not wed to this particular solution and would be glad to go another road if this seemed more promising.

In response, I expressed doubts about the import levy and described our own suggestion for establishing a relationship between imports and the domestic level of production on the basis of an international agreement. Although the industry and union were looking down different roads, they were closer than ever before on this subject. The union did not criticize the import levy plan as such but merely offered our opinion that, regardless of its merits, it could not succeed and a substitute should be sought.

The International Metalworkers' Federation Central Committee meeting was scheduled to take place late in September. We took advantage of the meeting to sound out European steel industries on the feasibility of our voluntary agreement plan. Also, we thought to notify the European Metalworkers Union and the IMF of our intentions. We requested that the subject of international trade in steel be placed on the Central Committee agenda, and indicated that we would speak on the subject with special reference to the steel import problem in the United States. Once in Europe, we emphasized our hope that the problem could be solved on a voluntary basis by government cooperation. I warned that pressures were mounting to such an extent that if an agreement could not be reached, there was a grave danger that a unilateral legislative solution would be imposed.

The union people in Europe raised strong objections to our proposals. In addition, Victor Reuther denounced the Steelworkers' proposal. He said that regardless of how we might try to disguise it, it was blatant protectionism, and he compared the Steelworkers' approach to our problem with "the courageous way" the United Auto Workers had resisted similar employer pressure with respect to imports of automobiles. The European unionists followed suit. They not only criticized our proposal, but also objected to our meeting with employers before taking up the matter with them. The European firms refused to admit that their exports to the United States were causing any difficulty, or could cause any difficulty. It came as something of a shock to them that efforts were underway to stop or restrict imports to the United States. They had received reports on the views of the U.S. industry, but simply did not take them seriously.

About this time, the U.S. industry changed its tack. It dropped its demand for a special import levy, and instead called for quotas. A number of other industries—textile, oil, and meat—were also asking for quotas and, by this time, the Senate Finance Committee had decided to hold special hearings devoted to these various bills. The steel industry program was introduced by Senators Hartke and Dirksen. The industry sought Steelworkers' support.

The bill provided for "orderly trade in iron and steel mill products." It was a relatively simple measure that sought to unilaterally impose quotas on countries exporting steel to the United States. It applied to the whole range of steel products plus pig iron. The president was authorized to negotiate multilateral or bilateral quotas. If the foreign countries agreed to accept the U.S. proposal "voluntarily," then the quotas would be established on the basis of the percentage of imports of mean average consumption during the years 1964 to 1966. These were years of highest imports, and the ratio worked out to 9.6 percent. If any country refused to accept such an "agreement," its exports to the United States would be based on the figures for 1959 to 1966. Since imports were considerably lower at that time, the quota for such countries would be far below the quota for countries accepting the "agreement." The arrangement would continually use the average of the last three years ao a base, and would run for five years when it would be reconsidered.[2]

The bill, of course, contravened the General Agreement on Tariffs and Trade. If a foreign country accepted an "agreement," it might well forego its right to retaliation. If it declined to come under the "agreement," its quota would be smaller, but it would have the right to retaliate by establishing limitations on exports from the United States.

The bill, however, did not meet the two main problems of the steelworkers. It did not deal adequately with a situation in which there was an inventory build-up during negotiations and a sudden cancellation of domestic orders as soon as the strike threat passed. Nor did it meet the problem of a steel recession, which could come upon us rather quickly as had occurred four times since the end of World War II.

Meanwhile, the Steelworkers' Executive Board had addressed the proposal of the industry that any differences between the union and the employers in next year's negotiations be turned to an arbitrator with a guarantee against strike or lock-out. The industry took this revolutionary step only after the major steel consumers had notified them that unless they (the consumers) had iron-clad assurance that there would be no strike in 1968, they would place massive orders for steel with foreign producers. Apparently this frightened the steel companies into making an arbitration proposal to the union. After much debate, the union rejected the proposal. The industry received this news with considerable dismay.

Obviously, there would now be a great increase in imports. The industry insisted that the least the union could then do would be to support their bill establishing import quotas. The union decided to do so. Its position quickly became purely protectionistic. We wanted quotas that would keep out foreign steel beyond certain limits. We never really defined what those limits should be, nor was any serious thought given to how such protection could be obtained. The Steelworkers simply supported any protectionist measure that came along. The steel industry became just as protectionist as the union.

In 1968, the Johnson administration decided to strive for a voluntary restraint agreement. There was little consultation with the union. (I do not know to what extent the industry was brought in.) When I learned the details of this non-enforceable limitation, I recommended to our union that we urge its rejection. The reasons were simple. The Voluntary Restraint Agreement provided that imports would start at a level of 14 million tons in 1969. This was less than the 18 million tons imported in 1968, but the 1968 figure was vastly inflated because of the negotiations and the strike threat and a more reasonable figure would have been less than half that amount. Secondly, the VRA provided that steel imports could increase at 5 percent per year. This was more than twice the natural growth level of the industry and, therefore, in time, imports would be taking over more and more of U.S. steel consumption. Thirdly, the growth was to continue regardless of the level of our own industry. In other words, we could be in a recession and, under the agreements, imports would nevertheless increase. Despite these objections, President Abel endorsed the Voluntary Restraint Agreement after a call from the White House conveying the suggestion of President Johnson.

The agreement was a failure. It is almost certain that imports would have been lower had the VRA never been signed. The reason is that foreign steel producers, having obtained such high quotas with the automatic 5 percent escalation, felt constrained to export up to their full allowance. In the middle of 1969 and early 1970, this was difficult because of a steel boom that had developed abroad. Foreign producers actually deprived their own customers in order to ship steel to the United States. This was not a total loss to us because we now had an opportunity to export more of our own steel and, indeed, we established an all-time record in so doing. But the Europeans and Japanese should have supplied the European and Japanese consumers and we should have supplied our own, which is what would have happened had there not been any Voluntary Restraint Agreement.

Steel was not the only industry hit by imports. Electronics, autos, and shoes, to name a few, were also badly hurt. The Trade Expansion Act of 1962 had provided that workers who were injured through increased imports resulting in major part from trade concessions could file a petition for adjustment assistance with the United States Tariff Commission. The Tariff Commission, however, quickly made a dead letter of this provision. It rejected every appeal submitted to it. For several years, until 1969, there seemed to be no point in even raising the matter. Then, in September of this year, I filed three petitions: two on behalf of the United States Steel Corporation, American Bridge Division, for transmission towers, and a third on behalf of the workers of Armco Steel in its Ambridge butt weld pipe mill. I had been one of the first to submit a claim for adjustment assistance right after the law went into effect. This first case involved an iron ore mine of United States Steel. Then, the company opposed the petition; but in 1969, the company's lawyers' attitude was entirely different. They now thought that there would be some advantage to the corporation in securing a favorable ruling. The same was true of Armco. Both companies, therefore, rendered available assistance in the gathering of statistics. I never could ascertain with any degree of assurance just what accounted for the Tariff Commission's change of heart, but at any event, all three petitions were approved.

The benefits were substantial. For example, 147 or the 320 Armco workers had elected to take early retirement. They therefore received the 52 or 65 weeks' benefits (depending upon whether they were under or over 60 years of age) on top of their pension payments. The others only received the difference between $85 a week and what they had already obtained in state unemployment compensation. Furthermore, the companies agreed to permit payment of supplemental unemployment benefits on top of the UC without any deduction for the adjustment assistance.

This was good and wholesome, but still only a palliative. The union continued to insist upon protection against imports. Finally, the AFL-CIO undertook to offer a joint protectionist measure, one that would address itself not only to imports of goods but to exports of capital and particularly to multinational companies. In principle, the bill is good. It is protectionist—no question about that—but generously so. It is fair. Its basic proposition is market sharing. It, therefore, avoids most of the evils of the Voluntary Restraint Agreement.

The bill also has a number of shortcomings and omissions. For example, it makes no mention whatever of fair international labor standards, which were even included in the Mills bill in 1970. It seems inconceivable for labor to introduce an overall trade bill and completely ignore fair international labor standards. Something should be done with respect to fair international labor standards. If the AFL-CIO was not ready to seek its adoption for imports generally, an alternative would be to introduce the principle where it would generate the least opposition and where the strongest justification could be made for it, namely, with respect to government purchases.

We already have a series of laws establishing social policy for American companies doing business with our government. Not only must minimum wages be paid, but there are other standards such as prohibition of child labor that must be met. Why not, on a reasonable basis, extend the same principle internationally? Why should American suppliers be held to certain rigorous standards while no labor conditions whatever apply to foreigners who sell to the American government?

This should not be a "Buy American" provision. Its purpose should not be to squeeze out foreigners. Its objective is simply the same as the Walsh-Healy Act—to compel foreign suppliers to comply with a fair social policy on the same basis as we now compel American suppliers to do so. I believe that this proposal could significantly improve U.S. trade law with regard to American workers.

Notes

1. The United States Steel Corporation had, in fact, opposed granting readjustment allowance to its iron ore miners. It argued that granting of this petition might adversely affect the anti-dumping charges that a number of American steel companies had filed against European and Japanese steel companies with respect to wire rod and other steel products.

2. To take care of the problem of exporters trying to get around the quotas on steel products by increasing shipments of items fabricated from steel products, there was a special provision that would put such fabricated merchandise under the same quota if imports on these items rose by 20 percent. To take care of the problem of inventory build-up during negotiations, no more than 60 percent of the annual quota in any category could be imposed during any six-month period.

15
On the Non-Equivalence of Import Quotas and "Voluntary" Export Restraints

C. Fred Bergsten

Introduction

Until the 1930s, tariffs were the dominant instrument of commercial policy. From the 1930s until the 1960s, quantitative import restrictions (QRs) acceded to that role. Since the early 1960s, "voluntary" export restraints (VERs) have moved up alongside both.[1]

Economists have analyzed the similarities and differences between tariffs and QRs.[2] But there has been no systematic effort to compare the economic and political effects of VERs and QRs, on the erroneous view that they are virtually identical.[3] This chapter will make such an effort.

Countries have restrained their exports for several reasons. A prominent motive has been national security, which throughout the postwar period has sharply limited the willingness of the United States (and Western Europe and Japan, to much lesser extents) to export to communist countries products that might strengthen their military capabilities. More broadly, exports have been restrained to deny the benefits of trade to importing countries, as with the embargo on oil sales to Italy maintained for a while by some League of Nations members in 1936, the embargo on sales to Rhodesia mandated by the United Nations in 1967, and the withholding of oil exports to the United States and Holland by Arab oil-producing countries in late 1973. A third motive has been the preservation of certain commodities for domestic consumption and to try to fight internal inflation, the traditional "short supply" criterion, which has recently prompted the United States and several other countries to limit their sales of a variety of agricultural and other products. A fourth is a conscious effort by an exporting country (or group of countries) to exploit an oligopoly position in a particular commodity market, as recently accomplished by the Organization of Petroleum Exporting Countries (OPEC). Individual industries or firms have also limited exports for oligopoly reasons—that is, through a division of markets among the subsidiaries of a given multinational firm or among independent firms in an industry that is cartelized internationally.

All of these types of exports restraint are initiated by the exporting country in pursuit of its own interests. They are presumably not welcomed by the importing country. They are *not* the subject of this chapter.[4]

I deal here with those export restraints that are adopted, by a country or by an industry, ostensibly[5] because of the problems the exports are causing for the country (or countries) *to* which they are flowing—and which are, therefore, perceived as a substitute for other actions, including restraints by the importing country of the same trade, to deal with those problems. Thus they are seldom voluntary, and I enclose the word with quotation marks throughout to indicate as much.[6] Such restraints are usually adopted in response to industry-specific pressures, as in the prominent cases of textiles and steel in the United States. They may also be adopted across a wide range of industries, in response to aggregate balance-of-payments or trade-balance pressures, as an alternative to exchange-rate changes (including revaluation by the surplus country) or import surcharges by the deficit country, as was announced by the Japanese in late 1972. Most of my examples will be drawn from VERs on sales to the United States, although the United States has by no means been alone in arranging such restraints in recent years.

VERs are limitations on export sales (a) administered by one or more exporting countries or industries (b) on the volume or value of their sales (c) to a single foreign market or several markets, or (rarely) the world as a whole, (d) triggered by pressure from the government or industry of the importing country or countries (e) carried out either bilaterally or within a multilateral framework (f) sometimes explicitly authorized or guided by domestic law, and sometimes not. There are thus numerous permutations among specific VER arrangements.[7]

A major distinction is between those VERs that are administered solely by the exporting country and those where the importing country uses back-up QRs to assure that the restraints are effective. In the U.S. case, the steel VER, negotiated between the U.S. government and the foreign industries, fits the former category.[8] So does the bilateral cotton textile VER negotiated with Japan in 1957, the precursor of the multilateral "Long-Term Arrangement on Cotton Textiles" (LTA), which governed the bulk of world trade in cotton textiles from 1962 through 1973. The LTA and its successor, the "Arrangement Regarding International Trade in Textiles," which commenced all-fiber coverage in 1974, fall into the latter category for the United States under Section 204 of the Agricultural Adjustment Act, which authorizes U.S. quotas once there exists a multilateral arrangement under which "a substantial volume of world trade" is covered by VERs. It also covers meat, under the Meat Import Act of 1964, which requires the president to trigger quotas if certain import levels—which therefore *de facto* set the VER ceiling—are exceeded.[9]

Indeed, some observers argue that this latter group of restraints should be viewed as QRs rather than VERs, because ultimate control rests with the importing country. Such a contention is only partly true. Even when the importing country has such control, it may choose not to exercise it in particular cases even when the VER ceiling is pierced, as has frequently been true with U.S. imports of particular categories of textiles. Thus the ceiling on imports, which is certain under QRs, is not certain even under VERs backed up by QRs. Even more important for the analysis of this chapter, the exporting country organizes the market under VERs even when they are backed up by QRs—and may even do so more efficiently by virtue of the QR threat standing behind its own VER. I will distinguish between these two types of VER when necessary in the analysis but will maintain the fundamental distinction between VERs and QRs.

There is no complete record of VERs, past or present, and hence no way to judge their aggregate importance in world trade.[10] In 1971, however, as shown in Table 15-1, more U.S. imports were covered by VERs than QRs. VERs covered well over $5 billion—about one-eighth—of all U.S. imports. There were three major QRs (oil, sugar, dairy products) and four major VERs (cotton textiles, synthetic and woolen textiles, steel and meat), as well as a number of both covering minor products.

The importance of VERs relative to QRs has grown since 1971. In mid-1973, a new VER was announced to cover exports from Korea to the United States of "certain rubber and plastic footwear."[11] The VER on meat was suspended, but was to be reinstated in 1975, and the elimination of the QRs on oil and sugar were much more important quantitatively. There were also signed a large and growing number of VERs on sales of a variety of products, mainly from Japan and a few other countries in the Far East, mainly to Western Europe[12] and Canada. And the new "Arrangement Regarding International Trade in Textiles" extended the scope for VERs to all textile fibers for all countries.[13]

The Relative Effectiveness of VERs and QRs

VERs and QRs can be set at identical levels of trade.[14] If such equivalence were actually achieved, the losses in economic efficiency caused by each would be equal. However, the differing natures of the two instruments virtually assure significantly different outcomes in practice, in terms of both the actual degree of restraint and the distribution of effects among exporting countries. In addition, VERs and QRs would produce different distributional effects between the importing and exporting countries involved in the restraints even if their aggregate effects were identical.

VERs are inherently less effective in achieving import restraint than QRs, for several reasons.

First, it is technically more difficult for most countries to control exports than imports. Most countries still have comprehensive import control machinery, while few have comprehensive export controls. In most cases, effective export control thus relies on truly cooperative behavior from the industry or the creation of a completely new government apparatus.[15]

Second, this technical problem is compounded by asymmetrical moti-

Table 15-1

Major U.S. Imports Subject to Voluntary Export Restraints and Import Quotas 1971

(In Millions of Dollars)

	VERs	QRs
Petroleum		3,278
Sugar		813
Dairy Products		70
Total		4,161
Cotton Textiles	590	
Synthetic and Woolen Textiles	1,840	
Steel	2,009[a]	
Meat	598	
Total	5,037	

[a]1969 figure, excluding several categories of steel products covered by the VERs. Thus the figure for total VER coverage should be somewhat higher. In 1973, the total coverage approximated $2.3 billion.

Source: Stephen P. Magee, "The Welfare Effects of Restrictions on U.S. Trade," *Brookings Papers on Economic Activity 3: 1972*, edited by Arthur M. Okun and George L. Perry, p. 662. © 1973 by the Brookings Institution, Washington, D.C. Reprinted with permission.

vations. Most export restraining countries do not really want to restrain. Indeed, they will often hope that the announcement of the new VER, along with some minimal attention to carrying it out in practice, will avoid action by the importing country. Even if the countries want to do so, their industries can often evade the efforts (as through transshipments, discussed below). Most import-restraining countries and industries, on the other hand, do want to maintain effective controls.

Third, and perhaps most important, VERs rarely cover all suppliers. They are usually sought only from the chief producers of "market disruption." The sales of small suppliers, or even large suppliers whose export growth is modest, or the occasional country that just won't agree (e.g., Canada in steel) remain uninhibited. The sales of these non-restrainers are in fact likely to be stimulated, both because of the limits on supply from restraining countries and because they will want to establish the highest possible level of sales against which to base the restraints they naturally fear they may be induced to accept in the future.[16] Companies in restraining countries may foster such developments by investing in new production facilities in non-restraining countries, as Japanese textile firms have done throughout Northeast and Southeast Asia.[17] QRs, on the other hand, are almost always global in their coverage, although discriminatory quotas —such as those levied by European countries against Japan and in favor of the overseas associates of the EC—are not unknown.[18]

Substitution by non-restraining countries can occur readily, because many of the industries that are most likely to become subject to pressures for import restraints embody simple technology and relatively unskilled labor. Textiles are the classic example, where production facilities in non-restraining countries have been set up very quickly to supplement sales from countries that accepted VERs. U.S. imports of cotton textiles from non-restraining countries, mainly Hong Kong, rose from $3.6 million in 1956 to $108 million in 1960, while the Japanese VER held its sales virtually constant. The same kind of geographical shifting in synthetic textiles accelerated after the United States extracted VERs from the four principal suppliers (Japan, Korea, Taiwan, and Hong Kong) in 1971.

Fourth, sales from restraining countries can be augmented by transshipments through non-restraining countries, including non-producers (or very small producers) of the product in question. This adds to the technical difficulty of actually controlling exports, even with the most sincere efforts on the part of the restraining government.[19] When U.S. meat prices soared in the early 1970s, for example, meat from Australia entered the United States via Canada in response to the price incentives to Canadian meat importers generated by the VER.[20] And Japanese steel has apparently entered the United States via Canada and Korea. QRs are of course applied at the border of the importing country; they encounter no such problems at all if the quotas are allocated on a global basis and can stop transshipments even under country quotas through strict rules of origin.

Fifth, VERs may actually *raise* the level of imports in some years. VER levels are usually negotiated annually, even when within the framework of a long-term agreement. Thus they are usually based on some negotiated growth factor over the actual results of the previous year. QR levels, on the other hand, are more likely to relate to a fixed base period. Thus a shortfall of exports in any VER restraint year, below the maximum permitted for that year, could reduce a country's allowable sales in all succeeding restraint years.[21] So countries may treat their *maximum* VER levels as *minimum* targets to be reached.[22] For example, European steel shipments to the United States might have fallen even more than 29 percent below restraint levels in 1970 in the absence of the steel VER, in view of the massive pressure of European demand on European steel-producing capacity. For similar reasons, there was widespread industry surprise that total U.S. steel imports in 1973 fell only 14 percent below 1972.[23] And the Japanese administrative apparatus for implementing the textile VERs, at least in the early years of the cotton restraints, penalized firms for not filling their quotas.[24]

Sixth, VER agreements are particularly likely to be ineffective during their last year. In the general absence of backup QRs or other sanctions on non-compliance, the incentive to exporters to restrain is further reduced. Even a provision for deductions from future VER levels has proven difficult to implement. Such "last years" can occur frequently. The meat restraints were annual. The steel VERs had durations of three years. So have many of the bilateral arrangements on cotton, woolen, and synthetic textiles. Only the first international arrangement on cotton textiles, which provided the umbrella over the cotton bilaterals, lasted even five years. On the contrary, terminal dates are seldom if ever set for QRs.

Finally, the terms of VERs are almost certain to be looser than the terms of QRs simply because they are subject to negotiation with the exporting country, in terms of such key variables as the overall level of restraint, the tightness of coverage of individual categories, shifting among categories, carryovers into previous and succeeding years, and so forth. Indeed, this is one of the major advantages of the VER alternative for the exporting country. From the standpoint of the importing country, the greater looseness reduces further the effectiveness of the import controls, relative to QRs, in limiting imports.

It is also frequently argued that VERs are less effective than QRs in restraining imports because they are politically easier to remove and thus likely to be of shorter duration.[25] It is true, as already noted, that VERs require frequent renewal while legislated QRs usually carry no termination date. But there is little evidence from U.S. experience that VERs come off more readily than QRs. It is true that the steel VER was permitted to expire in 1974. And the meat VER disappeared temporarily in recent years, but it was backed up by a U.S. quota law so the president in fact waived the back-up QR as well as the VER. But VERs may turn into QRs (as in oil) or into quasi-QRs (VERs backed up by QRs, as in cotton and now synthetic and woolen textiles), and their terms may tighten with renewal as in steel. And any QRs implemented under escape clause procedures, rather than legislated by Congress, do carry time limitations (though they can be renewed indefinitely). Finally, the recent unilateral U.S. import liberalization steps have focused more on QRs, with the elimination of the oil and sugar quotas and the expansion of dairy quotas, than on VERs.

The crucial issue determining the retention of both VERs and QRs is the balance of domestic political forces supporting and opposing them. Seen in this context, there is one important structural reason why VERs might last longer than QRs. VERs produce no overt compensation or retaliation. Thus they avoid any costs to other industries in the importing country, and avoid one important source of political opposition relative to QRs, where compensation and/or retaliation normally occurs.[26] Liberal trade interests thus develop sufficient power to terminate VERs only when price concerns become dominant, as recently in meat. They derive no support from other producing interests who, in seeking a termination of QRs, want termination of the compensation that reduced their own protection or the foreign retaliation that limited their own exports.

A related effectiveness question is whether VERs or QRs can be implemented more quickly.[27] That issue is also indeterminate. VERs have to be negotiated with other countries, QRs legislated by Congress or implemented through the lengthy procedures of the escape clause (Tariff Commission plus the president) or national security provision (study by the Treasury, formerly by the Office of Emergency Preparedness, and action by the president). In some cases, the executive has enough leverage with other countries to implement VERs quickly. However, many countries are becoming increasingly resistant to VER requests—note the reticence of Korea and Taiwan, as well as Japan, which balked at synthetic textile VERs for more than two years.

In sum, VERs clearly restrain trade less than QRs. This is of course a disadvantage to the industry seeking protection in the importing country, and an advantage to importers and consumers there as well as to the industry of the exporting country. (The advantage is greater for the former, because they benefit from continued imports from non-restraining countries.) Its effect on the overall balance between VERs and QRs can only be determined after the discussion of other considerations to which we now turn.[28]

Distributional Effects

Any increase in trade barriers reduces consumers' surplus. In Figure 15-1, which portrays the effect of an increase in prices from Pw to Pus due to the imposition of a new trade barrier, the reduction equals PwSRPus. Area E represents the transfer from U.S. consumers to the U.S. government, which results if the increase in barriers takes the form of a hike in the American tariff.[29]

A QR or VER, having the same effect on the level of imports, would under conditions of pure competition also raise prices from Pw to Pus.[30] However, there would be no transfer of revenue to the U.S. government unless it were to auction off quota tickets, which is not done under any existing QR. The disposition of the "tariff-equivalent revenue" of area E is thus indeterminate under a QR or VER. It will be shared between U.S. importers and foreign exporters, each of which will strive to maximize his share of the total.

There are two plausible bases on which this division might take place. One is the relative concentration of market power on the buying and selling sides of the trade. An oligopolistic industry selling to a competitive market of importers might well be able to capture most of area E, while an oligopsonistic set of importers buying from a market of competitive sellers might also be able to do so.[31]

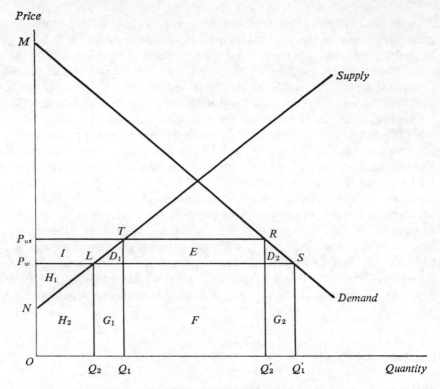

D_1, D_2 = Production and consumption deadweight losses, respectively;

E = Government revenue deriving from a tariff, or "tariff-equivalent revenue" in case of QR or VER:

$G_1 + F + G_2$ = Quantity imported in absence of restriction;

H_1 = Producers' surplus without restriction;

$H_1 + H_2$ = Level of domestic production under free trade;

$I + H_2$ = Producers' surplus with restriction;

MSP_w = Consumers' surplus without restriction;

MRP_{us} = Consumers' surplus with restriction.

Figure 15-1. The Economic Effects of Trade Restrictions.

A second possible explanation relates to the administration of the controls. Under QRs, the importing country organizes the market and assigns quotas. It may assign the quotas either to domestic importers (as in oil) or to exporting countries (as in sugar). If importers get the allocations, they should be able to capture most of the scarcity premia triggered by the restraints. On the other hand, under quotas allocated to exporting countries *or under VERs*, even when the VERs are reinforced by QRs in the importing country, the exporting country organizes the market and should be able to gain a predominant share of area E. In essence, restricting trade from the supply side strengthens the ability of the seller to maximize; restricting trade by a similar amount from the demand side strengthens the ability of the buyer to maximize.

The two explanations can be combined. The exporting country would be in the strongest position to maximize its share of area E if its export industry was relatively concentrated and if it also administered the controls, as via VERs. The importing country would be in the strongest position if its buying power was relatively concentrated and if it administered the controls via QRs allocated to domestic importers. The results would be less predictable if the criteria were mixed, especially under duopoly conditions where both the buying and selling sides of the market were heavily concentrated.[32]

Empirical work in this area is scarce. The evidence that does exist, however, suggests that administration of the controls largely determines the distribution of the tariff-equivalent revenue, at least in industries where neither oligopoly nor oligopsony dominates. The fact that VERs themselves foster added concentration in the exporting industry in question, as appears to have occurred in both textiles and steel, reinforces the dominance of this factor.[33] There would thus seem to be a significant difference between the microeconomic effects of VERs and most QRs.[34]

The clearest evidence comes from the oil, textile, and steel restraints. Under the oil QRs, "quota tickets" were allocated to U.S. importers. Some holders of these tickets exchanged them for domestic oil, instead of actually importing foreign crude or petroleum products, "which enables them to realize about the same value as they would receive from selling the ticket."[35] The imputed price of the tickets was basically determined by the difference between the U.S. and world price for oil (PusPw in Figure 15-1).[36] Hence the reduced U.S. consumers' surplus was captured by other Americans, through the operation of the quota system.[37] The oil industry is about equally concentrated on the selling and buying sides, so it appears that it was the retention of administrative initiative by the United States that determined the distributional effects.

Similarly, under the textile VERs in Japan and several other countries, export quotas are allocated to domestic firms largely on the basis of their historical market shares. Some of these quota holders sell some of their allocations to firms that will actually export to the American market.[38] The price of the tickets, again, presumably reflects most or all of the scarcity premia generated by the import restraints.[39] MITI has tried to assure this outcome in Japan by rejecting applications for export licenses when offer prices are too low, by penalizing firms whose prices are too low in the determination of quota allocations in subsequent years, and by providing bonuses in succeeding quota years for firms that most expand their total receipts.[40] Thus the textile exporters capture most of area E. The textile industry is highly competitive on both the exporting and importing sides, so it is again quite plausible that the administrative initiative is determinative.

Indeed, this particular VER has had a self-reinforcing distributional effect by promoting greater cartelization of foreign textile industries, as larger firms have bought out smaller ones explicitly to get their export quota allocations.[41]

However, U.S. textile importers and retailers report that they apply their usual markups to the cost of the VER ticket as well as to the usual, pre-quota price of the textile goods. They regard the tickets as an additional cost to them, on which they must pay import duties, financing charges, agents' fees, and so forth. If they cannot pass on this markup to their customers, their demand for the goods in question and hence the price of the VER tickets will decline. Since their combined markups may raise the final price of the product to consumers by a factor of three to six, the distribution thereof is central to the distribution of the overall scarcity premia. Some of it clearly goes to other Americans: the duty on the VER ticket component of the import price to the U.S. government, whatever share of the financing is provided by U.S. banks, and so forth. Some of it may go to foreigners other than the sellers of the product or the quota tickets, such as agents and other middlemen who operate on a percentage basis. These institutional arrangements render much more difficult any analysis of the geographical distribution of the price increases stemming from VERs, at least in the case of textiles.[42]

Foreign steel originally penetrated the U.S. market in significant quantity, in the late 1950s, because of interruptions of domestic supply resulting from strikes by U.S. steelworkers. It increased its U.S. market share further during each succeeding strike, or period of stockpiling by U.S. steel users who feared future strikes. But it always maintained most of its newly won share of the U.S. market, and even increased it further, after domestic production resumed. (The data are in Table 15-2.) The main reason was price, which became determinative after American producers learned (from necessity) that the quality and reliability of foreign steel was comparable to domestic production.[43] This competition from foreign steel was a major factor in the relative stability displayed by steel prices in the United States throughout the 1959 to 1967 period, despite the high degree of concentration of the U.S. industry. The U.S. steel industry admits as much.[44]

This price stability deteriorated rapidly with the inauguration of the steel VER in 1968. In response to the VER, European and especially Japanese steel producers radically changed their pricing strategy. They no longer sought to achieve and maintain growing shares of the U.S. market through price competition. Indeed, they explicitly priced their steel at a small discount below comparable U.S. steel—to compensate for "quality differences"—and raised their prices *pari passu* with each price rise by U.S. companies. Thus the difference between the U.S. and world prices for steel virtually disappeared, which clearly indicated that the foreign com-

Table 15-2
Steel Mill Products: Shipments, Exports, Imports, Apparent Supply, and Steel Trade Balance
(In Millions of Net Tons)

Year	Net Domestic Shipments	Exports	Imports	Apparent Domestic Supply	Imports as Percent of Apparent Supply	Steel Balance of Trade Millions of tons	Amount (millions)
1957	79.9	5.3	1.2	75.7	1.5	+4.2	+$577
1958	59.9	2.8	1.7	58.8	2.9	+1.1	+372
1959	69.4	1.7	4.4[a]	72.1	6.2	−2.7	−150
1960	71.1	3.0	3.4	71.5	4.7	−0.4	+152
1961	66.1	2.0	3.2	67.3	4.7	−1.2	+41
1962	70.6	2.0	4.1[a]	72.6	5.6	−2.1	−60
1963	75.6	2.2	5.4	78.8	6.9	−3.2	−163
1964	84.9	3.4	6.4	87.9	7.3	−3.0	−127
1965	92.7	2.5	10.4[a]	100.6	10.3	−7.9	−670
1966	90.0	1.7	10.8	99.0	10.9	−9.1	−788
1967	83.9	1.7	11.5	93.7	12.2	−9.8	−877
1968	91.9	2.2	18.0[a]	107.6	16.7	−15.8	−1,532
1969	93.9	5.2	14.0[b]	102.7	13.7	−8.8	−946
1970	90.8	7.1	13.4	97.1	13.8	−6.3	−948
1971	87.0	2.8	18.3[b]	102.5	17.9	−15.5	−2,060
1972	91.8	2.9	17.7	106,6	16.6	−14.8	−2,190

[a]Year of steel strike, or threat thereof due to negotiation of new labor contract.
[b]First year of steel VER.
Source: American Iron and Steel Institute, U.S. Department of Commerce.

panies were reaping virtually all of the increase in price triggered by the trade restraints.

International trade in steel is highly concentrated on both the selling and buying sides. Thus it is likely that the administrative arrangements of the controls largely determined this outcome. Despite the high degree of oligopoly maintained by virtually all national (or regional, in the case of the EC) steel industries within their domestic markets, price competition clearly did take place among them through foreign trade before the imposition of the VER. U.S. wholesale prices for iron and steel rose by 28.4 percent from 1967 through 1972, compared with a rise of less than 18 percent in wholesale prices of all industrial commodities,[45] after rising less than the aggregate price level in the earlier period. In addition, a U.S. district court has recently suggested that the steel VER probably violated the Sherman Antitrust Act and hence is illegal under U.S. law, thereby implying that trade was not so restrained before the VER. So there is strong evidence that the steel VER has sharply reduced competition in the entire U.S. steel market, and that the foreign producers have reaped most of the benefit from the higher prices of their sales into the United States.

The few estimates made by other authors support the view that foreign suppliers pick up most of the reduction in U.S. consumers' surplus when other countries administer the restraints, under VERs or QRs (sugar) that are allocated on a country basis, while Americans do so when QRs are allocated to them on a non-country basis by the U.S. government. Mintz[46] has estimated that the U.S. loss of "tariff-equivalent revenue" (area E in Figure 15-1 under a QR or VER system) to foreigners is negligible in the case of oil; about $300 million under the sugar QR, which as noted earlier is biased toward foreign suppliers because it is they who receive the quota allocations; and $53 million in 1970 for meat, where "the higher price paid under the quota...goes to the foreign exporters since the quotas are allocated to them." Magee[47] estimates that foreigners capture at least 66 percent of this "revenue" in steel, or about $175 million at the 1971 level of trade. He agrees with the above analysis on textiles, which suggests that foreign suppliers gained over $600 million in 1971 from the reduction in U.S. consumers' surplus. He attributes a loss of tariff-equivalent revenue of only $2 million to the dairy quotas, which are administered by the United States. Magee concludes that "loss of tariff-equivalent revenue accounted for almost a third of the U.S. social loss due to quotas [sic]," an outcome which is primarily attributable to administering two of the major restraints via VERs rather than via QRs allocated to U.S. importers.

Large amounts of money are thus involved in the allocation between Americans and foreign suppliers of the reduction in U.S. consumers' surplus triggered by VERs and QRs. The ability of foreigners to capture a much greater share of this total under VERs may play a major role in explaining why they are willing to accept such restraints, even at the cost of limiting the potential growth of volume of their sales.[48] Indeed, this phenomenon represents a significant degree of compensation to the restrained sellers—which is a politically more desirable form of compensation to the government of the exporting country than tariff cuts on some of its other exports, since the compensation accrues to the same people hurt by the restraints.[49]

Most businessmen, placing a high utility on reducing the variance of their sales and hence the possibility of overproduction (or underproduction, which may be psychically as well as financially costly in terms of lost opportunities), like nothing better than a predictable market, especially if they can dictate prices in that market. This phenomenon is particularly marked in industries that are already heavily oligopolized, such as steel, and may explain a good deal of the willingness—even eagerness—of the European and Japanese steel industries to restrain their exports to the United States.[50] Of course, it is far easier for an industry to cartelize in this fashion if it can point to a request for restraint from the importing country and conjure up worse consequences if it fails to do so. Under the blanket of the LTA, the Japanese may even have introduced quotas on some cotton textile items "for purposes of reducing competition among Japanese exporters and suppliers, (which) tended more to frustrate foreign buyers who were benefiting from the competition."[51] Correspondingly, the national cost of import restraints to the United States will tend to be significantly larger under VERs than under QRs, per dollar of deadweight loss, because of the loss of tariff-equivalent revenue in addition to the deadweight losses.[52]

A second distributional issue relates to the array of costs and benefits among the different supplying countries. VERs are usually applied only by the fastest growing suppliers, while QRs usually apply to all suppliers. Thus any small suppliers left outside the VER network obviously prefer VERs. Indeed, their market opportunity will be enhanced by the restraints on their largest competitors, and they will have an incentive to build their sales rapidly to hedge against the risk that they will subsequently be brought under the VER, or that the VER will turn into a QR.

Figure 15-2 modifies Figure 15-1 to depict this effect. A QR of $Q_2Q'_2$ would leave potential new suppliers with no scope for increased sales. A VER placing the same limitation ($Q_3Q'_3$) on traditional suppliers, however, would enable new suppliers, whose costs exceed those of the traditional suppliers but are less than those of suppliers in the importing country, to sell $Q'_3Q''_3$. Hence the U.S. price would rise only to P_{ns}, and the efficiency losses to the United States would be less than under QRs (only D_1+D_2). Area 1 would be the "tariff-equivalent revenue" contested between traditional suppliers and U.S. importers. Area 2 would be the loss of consumers' surplus relative to the free-trade alternative, which would however represent an increase in consumers' surplus relative to the QR alternative.

The largest supplier of a given product may also benefit from import restraints. Any such restraints tend to lock in market shares, and hence limit the scope for market penetration by new foreign suppliers who are also covered by the restraints.[53] QRs do this most completely because they cover all suppliers and may even benefit the strongest suppliers further if the quotas are allocated on a first-come first-served basis. But most VERs cover at least the several leading suppliers rather than just the single leader.[54] Thus the major losers among the exporting countries from VERs, relative to QRs, are likely to be the rapidly growing intermediate suppliers—who find the industry leader locked into his superior base even though he is no longer the most dynamic producer and their newly emerging competitors completely unrestrained. Korea and Taiwan in synthetic textiles are prototypes. The acquiescence of covered suppliers to the multilateralization of textile VERs into the LTA and its successor arrangement

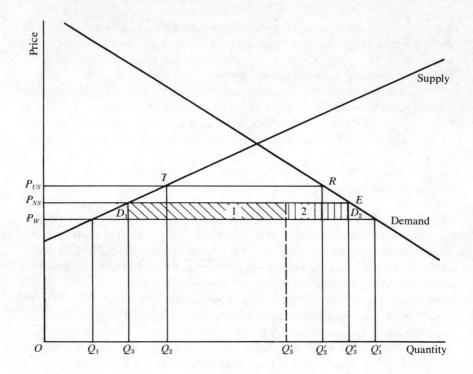

D_1, D_2 = Production and consumption deadweight losses, respectively;
1 = "Tariff-equivalent revenue" due to restrictions on traditional suppliers;
2 = Increase in consumers' surplus relative to QR alternative, due to imports from non-restrained countries.

Figure 15-2. The Economic Effects of QRs and VERs.

was motivated in part by precisely these kinds of concerns, though multilateralization was of course basically promoted by the United States and
other importers to increase the coverage of the overall restraint program.

Trade Policy Effects

VERs have several important effects on U.S. and world trade policy: the
possibility that their implementation can satisfy the protectionist demands
of individual industries and thus avoid import restrictions in additional
industries by avoiding altogether the legislative process, which would
otherwise be triggered as those protectionist industries sought QRs and
which is the only likely route to widespread protectionism in the United
States; the related erosion, by the same token, of domestic and interna-

tional rules and procedures for determining trade policy; and their impact in adding to the erosion of the most-favored-nation (MFN) principle.

Some liberal traders view VERs as "less bad" than QRs because of their lesser degree of trade restrictiveness, as outlined above. However, VERs and QRs may not really be alternatives if consideration is limited to a single industry. Few if any industries would seek protection via VERs if they thought they could obtain QRs. The U.S. administration argued that it had to negotiate a steel VER in 1968, but there was little risk that steel QRs would have been legislated at that time. A different administration made the same case for synthetic textile restraints in 1969, yet Congress failed to vote such quotas in 1970 despite eight months of effort. Any "advantages" that liberal traders might see in the greater flexibility of VERs might thus be more than offset by their greater ease of implementation in the first place.[56]

But VERs may well be "less bad" than QRs in terms of overall U.S. trade policy. For example, Congress might have passed a protectionist trade bill in 1970 had steel and meat not "been taken care of" with VERs in 1968. Abolition of the steel and textile VERs might well trigger major efforts by those industries, and leaders of their unions, to get legislated QRs. Such efforts could tip the political balance in the United States toward a protectionist trade bill.[57] And any such bill would almost certainly include quotas going far beyond steel and textiles, because Congress appears to oppose favored legislative treatment for particular industries threatened by imports.[58]

It is also true that VERs can help clear the way for trade liberalization. The first cotton textile VER with Japan, in 1957, made possible a four-year extension (the longest to that time) of the Reciprocal Trade Agreement Act and hence the Dillon Round of trade negotiations.[59] The Kennedy administration was able to assure Congressional support for the Trade Expansion Act, and hence the Kennedy Round, by first nullifying the opposition of the textile industry by negotiating a more comprehensive VER on cotton. The Nixon administration had no chance to achieve a liberal trade bill in the early 1970s, to authorize it to participate in a further round of trade negotiations, until it again satisfied the textile industry with a synthetics VER (and perhaps the steel industry by extending the steel VER). So, in trade policy terms, the relative merits of VERs and QRs must be considered in the overall context that exists at any given time rather than simply in terms of the different impact of the two approaches on the single industry in question.

The second trade policy issue is procedural. There are three major routes to import restriction in the United States. One is via existing law, which authorizes protection in cases of (a) "injury or threat of injury" from imports under the escape clause, (b) jeopardy to the national security, or (c) external threats to domestic agricultural support programs. Each of these authorizations lays out detailed procedural steps to assure that all interested parties will be heard before a decision is made.[60] The second is via new Congressional legislation, which by its nature triggers the airing of all sides of an issue both in public hearings and among Congressmen with different constituencies. The third is VERs, where no procedural requirements apply.

Democratic decision making is obviously fostered when provision is made for the input of all relevant considerations. VERs violate this basic principle. Industry representatives dominate the discussion, and financial support for political campaigns (as in textiles) and other acts of political back-scratching can easily dominate the outcome. No other voices may be heard at all—particularly if, like exporters and especially consumers, they are ineffectively represented within the government itself. So the interplay of national interests that attends all trade policy issues is least permitted to enter the decision-making process on VERs.[61] Indeed, as already indicated, the absence of such procedures may have actually led the government to violate the Sherman Act in negotiating the steel VER.

A similar, and related, loophole exists in the international trade rules. Article 19 of the GATT covers "Emergency Action on Imports of Particular Products" and applies only to increased imports resulting from "obligations incurred by a contracting party under this Agreement, including tariff concessions...," none of which relates to export restraints. Thus most observers conclude that the GATT does not cover VERs. But Article 11, aimed at the "General Elimination of Quantitative Restrictions," clearly states that "no prohibition or restrictions other than duties, taxes or other charges, whether made effective through quotas, import or *export licenses* ... shall be instituted or maintained on the importation of any product ... *or on the exportation or sale for export* of any product ..." (with the exception of agricultural, classification, or short-supply controls).

In practice, however, the GATT has exercised no jurisdiction over VERs.[62] Indeed, it has implicitly sanctioned both the cotton and all-fiber textile VERs by providing the forum within which they were multilateralized. Aside from textiles there has been no international guideline at all to which national laws and policies on VERs must conform. In turn, this has permitted the domestic situation just described in the United States. There is no requirement that an importing country seeking VERs provide compensation to the restrainer, or accept retaliation. As a result, an importing country can seek VERs for the benefits of a single industry without concern for any direct consequences for other industries. Both the procedural vacuum and the absence of other-industry effects add greatly to the ease of implementing VERs relative to QRs.

A final trade policy issue stems from the usual limitation of VER coverage to the major supplying countries, whereas QRs generally apply to all suppliers. The U.S. request for synthetic and woolen textile VERs, for example, was addressed solely to Asian countries although European countries supply a larger share of the U.S. market for some of the items covered.[63] The steel VERs covered both Japan and the Common Market,[64] but excluded Canada, some Europeans (e.g., Sweden and Austria) and some Asians (e.g., Korea and Australia). On the other hand, the meat VERs covered all major suppliers (but did exclude minor suppliers Canada and the United Kingdom). No firm conclusions can thus be drawn about the importance of this factor, and VERs do not seem to be promoting the formation of trade blocs. As long as the MFN rule continues to cover QRs (and tariffs), however,[65] VERs will provide a policy instrument that can be used in a discriminatory manner and thus heighten tensions between particular countries or geographic regions.

The Comparative Politics of VERs and QRs

VERs are alleged to raise fewer international political problems than QRs because of their greater flexibility, avoidance of repercussions on industries other than the one restrained (by avoiding compensation or retaliation under the GATT rules), and avoidance of spillover into broader issues of trade policy. My analysis of the economic effects, especially on this last point, tends to support the contention. And there have certainly been occasions when VERs were truly voluntary and hence raised no serious political problems. A recent example is steel where, as indicated above, the European and Japanese industries were as happy as the U.S. industry to eliminate the only arena in which they had previously been forced to compete.[66]

Some recent cases, however, are much less clear. Japan withstood major and accelerating U.S. efforts to induce it to adopt synthetic and woolen textile VERs from early 1969 until October 1971, when the United States applied the crudest and most blatant pressure to finally achieve Japanese acquiescence. Korea, Taiwan, and Hong Kong were equally unyielding over this period. Spain has wholly rejected U.S. efforts to induce it to accept VERs on shoes, and Italy has been unwilling to restrain on shoes unless Spain did.

Indeed, the United States suffered exceedingly high political (and economic) costs from pursuing the synthetic-woolen VERs so relentlessly with Japan. Part of the cost was the intangible but very real adverse impact which it had on overall U.S.-Japan relations, both because the Japanese felt they were simply being asked to redeem a campaign pledge made by President Nixon, which had no economic justification, and because President Nixon felt that Prime Minister Sato failed to deliver a VER after twice promising to do so. It is highly likely that the antipathy that the president developed toward these Japanese "betrayals" played an important role in his neglecting their sensitivities while dropping the "Nixon shocks" of July and August 1971 on Tokyo.[67]

More tangibly, the U.S. textile effort deflected the attention of both countries from the truly critical economic problems that were building up between them throughout 1969 to 1971: the mounting Japanese trade and payments surpluses, globally and with the United States, and the continued Japanese restrictions on imports (and capital inflows) that accelerated protectionist sentiments in the United States. The heavy costs associated with the international aspects of the New Economic Policy of August 1971 might have been avoided had these far more serious problems been addressed earlier, but the textile dispute kept them on the back burner.[68]

At the same time, the Japanese government proved unable or unwilling to force its textile industry to restrain. Hence it seemed finally to prefer that the United States take decisive action, so that it would avoid domestic political blame for "caving in to the American demands." U.S. QRs would probably have been less damaging to overall U.S.-Japan relations than the VERs that eventuated, particularly if they had been levied in 1969, but even had they been passed as part of a Mills bill in 1970 *without other protectionist elements*—which is precisely the legislation that the administration sought throughout the second half of 1970.

Any generalizations in this area are extremely hazardous. The relative desirability of VERs and QRs, in broad political terms, hinge on four factors: the political importance in the exporting country of the industry whose restraint is sought, the attitude of that industry toward restraint, the degree of overall national self-assertiveness (especially vis-à-vis the United States) in the country being asked to restrain, and the importance of that country to the United States. Politically, it is probably better for the United States itself to act via QRs versus a politically powerful industry that opposes restraint in a self-assertive nation of high importance to U.S. foreign policy. VERs would be more likely to minimize political costs if they were adopted by a politically weak industry that was willing to accept restraints (or even welcomed them, for the reasons outlined above, like the Japanese and European steel industries) in a relatively non-nationalistic society of lesser political importance to the United States. The attitude of the industry from which restraint is sought is probably the single most important factor. Of course, the degree of control sought will always be a major factor, as it was with Japan in 1969-71.

A second important international political implication of VERs is their discriminatory nature. As indicated above, most VERs cover only the most important supplying countries. Hence they deviate from the MFN rule that was installed at the center of the postwar trading system largely for political reasons. They carry especially high costs for those "middle countries" who have become significant enough to be covered under VERs but, unlike most leading suppliers, still have the internal dynamism and the market scope to grow a good deal more.

These considerations have related particularly to the relations between Japan and the other industrialized countries. Japan has been by far the major target of VER pressures, due to its phenomenal export success in a variety of industries. The United States has been a major applier of such pressure. But Europe has always done so as well, would doubtless have done so even more in the absence of its maintenance of discriminatory QRs against Japan on some of the same products, and is perhaps doing so even more rapidly now with the rapid rise of Japan's sales as it tries to diversify its export markets.

Yet Japan has also probably been more sensitive about foreign discrimination than has any other major country, particularly with regard to American policy.[69] So maximum discrimination and maximum sensitivity about discrimination have combined to heighten the political tensions surrounding VERs. The inclusion from the outset of the synthetic and woolen textile VER of Korea, Taiwan, and Hong Kong helped alleviate its discriminatory connotation, but an Asian bias clearly remained since no serious effort was made to exact similar restraints from several major European suppliers.

On the other hand, QRs raise problems with a larger number of suppliers precisely because they are not discriminatory. In the case of synthetic and woolen textiles, for example, U.S. quotas on European exports would clearly have damaged the Atlantic relationship at the same time that they relieved some of the strain on the Pacific relationship. So VERs may enable the importing country to avoid political problems too. It should also be noted that QRs, while usually less overtly discriminating than VERs, can also encompass discriminatory aspects: the allocation of U.S. sugar quotas to foreign countries, while based in principle on actual shipments in the 1963-64 base period, were in fact altered significantly in response to lobbying activities, and large and/or nearby countries are usually favored de facto by first-come first-served quotas that are allocated to domestic importers for other products.

The LTA on cotton textiles tried to resolve the discrimination problem by placing VERs within a multilateral framework within which importing countries "guaranteed" restraining exporters that other exporters would be covered as well. The meat VER tried to do so by including virtually all suppliers. So discrimination is not inherent in VERs, and can be avoided in several ways if it is deemed sufficiently important in particular cases. And discriminatory use of QRs may rise in the future, if the prohibition of such treatment is excised from the GATT as many observers now propose. Even if QRs are not overtly discriminatory, they can be used de facto to bite hardest on the most rapidly growing suppliers simply by setting an early base period against which all countries are permitted similar percentage increases. So the two may not differ too much on this count in the future, with the important political difference that the discrimination of VERs is overt while the discrimination of QRs can be much more subtle, and indeed be treated as non-discriminatory under the international rules. The desire of the importing country to achieve effective restraint and the desire of the covered exporting country to avoid discrimination (for both economic and political reasons) both suggest, of course, that VERs should either be generalized or QRs used instead.

Conclusions and Policy Recommendations

Barring significant changes in international and national trade policy and practices, efforts by importing countries to negotiate VERs are likely to continue to proliferate. This is certainly true in the United States.

Congress clearly likes VERs. The Meat Import Act of 1964 explicitly authorized negotiated VERs as an alternative to its mandatory QRs. The Mills bill of 1970 authorized the VER alternative in all of its QR provisions. The Trade Reform Act submitted by President Nixon in early 1973 made a similar proposal, which became law in the Trade Act of 1974. Even the Burke-Hartke bill would permit VERs to supersede the QRs that it sought on virtually all U.S. imports.

The executive also likes VERs. It would certainly prefer their flexibility to the mandatory nature of any QR legislation. It usually has a penchant for avoiding the limiting and time-consuming procedural requirements of present law. Individuals within the executive branch can pursue their special interests with such an under-the-table policy instrument. VERs enable any administration to play favorites both at home and abroad.

The analysis of this chapter suggests that VERs should be brought fully within the same domestic and international legal and procedural requirements that govern QRs. This would mean making them subject to Article 19 of the GATT, or any new "safeguard" provision which emerges from new international negotiations, and to the criteria and procedures of the escape clause in the United States. Action to do so is quite urgent in view of the strong prospects for their further proliferation.

VERs are far easier to implement than QRs because they are now subject to no domestic or international procedural restraints, and because they involve no other domestic interests through compensation or retaliation requirements. They restrict trade less than QRs, but there is no evidence that they are likely to be of shorter duration. Hence, on balance, their availability outside any legal or procedural constraints is quite likely to increase the degree to which international trade is restrained.

VERs may also raise even greater international political problems than QRs. Exporting countries are becoming increasingly reluctant to adopt VERs, which tendency can be expected to grow with the continuing decline of relative U.S. political and economic power and the accelerated sense of independence in most potential VER countries. Exporting countries, particularly Japan but also others throughout Asia and Latin America, will grow increasingly resentful of discrimination as their world role grows.

There is one case, of course, where VERs do not raise international political problems: where they are actually welcomed, or even sought, by the "restraining" industry to boost its oligopolistic position. By that very token, however, the VERs significantly exacerbate inflation in the importing country if, as is frequently the case, QRs are not likely to eventuate in their stead. In addition, the distributional effects of VERs add to their costs relative to QRs in the importing country. These effects argue against VERs for reasons of both global trade policy and national self-interest in the country seeking import relief.

Under present trade policies and practices, however, VERs provide two benefits relative to QRs. By providing the United States with an alternative to legislation to limit imports in particular sectors, they avoid the risk that protection will be accorded far more widely. And by permitting the exporting country to organize the restraints, they provide compensation within the restricted industry—the kind of compensation most needed by the government of the restraining country and most saleable to the "compensating" industry in the importing country. It is particularly important for the United States to be able to extend such compensation during periods when the president has no Congressional authority to provide compensation through lowering import barriers in other industries, as was the case from mid-1967 until the end of 1974.

Both of these benefits of VERs could be retained without VERs themselves, however. First, the United States should amend its escape clause so that it will be effective in permitting temporary QRs (or increased tariffs) for industries that are injured by imports. There is a widespread consensus in the United States that the escape clause has been too tight to deal with legitimate problems of import injury since 1962 and that it should be loosened by (a) eliminating the link between imports and previous tariff concessions and (b) requiring that imports be only "the primary" or "a substantial" cause of the injury rather than "the major" cause. These changes, which were in fact made by the Trade Act of 1974, should revitalize the escape clause, with its careful procedural safeguards, as a fair but effective avenue for import relief. Hence it would obviate the need for industries to seek legislated QRs to provide them with import protection, and the need for the executive to pursue VERs to avoid the wider manifestations of such Congressional action.

Once the criteria of such a modified escape clause were met through its standard procedures, the availability of VERs rather than QRs to provide the temporary import relief could be beneficial. The choice between the two instruments would turn basically on two issues: (1) whether the United States wanted to discriminate overtly among foreign suppliers, which is done more easily with VERs, and (2) whether it wanted to compensate the exporting country by letting it seize the scarcity premia generated by the VER itself or by extending trade concessions on other products. There would be policy advantages in retaining such flexibility once the VERs were brought within the same legal limitations as QRs—which was *not* done by the Trade Act of 1974, leaving the VER loophole intact.

Second, all such VERs and QRs (and increased tariffs) should henceforth take place within the framework of a new "import safeguard" mechanism negotiated internationally and embodied in an amended Article 19 of GATT. Such a mechanism should encompass the features recommended in the Rey Report: limited duration for all restraints, a declining degree of protection throughout their lives, and accompanying domestic programs to assure that they will in fact turn out to be temporary. In my view, even safeguards of this type should require compensation from the importing country and authorize retaliation by the exporting country, in the absence of satisfactory compensation, to assure that it will be no easier, from an international standpoint, to use the new safeguards than it was to use the old ones.[70] However, it should be possible to grant "compensation" within the restrained industry itself by letting the exporting country administer the restraints via VERs or by assigning QR allocations to each supplying country (as the United States has done with its sugar quotas).[71] This new type of compensation should not be granted when it would foster cartelization, however; in such cases, the traditional approach to compensation (via other industries) should be used instead.[72]

Third, developing countries should receive tariff preferences (preferably zero duties) for any of their exports to industrialized countries limited by VERs (or QRs) under the new safeguard mechanism. This would maximize their opportunity to expand their market shares at the expense of industrialized country exporters under non-country QRs and would at least help them fill the quotas allocated to them under either country QRs or VERs, without exceeding the aggregate level of imports sought by the importing country. It would also enable developing countries to improve their terms of trade at the expense of the treasury of the importing country, by charging sufficiently higher prices to capture the revenue formerly collected as customs duties. These gains would at least partially obviate the high costs of trade restriction to such countries, which would be particularly important under the proposed new trade regime in which (geographically non-comprehensive) VERs would by virtue of their being subjected to procedural limitations be used much less frequently, relative to (geographically comprehensive) QRs, than in the past. However, the U.S. Trade Act of 1974 explicitly *rejects* preferences for goods covered by VERs or QRs.

Each of these three changes in U.S. and international trade policy is desirable in its own right. It is suggested here that taken together, they would also turn VERs from an under-the-table device that permits countries to avoid both domestic and international trade rules into an acceptable, and perhaps useful, commercial policy instrument in the future. Benefits of both an economic and international political nature would flow to a variety of countries as a result.

Notes

1. To be sure, VERs have also existed since the 1930s. For an interesting short history see Stanley Metzger, *Lowering Non-Tariff Barriers* (Brookings Institution, 1974). Interwar VERs, such as those on French imports of Dutch and Italian agricultural goods and British, German, and Belgian manufactured goods, are discussed as "bilateral quotas" in Heinrich Heuser, *Control of International Trade* (George Routledge and Sons, 1939), especially chapter IX.

2. See especially Jagdish Bhagwati, "On the Equivalence of Tariffs and Quotas," in Robert E. Baldwin and others, *Trade, Growth and the Balance of Payments* (Rand McNally, 1965), pp. 53-67; the comments thereon by Hirofumi Shibata, "A Note on the Equivalence of Tariffs and Quotas," *American Economic Review,* Vol. LVIII, No. 1 (March 1968), pp. 137-42; and the reply by Bhagwati, "More on the Equivalence of Tariffs and Quotas," ibid., pp. 142-46. For the critical differences that result in a dynamic model see Mordechai E. Kreinen, "More on the Equivalence of Tariffs and Quotas," *Kyklos,* Vol. XXIII-1970-Fasc.1, pp. 75-79, and Ingo Walter, "On the Equivalence of Tariffs and Quotas: A Comment," *Kyklos,* Vol. XXIV-1971-Fasc. 1, pp. 111-2.

3. The only exceptions I could uncover were Shibata, *American Economic Review,* in three paragraphs, and brief references to their different distributional effects in Richard E. Caves and Ronald Jones, *World Trade and Payments: An Introduction* (Little, Brown & Co., 1973), p. 289, and Robert Stern, "Tariffs and Other Measures of Trade Control: A Survey of Recent Developments," *Journal of Economic Literature,* Vol. XI, No. 3 (September 1973), p. 870.

4. Most of them are analyzed in C. Fred Bergsten, *Completing the*

GATT: Toward New International Rules to Govern Export Controls (British-North American Committee, 1974).

5. I inject here the caveat "ostensibly" because we shall soon see that VERs bring sufficient benefits to exporting countries or industries that, in some circumstances, they may actually be welcomed by those countries or industries.

6. The term "orderly marketing agreements" avoids this problem, but "voluntary export restraint" is less inaccurate and understood more widely so I use it in this chapter.

7. There are also numerous trade-restraining agreements that have the same effect as VERs. An example is the Automotive Products Trade Agreement of 1965 between the United States and Canada, under which the United States essentially limited its exports of automobiles and parts to Canada by promoting growth in Canadian production of those items—to avoid a perceived threat that Canada would impose its own limitations on automotive imports in the absence of some such U.S. action. And multinational firms may sometimes be permitted to invest in a host country only if they limit the imports of the new subsidiaries from the parent firm. The sharply different institutional features of such arrangements differentiate their effects from the straightforward VERs under consideration here, however, and they are excluded from the analysis.

8. The U.S. government denies playing any formal role in the arrangements, and its position is supported by the absence of any U.S. machinery to back up the VERs. However, it clearly negotiated them with the foreign industries in 1968 and again in 1971.

9. Unless the president waives the quotas themselves for overriding "national interest" reasons, as he did in 1972, 1973, and 1974.

10. Even a complete list of VERs and their trade coverage would not provide a satisfactory basis for assessing their significance because of the familiar problem that the volume of trade is *reduced* as the VERs (or QRs) are *tightened*. For a partial listing of the widespread use of VERs through the early 1960s see Gardner Patterson, *Discrimination in International Trade, The Policy Issues 1945-1965* (Princeton University Press, 1966), pp. 295-6. For a detailed discussion of interwar VERs see Heuser, *Control of International Trade*.

11. Press Release #183, Office of the Special Representative for Trade Negotiations, June 19, 1973. Imports of these shoes, primarily sneakers, were valued at about $40 million in 1972.

12. An EC Commission working party has reportedly listed 55 cases in which Japan has introduced VERs "in the hope of avoiding restrictions by the Community." *Journal of Commerce* (August 3, 1973), p. 9. And addi-

tional Japanese VERs on sales to Europe (e.g., television sets to Britain and tape recorders to Italy) were announced after that date.

13. A new area for the growth of VERs may occur in East-West trade. The U.S.-Soviet commercial agreement of 1972 calls for VERs by the exporting country in any product where the importing country declares unilaterally that "market disruption" has occurred.

14. There are of course other similarities between VERs and QRs, that will be ignored in this analysis. For example, either type of restraint on trade to a single market deflects trade in the restrained product into other markets; but there is no systematic difference between VERs and QRs in this regard.

15. For a fascinating account of the complex machinery that the Japanese government and industry associations had to create to administer the original cotton textile controls, see John Lynch, *Toward An Orderly Market: An Intensive Study of Japan's Voluntary Quota in Cotton Textile Exports* (Tokyo: Sophia University, 1968), especially chapter 6.

16. For example, the share of U.S. steel imports obtained by non-restrainers doubled, from 12 percent to 23 percent, between 1969 and early 1973. This issue is discussed in Caroline Prestieau and Jacques Henry, *Non-Tariff Trade Barriers As a Problem in International Development* (Private Planning Association of Canada), especially p. 158.

17. Evasion of VER limits is not the only motivation for Japanese foreign direct investment in textiles. Indeed it is conscious Japanese policy to upgrade Japan's industrial base by exporting its lowest wage, lowest productivity industries—such as textiles—particularly if they are also major polluters and heavy users of energy. One implication is that the Japanese textile VER may have become unnecessary even from the stand-point of the U.S. textile industry, which view is supported by the failure of the Japanese to fill their quotas in many commodity categories in recent years.

18. There are also numerous proposals to relax the non-discrimination rule, which has governed QRs throughout the life of the GATT, in the future. Such proposals are made by Anthony Solomon in Chapter 16 and Eric Wyndham-White in Chapter 19, and in the U.S. Trade Reform Act of 1974.

19. Warren Hunsberger, *Japan and the United States in World Trade* (Harper and Row, for the Council on Foreign Relations, 1964), p. 323, called this "The most serious administrative difficulty" of the cotton VER in its early days.

20. The response of the U.S. government provides a fascinating anecdote in the history of trade controls. Overruling all of his advisors who had concluded that this Canadian loophole had to be plugged, both to implement faithfully his policy of limiting meat imports and to be fair to suppliers who could not take advantage of it, President Nixon in early 1970 refused—due to the rise in meat prices—to authorize the imposition by the United States of QRs on meat imports from Canada. As a result, the VER limits were sharply liberalized at the first opportunity to accommodate (rather than stop) the transshipments.

21. This "problem" could be avoided by basing restraint levels on a constant *share* of the market in the importing country, to be monitored *ex post*. In practice, however, both QRs and VERs are almost always defined in absolute volume or dollar terms.

22. The tighter the VER restraints, in terms of barring carryover of shortfalls from one year to the next and shifting of allowables among restrained categories, the more likely is this result.

23. *Journal of Commerce* (February 22, 1974), p. 6. Meyer Bernstein, for many years Director of International Affairs of the United Steelworkers of America, attacks the steel VER as perverse on precisely these grounds (see Chapter 14).

24. Lynch, *Toward an Orderly Market*, p. 157.

25. Hunsberger, *Japan and the U.S. in World Trade*, p. 364 and Patterson, *Discrimination in International Trade*, p. 298.

26. I include the modifier "overt," because VERs may provide compensation to the restraining country *within* the industry being restrained and because they may levy costs on the importing country in terms of its broader economic and even political relations with the country on which export restraint is urged. These issues are discussed in the text.

27. As distinguished from the more important question of whether VERs or QRs are more likely to be adopted *at all,* which is discussed in the section on "Trade Policy Effects."

28. There is no way to generalize about the relative effectiveness of VERs and tariffs. But Shibata, "A Note on the Equivalence of Tariffs and Quotas," p. 141, is clearly wrong in stating that "the protectionists are essentially indifferent between quotas and tariffs," for the reasons pointed out by Kreinen, "More on the Equivalence of Tariffs and Quotas": an increase in demand in the importing country leads to increased domestic production and/or prices under quotas, but (at least partially) to increased imports (with smaller price rises) under tariffs.

29. Area I represents the transfer to American producers. Areas D_1 and D_2 are the production and consumption deadweight losses that reflect the reduction in efficiency generated by the increased tariff.

30. Bhagwati, "On the Equivalence of Tariffs and Quotas." See also Rachel McCulloch and Harry G. Johnson, "A Note on Proportionately Distributed Quotas," *American Economic Review,* Vol. LXIII, No. 4 (September, 1973), pp. 726-32, who demonstrate that the price-quantity equilibrium "does not depend on whether consumers or producers receive the import licenses." When competitive conditions do not exist, this equivalency between a tariff and quota may break down; for a survey of the literature, see Stern, "Tariffs and Other Measures of Trade Control," pp. 868-70. The present discussion focuses solely on the differential distribution of benefits under QRs and VERs, whose overall effect on price and import levels is assumed to be equivalent.

31. As suggested by Shibata, "A Note on the Equivalence of Tariffs and Quotas," pp. 139-42.

32. When retail prices are frozen, as they were in the United States under Phase I and Phase III ½ of the Nixon incomes policy in 1971 and mid-1973, foreigners should be able to seize any increase in the scarcity premia caused by trade restraints even under QRs. This is because increases in the "landed cost of imports," though one of the few exceptions permitted from the freeze, can be passed on only dollar-for-dollar. Thus all increases in scarcity premia accrue to the foreign seller (assuming no illegal kickbacks to the U.S. importers to circumvent the freeze). Similar results occur under any type of price controls for any increases in the scarcity premia that exceed the price increases permitted by the controls. I ignore this case in the analysis in the text.

33. For textiles, see the discussion in the text. For steel, *Economic and Foreign Policy Effects of Voluntary Restraint Agreements on Textiles and Steel,* A Report by the Comptroller General of the United States, March 1974, p. 24, concluded that the ". . . 1969 arrangements reduced competition among Japanese steel companies." Heuser, *Control of International Trade,* p. 121 concluded that "combination (oligopoly) . . . undoubtedly receives a new impetus from the practice of bilateral quota restrictions (VERs)."

34. Another issue is whether consumers really get the "consumers' surplus." The more concentrated an industry, on either the selling or buying side (or both), the less likely are they to do so. For example, a reduction in trade barriers in a monopsonistic industry may simply increase importers' profits. This issue arises irrespective of the nature of the import restraint in place or being removed, however, and hence is not treated in this chapter. Anticipating the conclusion to be reached shortly in the text, it does suggest that, in the real world, the effect on consumers of a trade restriction can range across a wide spectrum: from 100 percent of the theoretical consumers' surplus in a highly competitive industry where

trade is restrained via a VER, to nothing in a highly concentrated industry regardless of the method of control.

35. Cabinet Task Force on Oil Import Control. *The Oil Import Question* (Government Printing Office, 1970), p. 86.

36. Pro-rationing of U.S. domestic production of course played a major role, along with the import quotas, in preserving this price differential.

37. Auctioning rather than allocating the quota tickets would also "assure that the benefit of permitted low-cost imports is fully realized by [the public of] the importing country," Cabinet Task Force on Oil, ibid. A similar issue arises under VERs with regard to distributing the benefits within the exporting country. Export quota tickets could be auctioned or sold at a fixed price, as was done by the Dutch government on its restrained level of butter exports to France in the 1930s (Heuser, *Control of International Trade*, p. 114) instead of allocated free.

38. Lynch, *Toward an Orderly Market*, p. 157, reports that Japanese firms were assessed fines by the Japanese government under the cotton VER if they did not use all of their export quotas, so had an incentive to "transfer" their tickets instead. (On the other hand, their quotas were determined on the basis of each previous year's sales so they had an even greater incentive to actually fill their quotas, as indicated above.) There are unverified industry reports that quota tickets have been sold by holders in one restraining country to sellers in a second restraining country.

39. Richard Ward (Director, Foreign Buying, Montgomery Ward), "Remarks to Republican Task Force on International Trade," January 29, 1972, reports that the price of export "tickets" often amounted to $2.50-4 per dozen units, raising the price to U.S. importers by 10 percent or more. Industry sources report more recently that the premia often amount to 15 to 30 percent of the ex-quota prices, Comptroller General's Report, pp. 26-27.

40. Lynch, *Toward an Orderly Market*, pp. 152, 156, indicates that price levels of actual sales were accorded a 30 percent weighting in the formula for determining future quotas.

41. The seizing of the scarcity premia by foreign textile producers can also be inferred from the findings in G. C. Hufbauer, Naygara Aziz, and Asghar Ali, "Cotton Textile and Leather Exports: What Cost Foreign Exchange?" *Pakistan Development Review*, Vol. IX, No. 3 (Autumn 1969), pp. 330-3. They conclude that "profits on some exports are so large that the goods could be sold abroad at a gain to the manufacturer, but at a loss to the nation."

42. The Comptroller General's Report, pp. 26-28, concluded that only about one-third of the price increase induced by the quotas went to foreign suppliers while the rest went to U.S. importers and retailers. In discussing

the interwar VERs, Heuser, *Control of International Trade,* pp. 115, 118, points to such a division of the scarcity premia between exporting and importing countries under VERs. He notes that French retailers, who first opposed the VERs bitterly, proposing QRs instead so that *they* could reap the scarcity premia, soon accepted them because they began to get enough of the induced price increases to offset the effect on their profits of the reduced volume of trade.

43. The latest evidence of the importance of price in this industry is the shift back to U.S. steel by a number of U.S. steel users in the wake of the 1971-73 exchange-rate changes, through which the Japanese yen and German mark (including its 1969 revaluation) have both appreciated sharply against the dollar.

44. Stewart S. Cort (Chairman of Bethlehem Steel and spokesman for the U.S. steel industry), Statement before the House Ways and Means Committee, June 7, 1973, p. 18: "Production costs are not the determining factor in steel export prices of foreign producers. They frequently price the product to get into our market to achieve domestic economic objectives." Cort used this argument to support protection for U.S. steel, charging predatory pricing by foreign companies. In so doing, however, he clearly recognizes the reduction in prices to U.S. steel users from such imports; foreign sellers covered by the VER hardly need to cut prices "to get into our market."

45. *Survey of Current Business* (January 1974), pp. S-8, S-9. This difference narrowed in 1973, but almost wholly because of the effect of the explosion of fuel prices on the all-commodity index. Kurt Orban, president of a steel-importing company and president of the American Importers Association, has testified before Congress that "the true market price [of steel] has risen much more, because of all kinds of hidden increases." See his statement on the Trade Reform Act of 1973 before the House Ways and Means Committee, May 14, 1973, p. 6. To be sure, factors other than the VER have affected U.S. steel prices in recent years, and high demand for steel in foreign markets held U.S. imports even below VER levels in 1969. Nevertheless, the close correlation between institution of the VER and the dramatic acceleration of U.S. steel prices, relative to other U.S. prices, strongly suggests that the restraints are a major cause thereof.

46. Ilse Mintz, *U.S. Import Quotas: Costs and Consequences* (Washington: American Enterprise Institute for Public Policy Research, 1973). Her estimates cited in the text are drawn from pp. 78, 40, and 76, respectively.

47. Stephen P. Magee, "The Welfare Effects of Restrictions on U.S. Trade," *Brookings Papers on Economic Activity 3; 1972,* pp. 671-4.

48. At least some of the interwar VERs seem to have been negotiated for precisely this reason. See Heuser, *Control of International Trade*, p. 112.

49. Still another alternative would be a lump-sum payment (e.g., foreign aid) from the United States to the exporting country in lieu of the higher prices it could charge under the VER. Rachel McCulloch, "Import Quotas and Resource Allocation" (unpublished Ph.D. thesis, University of Chicago), pp. 54-56, has demonstrated that both the monopolist and the importing nation can improve their welfare through such arrangements. However, such compensation would require fiscal appropriations in the United States, whereas one of its basic objectives in pursuing the VER route is precisely to avoid the legislative process (see text discussion), and it remains unclear how importers could be prevented from exploiting the scarcity premia themselves. Such a lump-sum payment, of $375 million, was apparently pledged by the United States to get Korea to agree to the VER on synthetic textiles in 1971; a "U.S. Embassy official" in Korea is quoted to that effect in the Comptroller General's Report, p. 29.

50. Striking evidence of this eagerness was recently provided as a by-product of the suit filed against the steel VER by Consumers Union. Early in the legal proceedings, it appeared that questions might be raised about the standing in court of Consumers Union to prosecute the case. Efforts were thus made to find steel importers or end-users of steel in the United States to join the suit. Despite major efforts, including discussions with importers who had publicly complained of shortages of steel resulting from the VER, not a single additional plaintiff could be found. All expressed fear that they would suffer retaliation from their foreign suppliers if they made such an effort—despite the fact that the suit sought to eliminate the restraints that had been "forced on" those very suppliers by the U.S. government!

51. Lynch, *Toward an Orderly Market*, p. 195. Hunsberger, in *Japan and the U.S. in World Trade*. also notes the irony of U.S. promotion of cartelization of the Japanese textile (and later, steel) industry after its major effort to break up the *Zaibatsu* after World War II. See also the commentary by Komiya following Chapter 15.

52. On the other hand, as noted above and in Figure 15-2, the decrease in imports and hence deadweight losses—areas D_1 and D_2 in Figure 15-1—are usually less under VERs than QRs.

53. The U.S. textile restraints have probably perpetuated the life of parts of the Japanese textile industry, for example, that might have moved abroad more rapidly had they not been assured a particular share of the U.S. market.

54. Japan has been frequently singled out, however, as in many of the VERs on sales to Europe and in the original cotton textile VER with the United States in 1957.

55. The U.S. textile industry vetoed a U.S. government proposal that might have produced U.S.-Japanese agreement on a very tough synthetics-woolens VER in December 1970 because they still thought that the Mills bill, with its all-fiber QRs, might become law.

56. George Ball, *The Discipline of Power* (Little, Brown & Co., 1969), p. 193, has noted that voluntary agreements, "since being too easy to work out, have tempted hard-pressed government officials to yield to industry pressure."

57. For an analysis of that balance, see Chapter 20.

58. The "Byrnes basket" provision of the Mills bill of 1970, which would have presumptively triggered QRs for any industries that met certain numerical criteria and which passed the House of Representatives, is the latest evidence of such a view. The president and Congress agreed on the desirability of textile QRs in 1970 but could not agree on whether other industries should receive similar treatment and hence no action resulted.

59. Hunsberger, *Japan and the U.S. in World Trade,* p. 355.

60. The procedures may not always be totally effective in achieving that purpose. Nevertheless, they do provide a basis for the consideration of all relevant viewpoints.

61. In his assessment of the textile and steel VERs, the Comptroller General, p. 33, reported that "We did not find evidence that responsible agencies had made this assessment [of the costs and benefits of import restraint, and of different methods of achieving a desired level of restraint]. Restraints continue without regard to current or prospective conditions."

62. Patterson, now Deputy Director-General of GATT, indicated in *Discrimination in International Trade,* p. 298, that VERs "do not legally violate GATT rules."

63. There was also a request to Israel, a minor supplier, that never produced any results.

64. One early "benefit" to the United Kingdom of joining the EC was the entry of its steel exporters into the steel VER.

65. Except where superseded by the GATT authorization for customs unions and free-trade areas, and the "transitional" arrangements of article XXXV that continue to provide a justification for Europe's discriminatory barriers against Japan.

66. The Commission of the EC formally expressed unhappiness about the steel VER, but no national governments voiced displeasure. Lynch, *Toward an Orderly Market,* p. 193, also believes that the original postwar

Japanese cotton VER in 1956 was at least partly voluntary: "The Japanese wanted peace, and an end to a messy campaign that may possibly hurt their business and name at a time when they still had an international inferiority complex. The enticing offer of compromise and a chance to bury one more unpleasant memory of the late Pacific war were tempting tidbits that the Japanese finally accepted." The "messy campaign" of course means that the Japanese, even in this case, were not acting wholly on their own initiative.

67. For a detailed and absorbing analysis see I. M. Destler, Haruhiro Fukui, and Hideo Sato, *The U.S.-Japan Textile Negotiations of 1969-1971: A Study in Bureaucratic and International Politics* (Brookings Institution, forthcoming).

68. In May 1969, before Secretary of Commerce Stans made a major trip to Japan, the National Security Council was presented an options paper that analyzed the four major problems in U.S.-Japan economic relations: their bilateral payments imbalance, Japan's import restrictions, Japan's investment restrictions, and textiles. The paper concluded that the United States would have to clarify its priorities among the four issues in order to make any progress at all and recommended the ordering just indicated. The president was unwilling to set any priorities, however, the practical effect of which was to focus most of the U.S. policy effort on textiles.

69. See Chapter 12.

70. For a contrary view see the two-track import safeguard mechanism proposed by Anthony M. Solomon in Chapter 16. He would exclude compensation and retaliation in cases where countries adhered to the new international rules and require such treatment only when they violated those rules. This approach is conceptually sound, but could lead to frequent action outside the new rules due to the internal political temptation to impose new restrictions without a clear requirement for compensation retaliation and the strong possibility that a country applying safeguards, especially a powerful country like the United States, could then successfully "justify" its actions as coming fully within the new framework whether in fact they did so or not.

71. A further wrinkle could be for the *government* of the exporting country to auction off the export quotas or levy an export tax, seizing the scarcity premia generated by the trade restraints for its public as a whole rather than letting them accrue to the protected industry. The same reasoning suggests that an importing country should auction off QRs (to a large number of buyers) so that its public will gain back the cuts in consumers' surplus generated by the quotas, rather than handing price increases as well as quantitative protection to the injured industry.

72. Implementation of this principle could prove difficult. Is cartelization strengthened more by giving more market power to an industry that is already heavily concentrated, as in the steel VER, or by providing an impetus to cartelization in an industry that is highly competitive, as in the textile VERs? Guidelines would have to be developed to indicate when each type of compensation would be appropriate.

Chapter 15
Commentary

Ryutaro Komiya

It is not easy to define Voluntary Export Restraints (VERs). Restrictions on exports established according to an international agreement, whether bilateral or multilateral, should be called "compulsory (or contractual) export restrictions," not VERs. They are not at all voluntary, and should be considered separately from other VERs.

There remain then two types of VERs: (1) those enforced ' "voluntarily" by the government of the exporting country, and (2) those established by exporters or industries, which are "triggered by pressure from the government or industry of the importing country or countries," to use Bergsten's words.

In case (1), it is usually easy to determine whether the restrictions in question respond to explicit or implicit requests or pressure from foreign countries. To the extent that such requests or pressure are imminent, a VER under (1) is not really "voluntary."

In case (2), it is more difficult to confirm the foreign pressure. Such VERs are almost indistinguishable from simple export cartels. A really "voluntary" VER is nothing but an export cartel. Under Japanese antitrust laws export cartels are exempted from the general prohibition of cartels, and there are now slightly fewer than 200 export cartels in Japan. Almost all of them mention, among their purposes of organization, something such as "the maintenance of orderly conditions in export markets in view of the pressure from the governments or industries of importing countries."

It should be pointed out that the export cartel is one of the areas where research up to now has been very inadequate, and government policy is confused. Many of these cartels probably violate antitrust laws in the United States and the EEC, or at least in West Germany. The government of the importing country requests, on the one hand, the organization of cartels in the name of VER, and prosecutes, on the other hand, export cartels as restricting competition in their domestic markets! There are few other areas where government policies are so contradictory and confused.

Bergsten mentions a recent U.S. District Court decision in which it was suggested that the steel VER probably violated the Sherman Antitrust Act. Japanese TV manufacturers have been involved seriously in a triple damage antitrust suit in the United States. In Germany, Japanese exporters of electronic products were suspected of violating the German anti-cartel law, although the German authorities dropped the case later.

Short of some new legislation, it seems quite probable that most VERs of category (2) are, at least in theory, in violation of antitrust laws in the

United States, the EC, and Germany. Thus, most of what are generally called VERs are either involuntary or illegal within importing countries.

Bergsten mentions cotton textiles, synthetic and woolen textiles, steel, and meat as four major VERs, and one might have an impression that there are few other VERs in which the United States is a party on the importing side. If my understanding is correct, however, there have been more than 50 VERs "forced upon" Japanese exporters by foreign countries, especially the United States, in which the government of the importing countries is involved. They have covered a wide range of products such as canned fish, ceramics, sewing machines, cameras, baseball gloves, umbrellas, stainless steel silverware, and some chemicals.

The ways in which the government of the importing country is involved are varied. For example, following a rapid increase in imports, there takes place a move toward raising tariffs, establishing quotas or tariff quotas, or starting antidumping procedures. Then the Japanese government establishes a VER in consultation with exporters, and notifies the government of the importing country of its details. The move towards import restriction is thereby stopped or postponed. Or in the case of a European country, the governments agree under a bilateral trade agreement to establish a VER on certain Japanese exports, the details of which are to be worked out on an industry-to-industry basis in consultation with the governments. From Japan's point of view, these VERs are forced upon her by foreign governments.

Bergsten states that exporting countries are becoming increasingly reluctant to adopt VER. While one should not generalize too easily, I think that he is perhaps right as far as Japan and other Far Eastern countries are concerned. VERs of category (2) run a risk of antitrust prosecution. On the other hand, if the government of the exporting country enforces export restriction on exporters under category (1), the latter may request compensation from the government. The cost would be high, as in the case of the recent VER on synthetic and woolen textiles; if it had been an import quota by the United States, instead of a VER agreed upon bilaterally, the Japanese government would not have had to offer compensation, nor be blamed for what the industry and the public at large considered as an unnecessary compromise.

VER is clearly a breach of the GATT rules, and constitutes a serious erosion of GATT's MFN principle. Discussing the relative desirability of VERs and QRs, Bergsten suggests that from the U.S. point of view, a "VER would be more likely to minimize costs" (what costs?) if enforced upon "a politically weak industry" in "a relatively nonnationalistic society of lesser political importance to the United States." But this is sheer power politics. If big powers engage themselves in such international economic power politics, smaller countries and politically weak groups will be victimized and world trade relations will deteriorate into disorder.

I think that it is therefore most desirable if all VERs were abolished and emergency import restrictions were allowed only under a properly revised Article 19 of GATT. But such a proposal may not be accepted by countries whose exports are now under VER since they will be afraid that all existing VERs would be replaced by more rigid import quotas administered by importing countries, which could be perpetuated without limit as with the case of cotton textiles.

16 Safeguard Mechanisms

Anthony M. Solomon

Accepting the basic postulate that the world is increasingly interdependent economically—that this is both inevitable and desirable—limits fairly sharply the possible forms of an international safeguard mechanism.[1] Since however it is generally accepted that each nation-state has the responsibility for reconciling its own economic growth and stability objectives, it is both desirable and politically realistic that there be sufficient flexibility in any international safeguard mechanism for different governments to have different mixes of trade policy and/or trade practice. This can probably be best accomplished by modifying Article 19 of the GATT to provide for the following type of two-track system.

Track 1. Where a member of GATT adheres to an internationally agreed upon procedure (more or less as follows), compensation or retaliation would *not* be in order.

1. Internal public hearings in which interested parties (both domestic and foreign) can participate and which result in a public determination (or not) that serious injury exists for a particular industry (or segment) due in substantial part to like or competitive imports increasing both absolutely and relatively (to domestic production). This public hearing should also assess the cost to the consumers of import restrictions.
2. Notification to the GATT of an affirmative determination and decision to take action by the government.
3. Multilateral consultations in a specially created group of the affected supplying countries on the remedial actions the importing country plans—including not only import relief but customarily as well a general idea of the governmental adjustment assistance for the injured industry.
4. Import relief limited to five years and modestly degressive during that five year period.
5. No extension except one (for another period up to five years), and that only where an up-to-date report is made and where a specific adjustment plan is presented—and where there is no formal expression by a majority of the group that the extension is not reasonable.

Track 2. Where a national government does not adhere to the internationally agreed upon procedure, it would still be permissible to invoke import relief, but the obligation to give compensatory trade concessions or accept retaliatory action on a roughly equivalent scale would still apply.

The conditions that would still have to be met by the country taking import-restrictive action would be that a public hearing was held in that country (irrespective of the final determination), import relief would be limited to five years and be modestly degressive and that if the import relief action were later extended (up to another five years maximum) double voluntary compensation or compensatory retaliation might well be in order. Whenever there is disagreement on the scale of voluntary compensation or retaliation, the matter should be settled by a compulsory arbitration panel in the GATT.

In both tracks, import relief should be utilized on a bilateral or discriminatory as well as on an MFN basis; it should be limited to a maximum of two five-year periods; and government could switch from one track to the other at the beginning of the five-year extension if it met the relevant conditions of the new track.

The reasons for this two-track safeguard mechanism and for the specific steps and conditions of the two procedures outlined above are mostly self-evident. Other reasons that are less self-evident are the following.

1. It does not seem to be feasible, contrary to my first thought, to develop a quantitative formula or mathematical trigger for invocation of the safeguard mechanism in place of a case-by-case hearing to determine whether there is serious injury (or threat of). Even "sudden and sharp increase" in imports have widely different dimensions for different products and widely different implications for the question of serious injury, and no mathematical trigger could be universally applicable.

2. A separate concept of "market disruption" has practical meaning only where serious injury (or threat of) *cannot* be proven. If, notwithstanding this, the importing country feels compelled for political or other reasons to give import relief it should be handled under Track 2, and there seems to be no advantage in cluttering up the negotiations and administration of the multilateral and national safeguard mechanisms with separate provisions for market disruption.

3. It no longer seems sensible to require that the serious injury finding depend upon proving a direct link to previously given tariff concessions. This existing condition of Article 19 has proven to be a dead letter since the cumulative import of all the tariff concessions since the end of World War II makes it virtually impossible to deny a link on the one hand and yet hard in some cases to prove a specific link to a particular concession. Trade diplomats agree that this criterion is no longer considered meaningful in GATT discussions.

The "safeguard mechanism" concept is broader and less legalistic than the "escape clause," which is thought of as action by a country to derogate temporarily previously tendered trade concessions to others. In contrast, the safeguard mechanism concept, particularly when administered in two tracks, deals with any import problem that is serious enough in its merits, irrespective of whether the existing tariff is legally bound or not: also compensation would no longer hinge on whether the import relief action infringes on a previously granted legal concession but whether the multilateral safeguard procedure (Track 1) or the national safeguard procedure (Track 2) were followed. Replacing the escape clause concept with the safeguard mechanism also makes it unnecessary, at least in most cases, to negotiate those special "exceptions clauses" that would permit future import restrictions without payment of compensation. Finally, since the safeguard mechanism could be used whenever serious injury due substantially or primarily to increasing absolute and relative imports was proven (irrespective of the reason for that import increase) it could of course be used for serious injury cases arising in the future from elimination or reduction of non-tariff barriers.

4. The requirement that the Track 1 mechanism involve internal but *public* hearings arises from an examination of the actual use of the Article 19 escape clause in the different major trading countries. U.S. law requires public hearings before its Tariff Commission to prove serious injury, but even in the United States this has not been observed when voluntary bilateral or discriminatory agreements have been sought outside the Tariff Commission procedures. In Australia the individual appointed as Special Advisory Authority on the particular trade problem holds informal private hearings. In Britain the procedure is also loose—views on injury are frequently presented orally in informal discussions with Board of Trade officials and submission to the BOT can be made "in confidence." EEC regulations do not provide for public hearings in escape clause actions; the Council of Ministers has discretionary authority to accept, reject or modify commission proposals and makes its decisions on import permits "when the interests of the community requires it." In Japan the relevant body, the Customs Tariff Council, has never held public hearings in connection with an emergency action on imports although they are theoretically possible. In Canada the procedures are varied—investigations preceding action under the Customs Tariff Act or Export-Import Permits Act consist of informal administrative determinations while more formal investigative procedures, usually although not necessarily including public hearings, are held under the Anti-Dumping Act and Tariff Board Act. In none of these different national procedures is it mandatory, or even customary, as best I can determine, to analyze and publish the cost to domestic consumers of a proposed import-relief action.

5. The reason for my recommendation that the safeguard mechanism can be applied by the importing country on an MFN or discriminatory basis (presently not permitted under Article 19) is, first, that the proliferation of hundreds of bilateral orderly marketing agreements has demonstrated the

need for this flexibility[2] and, second, a fairly widespread view among representatives to the GATT that exporting countries not creating the injury problem should not be penalized. Third, in the case of the United States, if the executive is to be asked to give up his present power and practice of making voluntary bilateral agreements without a public hearing and a finding by the Tariff Commission, then in the event of a finding he must be permitted to invoke the import relief in the most practical and least disruptive manner—and that may be either a bilateral orderly marketing agreement or a quantitive restriction against the country creating the problem. Finally, it is unrealistic to believe that the European Community would relinquish its bilateral safeguard provisions in existing treaties with Japan for a multilateral safeguard mechanism that must always work on an MFN basis.

6. Although the multilateral Track 1 safeguard mechanism procedure customarily includes an adjustment program for the industry found to be seriously injured (or so threatened), I wish to emphasize that it does not automatically follow that the eligibility criteria for a serious-injury finding leading to import relief must be the same as for extending an adjustment assistance program. Those adjustment assistance criteria should be easier to meet and much more anticipatory in nature.

7. One of the differences between these recommendations and those of the Rey group in regard to a modified safeguard mechanism is that I have omitted the group's proposed conditions that the level of temporary import relief should not reduce imports below existing levels, and that it should allow imports to increase at a reasonable rate. The disadvantage of these two conditions is that they force the importing country to use predictable quotas rather than leaving them the option of raising tariffs temporarily with much less predictable results. I think it sufficient therefore to require that the level of temporary import protection be modestly degressive within the five-year maximum.

8. In practice, very few countries other than the United States have engaged in prior consultation before invoking import-relief escape-clause action—most have used the "emergency" alternative of Article 19 and consulted after the action. Under a modified Article 19 two-track safeguard mechanism, there would no longer be the need for an alternative "emergency" procedure since the importing country would either follow the national Track 2 procedure (where prior consultation is not required but compensation is paid) or the multinational Track 1 procedure that in any case requires as a first step, internal but public hearings and an affirmative determination of serious injury, and secondly, notification to the GATT of the determination followed by multilateral consultation in the specially created group of affected trading partners on the proposed import relief action (and adjustment assistance program).

There would be an advantage if a long-term provision could be made in a modified Article 19 for future, modestly flexible interpretations of the agreed-upon Article 19 mechanism to be made by a panel (with only very major changes requiring parliamentary and congressional action).

The heaviest user in the past, and probably in the future, of safeguard mechanisms has been the United States. It is true that U.S. policy faces a dilemma—the U.S. Congress will not pass trade legislation with negotiating authority for the president unless it also revises its national safeguard mechanism, and yet the modification of the Article 19 safeguard mechanism can only be achieved in the course of the subsequent multilateral trade negotiation. It is very possible that any revised U.S. safeguard mechanism will be consistent with Track 1, but it is unlikely that U.S. legislation will also provide a sufficient basis for the U.S. executive to agree to a multilateral Track 2-type mechanism without returning to the Congress after the trade negotiations for additional legislation. However, this would be true of any truly meaningful multilateral safeguard procedure, and the advantage of the flexible option (to follow either Track 1 or 2) plus the advantage of the no-compensation or retaliation feature in a track 2 procedure should be clearly apparent to Congress as well as to other governments.

Note

1. This chapter does not deal with balance-of-payments-related escape clauses. However, it may be worth recording my agreement with the frequently expressed need for a change in Article 12 of the GATT to make permissible temporary import surcharges (in addition to, or in place of, QRs) and that the emergency balance of payments authority should be symmetrical—that is, surplus countries could and would reduce their import restrictions temporarily by up to the agreed percentage if they believed a revaluation of the exchange rate was not indicated.

2. See Chapter 15.

Chapter 16
Commentary

Ryutaro Komiya

Both Sir Eric Wyndham-White and Anthony Solomon propose a modification of Article 19 so as to permit the discriminatory use of safeguard mechanisms—that is, temporary import restrictions imposed on certain imports coming from particular sources that are identified as causing the market disruption.

Under the present Article 19 the safeguard must be applied on a nondiscriminatory (MFN) basis—that is, the temporary import restriction or withdrawal of tariff concessions must be applied to imports coming from any member countries. This means that the country wishing to apply the safeguard is obliged to offer compensation to, or accept retaliatory actions from, all member countries having interests in the imports in question.

The reason for legalizing discriminatory safeguards is twofold. First, by so doing, the temporary import restrictions will be confined to particular bilateral trade that is rapidly expanding and causing market disruption, without affecting orderly imports that are not disrupting the market. Second, the requirement of non-discrimination in safeguards has been felt to be so onerous for countries seeking safeguards that many of them have tried to solve the problem outside of the GATT rules.[1] By allowing discriminatory safeguards, it is hoped, a much larger number of cases of market disruption and safeguards will be brought under the legal framework of GATT.

I see the points in these arguments, yet I still feel strongly that the principle of non-discrimination should not easily be compromised. One of the functions of the principle of non-discrimination is to ensure multilateral surveillance and to establish a degree of equality among countries with unequal economic power. When discriminatory safeguards are legalized, countries that will be hurt most in the future are likely to be smaller countries in the early stage of industrialization. Big countries such as the United States, the European Community, or Japan have the power to negotiate seriously and could retaliate against discrimination if they choose. Also, since their exports are well diversified, other countries' use of safeguard mechanisms against their rapidly increasing exports hits only a small portion of their total exports.

But suppose that a relatively small country in the early stage of industrialization believes in GATT and shifts from a protectionist policy of import substitution to a development policy based on an international division of labor. Resources will then be moved from hitherto protected import-competing industries to export industries in which its inherent

283

comparative advantage lies. When the country succeeds in developing such industries, the rate of industrial growth can easily be as high as 10 to 15 percent per year. When discriminatory safeguards are applied to such a newcomer exporting country and only 2 to 3 percent annual growth is allowed for its exports, the country will simply face stagnation.

It might be suggested that a small country, being small relative to a large market, is unlikely to cause market disruption in major markets or that such a country should not heavily concentrate in narrow product lines but should diversify its products and export markets. It may be recalled, however, that the United States, the United Kingdom, and other countries requested Hong Kong, whose population is only about four million, to establish VERs on cotton and other textiles and several other items. Also, although it is not an example of an independent state, the United States now levies a countervailing duty on tires made in Nova Scotia under its regional industrialization program. Nova Scotia's population is about three-quarters of a million. These examples indicate that small countries will not be free from the discriminatory imposition of import restrictions by big ones.

Second, in order to achieve economies of scale in the early stage of industrialization, it is not surprising that such a country concentrates its export effort in a few product lines. It is not uncommon that a region in a large country with a population of a couple of million specializes in one or a few industries as far as its ''exports'' to other regions or other countries are concerned. Moreover, if the government does not intervene considerably with industries, it could happen that their exports concentrate in a few markets.

While it is difficult to agree upon what is fair and what is unfair, one can argue that it is unfair to discriminate against such newcomer exporting countries while other exporters enjoy the status quo ante. For smaller countries, retaliation or compensation mean little. They have a high stake in some mechanism of multilateral surveillance. The non-discrimination principle is perhaps the surest way of guaranteeing multilateral surveillance in the matter of safeguards.

Note

1. For example, illegal import quotas, clauses of bilateral trade agreements, voluntary export restraints, and arrangements under cotton textile LTA. See Chapter 15.

17

Economic Adjustment to Liberal Trade: A New Approach

Task Force on Adjustment Assistance,
U.S. Chamber of Commerce,
C. Fred Bergsten, Chairman

Introduction

The Chamber of Commerce supports a liberal trade policy for the United States. The Chamber in fact believes that liberal trade is now more important to our national interest than at any time in the postwar period, for both economic and political reasons.

Economically, the United States is likely to continue to face persistent problems of both high unemployment and inflationary pressures. The Chamber rejects the notion that unemployment can be reduced to acceptable levels only by pushing inflation to unacceptable levels or vice-versa. However, skillful public policy is needed to solve the two problems simultaneously.

Fiscal and monetary efforts provide much of the policy response, but it is too much to expect that they can do the job alone, particularly since each problem is caused in part by structural difficulties rather than inappropriate levels of aggregate demand. Selective measures are thus needed as well. One such measure is the present program of wage-price controls, which is necessary at this time but which violates the basic precepts of the free market that are essential to the continued success of the American economy. The controls should thus be phased out as soon as possible.

But a number of other selective measures both conform to the precepts of the market and offer the possibility of major help in fighting unemployment and inflation. One is free trade. Import restrictions levy heavy costs on our economy. Tariff and quota restrictions were raising prices to our consumers by close to $20 billion per year before the administration wisely liberalized the oil and meat quotas to help fight inflation. They undermine our competitiveness, by raising costs to our producers and by shielding important sectors of our economy from the stimulus of foreign competition. They do not save jobs; indeed, they cost American jobs by triggering foreign barriers to our exports and by retarding the historic and natural evolution of our economy into ever more efficient and higher-wage industries. Indeed, the Chamber believes that new import restrictions would deal a devastating blow to the American economy and undermine over time both our standard of living and the basic economic system on which our nation is based.

At the same time, foreign barriers to trade continue to impede the U.S. economy by restraining our exports in industries (including agriculture) where we possess marked comparative advantages. These barriers cost us high-paying jobs and reduce the competitive incentives to our firms and workers. Our major national interest in their reduction can be realized only within the framework of an international negotiation in which all major countries agree to renew their progress toward freer trade.

A second selective approach, which can help combat both unemployment and inflation, is manpower policy. The skill mix of our labor force can of course never mesh precisely with the needs of the shifting patterns of production; there will always be some unemployment. But effective manpower programs can reduce the level of unemployment by equipping workers to fill available jobs. They can reduce inflation by increasing the productivity of our labor force and by reducing the costs of unemployment compensation. Indeed, they can represent a highly productive investment in the future of our nation.

Similar in principle to manpower training is assistance to smaller firms that also need help in adjusting to the rapid changes triggered by modern economic forces such as foreign trade. Their contribution to our overall economy can be promoted if they can be helped to improve their competitiveness in their present industry or shift their resources into more promising endeavors.

Freer trade, manpower programs, and industrial assistance are integral components of the foreign economic policy that the Chamber believes must be pursued by the United States in the 1970s. Each is highly desirable in its own right, as just indicated, and the relationship among them is straightforward. Freer trade causes dislocation for a few in order to benefit all. The personal hardships that result are often severe and must be alleviated. Those who are hurt by a policy that is thus pursued in the general interest should be compensated adequately for their losses, and the opportunity should be seized to enable them to increase their contribution to the national welfare. The Chamber is confident that the benefits of such a foreign economic policy to our nation far exceed its costs, as will be demonstrated later.

The Chamber also wishes to emphasize the importance of freer trade to the foreign policy of the United States. Economic issues now play a central role in U.S. relations with virtually every country in the world, especially our closest allies in Canada, Europe, and Japan. New U.S. trade restrictions could severely injure those relations. Steady progress toward freer trade could smooth them. Since amicable U.S. relations with both Europe and Japan are an essential component of continued improvement in our relations with the Soviet Union and China, a successful and cooperative U.S. foreign economic policy will play a central role in realizing our hopes for a generation of peace.

A New Program of Economic Assistance

The concept of "adjustment assistance" to workers and firms displaced by imports was embodied in the Trade Expansion Act of 1962. The Chamber believes that the program authorized by that Act, however, is wholly inadequate for the following reasons:

1. It generates little real adjustment to economic change for dislocated workers, providing only temporary supplements to unemployment compensation.
2. Its assistance commences long after dislocation has occurred, and it delivers this long-delayed assistance far too slowly.
3. Its level of compensation to workers for their loss of jobs is inadequate and frequently amounts to less than one-half their previous earnings.
4. The program provides no help whatsoever for communities.
5. There is no high-level governmental attention to the program, and no central direction to it.

None of these problems are inherent in the concept of adjustment assistance. The Chamber believes that each of them must be solved in order to construct a program of economic adjustment that will enable the United States to pursue a liberal trade policy in the 1970s, and that such a program can be devised. It believes that such a program must compensate those whose skills are rendered unprofitable by trade for their losses *and,* more importantly, help them adjust into new endeavors. The Chamber offers the following proposals to that end.

1. Eligibility

Under present law, firms and workers are eligible for trade adjustment assistance only if a majority of the Tariff Commission concludes that they are suffering serious injury (or are threatened with serious injury) and that the major cause of their injury is an increase in imports, which was in turn triggered in major part by U.S. tariff concessions. This formula has proved exceedingly restrictive. It ignores the vast bulk of our imports, since they are not caused by U.S. tariff concessions. It is often difficult to prove conclusively that imports are the major cause of a particular dislocation.

There has been no basis for helping those affected indirectly by imports, either as suppliers to firms directly affected or living in communities whose "gross community product" is retarded. The procedures for determining eligibility and extending benefits are so cumbersome that severe delays in both are inevitable. And there has been reluctance to determine eligibility, both at the Tariff Commission and in the White House, because the identity of the criteria for "adjustment assistance" and for protection from imports under the escape clause has raised the spectre of trade wars any time that assistance is provided—although the intent of the legislation was to authorize such assistance as a clear alternative to import quotas and tariff increases.

The Chamber recommends a basic change in the eligibility criteria:

1.1 *Workers employed continuously by a firm for more than six months should be presumed to be eligible for assistance if layoffs affect a significant share (perhaps 5 percent) of those engaged in producing a product in which total domestic output and the output of their particular firm have declined, and imports of a like or directly competitive product have increased, over a representative period of time (perhaps the latest twelve months for which data are available compared with either of the two previous twelve month periods, or an average of those two periods).*

1.2 *Firms would be presumed eligible if their own output and total national output of the product declined while imports rose, and for certain forms of assistance when there was serious threat of such developments, if the product represented a substantial share of the total output of the firm, unless the imports were generated by the firm itself.*

The combination of these two changes—reduced domestic output and increased imports for both workers and firms—of course implies a rise in the ratio of imports to domestic production. This approach is superior to formulas that would trigger assistance solely on the basis of some given increase in the import/domestic production ratio, however, because such increases frequently take place for products for which total demand is growing rapidly.

1.3 *Firms, and workers thereof, whose output declined and 50 percent of whose output represented inputs to product lines that met this new injury test themselves would also be eligible; other supplying firms could become eligible if they could demonstrate that their own problems were substantially due to the effect of import competition on their customers.*

In all of these cases, a "product" would be defined narrowly in order both to permit help for small groups of workers and, conversely, to avoid paying benefits to those for whom they were not justified.

1.4 *Communities would automatically be eligible when a significant share (perhaps 5 percent) of their total workers have been declared eligible for the program themselves. Communities could qualify in any event by demonstrating that their own problems were substantially due to the effect of import competition.*

1.5 *In all of these cases, there would thus be a presumption that injury existed and eligibility for assistance established when rising imports and reduced output coincided. The presumptions could be challenged by the administering authority in cases where it felt that imports were not a substantial cause of the dislocation,* as could often be the case for firms where poor management (including failure to anticipate competition from imports) was the crucial factor.

Indeed, cases can be envisaged where workers of a firm would receive full benefits whereas the firm would not be eligible. Particularly for workers, however, the presumption would be realized in most cases.

Under the Automotive Products Trade Act of 1965, an analogous formula was used to provide assistance for the dislocations caused in the course of the restructuring of the North American automobile industry under the U.S.-Canada Automotive Agreement of that year. Under that arrangement, the legal presumption was never challenged and the eligibility criteria of the adjustment program were regarded by all parties—the unions, workers, firms and U.S. government—as a complete success. The Chamber is confident that the approach can work successfully for U.S. trade policy as a whole.

Under the program proposed here, the criteria would encompass dislocations caused by imports both from foreign-owned firms and from the foreign affiliates of U.S. firms. It is recognized that there are problems of comparability between the present U.S. data for imports and domestic output and that improvements in these data are needed for a wide variety of purposes, but the technical problems have been met so far and can be met in the future.

2. Speed of Delivery

At present, there are two routes to obtaining "adjustment assistance." Under the escape-clause procedures, firms and workers in an entire industry can obtain help. The process in this case takes up to six months in the Tariff Commission; a subsequent decision by the president, which may take 90 days; subsequent certification of individual firms and workers by the Departments of Commerce and Labor, respectively; and delivery of the benefits through specific agents. When individual firms and groups of workers apply for assistance, they must undergo scrutiny by the Tariff

Commission for 60 days; presidential consideration if the Tariff Commission vote is tied, as has frequently been the case; certification by the relevant department; and then delivery. In both cases, interminable delay has been the rule.

The proposed changes in adjustment assistance eligibility criteria (we are proposing no changes in the criteria for tariff increases, or the applications of quotas, under the escape clause) would themselves go far to speed the delivery of assistance. The simple correlation between declining output and increasing imports would be easy to verify, particularly in comparison with the complex investigation of "serious injury" and two-stage causality under present law. The dissociation between the new criteria for economic adjustment and the criteria for imposing new import restrictions would relieve concerns that the former might trigger the latter, and hence remove another impediment to a speedy delivery process.

Further steps are needed, however, both to anticipate and hence avoid dislocation caused by trade flows and to assure prompt relief when dislocation does occur. Early warning of impending dislocations is needed well before firms begin to slide competitively. The government, which now enters the adjustment process far too late, can help in this process by improving its analytical capacity. To do this, however, the government must get close and continuing advice from those directly affected, who are likely to first pick up the signals of impending change—the firms themselves.

Recommendations to improve speed of delivery are as follows:

2.1 *The government should actively contact firms (and trade associations) to keep abreast of their judgments concerning trade trends, and inform firms of problems that appear to be developing.* (A two-way process is needed, however, so that the information can be effectively utilized.)

2.2 *Firms should actively consult the government to check out their own individual views as they make their future investment and marketing plans.*

Such information should be particularly helpful for smaller firms, who usually suffer most from import dislocation. Acting as a broker, the government could assure the confidentiality of information of commercial importance to individual firms. In the consumer goods industries, where imports have been rising sharply, retailers—who are frequently in the best position to spot changing patterns of production and hence pending economic dislocations—should be consulted.

The objective would be to develop and share information on the outlook for foreign competition in the U.S. market, in an effort to spot emerging trends better than could be done by individual firms on their own. Firms would then have an earlier opportunity to adjust on their own and avoid import dislocation.

2.3 *The Chamber also recommends that firms be eligible for technical assistance from the government, on both a grant and reimbursable basis, when the administering authority determines in advance of the actual manifestation of any injury that they face a "threat of serious injury" from imports.*

The concept of a "*threat* of serious injury" is encompassed in the present "adjustment assistance" legislation, but it has been interpreted to require that the threat be imminent. Under the proposed new approach, it would encompass a much longer lead time than has been required heretofore.

The primary responsibility for early warning to workers rests with private firms, however, because it is they who face the pressure of increased competition and must make decisions to respond to it. Many U.S. firms already give such warning, and many agree to do so under their management-labor arrangements. Several countries require their companies to give a minimum amount of prior notice, which ranges from four to sixteen weeks, to workers who are to be laid off.

2.4 *The Chamber views it as the responsibility of U.S. firms to give the maximum possible advance notice to workers whom they will be laying off and to provide them with full information concerning the available benefits under the proposed program. It urges all firms to comply with this principle.*

In combination with the speedy delivery of benefits permitted by the new assistance criteria and promoted by the new administrative machinery to be discussed below, and the improvement in compensation and adjustment aids to be discussed next, these early warning mechanisms should go far to assure workers that they would have both the time and the means to transit from present to future employment with minimum personal disruption. Indeed, early action by firms to preempt import penetration would, if successful, obviate any dislocation to workers at all. The proposed program, taken in its entirety, should thus significantly reduce their resistance to import-induced change.

3. Compensation Benefits for Workers

Under present law, workers declared eligible for "adjustment assistance" receive 65 percent of their previous wage *or* 65 percent of the average manufacturing wage, whichever is less. These benefits are not taxable. There is no compensation for lost fringe benefits. Present benefits thus range from about 40 percent of previous net earnings (for workers with above-average wages and large fringe benefits) to as much as 70 percent of previous net earnings (for those workers with higher tax liabilities than fringe benefits and below-average wages), with most clustered about 50 to 60 percent.

The Chamber agrees with the judgment of the House Ways and Means Committee, the entire House of Representatives, and the Senate Finance Committee, as recorded in their passage of the Trade Act of 1970, that these levels are inadequate. Workers have invested considerable time, and often money as well, in acquiring their skills. Time, and often money, will always be required to reemploy or replace those skills to rebuild the worker's earning capacity. Individual workers should be adequately compensated for losses imposed on them by government policies, such as liberal trade, which are pursued because they serve the overall national interest.

The House and the Senate Finance Committee, in 1970, voted to provide eligible workers with 75 percent of their prior earnings, or 75 percent of the average manufacturing wage, whichever is less, non-taxable.

Proposals for compensation benefits for eligible workers are as follows:

3.1 *The Chamber believes that 75 percent is a reasonable level of compensation and recommends that it replace the present level (with a ceiling of an annual rate of $12,000 for any individual worker).*

However, the Chamber feels that it is inequitable to penalize a worker because his wage is higher than the national average for manufacturing. Every worker should receive a like proportion of his previous wage—75 percent, on this recommendation.

3.2 *There should thus be no alternative calculation based on the national average.*

The resource cost of these benefits would of course be simply their excess above the level of unemployment insurance that virtually all displaced workers would otherwise receive.

3.3 *For those few workers affected by imports who are not covered by unemployment insurance, the assistance program would have to finance all benefits.*

Salaried workers, as well as those who are paid an hourly wage, would of course be eligible.

Fringe benefits now comprise a major part of a worker's income; they average about 15 percent beyond money wages for all workers but amount to as much as 30 to 40 percent for some. An important share of these benefits is not transferable as the worker moves from one firm to another, unlike the case in many countries, which greatly increases his reluctance to do so. Indeed, there is no way to provide compensation for a number of important fringe benefits, such as guaranteed overtime pay and seniority rights, even if it were deemed desirable to do so. A number of the most important fringes, however, represent health and life (and perhaps disability and other) insurance whose lapsing could levy heavy costs on a displaced worker and his family. There should be no reduction in the level of benefits available to displaced workers under these plans.

3.4 *The Chamber thus recommends that the government assistance program pick up whatever premiums the companies had previously been paying, at the group rate prevailing before the worker was laid off, to enable all dislocated workers to maintain in full their insurance plans.*

3.5 *In cases where workers were enrolled in local plans that could not be maintained, if they moved elsewhere to train or pursue jobs, they could join the insurance plans for employees of the governments of the states to which they had moved for the temporary period in question.*

Some other important fringe-benefit problems, such as vesting of pensions, may be met by changes in the relevant legislation that are already under consideration. Older workers, who often find it particularly difficult to find a new job, could get added benefits as will be outlined below.

4. Adjustment by Workers

The Chamber believes that economic adjustment to liberal trade should focus most heavily on helping workers adjust into fruitful new occupations as quickly as possible.

4.1 *Workers would thus have to be actively seeking employment to receive any of the compensation benefits just described.*

Workers receiving benefits would cease to receive them once they were offered suitable jobs.

4.2 *Workers would also have to apply for retraining programs to qualify them for suitable jobs, that were identifiable as available, to use the skills when they were trained for them, and join those training programs as soon as openings developed.*

These two requirements would assure that the enhanced level of compensation benefits promoted, rather than deterred, the likelihood that the trade-impacted worker would find new employment as soon as possible. The higher the level of employment in the economy as a whole, the less need would of course exist for the actual payment of compensation benefits— although structural problems will always exist even when aggregate unemployment is very low.

Under present trade adjustment assistance, a worker can receive compensation benefits for 52 weeks plus 26 additional weeks if he is undergoing retraining plus an additional 13 weeks if he is over 60 years of age. The Chamber believes that this period may be too long for some workers, and—in the absence of the "accept suitable employment and apply for retraining" requirement included here—reduce the incentives for them to seek new jobs. At the same time, it recognizes that the average duration of unemployment of workers who have received trade "adjustment assistance" in the past is ten months. This compares with the national average of one and a half to three months, which fluctuates with the level of aggregate unemployment. It also recognizes that appropriate retraining programs are not always available immediately and may take some time to complete. It is to be expected, of course, that workers displaced by imports—who generally come from industries that are less productive than the industries employing the "average worker," much of whose "unemployment" is due to voluntary quits as he moves from job to better job—will suffer periods of joblessness far longer than the average.

It should be recalled that the requirement exists for an eligible worker to accept an offer of a suitable job or to apply for retraining for a job that will be available to use his new skill.

4.3 *The Chamber therefore recommends that the full compensation benefits as outlined above be paid for the durations specified in the present act, except that the extension period for workers in training programs be increased from 26 to 52 weeks.*

This extension will enhance the likelihood that such training will have a full opportunity to provide real adjustment for them.

4.4 *Workers 55 or older would be eligible to receive the same benefits.*

It is often much more difficult for their older workers to obtain new jobs, however, even with retraining, both because employers are frequently reluctant to hire them and because these older workers may be less adaptable themselves. And experience demonstrates that the number of older workers laid off due to imports constitutes a large share of the total problem.

The Chamber therefore recommends that older workers be offered the alternative of early retirement, with immediate commencement of benefits (at the level otherwise available at age 62 for those retiring before 60, at the level available at age 65 for those retiring at 60 or over) under their private pension plans and the Social Security and Medicare systems.

4.5 *The additional costs of such early retirement would be reimbursed to the private firm or Social Security system by the new government assistance program.*

Real adjustment into new positions will often require retraining and relocation to areas where new jobs exist, in addition to proper incentives to workers to seek and accept such jobs. Such steps can be most effective in reducing the costs of dislocation if they are initiated as early as possible in the dislocation process. Thus proposals have already been made to assure early warning of pending dislocations, to require entry into training programs for workers to qualify for the proposed compensation benefits, and to provide financial incentives (the additional period of compensation benefits) for those workers who are dislocated to stay in retraining programs. The narrow "product" definition of the eligibility criteria also enhances the potential for adjustment, by enabling workers producing the impacted product to receive (presumably on-the-job) training to fill a new position with the same (multi-product) firm. More specific measures are also needed, however, to reduce hardships to individuals and the costs to society as a whole of unemployment triggered by trade flows.

A successful adjustment program for trade-dislocated workers requires four key components. The first is early attention to the problem. Part of the success of the Office of Economic Assistance in the Department of Defense in helping whole communities adjust to cutbacks in defense expenditures can be traced to its early knowledge of developing problems. It would be difficult to replicate as much early warning in the private sector, of course, since the Defense Department usually knows where defense cuts are coming. Nevertheless, the suggestions already made to provide early warning of pending problems would permit much earlier triggering of adjustment efforts, including efforts to preempt the dislocation from occurring at all. (Such early warning would also assure timely commencement of compensation benefits when they become necessary.)

The second requirement is that job training be geared to jobs that will in fact be available when the training is completed. This suggests a focus on on-the-job training, under which the new employer receives government payments for each new worker hired during the training period.

4.6 *To utilize effectively both the on-the-job and institutional programs, sharp improvements are needed in the federal-state employment service and computerized job-worker matching, including better statistics on "jobs available" and continuous updating of job definitions.*

4.7 *All dislocated workers should receive sharply improved counselling services to bring workers and jobs together.*

The counselling should be of the type that facilitated the adjustment of workers laid off when Studebaker folded in 1964.

4.8 *Workers should be authorized to use private counselling services approved by the government, but under its continuing surveillance, and be reimbursed for the costs thereof.*

A final requirement is conscious effort by the employment service to pinpoint emerging job opportunities, preferably in the same or neighboring geographical areas, that will be available to job trainees. Job searches by the employment service for the relatively small number of workers displaced by imports might be a particularly useful area in which trade adjustment could be a pilot program for broader manpower programs in the future, as advocated at the outset of this report, since major improvements in the federal-state employment service would have to be a major part of such improvements. The effort could draw on the successful computerized job placement system maintained by the Department of Defense to direct retiring defense personnel into civilian employment.

Third, adequate training programs are needed. There is much present criticism of the effectiveness of current manpower training programs. Few of the present government programs bearing that name, however, have aimed at the kind of adjustment discussed here. Most of them have been adjuncts for the poverty program, aimed at the most disadvantaged and least skilled of all Americans. Even so, a number have achieved real adjustment—even in extremely difficult circumstances, such as Appalachia. Specific programs for specific circumstances have worked—the Studebaker and Armour reconversions and the Defense Department programs to smooth the adjustment to reductions in defense spending in Wichita and dozens of other locales. Manpower programs have worked effectively in other countries, where they have received a higher priority from national governments, have had longer periods of experience from which to learn, and have operated within a context of low unemployment. Such programs have worked in individual states in our country in that they have attracted firms by training workers to meet the firms' specific job needs.

4.9 *Trade-dislocated workers should be eligible to participate in all present programs, and the new counseling programs must assure that workers will be aware of all alternatives available to them.*

The most important reason why the Chamber is confident that current training programs can achieve adjustment to trade dislocations, however, is that the workers displaced by trade flows are far superior to the participants in most current manpower efforts—who are essentially recipients of poverty help. Trade-impacted workers have been working, often for many years and even decades. This means that they have demonstrated work skills. Even more importantly, they have a proven desire to work—the work ethic is clearly alive in this group. They are thus likely to be highly employable relative to the average participant in current manpower training programs, many of whom have little work experience or education. (A possible exception is older workers, for whom special compensation provisions have already been suggested.) They are superior to the average unemployed worker, who is a new entrant to the labor force or re-entrant to it after periods of absence that are often quite extended.

There is thus real reason to expect that trade-impacted workers, if given appropriate help including proper incentives, will be able to adjust effectively into new occupations. We believe that the proposals made in this report will strongly enhance that possibility. We see little risk that the proposals would create disincentives to work: the compensation benefits represent a cutback from previous earnings, their duration is limited in time, no benefits are available unless the worker meets the job test and applies for retraining. The workers involved would have already demonstrated their desire and ability to hold the job. Indeed, serious efforts to train the relatively able workers dislocated by trade flows could provide valuable lessons for the broader manpower programs that, as indicated in the introduction to this report, can play a major role in helping to win the fight against inflation by upgrading the skills of our national labor force.

Fourth, adequate relocation reimbursement is needed. Efforts should be made to avoid the need for workers to move geographically to obtain new employment, because of the disruption of their lives that results. The community assistance programs discussed below should help meet that objective, as should the inducement to multi-product firms to shift workers displaced from producing their trade-impacted product to producing more competitive items. However, geographical moves will be needed in some cases.

4.10 *The costs of such moves should be completely financed by the trade adjustment program.*

This assistance would be similar to that in the Amtrak settlement promulgated by Secretary of Labor Hodgson in 1970 as part of the creation of our new national passenger railroad system. This includes the search process for a new home and the loss to the worker, if any, of selling his old home in a depressed market or breaking an apartment lease. The Homeowners Assistance Program of the Department of Defense, and the forebearance authority of HUD, could be mobilized to assist this effort.

4.11 *All dislocated workers, not just heads of families, should be made eligible for relocation expenses.*

In making all of these proposals, the Chamber is aware that some observers argue that special adjustment programs for trade-impacted workers are illogical, because these workers are no different from those Americans dislocated by other changes, of purely internal origin, that affect our economy. In response, it would note that Congress has judged for over a decade that special adjustment to trade dislocation is needed; the only issue would seem to be the effectiveness of that adjustment program. In addition, however, the Chamber supports the judgment of Congress. The trade adjustment issue will have to be faced head-on in the near future in the context of trade legislation alone. The costs of an adequate liberalization of compensation benefits (such as unemployment insurance benefits) for workers dislocated by all types of economic change, and a total new manpower program, are widely regarded as excessive under present conditions. Perhaps most important, a pilot project along the lines suggested could try out the needed new approaches in a policy area in which much greater knowledge is necessary. The Chamber thus feels that it is sound policy to propose a special program for trade-impacted workers.

5. Adjustment by Firms

This report has stressed the need for reformed economic adjustment for workers, because the Chamber believes that management should itself generally be responsible for the response of firms to dislocation from imports (as other disturbances) and that the responsibility of government to provide assistance is thus primarily to workers. There should be no compensation benefits for firms. Indeed, firms that fail to adjust to competition from imports, either by improving their ability in their present product line or by shifting to a new product line, may have to go out of business entirely.

There is often a need to help smaller firms really adjust, however, as provided for under present trade legislation. Changes should be made in the application of that legislation to firms to parallel the changes already proposed for workers. Depending on the particular case, the objective of the assistance should be to help the firm restore competitiveness in its present industry or adjust into a new line of endeavor. Despite the limited nature of the experience gained so far under the existing program, it appears that both objectives can be achieved.

The most necessary improvement in aid to firms is increasing its timeliness. Firms must adjust rapidly to avoid major losses that may undermine their positions for years, or even lead to total collapse. Most of the failures to promote firm adjustment under the present program can be attributed to its slowness to identify a problem and then provide the available assistance. Early help is more effective and cheaper as well.

The needed speed-up should be achieved through liberalization of the criteria for eligibility and an improved delivery system. As already proposed, new approaches to early warning and technical assistance to firms facing a threat of future injury could play a critical role in preempting dislocation from imports for firms (and through them for their workers), if expert management consultants were employed at an early stage to analyze the firm's problem and propose a plan of action.

The criteria for eligibility (1.2) after most import injury has occurred would be similar to those proposed for workers: *an increase in imports coupled with a decline in output, both by a firm and nationally for the given* product, if the product represented a significant share of the firm's output, would make the firm eligible for assistance with discretion to the adminis- tering authority to challenge the presumption of injury if it felt that imports were not a substantial cause of the dislocation. Firms and workers in those firms should in fact be encouraged to apply for help together; the use of similar eligibility criteria will promote that objective.

The benefits available to firms in present legislation include eligibility for tax loss carrybacks for two years beyond normal practice, preferential access to government credit, and technical assistance to help them achieve a viable business position. These aids to adjustment should be maintained, but several should be added.

5.1 *Government guarantees should be extended–for a fee–to enable eligi- ble firms to obtain credit from private sources.*

This recommendation, which would possibly save money for the govern- ment, requires two changes from present law.

5.2 *The interest rate on guaranteed loans should not be tied to the borrow- ing rate of the Treasury.*

The Treasury is obviously a far better credit risk than firms threatened by import competition.

5.3 *Guarantees should cover 100 percent of the private loans (instead of the present 90 percent ceiling) if they were arranged sufficiently early in the adjustment process to provide high promise of saving the firm.*

5.4 *Technical assistance, including consideration of mergers and sales of a firm's assets, should be expanded through additional use of private consultants approved by the government and under its continuing surveillance, at the earlier instances made possible by the new system of early warning, the new criteria, and the improved administration.*

6. Adjustment by Communities

Communities are not eligible for "adjustment assistance" under present law. Yet many of the most severe dislocations caused by trade flows fall on those affected indirectly—the firms and people who provide services and inputs to the firms and workers who compete internationally. Indeed, communities may wither even if firms and their workers affected by im- ports successfully resist the new competition by moving elsewhere. The problems of direct suppliers would be met by the proposals made above for them to become eligible for all of the new adjustment benefits. Action is needed at the community level, however, to meet the problems of many others.

Communities should therefore automatically be eligible for aid under the new program when a significant share (perhaps 5 percent) of their workers themselves had become eligible under the new criteria applicable to them. Even if these particular workers found jobs elsewhere, their eligibility would enable the community in which they were laid off due to trade dislocation to receive benefits—providing a means to deal with the local problems caused by "runaway plants." *Other communities could apply for eligibility on the grounds that imports were a substantial cause of their problems.*

6.1 *Eligible communities should then receive attention of the type carried out successfully by the Office of Economic Adjustment in the Department of Defense, in recent years on behalf of the President's Inter-Agency Adjustment Committee, for over 160 large and small communities* (including entire counties) *impacted by changes in defense spending since 1961.*

The primary thrust of this effort is to help affected areas mobilize their own resources effectively, and by doing so attract private resources from outside the area to add to the adjustment. (In Wichita, for example, $40 million of federal funds played a key role in attracting $700 million of private money.) The Department of Defense sends teams of experts into impacted areas to analyze their problems and devise rehabilitation efforts. Local leaders—from business, labor, and other groups—are brought together to agree on a plan of action, assign responsibility for its implementation, and monitor the follow-through.

6.2 *Financing from ongoing government programs should be available under the new trade adjustment program as well.*

Agencies such as the Small Business Administration have provided key seed money in some cases, but the primary emphasis would be on technical assistance of all types, to help the communities realize their own potentials for adjustment.

7. Administration

This report has stressed the need for major improvement in the administration of the program of economic adjustment for those firms and workers who suffer dislocation as a result of the maintenance of a liberal trade policy by the United States. The present program is badly fragmented; delay and lack of coordination are inherent. The Tariff Commission must first find injury from imports. In industry-wide cases brought under the escape clause, the president must then determine whether adjustment assistance is the proper remedy. (He may also break ties in cases limited to specific firms and groups of workers.) Individual firms must be certified as eligible by the Secretary of Commerce, and the process has been extremely clumsy and prolonged. Individual groups of workers must be certified by the Secretary of Labor. There is no early warning, and no early action.

7.1 *A single agency is needed to administer the adjustment program under tight time limits specified in the authorizing legislation.*

It would be responsible for the participation of the government in the new system of early warning, economic analysis, eligibility findings, packaging of appropriate benefits, delivery of benefits to firms and communities, monitoring, evaluation, publicity of results, and accountability to the president and Congress. (Benefits to workers would continue to be delivered through the local Employment Service, under close surveillance from the Trade Adjustment Agency.) Such an integrated approach would permit early attention to emerging dislocations and rapid delivery of the new and liberalized help to meet them.

Such an agency could closely link, in time and in the decision-making process, determinations of eligibility and packaging of benefits—instead of the sequential process of the present program, which has proved to be ineffectual. It would build on previous experience, which suggests that the best-managed government programs are those of specialized agencies with unitary purposes—and that the worst of all worlds, adopted so far for "adjustment assistance," is to attempt to manage a unitary program by parceling out various aspects to a combination of old-line agencies and regulatory commissions. To insure full coordination of the assistance program with overall foreign economic policy, its director should be made a member of the Council on International Economic Policy (or any successor body created to coordinate foreign economic policy). To insure full coordination with overall economic policy, including structural adjustment efforts, he should also be a member of the Council on Economic Policy.

The Chamber shares the general distaste for new government agencies. Nevertheless, they may have to be created when a particular need arises. The Chamber believes that domestic adjustment to trade flows represents such a case.

7.2 *The Chamber recommends the creation of a new government agency independent of all existing departments.*

The agency would be along the lines of the Export-Import Bank or the Federal Home Loan Board. It would operate with a small cadre of top-flight administrators, manpower specialists, business and financial analysts, and economists.

7.3 *In view of the long-run and continuing nature of the adjustment prob-*

*lem the new government agency should operate under a multi-year
authorization.*

7.4 *The policy direction of the agency, within the framework legislated by
the Congress, should be set by a mixed board comprising the relevant
government officials* (e.g., at present, Assistant to the President for
Economic Affairs, Assistant to the President for Human Resources,
Secretary of Labor, Secretary of Commerce, Special Representative
for Trade Negotiations) *and representatives from the private sector*
(including labor union officials and corporate executives).

The Costs of the Proposals

The maximum resource cost of the proposed program is estimated at about
$300 million in its first year of operation. By its tenth year, the resource cost
could rise to about $350 million annually as the early retirement benefits
accumulated for older workers who took advantage of them. If present
procedures are continued, the budgetary cost to the federal government
would be $100 million per year higher as it replaced the state unemployment
insurance funds in paying compensation benefits to trade-impacted workers (or reimbursed the funds for their payments of unemployment compensation to such workers in cases where the trade assistance program did not
move quickly enough to provide payments as soon as the workers were laid
off). This is simply a substitution of one payment for another with no
inflationary effect on the economy, however, since the workers would have
received the unemployment compensation anyway. In addition, there
would be offsetting resource gains (including tax payments) in productivity
of the retrained workers and the reduced likelihood that they would ever
again require unemployment compensation.

Detailed analysis of the experience of 1967-69 suggests that 60,000
annual job layoffs were directly attributable to increased imports. Imports
increased very rapidly in those years, and domestic output of the imported
products did not decline in all cases; so this number may err on the high side
as a guide to eligibility for trade assistance in the future. On the other hand,
the size of the labor force has increased since then. But 60,000 appears to be
a reasonable estimate of the maximum number of workers who might be
eligible for benefits under the new program as a direct result of import flows.

Educated estimates suggest that another 20,000 layoffs annually could
be attributed to the indirect effects of import increases. Under the
liberalized criteria proposed, the annual number of workers laid off due to
trade flows could thus number about 80,000. The following calculations will
be based on this number, implicitly assuming that none of the 80,000 find

new jobs on their own. This is obviously unrealistic. Only 65 to 75 percent of the workers eligible under the Trade Expansion Act have actually sought help, and the percentage of workers seeking help under liberalized criteria would undoubtedly be smaller because this group would include far better workers—who would find new jobs quickly—then were eligible under the restrictive approach of the present law. The estimated costs would thus be adequate to cover a much larger number of displaced workers (probably 100,000 or more) if some did find work on their own, as they certainly would, and are undoubtedly biased toward erring on the high side.

The Department of Labor estimates that 17.5 percent of the dislocated workers could quickly find on-the-job training, with the government compensating their new employers at the average current rate of $60 per week for an average of 26 weeks. Thus, 14,000 workers would require little or no compensation benefits, at a cost to the government of about $22 million per year.

The other 66,000 workers would receive compensation benefits. The average manufacturing wage is now approaching $140 per week, 75 percent of which is $105. Unemployment insurance benefits already average $62 per week, however, so the supplementary trade benefit is only $43. To this must be added a maximum of $10 per week for government takeover of the health, life, and other insurance premiums previously contributed by the firms that laid off the eligible workers. The net economic cost of the compensation benefits is thus about $53 per week for the 66,000 workers.

It is estimated that the average duration of benefits will be 26 weeks. Under the assistance provisions of the Automotive Products Trade Act, the average duration was 20 weeks. This program took place in 1967-68, however, when aggregate U.S. unemployment was low and declining, and covered auto workers whose productivity (and hence potential for finding new work) was above average. It is probably too low a figure for the future program.

On the other hand, the 30-week average of the present trade "adjustment assistance" program is probably too high. Most of its experience came during 1970-71, when aggregate unemployment was very high. In addition, the workers who finally became eligible under the tight criteria of the present law are probably less productive, and hence less employable, than the average trade-impacted workers. And the early warning provision of the new program would permit an earlier start on searches for new jobs and retraining, so that fewer workers would now need the maximum duration of benefits. Thus an average benefits period of 26 weeks per worker over an entire business cycle under the liberalized criteria appears reasonable and again likely to err on the high side. The annual cost of compensation benefits to workers could thus average about $90 million.

This figure represents the *additional* payments to laid off workers above the unemployment insurance benefits they would receive anyway and is thus the best measure of the real resource cost of the new program. Under the present trade adjustment program, the federal government, out of trade assistance funds, reimburses the state unemployment insurance funds for all unemployment insurance benefits paid out to these workers. Most estimates of the cost of a new trade adjustment assistance program *include* this reimbursement, which would total about $100 million for the number of workers here estimated to receive compensation benefits due to trade dislocations. (In the new approach proposed here, of course, the emphasis on early warning and early action would often enable the trade assistance program to pick up the benefits for many workers as soon as they were laid off, so standard unemployment compensation would never enter the picture.) Whether or not such reimbursement is continued, however, the real resource cost of the program is limited to the *additional* benefits that it makes available.

In addition to on-the-job training, the proposed program would include institutional training. The Department of Labor estimates that 13 percent (10,000) of these dislocated workers can benefit from such programs. The programs cost the government about $2,000 per worker, so add about $20 million to the annual bill.

The Department of Labor estimates that relocation costs would amount to about $250 per worker, and that 20 percent of dislocated workers (16,000 annually) will relocate. This adds $4 million to total program cost.

Acceleration of Social Security benefits requires reimbursement to the Social Security Fund of about $2,600 per worker per year. The Department of Labor estimates that 20 percent of all dislocated workers (16,000) are 55 years or older, so this aspect of the program would add about $20 million to its total cost in the first year if even one-half of those eligible opted for early retirement. This reimbursement to the Social Security Fund would have to be paid for each worker for each year prior to the year in which he would have normally retired—probably an average of about 5 years later. By the tenth year of the program, the cost of this provision could thus rise to about $100 million annually—again assuming that one-half of all eligible workers opted for early retirement. Small additional expenditures would be required to reimburse individual firms for the early commencement of retirement benefits to workers with private pension plans.

The total cost of the proposed program for workers would thus be well under $200 million in its first year, and rise to a long-run equilibrium level of no more than $250 million annually after ten years. About 10 percent of all dislocated workers would be over 55 years old and are assumed to take advantage of the early retirement option. About 30 percent would benefit from on-the-job and institutional training. The rest would be able to find new jobs without such programs, assisted by the improved counselling or simply due to the inducements provided by the job test and the limited duration of compensation benefits, within an average period of six months.

It is extremely difficult to estimate costs for firms and communities. The relatively few firm cases to date have cost about $2 million each. Some of the proposals made above would actually reduce government costs per case, by substituting loan guarantees for loans, and promoting earlier—and hence cheaper—help. On the other hand, the new eligibility criteria may well produce more cases. Until experience is gained with the new program, it will be impossible to say how much it might cost. The same is of course true of the completely new program for communities. The Chamber therefore proposes an initial budgetary ceiling of $100 million for the two together, with that figure to be adjusted in future years in the light of whatever experience is gained to that time. The total annual resource cost of the proposed program would thus rise from a maximum of about $300 million in its first year to a maximum of about $350 million in the longer run.

The annual costs to the economy of the Burke-Hartke import quotas would rise from at least $4.5 billion in its first year—$3.4 to 6 billion from the rollback of imports, $1.1 billion from the new proportional quotas—to $5 to 10 billion (the $3.4 to 6 billion from the rollback, plus $3.5 to 7 billion from the proportional quotas, whose cost rises as time passes) in later years.[1] The annual costs to the U.S. economy of present trade restrictions, both here and in other countries, average $7.5 to 10.5 billion (and are rising over time). All of these costs are economic, and very conservative because standard economic analysis cannot capture dynamic and monopoly effects. The estimates do not even attempt to include the incalculable costs of such trade measures to U.S. foreign policy and to our national security. If the proposed new program of economic adjustment to liberal trade were instrumental in permitting an elimination of present restrictions as well as avoiding the Burke-Hartke quotas, its benefits would thus amount to $15 to 20 billion per year plus the avoidance of major national security difficulties, compared with its resource costs of $300 to 350 million per year.

Conclusion

The Chamber believes that the benefits of the proposed program far outweigh its costs. Indeed, the Chamber believes that the liberal trade policy which this program makes possible is essential for U.S. economic welfare and for the maintenance of our national security. It believes that the proposed program will work, building as it does on a number of precedents in different areas that have existed for many years, and may in fact provide a basis for much more extensive structural adjustment programs in the future that could play an even greater role in promoting the efficiency and growth or our economy. The Chamber urges the early adoption of such a program by the Congress, as part of legislation that will establish a new and constructive U.S. trade policy for the 1970s and beyond.

Note

1. Stephen P. Magee, "The Welfare Effects of Restrictions on U.S. Trade," *Brookings Papers on Economic Activity 3: 1972.*

18 International Adjustment Assistance

David Lea

Several proposals have been put forward for schemes of international cooperation in financing industrial adjustment programs necessitated by changes in the volume and pattern of world trade.

In 1967 the Trades Union Congress of the United Kingdom (TUC) put forward a plan for an OECD Development Fund that had two objectives: first, to internationalize the costs of adjustment assistance, with a view to permitting an increased flow of manufactured imports from the developing to the developed countries; and second, to encourage an increased flow of official aid, by a mechanism for alleviating temporary balance-of-payments difficulties faced by individual aid donors. However, in subsequent discussion it became apparent that there would be considerable difficulties, of both a political and practical nature, in setting up a scheme to insulate official aid payments from the balance-of-payments difficulties faced by individual developed countries. There would in particular be difficulties in reaching agreement about the basis and conditions of aid allocations to individual developing countries. From the development point of view, improvements in official aid and technical assistance are likely in many cases to be more beneficial than trade concessions—particularly so far as the least developed countries are concerned. This reinforces the need for progress on reform of the international monetary system, including the adoption of arrangements for the speedy adjustment of parities by countries in situations of fundamental balance-of-payments surplus or deficit. Following discussion of the TUC's proposal by the Trade Union Advisory Committee to OECD, in 1968 TUAC put forward a proposal for an OECD fund that would have as its main function the internationalization of the costs of adjustment assistance.

The TUAC proposal was the subject of further discussion during 1972, when it was proposed in a paper submitted by TUAC to the OECD High Level Trade Group under M. Jean Rey. The proposal assumed an additional interest at this time in view of the increasing concern being voiced by American and European unions at the adverse impact on employment of increasing manufactured imports from developing countries. Despite this renewed interest, however, the TUAC proposal has been discussed only in general terms. This chapter discusses in greater detail the possible objectives and functioning of an international adjustment assistance fund on the lines proposed by the TUAC.

308

Objectives of an International Fund

The ultimate aim of the fund would be to promote a transfer of resources from rich to poor countries, by removing political obstacles to the expansion of trade between these two groups of countries. All developed countries would contribute to the fund, which would be used to help finance adjustment programs in individual developed countries, where an industry was faced with contraction due to increased trade with developing countries. The adjustment programs would need to conform to certain common principles; a second, and important, objective of the fund would be to promote "upward harmonization" of the adjustment policies operated by individual countries.

The Fund as a Form of Aid

The fund proposal is based on assumptions that implicitly contradict "the comparative advantage" theory of international trade, at least so far as trade in manufactures between developing and developed countries is concerned. Thus, the traditional theory would assume that increases in trade produce overall increases in economic welfare for both trading countries. The theory would allow the possibility of reductions in economic welfare affecting particular industries or regions of any individual country, but would assume that such losses would be more than compensated for by economic gains to the country as a whole. Thus, for example, the economic gains to the country would include the availability of cheaper imports and improved export opportunities in the medium and longer term. The economic losses in particular sectors would include increased payment of social security benefits and reductions in tax revenue; it would also include important non-measurable elements, mainly the psychological and social costs falling on workers and their families due to unemployment and not compensated for by financial means. Assuming that all these gains and losses could be quantified, the theory would predict that the gains would be more than sufficient to pay for the losses. The country in question would be able to finance any necessary adjustments without entirely forfeiting the gains from trade. It could do this, for example, by levying more tax on consumers (whose real incomes had increased as a result of the availability of cheap imports) and by taxing the profits from increased exports; this revenue could be spent on job-creation and income-supplementation programs in the adversely affected industries and regions.

If it is assumed that the importing country benefits in overall economic welfare terms as a result of increased trade, there would be no case for seeking "compensation" from an international fund to help finance adjustment programs for industries affected by imports. The proposal for a fund is based on the assumption that in many cases, and particularly in the case of developed countries' imports from developing countries, the economic welfare gains from trade may be insufficient to offset the welfare losses. The likelihood of this happening reflects two recent developments in particular: first, the increased pace of change of trade patterns and industrial structures; and second, the fact that the existence of an articulate workforce, with rising social expectations, compels governments to attach greater weight than ever before to the non-measurable social costs of adjustment.

To the extent that the existence of the proposed fund had the effect of reducing political resistance to trade, and thus of promoting increased imports from developing countries that would not otherwise occur, it can be regarded as a form of aid—although it remains true that consumers in the importing countries would benefit as well. More specifically, it can be thought of as a mechanism for reallocating the costs of this "aid" more fairly among the developed countries. The fund would be of most relevance in the context of generalized, non-reciprocal tariff concessions granted by the developed to the developing countries. It would be of particular value in helping to promote the more widespread application by developed countries of the OECD Generalized Tariff Preference Scheme. It would, as with the OECD GTP scheme itself, be necessary to define a common list of developing countries, whose imports would be covered in principle by the fund.

The Role of Trade Liberalization in International Development

Given that the fund proposal is regarded as a form of aid, the case for such a fund rests on the assumption that expansion of manufactured exports is beneficial to the development efforts of developing countries. This proposition has been repeatedly endorsed by development economists and by the international agencies concerned with development. However, it is clear that the extent to which export growth improves development prospects and the living standards of the general population may vary greatly between different developing countries, according to the way in which the exporting industries are organized: whether they are domestic or foreign-owned; the standard of wages and conditions; and the financial relationship to the government.

The growth in the scale of the operations of multinational companies in developing countries raises a new set of questions concerning the effects of trade on the development prospects of these countries. A major reason why some trade unions—and particularly, American trade unions—have resisted proposals for liberal trade with developing countries is their belief that, while trade liberalization involved job losses at home, a very large part of the gains of such concessions accrue to the shareholders of wealthy multinational companies. It would therefore be essential for the establishment of an OECD Fund for adjustment assistance to be accompanied, first, by research into the effects of multinational companies' activities on the development prospects of developing countries, and second, by international agreement on a Code of Conduct for multinational companies operating in such countries. A detailed discussion of the contents of such a code is beyond the scope of this chapter, but the code should include a requirement to observe ILO fair labor standards, to comply with national social laws, and to recognize and negotiate with independent trade unions.

The Functioning of an OECD Adjustment Assistance Fund

Situations in Which Help Could Be Claimed from the Fund

Applicants for assistance from the fund would have to show that (1) the industry in question was experiencing a permanent reduction in employment levels and (2) the cause of this decline was an increase in competition from developing countries.

It is clear that considerable difficulties would arise in practice in identifying situations in which a decline in employment was directly attributable to an increase in imports from developing countries. In many cases the causes of decline would be more complex and would, for example, also include loss of export markets, and increasing capital intensity in an effort to remain competitive. It would therefore be preferable to define more broadly situations in which the fund would apply: the definition might cover situations where a loss of employment could be related to a decline in the industry's *world market share*, and this was shown to be due primarily to increased production by developing countries. A definition of this type would require continuous independent monitoring of world trade developments, a role that could be performed by OECD.

Activities for Which Assistance Would Be Provided

The aims of the various forms of assistance provided by participating countries should be two-fold: (1) to promote the adaptation of industrial structures into more permanently viable forms (either by the adaptation of the industry itself, or the transfer of resources into other activities) and (2) to alleviate the social problems caused by the loss of jobs. Activities eligible for assistance under the fund should ideally include: retraining and resettlement schemes; income support for workpeople in the form of training allowances, tideover payments, or early retirement on full pension; and financial assistance (including low-interest loans and employment-related grants) to firms to encourage new job creation. Although there might be advantages in also providing selective assistance to convert the structures of affected industries into more viable forms, in practice there would probably be considerable political difficulties in reaching agreement on acceptable forms of subsidy, and it might thus be preferable for adjustment measures of this kind to remain the sole responsibility of individual governments.

Applications for Assistance under the Fund

It is proposed that the fund should reimburse a part—say, 50 percent—of expenditures by national governments on approved schemes of the kind described above. Applications would have to come from public authorities, and projects for which help would be given would have to conform to certain common principles agreed by participants in the fund. These common principles should cover: (1) minimum levels, and coverage, of income support schemes for workpeople displaced by industrial restructuring; (2) clear obligations on employers to cooperate with the schemes in question, in particular by providing adequate advance notice of redundancies, and by giving workpeople time off work for retraining and job interviews; and (3) a government commitment to advance planning of manpower requirements at national, regional, and industrial levels.

The grant of asissistance under the fund would be conditional on it being established that the adjustment measures were necessitated primarily as a result of increases in competition from less-developed countries (see above). Finally, since the resources under the fund would be limited in total, it might well prove necessary to choose priorities for expenditure from a number of eligible projects. The procedure for examining this aspect is discussed below in relation to the question of how the fund would be constituted.

Assessing Individual Countries' Contributions to the Fund

The TUAC proposal suggested that individual countries' contributions to the fund should be calculated on a formula reflecting (1) each country's national income, (2) its national income per head, and (3) the inverse of the share of imports from developing countries in its national market.

The intention of item 3 is that the financial structure of the scheme should favor countries that import a relatively large share of manufactures from developing countries and should thus encourage other countries to increase their imports. However, the merit of this proposal is doubtful, for two reasons. First, it has been suggested above that the volume of actual import competition is in itself an insufficient indicator of the damage suffered by an industry due to competition from developing countries— account should also be taken of competition from developing countries in third markets. Second, the structure of the scheme should not be designed to "reward" countries for past performance. (In many cases this would be manifestly unfair; for example, the United Kingdom's high level of import penetration in the textiles sector to a large extent reflects the system of Commonwealth Preference from which, overall, the United Kingdom greatly benefited.) Instead, the scheme should aim to promote better performance in the future, and the criteria for assistance under the fund itself gives a positive incentive to countries that have restricted the access of manufactured imports to their markets, to liberalize these. It is therefore suggested that individual countries' contributions to the proposed fund should be calculated on a basis reflecting the national income per head of each country, weighted by the country's total national income.

Constitution of the Fund

Decisions about the allocation of assistance under the fund would involve conflicts of interest between participants in the fund. The TUAC proposal that the fund should be under OECD auspices was based on the view that obtaining the full advantages of the proposal would to a very large extent be dependent on obtaining the active cooperation of the United States and Japan, as well as the Western European countries. An OECD Fund would however clearly have to be administered by an executive body representative of participating governments at a political level. This executive body would consider applications for assistance under the fund and would, as necessary, select priorities from these applications. The body might be serviced jointly by the Trade, and Manpower, and Social Affairs Directorates of OECD, which would analyze the degree to which proposed adjustment programs were necessitated by increasing competition from developing countries.

It might be argued however that in practice, given the OECD's lack of political authority, it would be difficult to obtain the commitment of individual governments to a fund run under OECD auspices. A fund that failed to gain the support of major developed countries would be of little value. It might be argued that a more practicable objective would be to establish special machinery within an enlarged European Economic Community. If this approach were adopted, it would be essential to consult with the other main developed countries—the United States and Japan—in drawing up common principles for adjustment programs in individual countries, and these countries should be urged to conform to the agreed principles. OECD would be the appropriate body for coordinating consultation on these common principles and for monitoring progress in individual participating countries.

The forms of assistance proposed in this chapter would share certain of the objectives of existing Community schemes: for example, income support measures under the Social Fund; job creation in agricultural areas under the Agricultural Guidance and Guarantee Fund (FEOGA); and job creation and resettlement provisions under the E.C.S.C. Convention. However, separate machinery would be essential for the proposed scheme, because the criteria for assistance under the scheme would be very different from the criteria of existing EEC arrangements; specifically, the aim would be to promote industrial restructuring in circumstances where industrial decline is due to competition from developing countries, which is quite distinct from other Community objectives. The basis for fixing individual countries' contributions would also—reflecting the objectives of the scheme—be significantly different from that of the EEC budget.

Though adjustment assistance could in principle be dealt with on a national (or in the case of the EEC, a European) basis, this could with great advantage be underpinned by an OECD approach. The EEC, Japan, and the United States would then be publicly committed to programs of adjustment assistance as a positive alternative to excessive reliance on import safeguards. But as the concept of "active industrial policy" becomes generally accepted, some surveillance will be needed to avoid the danger that policies for "adjustment assistance" will entail permanent subsidies. In the light of its responsibilities in the field of industrial policy, as well as balance-of-payments policy and generalized preferences, the OECD would appear to be ideally suited to this purpose.

Part IV
Commentary

Sidney Golt

In the wealth of material in the chapters concerned with the subject of Part IV, it is impossible not to be selective. I shall deal primarily with safeguards and to some small extent with export restraint.

Dr. Düren's Chapter 13 has given an all-around picture of the adjustment process in the creation of the European Community. It is remarkable how smoothly, at any rate on the trade side, adjustment has taken place, especially in relation to the magnitude of the changes carried through and the comparative shortness of the period provided. It would have been quite extraordinary if this process had gone through without some frictions and difficulty; in the event, the number and size of the problems have been quite extraordinarily small.

Dr. Düren also shows that there has been no single actual use of the safeguard clause. There has been only one case of even an application by any country to use it and in that case—the French domestic appliance industry's difficulties following the success of Italian competition—the refusal of the application was followed by successful adaption to the circumstances.

Similarly, the EFTA lived its life through and completed—in a period shorter than the original convention provided for—the total abolition of tariffs and restrictive quotas on manufactured goods without any use of the safeguard clauses. Nor should we overlook the worldwide process that has gone on over the whole period since the early 1950s. Tariffs are not yet entirely insignificant as a trade barrier, but the very fact that the point has to be made is an indication of the distance traveled since the first GATT tariff negotiations. And, until very recently, the use of escape mechanisms by the main trading countries has been very small when measured against the total amount of trade involved and the amount of adjustment that has been carried through with no intervention and without significant concern.

This may seem an optimistic picture of what has happened and of the present situation. But it does not seem to me an exaggeration, and I think it needs to be recalled for two reasons: first, to remind ourselves, in our natural concentration on today's problems, that a great deal has been accomplished in a comparatively short time; second, to remind governments of what is at risk if exaggeration of the problems of adjustment were really to set the world moving back instead of forward.

Against this indication of my own general approach, I turn now to the topic of safeguards in any forthcoming trade negotiations. The first question is why this has seemed to become the central issue in discussion, when it was so subsidiary a matter among the Six at Messina, among the Seven at Saltsjobaden, and in the whole process of tariff reduction from Geneva through Torquay and Annecy and up to and including the Kennedy Round.

Like so much else, this must be a reflection of the change in the trading power pattern in the postwar world, and in particular the change from the well-shaped world of the early years of the quarter century—the United States at the hub and the rest of us round the rim, with the most important trading relationship for all of us the connecting spoke—to the triangular world formed by the three, much more nearly equal, giant trading partners of today.

I associate with this change three further developments. First, the trading world for which and by which the rules of the GATT were written consisted of some two dozen countries, differing certainly among themselves in the weight of their share of world trade, but all playing a significant separate part and all separately contributing, on more or less equal terms, to the world debate. The reduction of this cohort of nations to three giants, with perhaps three or four others of any significant weight at all in world trade, is a change in fundamental character that affects all the terms of the equation, not excluding the MFN rule. In this connection, moreover, the world outside Europe (as well as Europe itself) must now begin to accustom itself to the concept of the European Community as one entity for trade purposes, and to stop thinking about intra-Community trade as any more discriminatory than trade among the states of the United States.

Secondly, the failure of the monetary mechanism to keep in step with the change in the relative economic strengths of the major countries has in itself been a contributory exaggerating factor in the process of change.

Thirdly, partly as a result of this monetary dislocation, but for many other reasons also, neither the United States nor the Community has yet sufficiently digested or been able to accommodate to the new position of Japan, especially the pace at which Japan's growth has occurred.

The problem of safeguards, therefore, is largely a problem of wariness in reaction to a new and unfamiliar situation that has developed with startling speed. It would be skirting the truth not to admit that the present preoccupation stems largely from U.S. and European fears of rapidly growing and seemingly uncontainable competition in a succession of industries, first from Japan and then three or four other countries that are at present still comparatively small, but may have the potential and the entrepreneurial skills that could enable them to emulate Japan's export surge.

In making this point, I do not at all disregard the very cogent argument that Professor Komiya has put forward in his comment on U.S. foreign economic policy (pages 359-63). Indeed, I agree very substantially with his criticism of U.S. policies on exchange rates, and, especially, of the tactics of U.S. negotiations in the period following August 15, 1971.[1] But I would make one comment in reply to his question, "What would have been the U.S. reaction if the rest of us (during the period of U.S. surplus in early postwar years) asked her to reduce tariffs unilaterally, and so forth, without making any trade concessions in return?" This is a very nearly exact representation of what, in effect, *did* actually happen. Of course, we all, in form, reduced our tariffs in the negotiations. But, with U.S. acquiescence, we retained the QRs that frustrated the imports which would have resulted from these reductions.

This leads to my concluding points about safeguards in light of the differences between 1947 and 1973. The GATT, written in the circumstances of 1947, saw the world's principal problem as being the persistent and perhaps permanent inability of other countries to earn enough dollars to buy from the United States all they needed. The provision for the use of discriminatory quantitative restrictions was related to the balance of payments precisely because it dealt with a balance-of-payments problem, vis-a-vis one country. It was not needed to protect the domestic industries of other countries against U.S. trade competition, but to enable them to ration their dollar resources among their own competing claims. In effect, it used trade mechanisms to deal with the monetary problem.

The 1973 problem, as both governments and industry in Europe and America see it, is on the contrary the trade problem of coping with what seems to be uncontainable competitiveness. No doubt that concern is greatly exaggerated. No doubt also the right remedy for it is the monetary one—getting the exchange rates somewhere near right and devising the machinery to ensure that they don't go so disastrously wrong again.

But, meanwhile, we should recognize that if major trade negotiations are going to be possible at all (and I see no certainty that they are) a safeguard clause that will be a sensible part of them will have to be related to the substance of what it is needed for. There seems no alternative, therefore, to having one that, provided it is subject to reasonable international procedures and supervision, could be used discriminatorily. I agree particularly with Mr. Solomon (Chapter 16) that a temporary tariff increase might be a more appropriate method than QRs; but I think that the criticisms of his mechanisms that Dr. Bergsten has made, in Chapter 15 on "voluntary" export restraints, have considerable substance.

As to "compensation" or "retaliation," should we not return to first principles? The first question is surely whether the action taken nullifies a previous bargain freely arrived at between the parties concerned. If country A, in applying the safeguard against country B, increases a tariff that has been bound to B then B must certainly have at least a prima facie case for compensation.

There are, however, two additional points to be made. First, on the assumption that other things—and especially world monetary arrangements—that affect trade are put right, I see no reason why such a safeguard clause should be used more often or widely than its analogues were before 1971. Second, and perhaps more important, the effective and reasonable operation of any system that includes international participation calls for a quite substantial change of attitude on the part of many governments, and in particular—since it is they who have the influence to determine these matters for the world—of the governments of the United States and the European Community. They will simply have to return to an acceptance of the rule of law in trade affairs which was fundamentally the style of the fifties rather than of the sixties, much less of our present decade so far. On the prospect for this, at any rate in the short term, I am no optimist.

I turn now very briefly to the interesting and innovative chapter by Dr. Bergsten on "voluntary" export restraints. I would only say that I think he has rightly concluded that they are a dangerous and unwelcome addition to the armory of trade restrictions. They are particularly pernicious because they are in their essence instruments of bilateral power bargaining, and both their "voluntariness" and their extent are reflections of the power relationship between the participants. If the postwar settlements meant anything, it was that trade (and monetary) relations would be determined not by the exercise of bilateral political and economic power, but within the framework of the multilateral institutions, and that the relations between any two members that might affect the working of the system were the concern of all. Professor Johnson has described this as the "civilization of international economic relations,"[2] and Professor Cooper has illuminated the topic in his discussion of the role of economic affairs in foreign policy.[3]

The GATT once seemed to be moving towards having two classes of members—the Contracting Parties and the Expanding Parties. The danger now is of a concerted move towards being Contracting-out Parties. But perhaps it is into the hands of the newest great participant in international trade, Japan, that the torch of defense of the principles of the GATT should now pass.

Notes

1. See also C. Fred Bergsten, "The New Economics and U.S. Foreign Policy," *Foreign Affairs* (January 1972), pp. 199-222.

2. Three Banks Review, London, June 1972.

3. "Trade Policy is Foreign Policy," *Foreign Policy* 9, Winter 1972-73, pp. 18-36.

**Part V
World Trade Policies for the
Future**

19 Negotiations in Prospect

Eric Wyndham-White

There are few who would deny that the GATT rules for international trade have played a major constructive role in the last two decades. It is equally true that many voices are now raised to question their validity and relevance in the present and predictable future. Before coming to any judgment and, if the judgment supports the sceptics, making suggestions for an alternative commercial code it would be judicious to examine the raison d'etre of the GATT regime and also to analyze its essential characteristics.

The origins of the GATT rules are to be found in two distinct but closely related sources. The first may be termed ideological and political. Cordell Hull and Will Clayton—and the thinking they personified—placed an orderly and acceptable commercial system amongst the high priorities of international political order and solidarity. They perceived autarchic commercial policies, protectionism, and above all discrimination, as major factors of international political conflict. Accordingly, side by side with the financial institutions of Bretton Woods, they envisaged a multilateral, non-discriminatory, trading system as an essential element in the new order that should emerge from the catastrophe of world war. Hence the abortive attempt to construct—within a world political order embodied in the United Nations Charter and the financial cornerstones of Bretton Woods—a charter for international trade that would complete the grand design of a world society based upon equality, justice, and equity.

Reasons of timing and unpredictable political developments condemned the trade charter to stillbirth. Meanwhile, however, the architects of this ill-fated endeavor had agreed upon a major commercial negotiation requiring for its effectiveness a minimum of agreed rules of commercial policy to protect the specific trade concession that would be exchanged in the negotiations. The expedient adopted was to incorporate in the General Agreement on Tariffs and Trade the bulk of the provisions on commercial policy that formed part of the more ambitious charter for international trade negotiated in successive stages in London, Geneva, and Havana in 1947-48.

Disregarding this ideological umbilical cord, the code of commercial conduct can be regarded as essentially a set of rules designed to protect the specific tariff concessions negotiated initially in Geneva in 1948, and subsequently in Torquay, Annecy, again Geneva, and finally in the Kennedy Round. But this would involve ignoring the historical process whereby these rules—in the vacuum created by the foundering of the Havana Charter—became the accepted ground rules for the international trading system that contributed in large measure to the astounding growth of international trade and national economies in the last two decades.

There is therefore good reason for caution in approaching the question as to whether it is prudent or appropriate to tinker with a system that has proved its value in demonstrable and practical terms. It is certainly unwise to blow up a bridge—even an imperfect one—unless one is sure that an effective tunnel can be constructed to take its place.

The first thing then is to examine what are the fundamentals of the GATT rules and to confront these with the circumstances and exigencies of the present and future of international trade, without impairing this analysis by preconceived ideological concepts.

Non-discrimination

The fundamental cornerstone of the GATT is the rule of non-discrimination. Its principal expression is the unconditional most-favored-nation clause (Article 1). From the outset it suffered some emasculation. Strong political and emotional factors made it necessary to exclude existing preferential systems, notably the controversial Ottawa preferences, but also French colonial and U.S. pseudo-colonial preferences, subject only to an interdiction against increasing the margins of preference and a commitment to include in commercial negotiations the reduction and elimination of existing margins. Equally, insofar as the rule inhibiting the use of quantitative restrictions of imports admitted of exceptions, the restrictions were enjoined to be non-discriminatory except insofar as discrimination could be justified on balance-of-payments grounds within the highly permissive transitional provisions of the International Monetary Fund. This somewhat extraordinary provision is discussed from a different viewpoint subsequently in this chapter.

A broader and more philosophical exception to MFN was the provisions (Article 24) relating to customs unions and free trade areas. At the time of the negotiation of the Havana Charter, the theme of regional economic groupings was very much in the air, and some of the provisions of Article 24 reflect this fact. But the thinking was vague and unfocussed with the result that the conditions and safeguards embodied in Article 24 followed a traditional pattern and were to require considerable bending to cover the eventual situations for which they were invoked.

It would strain credibility too far to assert that the application of most-favored-nation treatment is a characteristic feature of the international trading system as it operates today. The major trading countries of

Europe (including now the United Kingdom) conduct their mutual trade within the terms and conditions of the Treaty of Rome, which predicates inter alia a customs union with free trade between its members and a common external tariff to be applied to imports from outside the European Economic Community. In practice this common external tariff is far from common in its application. Under the impulse of a variety of factors —mostly, but not exclusively, political—the Community has for some years accorded duty-free entry to products of the former French and Belgian colonial territories and in turn enjoyed preferential entry to the markets of the associated African states. This arrangement has been euphemistically presented to GATT as a free-trade area. Although GATT has never officially accepted this claim, it has for understandable reasons never attempted to close the doors to this particular equipage of coach and horses that the Community saw fit to drive through the conceptually narrow door of Article 24. Nothing succeeds like success, and "association" agreements have been found an elegant technique for dealing with a number of aspirants who were clearly not—or not yet—Community material but could not be ignored politically. Thus special arrangements have been worked out with Greece and Turkey (the acute political observer will identify these countries as the Eastern fringe of NATO) on the hypothesis that these are interim stages in the accession of these countries in a long and vulnerable transitional period. It was a short step thereafter to work out special preferential trading arrangements with other third countries that were either politically important or importunate. If this course had to be followed at all—and the author has always questioned its validity or necessity—it would at least have been preferable that the Community should have limited itself to benevolence without loading the "associations" and "arrangements" with reverse preferences for the benefit of the Community's exports.

The EFTA countries that have not acceded to the EEC apparently intend to continue to apply the Stockholm Convention—which provides for duty free treatment of industrial products, and special arrangements on agriculture—to their intra-trade, and an agreement on relatively comprehensive industrial free trade—accompanied of course by special arrangements for agriculture—is the device adopted by the Community for satisfying the aspirations of the EETA non-acceders.

If we add to these major phenomena the proliferation of regional economic groupings elsewhere in the world with preferential consequences—usually, of course, they rely on an avowed intent to move towards the elastic framework of Article 24—and the various and variable preferential schemes in favor of (and occasionally between) developing countries, it becomes difficult to sustain that the unconditional most-favored-nation clause is a basic pillar of the international trading system.

We shall examine at a later stage whether the interdiction of the use of quantitative restrictions in imports or exports for commercial purposes is equally illusory. Insofar as non-discrimination in the use of quantitative restrictions—assuming they are valid in the first place—is concerned, there might at first sight appear to be some reason for complacency. But the widespread use of quantitative restrictions against imports of a major trading nation such as Japan—even when the legal niceties are observed by invoking the provisions of Article 35 of GATT—and the systematic use of QRs as a method of negotiating bilateral agreements with the communist states raise some doubts as to the justification for such complacency. It is also an unhealthy sign when a major trading country like the United States, for national reasons of its own determination, decides to bring an important sector of its trade under quota control and to discriminate in the operation of the quotas in favor of friendly neighbors. This preferential quota system for oil is now being abandoned not for reasons of principle but because of an acute shortage of energy in the United States. It remains on the books as a disquieting precedent.

The Interdiction of the Use of Quantitative Restrictions on Imports and Exports

It is another basic concept of GATT that protection shall in general be afforded exclusively by the customs tariff, the use of quantitative restrictions on imports for protective purposes being completely excluded. This interdiction—like everything else in GATT—is subject to exceptions, strictly conditional in the case of agriculture, unqualified when reasons of national security are invoked, and broad—though in the author's view spurious—in the case of acute balance-of-payments difficulties. Generally speaking, therefore, the interdiction of QR for overt protective purposes is both sweeping and fundamental. On the face of things, this basic rule appears to have been largely respected. Unhappily this rare acceptance of the rule of law is more apparent than real. When the rash of balance-of-payments QRs was swept away, it was found that there were a number of restrictions that in fact had come to have—even if one assumes charitably that this was not the initial intent in imposing them—a protective effect on certain "sensitive" (this is generally an euphemism for "economically inefficient") industries. It was therefore proposed that a formal procedure—which would include temporary legal cover—should be established to ensure the elimination of these residual restrictions within a defined time period. This was the origin of the so-called "hard core" waiver. So far no contracting party has invoked the benefit of this procedure, and a significant number of residual restrictions has continued to be maintained illegally and for protectionist reasons. A large number are of course in the agricultural sector, which is hereafter treated separately, but there are enough in other areas to weaken considerably the effectiveness of the GATT rules.

Some contracting parties have preferred to wear the mantle of righteousness—which apart from its spiritual comfort is also a useful garment to wear when seeking compliance from others—by shifting the burden of restriction on to the country or countries whose exports are disturbing domestic producers. This device—usually seductively described as "voluntary" export restriction—was invented many years ago by the United States in its bilateral dealings with Japan. It appears to be gaining in popularity. Its most dramatic and significant debut on the international scene was in the well-known GATT cotton textiles agreement. Faced with the threat of unilateral—and certainly severe—import restrictions by the United States, accompanied by the real and horrendous probability that once quotas were enacted in one sector they would spread like wildfire to others, the United States persuaded Japan, Hong Kong, India, and other "low-cost" textile producers to place quantitative limitations on their exports to the United States whenever these were causing or threatening to cause serious disruption of the U.S. industry, with the United States reserving the right to determine whether or not such a threat existed. Other countries were of course not hesitant to use the agreement to give a cloak of respectability to the import restrictions they also maintain against cotton textile imports from the same countries.

Whilst there are valid grounds for considering the Textiles Arrangement (which like most temporary devices has taken on every appearance of permanence) as a legitimate opportunism that avoided something that could have been far worse (even for the immediate victims), it would be unrealistic not to recognize the violence it does to GATT concepts, since the device of "voluntary" export restriction has since been applied to steel and has many advocates for application in other areas. The device does not even avoid open breach of the rules since, as is usually conveniently forgotten, the interdiction of the use of quantitative restrictions applies equally to export as to import restrictions (Article II). It is also by nature and intent discriminatory.

The foregoing suggests, without taking into account the abuse of the permitted use of quantitative restrictions for balance-of-payments reasons and the general license applied to agriculture, that the GATT system is not in perfect health in yet another basic area.

GATT and Balance of Payments

The most sweeping permitted exception to the GATT prohibition of QR is that which allows contracting parties confronted with a serious decline in monetary reserves to impose quantitative restrictions on imports to the extent necessary to eliminate the threat or to reinforce an inadequate reserve position. The restrictions must be non-discriminatory except insofar as discrimination in exchange restrictions is permitted under the IMF rules. The GATT is required to accept the findings of the IMF as to the facts of the balance of payments and reserve position of the country invoking the exception. In theory, the judgment as to whether the invocation of the balance-of-payments exception is justified and the extent of the restrictions commensurate with the gravity of the situation rests with the GATT. In practice the certificate provided by the IMF at the outset of the consultations is so drafted as to render the rule of the GATT on the basic issue purely symbolic. The consultations in the GATT are, therefore, in part an unnecessary duplication of what has been done more professionally in the IMF; but they do provide a useful examination of the trade effects of the measures adopted by the deficit country on its trade with other contracting parties. These consultations have occasionally yielded practical results in mitigating some of the peripheral or marginal trade effects and in any case clearly underline that the measures, though in form commercial, are in fact solely justified as exchange measures to arrest declining or to fortify weak reserve positions. It is accordingly highly doubtful whether these provisions should appear in the GATT. In the author's view their inclusion—at least in their present form—is an anomaly explicable on the basis of the facts and the atmosphere in which the treaty was negotiated. In 1947 many of the negotiators were still haunted by memories of 1929-31, and though they welcomed the apparent constructive change in U.S. attitudes, they were unwilling to tie their hands unconditionally on commercial policy to an extent that would leave them powerless to ward off or insulate themselves from a deflationary pressure exerted by the United States in a future hypothetical depression. In this context, they eyed with some apprehension the domination that heavy-weighted voting secured to the United States in the IMF. They sought in the ITO Charter and carried over into GATT a freedom to take defensive measures through commercial policy that might be blocked by negative-weighted voting in the monetary area. The same apprehensiveness explains the odd provision in Article 23, which enables the GATT by a majority vote to relieve a contracting party of its obligations if the benefits of the agreement are being impaired by "any other situation."

To a large extent, these fears no longer exist and, of course, the weighted voting in the IMF has undergone considerable modification. Accordingly, the time has now come to recognize that the provisions relating to the use of QR for balance-of-payments reasons are inappropriate in what purports to be essentially a trade agreement. Commercial measures adopted exclusively for balance-of-payments reasons are essentially exchange restrictions applied by a particular technique and should be dealt with as such. When they are widespread—or even massively applied by one major trading country—they tend to have a misleading appearance and to bring unjustified discredit on the trading system as such. One other mild advantage is that their elimination would prevent the GATT being put into the future, as it has been in the past, in the rather absurd position of urging countries to adopt a highly restrictive technique such as quota restriction in the place of temporary import surcharges for which even this catholic institution provides no blessing.

Other Trade Measures

As elsewhere what is said here excludes agricultural trade that is dealt with separately. Next in importance are the rules relating to subsidies. By and large, in the industrial area—and excluding the special sector of shipbuilding—the rules on subsidies have been reasonably respected so far as they go. But they do not in fact go very far, since they are confined to the more obvious and easily identifiable direct subsidies on exports. They do not cover—or at least are deemed not to cover—the more sophisticated devices that have similar trade diverting or restrictive effects (e.g., competitive export guarantee facilities, tied loans, investment credits and subsidies, tax rebates, and so forth). The anti-dumping provisions are well drafted but not uniformly applied, although the supplementary anti-dumping code negotiated in the Kennedy Round was an important step forward.

The state trading provisions are entirely inadequate to provide a basis for the accession on a meaningful basis of countries whose trade is totally conducted through state agencies. They are largely ignored in the operation of state or parastatal institutions in otherwise free enterprise countries.

Accession and Membership

There are two methods of accession to the General Agreement. The standard form is the submission of an application in which the applicant expresses the desire to acquire the benefits and accept the obligations of membership. The application is examined by the GATT and submitted to a vote requiring a positive vote of two-thirds of the existing contracting parties. The approval normally requires that the applicant pay an entrance fee to the extent of negotiating with the other contracting parties tariff concessions equivalent to the benefit the applicant automatically acquires to all the tariff concessions hitherto negotiated and bound in the GATT schedules.

The negotiations with state trading countries are more complicated since they involve the negotiation of terms of accession that give some meaning to obligations to be assumed by the acceding country in whose case the rules of GATT, as they now stand, in terms of providing any real reciprocity in exchange for full GATT treatment, are largely meaningless.

Accessory to the normal accession procedure is one glaring anomaly that is again explicable on historical grounds. Any contracting party is free, on the accession of any new member, to refuse to enter into negotiations with the newcomer and to withhold GATT treatment from it (Article 35). Article 35 being thus invoked, there arises the anomalous situation of two countries participating together in the world trading system and institutions but having no GATT relationship between them. Nevertheless, in theory, either can participate in the voting on the other's rights and obligations. Usually good taste excludes this in practice, but the right curiously enough exists.

In the first instance, the inclusion of such a provision was necessitated by the circumstances of U.S. participation. The United States participated in the negotiations establishing the GATT on the basis of the negotiating authority delegated to the administration by the Reciprocal Trade Agreements Act, and its continued participation in GATT and in the negotiations sponsored by GATT has continued to be based legally on that statute as periodically extended by Congress. This legislation limits the extension of trade concessions to countries with whom the United States has entered into negotiations on a basis of reciprocity. Unfortunately other countries fastened on this technicality to endow Article 35 with a more dangerous potential by allowing any contracting party to invoke it against any new acceding country without having to justify or motivate its action. The full negative implication of this provision was brought clearly into the open when Japan acceded to the GATT. Immediately, an important number of contracting parties invoked the Article 35 provision in order to be free to discriminate against Japan. This is not the place to enter into a critique of this curious act of politico-economic statesmanship. Enough has been said to provoke some question whether such a provision is a desirable element in a generally applicable set of trade rules.

Loosening the Bonds

The great advantage of the GATT over all previous attempts to organize the international trading system is that the provisions of the GATT represent legal rights and obligations of the member countries. This means that if any country strays out of line, it has to compensate by substituting comparable benefits to those it withholds or suffer equivalent retaliation by the injured members. This, in addition to the general reluctance to be held in breach of international obligations, has been a poweful force in sustaining respect for the GATT rules.

Generally speaking—and even allowing for the loopholes to which attention has been drawn above—the commercial code embodied in the GATT is a strong one, and unless there had been—more or less unwittingly—built into it a mechanism for providing some degree of flexibility, it is likely that the GATT mechanism would have broken down long ago. This flexibility was achieved by yet another distortion of a provision inserted initially for quite limited reasons.

Article 25 enables the GATT, by a two-thirds vote, "in exceptional circumstances not elsewhere provided for in the Agreement," to grant to an applicant contracting party a waiver of particular obligations under the agreement. This article was intended originally to be extremely limited in its application—that is, to cover natural disasters, national emergencies, and so on. Hence it has come to have exceedingly wide coverage since it has been held to extend even to the obligations relating to the tariff concessions and MFN treatment that cannot be amended except by unanimous agreement.

Article 25 has in practice proved to be one of the most actively—and, on balance, constructively—invoked provisions of the General Agreement. Waivers have, in general, been accompanied by carefully negotiated conditions and safeguards designed to protect the interests of other members against an abusive use of the flexibility accorded to the applicant. Moreover, the existence of a waiver does not override another contracting party's right to resort to the nullification and impairment provisions of the agreement.

There comes a point, however, when the ready appeal to this instrument of flexibility suggests that the time may have come to have another look at the rules themselves. This feeling is reinforced by a growing tendency to assert the flexibility whilst foregoing the formalities of Article 25.

Sanctions

It is axiomatic that any rule of law must have behind it a system of enforcement and sanctions for violations. The contractual nature of GATT determines the nature of its provisions for enforcement and sanctions.

In the first place the mechanism can only be set in motion at the initiative of an aggrieved member. The GATT, as an institution, cannot initiate proceedings against the offender. Any contracting party that feels the benefits it expects to derive under the agreement, because of the action of another contracting party whether or not they are inconsistent with the agreement, can invoke the intervention of the organization. After exhausting the possibilities of conciliation, the GATT can rule on the matter, make recommendations to the parties, and in the last resort can relieve the plaintiff of obligations equivalent to the loss that it is found to be suffering.

The sanction is negative and weak, but the conciliation possibilities inherent in the procedure are of great value and have been used very effectively. The very existence of the possibility of appeal to the organization has a salutary disciplinary effect.

This then has been a very positive aspect of GATT's operation and is capable of further positive development in the future.

Membership

Given its contractual character GATT is not, like the specialized agencies of the United Nations, a universal organization. Accession, as we have seen, requires negotiation with and the agreement of the existing contracting parties. The membership has in fact grown very fast—perhaps too fast to sustain the validity of its contractual character. For this there are two reasons. First, the provision whereby a newly independent state, previously under the colonial rule or authority of a contracting party to the General Agreement can, upon application and with the sponsorship of its former suzerain, automatically accede to the agreement. The rapid liquidation of the old imperial empires brought in a large number of new adherents, many of whom were motivated principally by considerations of prestige and partly by a natural desire to retain any benefit in the trade area that their previous indirect membership secured to them. There is rather more doubt as to whether they are conscious of or sensitive to the obligations involved or realistically in a position to assume such obligations in any meaningful way.

Secondly, the GATT—perhaps apprehensive of a takeover bid—has been very lenient, one might even say lax, in the consideration of applications for accession by developing countries. Indeed it has sometimes seemed to be operating a recruiting station rather than a screening operation.

For these reasons there has been a vast overloading of the membership by countries that despite their benefiting largely and depending heavily on expansion of trade as the GATT has fostered, appear to derive little direct or easily identifiable benefit from the GATT provisions and that are far from willing (unwisely, in their own interest, in the author's opinion) to accept the obligations and disciplines membership of GATT entails.

There was a serious risk at one stage that GATT, because of its large and heterogeneous membership, would lose its practical and businesslike character. Nothing could be less glamorous or exciting than the agenda of a good annual meeting of the "Contracting Parties," but few annual meetings produce equally relevant, practical, and useful results. Ironically this fact ensures them a nil or even negative press.

Happily, the unrest of the developing with their position in international commerce was institutionalized in UNCTAD, which provides a far more appropriate forum for the ample and time-consuming international discussion of these important and highly complicated issues.

Provisional Application

The supreme oddity of the GATT is that it has never been legally accepted or entered into force for any of its members. It is applied through a Protocol of Provisional Application, which binds contracting parties to observe the provisions of the agreement to the fullest extent not inconsistent with existing legislation. This means that the executive power is bound to act in accordance with the GATT except only in circumstances where it is not bound to act otherwise by legislation already existing when it acceded (for the most important countries this means 1947).

Once again this curious situation derives from the peculiarities of the U.S. Constitution. It has enabled the United States in effect to participate in an international trade organization without benefit of clergy, if one may refer in such terms to direct approval by the U.S. Congress.

It is predictable—and one of the risks of undertaking an overhaul of the system—that ratification by Congress and by other legislatures would be a major problem in giving effect to any new order resulting from negotiation. Against this must, however, be set the undoubted fact that if unrest with the present system continues to mount, national legislatures will not be unduly tender in overriding what the U.S. Congress has from time to time described disdainfully as "that Executive Agreement known as the General Agreement on Tariffs and Trade."

Agriculture

The complicated problem of international trade in agricultural products has been left as the last item in the review since in a sense it pervades the whole.

It has occasionally been said that the GATT has never applied to agriculture. This is a considerable exaggeration. Over the years a large number of valuable concessions on agricultural products have been successfully negotiated, and a substantial volume of international trade has been carried on under GATT rules. Agricultural exporters have recognized too that the GATT has provided the most useful forum for airing and discussing agricultural trade problems even if discussion has so far failed to provide satisfactory solutions to the problem.

It is true that on basic agricultural products few, if any, countries have felt in any way bound to adapt their national policies in order to comply with GATT rules. Already in the original agreement the important rules on quotas and subsidies leant heavily in favor of a degree of controlled agricultural protectionism. But the limitations were generally ignored, and indeed one major contracting party—with a certain puritanism that was to prove more embarrassing to itself than to others—sought and obtained a waiver that entirely freed its agriculture from GATT restraints, subject, it is true, to prolonged and penetrating annual consultations that were not without some marginal practical results. Most other countries went their various ways without the benediction of the GATT and equally without regard to its provisions. They no doubt argued that other countries had the mechanism for complaint at hand in the General Agreement if their sense of grievance was strong enough and their own conscience sufficiently clear.

This uneasy modus vivendi was broken by the establishment of the common agricultural policy of the European Economic Community. Whatever its merits or demerits in terms of the Community itself and however ingeniously it may be demonstrated that it does not overtly violate any GATT provision, the fact remains that the effect of the CAP is to insulate Community agriculture from the world market, except for the negative effects resulting from its off-loading surpluses with massive subsidies on world markets. The inclusion of the vital U.K. market in the Community system adds a new dimension to an already explosive problem. The author has made elsewhere some suggestions for handling this problem which are included by reference in the negotiating proposals put forth below.[1]

Negotiations in Prospect

This summary critical review of the system as it stands provides the background of what should be sought in the new negotiations, which many are pressing with more fervor than apparent forethought.

It seems to the author that the circumstances call for negotiations at two different levels, although there would be some advantage in combining them in a single operation.

The first and lowest level of negotiation relates to comparatively minor problems that nevertheless create disproportionate frictions, as well as a number of adjustments calling for negotiations under the existing provisions of GATT (e.g., tariff adjustments consequential upon the accession of the United Kingdom and other countries to the European Economic Community). The irritants include some of the peripheral effects of the common agricultural policy that are capable of negotiation without going to the heart of the problem. It would be unwise to talk up these issues into major problems just for the sake of mounting or appearing to mount a major negotiation. After all, international trade is in a pretty healthy condition and is likely to continue its favorable trend for some time to come, even if the evident defects in the system are not immediately corrected.

On the other hand, there is mounting dissatisfaction with the present international trading system, not as we have seen without reason. It would indeed be strange if the rules negotiated in the context of 1947 would be appropriate to that of the 1970s and 1980s. In the author's view therefore—particularly when the international monetary mechanism is about to undergo a comprehensive overhaul—it is timely to initiate with careful preparation a renegotiation of the GATT that would, as in 1947, include important negotiations on the reduction of remaining trade barriers and the drafting of a commercial code appropriate to the circumstances of today and the future we foresee. This negotiation will be long and difficult. The 1947 settlement, which was comparatively an easy matter, since there was a large measure of agreement on the major issues between the principal countries was a long drawn out and hard fought affair. It required a Preparatory Committee whose work spread over the years 1946 and 1947 and a full scale international conference lasting nearly six months. The negotiations in prospect will be more difficult as there is less basic agreement on the fundamentals, and the issues are, if anything, more complex.

There follow some suggestions as to how to go about the business.

At a reasonable early date the major trading countries should agree to enter into negotiations, within the framework of GATT, to deal with the issues at both levels indicated above.

In order to show the seriousness of their intent the major negotiators should obtain through the appropriate constitutional processes a comprehensive negotiating mandate, sufficiently broad to cover the wide scope of the negotiations but not so specific as to limit the room for maneuver of the negotiators. The experience of the Kennedy Round suggests that this definition of the scope of the negotiations will be the most important element in the pre-negotiation stage. It involves a new approach both for the EEC and for the United States. Hitherto the Council of Ministers has tended to give the commission an initial, rather vaguely defined, negotiating mandate and to dole out specific mandates from time to time as the negotiations proceed, often so detailed as to limit the commission's role to that of a post office. The commission's role as a negotiator is still further diminished by the absence of security in Brussels. The discussions and decisions of the Council of Ministers are immediately reported in the press—and in more sophisticated detail by the assiduous delegations of other countries accredited to the EEC. In consequence, the commission negotiates not only with limited cards, but the hand is always fully exposed to its negotiating partners. The practice in the United States has been to seek from Congress a delegation of powers that by definition limits the negotiating power of the executive within the limits to which the legislature is prepared to delegate in advance. This has obvious disadvantages since it discloses the maximum U.S. position ab initio and inhibits the possibility of adapting its negotiating position to the full possibilities that unfold in the course of negotiation. The painful and abortive negotiation on American Selling Price in the Kennedy Round sharply illustrates this difficulty. The same example illustrates the risks—both for the U.S. executive and for its negotiating partners—of negotiating subject to Congressional ratification. European negotiators have always been wary of being put in the position of being called upon later to pay an additional price for ratification by Congress. Despite these evident risks, there would appear to be no alternative if negotiations of the scope here envisaged are to be successfully undertaken. It is therefore a question of limiting the risks through a more intimate congressional/administration relationship in the negotiating process. This might be achieved by a joint congressional resolution embodying a negotiating mandate on the lines already suggested. Provided the negotiators keep within the broad limits defined by the resolution, it may be doubted whether Congress would in the last resort show sufficient bad faith as to refuse ratification of the negotiated package. As an additional safeguard the practice of including congressional representatives in the U.S. delegation should be retained, but with a greater degree of involvement than has hitherto been the case. On the side of the EEC it would be equally desirable to delegate to the commission far greater flexibility and discretion in negotiation, subject to ex post ratification. This raises political and constitutional issues that are still unresolved in the Community. But if the commission is to be an effective negotiator, these inhibitions have to be overcome.

Only after these basic procedural steps have been taken can real substantive negotiation begin on the basic issues. First let us examine the specific trade concessions that might be the objectives of negotiation. In the industrial sector would be the automatic, progressive elimination of tariffs spaced over a period of years. The difficulty here is clearly the existence of sensitive areas that will seek exclusion from the operation and will mobilize powerful political support for their case. Textiles and shoes come at once to mind in the United States, but Europe also has its soft areas. Experience suggests that these cases should not be dealt with by an exceptions procedure, which inevitably leads to escalation and an arid exercise in ingenious justification rather than to a serious negotiation on trade liberalization. Since it is proposed that the elimination of duties should be spread over a period of years, there should be ample time for adjustment in particular sectors: it might also be practicable to have a rather longer transitional period for the more sensitive products. The more constructive approach, however, is to follow the example set in the Rome Treaty and the Stockholm Convention in providing effective safeguards if the elimination of duties threatens to lead to serious (demonstrable) disruption in particular sectors of production. The existing safeguard provided by Article 19 of the GATT should be re-examined and adapted to this end. But if it is to provide a really effective and credible degree of security to the interests concerned, the contracting party invoking it should be prepared to submit the case to international examination and judgment. Given this acceptance it would obviously be necessary—since the procedure of examination and judgment must necessarily be time-consuming—to provide latitude for unilateral emergency action, provided that the case is submitted promptly to the organization with the understanding that the emergency measures will be discontinued if the case is not upheld. The safeguard clause should contain clear and precise criteria for determining the circumstances that would justify the withholding of measures of liberalization or, in the case of need, the imposition of measures of protection. It should require the applicant to demonstrate injury or serious threat of injury, that such injury or threat thereof results from exceptionally severe import competition and not from other causes, and that all available methods of adjustment have been examined and found ineffective. Given strict criteria and the intervention of an objective judgment, the safeguard clause should in appropriate circumstances permit action directed to particular sources of supply identified as the prime cause of the disruption of the domestic market of the applicant. Article 19 of the GATT, logically enough, since it operates within the context of the MFN clause, can only be applied on a non-discriminatory basis. It has from time to time been argued —particularly in connection with especially aggressive competition from Japan and Hong Kong—that this is a serious imperfection since it obliges the injured party to take restrictive action—and hence run the risk of retaliation—against all its trading partners even though competition from these other sources is normal and acceptable. Since the essence of the safeguard clause is to provide participants with sufficient assurance to eliminate the remainder of their protective tariffs, it would appear to be wise—even if the theoretical basis of the arguments is doubtful—to concede the point so long as the criteria are strict and the ultimate judgment is not subjective. This is probably the most thorny point of all. Ex hypothesi the application of the safeguard clause involves very sensitive political areas of national interest, and it will require some courage on the part of governments to commit themselves to accept objective judgments in such situations. But unless they are prepared to do so it seems unlikely that sufficiently broad and credible safeguards can be written into the trade rules.

Admitting the principle, the question arises as to who the judge or arbiter should be. It clearly cannot be the trade organization itself since this would open the whole procedure to discredit because there could be no guarantee that judgments would be objective and free of taints of politics or interest.

The GATT, in the administration of the very mild provisions of Article 23, found it necessary to give an appearance of impartiality to its judgments by the use of panels to examine and to report on charges of nullification and impairment. The panels are composed of national civil servants chosen for their technical competence and wherever possible from countries having no direct interest in the dispute or in close relationship with either of the parties. The recruitment of such panels has become increasingly difficult and would be virtually impossible for the far more exacting task we are now considering. What is needed is a sort of international court of justice for trade matters, but one able to work with speed and authority. There could be established a list of eminent persons whose integrity and competence was beyond question. At their head would be a permanent chairman of international standing. The chairman, in consultation with the Director General of GATT (who by the nature of his functions would also be close to the parties in dispute) would for each case submitted to the organization appoint from the list a panel (over which he himself would preside) and to make appropriate findings, recommendations, and decisions. As in the case of the present GATT Article 23 panels, the parties, and any other interested contracting parties should be heard and also given an opportunity to comment upon the draft of the findings. But once these are finalized, they should be accepted as binding on the parties.

This is a subject that could be developed more extensively, but the GATT archives (particularly those recording the lengthy if inconclusive discussion of market disruption) as well as those of EEC and EFTA would provide the negotiators with ample materials for their discussions.

It is now time to turn to the trade rules. In the earlier analytical part of this chapter, the author has taken the position that the present rules are inadequate and inappropriate. It is a logical concomitant that we should examine what might be considered adequate and appropriate.

The Parties in Presence

For a variety of reasons the present composition of GATT is unrealistic and unwieldy. The first anomaly is the position of the European Economic

Community. The Community asserts a common commercial policy, which, in part, is not yet fully evolved. Complete or not, the Community negotiates in GATT as a single entity. On the other hand, the constituent states are each individually and separately members of GATT. There is an evident contradiction here that should be removed as an essential element in reframing the rules.

The GATT has also admitted to membership a number of countries with centrally planned and entirely government-controlled economies. The terms of admission are various and in the case of Czechoslovakia— the product of an accident of timing—with no special conditions at all. It should be an object of the negotiations to arrive at a realistic and mutually acceptable basis for trade between these countries and the free enterprise economies. Once this is arrived at, contracting parties should renounce bilateral and discriminatory arrangements with the communist countries and base their trade relations with them on the agreed rules. There is little reason to doubt that most of the communist countries—and perhaps by now even the Soviet Union—would welcome such a development.

Next comes the controversial subject of the position of the developing countries in GATT. It is fashionable to argue that the developing countries (lumped together in a somewhat unhelpful generalization) derive no benefits from GATT membership because the GATT is basically a rich man's club with rules designed and operated only for the benefit of the wealthy industrialized countries. Looking at the past, this view is somewhat of a travesty of the facts. The developing countries have been both directly and indirectly—and without any concomitant restraints—beneficiaries of the GATT system. They have—at least until recently—been largely sheltered from discrimination in their export markets, at least in the industrial countries, and have received the benefit, both MFN and contractual, of all the tariff concessions negotiated in GATT, as well as of all the restraints imposed by GATT on various instruments of commercial policy to which the developing countries, being poor, are particularly vulnerable. Indirectly too their stake is high since they are more vulnerable than their wealthier partners to recessive movements in international trade and therefore have a strong interest in an international system that promotes its regular expansion.

At the same time, both explicitly and by acquiescence, the developing countries "enjoy" complete freedom in their own commercial policies. The word "enjoy" is placed in quotation marks because it is arguable that a closer conformity with GATT obligations and principles might serve these countries better, and they are of course on the receiving end of restrictive policies pursued in other developing countries.

Given the existence of UNCTAD, which could, with a little more system and discipline, provide a forum for the discussion of major general trade issues between the developing countries as a whole and the industrialized countries, there would be advantage in confining GATT membership to those countries that are sufficiently advanced economically to participate meaningfully and on a basis of equality in the working of the international commercial system. This would spare those countries whose direct interest in GATT is marginal or nil the expense and inconvenience of having to staff delegations both to UNCTAD and to GATT while affording those countries that are able and willing to participate effectively in GATT to do so. Their numbers would increase progressively as more of them moved forward to more sophisticated economic and commercial policies. Crudely stated, this would mean that accession to the new GATT would require a stricter assessment of the ability of would-be members to accept the obligations as well as the benefits of membership.

The Rules

For the reasons already given, the provisions of Article 1 providing— with specified but largely outmoded exceptions—for unconditional most-favored-nation treatment should be substantially revised. Instead of resorting to the questionable expedient of waivers under Article 25 or the even more questionable practice of turning a blind eye to distortions of the customs union and free trade provisions, provision should be made for negotiated exceptions to the most-favored-nation clause. All interested parties should be joined in the negotiations, and a substantially interested party—without being given an absolute veto—would be given the right to a suspensive veto that should be ruled upon by the arbitral body described in the discussion of safeguards. If the panel found that the dissatisfied party was unreasonably withholding assent, its objection would be overruled. If upheld, the negotiations would continue until a reasonable accommodation was worked out.

Existing preferential arrangements would be reviewed and subjected to a similar negotiating procedure. At first sight this may appear a somewhat startling suggestion. But if industrial free trade is accepted as an objective, its impact on industrial products would at the worst be transitional and agricultural problems would be subsumed in the continuing negotiating process that is suggested for this area of international trading relations.

The subsidy provisions require substantial overhaul. Their coverage should be extended to include a variety of governmental interventions that—though not within the conventional definitions of subsidy—have comparable effects on trade.

Consideration should also be given to establishing a code for international investment and for the regulation of international corporate activities, which while permitting sufficient freedom of action to preserve the dynamic effects of investment and multinational corporate activity, would recognize the right of governments within acceptable limits and subject to consultation to take measures to preserve legitimate social objectives.

The specific trade negotiations will no doubt embrace a number of non-tariff barriers, and insofar as these indicate that some areas (e.g., prescription of standards, health and safety regulations) permit the definition of some standard practices, it would be desirable to codify these in the new agreement. In this context, without going so far as to suggest another attempt to draw up an international code on restrictive business practices, a further study and review of the hitherto abortive exercises in GATT and elsewhere on this difficult subject should certainly be undertaken.

Assuming a rather radical revision of Article 1, no very detailed revision of the customs union and free trade area provisions (Article 24) would be necessary, although it would be desirable to clarify some of the ambiguities in the existing provisions that experience has brought to light.

The prohibition of import and export restrictions should be maintained since any necessary exceptions would be dealt with in the application of the safeguard provisions (above).

The balance-of-payments exception should be eliminated altogether and indications made that restrictions of trade by commercial policy techniques exclusively for balance-of-payments reasons are to be considered as exchange restrictions to be dealt with by the International Monetary Fund. The GATT should be required to seek an agreement with the IMF whereby whenever the latter is called upon to deal with exchange restrictions effected by trade measures, it will consult with the GATT about the trade effects of such measures and take fully into account the findings of the GATT in consultation with the countries concerned.

It follows from what has been said about membership that the confused and unsatisfactory provisions of Part IV of the GATT would be deleted.

Finally the obnoxious and potentially dangerous provisions of Article 35 (the unilateral "blackball") should be eliminated.

Institutional Arrangements

The renegotiation of the GATT would furnish the opportunity to endow it with an adequate organizational structure that should maintain the present economy in operation but endow the organization and staff with a standing and security that the present makeshift arrangements lack.

Present arrangements for cooperation with the IMF should be substantially revised and extended. In some respects, the fusion of the two organizations would be the ideal solution, but this would doubtless be too difficult and cumbersome to negotiate at the present juncture. Instead, there should be instituted a close and continuous collaboration between the two organizations that would include provision for a joint meeting twice annually —and ad hoc as required—of financial and trade officials from national capitals to review the evolution of world trade and payments and formulate recommendations to guide the two institutions in their day-to-day operations. This institutional link would provide an "early warning" system, which when intelligently applied, might obviate the necessity for hasty and ill-considered policies in periodic crises that even with a more rational management of affairs will disturb the system from time to time.

With Part IV having been eliminated from GATT (inclding GATT's joint responsibilities with UNCTAD for the International Trade Center), it will be necessary to establish formal institutional relationships between GATT and UNCTAD, so that the former would be closely informed of the development of thinking in UNCTAD on trade developments of particular concern to the developing countries and that UNCTAD could express in an authoritative way its views and recommendations as to how these concerns should be reflected in the operation of GATT. On the other side, GATT should provide UNCTAD with technical advice and access to its discussion of general commercial policy matters.

Finally, in order to prevent the coexistence of the old unrevised GATT with the revised version, the principal trading nations should give notice at the outset of the negotiations of withdrawal from GATT to take effect upon the ratification of the new trading arrangement and institution by countries representing a preponderent share of world trade.

These then are a few suggestions for a modernized and streamlined GATT. They are not exhaustive and may well be ill-conceived. It is hoped, however, that they will stimulate others to approach the coming negotiations in an imaginative way. This is not a case for patching and tinkering —what is required is imagination and innovation to build a trading system that looks forward to the eighties and not back to the forties.

Note

1. Eric Wyndham White, "Negotiating on Agriculture," paper prepared for the Committee of Nine, August 1972, processed.

20 Future Directions for U.S. Trade Policy

C. Fred Bergsten

The Setting

The United States now faces a clear choice between alternative trade policies. On the one hand, the AFL-CIO and some others actively support unilateral U.S. imposition of a new regime of comprehensive import quotas. If erected in the form that these groups presently propose, the Burke-Hartke bill, the new regime would *reduce* U.S. imports by at least $11 billion from the 1971 level and limit their growth to a fixed share of U.S. consumption thereafter.[1] Any such cutback in U.S. imports would cut back U.S. exports by at least a like amount, in view of foreign income effects, overt retaliation, and emulation by other countries of the U.S. moves. Thus the decline in world trade would be roughly double the size of the U.S.—about 8 percent of the level in 1971.[2]

The Burke-Hartke bill is highly unlikely ever to become law in its present extreme form. But a new "orderly marketing" regime, which would limit future import growth to some given share of the U.S. market, implemented either by the United States or through the favored new technique of "voluntary export restraints" by foreign suppliers, remains distinctly possible.[3] Indeed, the United States has instituted such restraints in several key industries since the early 1960s (e.g., cotton textiles, meat, steel, and synthetic and woolen textiles), and such a generalized approach would in one sense represent a culmination of that trend.

On the other hand, the U.S. administration and numerous private groups have been actively calling for new international negotiations to resume the earlier efforts to reduce national barriers to world trade and to devise new international rules and mechanisms to govern those barriers that will continue to exist in the future. This approach is partly motivated by the traditional foreign policy desire to use economic negotiations as a functional means for expanding global cooperation. It has received added impetus (as in other countries) from the contribution that trade liberalization can make to combatting inflation, which has led the administration to unilaterally eliminate or reduce existing barriers to imports of oil, meat, and cheese. The administration also asked the Congress to authorize temporary, unilateral across-the-board cuts in U.S. tariffs to fight inflation, and such authority was provided in the Trade Reform Act passed by the House of Representatives in late 1973.

341

The call for new negotiations is primarily motivated, however, by the realization that trade policy is dynamically unstable and that a theoretical third trade policy alternative—maintenance of the status quo—is untenable. Protectionist efforts by special interests can be countered only by trade liberalization in pursuit of the general interest. Steady movement toward trade liberalization is necessary to avoid new trade restrictions, and it is widely believed that such liberalization can be achieved only through international negotiations. If more proof of the instability of trade policy were needed, it is provided by the impressive success of U.S. special interests immediately after the completion of the Kennedy Round in obtaining new import protection (steel, meat, the pledge on synthetic and woolen textiles by both presidential candidates in 1968, which culminated in new restraints in 1971) and in altering the overall thrust of U.S. trade policy (severe tightening of the administration of the anti-dumping and counter-vailing duty laws, the import surcharge of 1971, the near-passage of the Mills bill in the face of administration ambivalence in 1970, and the presentation by the Nixon administration in early 1973 of a major trade bill that would have been regarded a decade earlier as overtly protectionist).

Indeed, the primary impact of the Kennedy Round on world trade flows was not its tariff cuts. Its major achievement was in providing governments around the world with a broad international initiative of sufficient political importance to enable them to reject the entreaties of particular domestic groups seeking trade restrictions that would have rendered its completion impossible. Again, the U.S. evidence is clear: demand for the restrictions that were implemented after 1967, as outlined above, grew rapidly during the 1960s despite the steady growth of profits to record levels and the steady decline of unemployment to post-Korea lows. They probably could not have been forestalled without the simultaneous presence of a major trade-liberalizing initiative. Unless inflation remains so rampant that everyone can see the absurdity of new import barriers, a decidedly unhappy prospect despite its beneficial side effects on trade policy, they would be even harder to forestall now with the far less satisfactory state of our domestic economy and external economic position.[4]

It is even highly unlikely that individual industries can any longer be "bought off" by restrictions limited to them alone, in view of the political pressure for "equitable treatment" of all. Precisely this view motivated the "Byrnes basket" provision of the near-miss Mills bill of 1970, which made eligible for import quotas all products where imports satisfied certain numerical criteria—a total of $7 billion of trade at that time.

In the absence of new trade liberalization, either unilaterally to fight inflation or through a multilateral negotiation, new trade restrictions are therefore likely in the United States. The ultimate choice between the highly polarized alternatives could be very close. It will probably turn on five key issues.

The Link to International Money

All theories of international trade that conclude that maximum freedom of trade maximizes world welfare rest on a variety of assumptions. One of these assumptions is the existence of equilibrium exchange rates. The absence of a monetary system which provides a mechanism for assuring equilibrium exchange rates thus severely jeopardizes the economic case for free trade. It certainly undermines political support for freer trade, by eroding the competitive position of industries in countries with overvalued exchange rates and thereby generating additional desires for protection.[5] This is the real link between trade policy and international money.

Until August 1971, however, the United States did not seek an equilibrium exchange rate for the dollar. Indeed, the international monetary policy of the United States throughout the previous postwar period was aimed primarily at assuring financing for U.S. payments deficits, primarily through the key currency roles of the dollar. The adjustment mechanism in the dollar-centered monetary system was in fact biased against the United States, and the dollar actually appreciated against a weighted average of the other major currencies during the 1960s despite the persistence of U.S. payments deficits.[6]

Some observers argue that the dollar had become overvalued by the late 1950s. Others view the overvaluation as occasioned solely by the inflation associated with the Vietnam war. Whatever the timing, however, it is clear that a fundamental contradiction pervaded U.S. foreign economic policy: the United States sought to lead the world toward freer trade, but made no effort to lead the world toward a monetary system that produced equilibrium exchange rates.[7]

Perhaps ironically, the victim of that contradiction was the United States itself. In August 1971, the United States decided that it *wanted* to adjust its exchange rate—largely for domestic reasons, but also in belated realization that it had to do so to restore the prospects for a liberal U.S. trade policy.[8] However, it found itself confined by a monetary system that made it very difficult for the United States to devalue, the only economically effective means of adjustment that would be politically acceptable in the relatively closed U.S. economy. It was thus caught in its own policy contradiction.

The United States was able to evade this contradiction until 1971 for two reasons. In the 1950s, it faced little serious international competition. Throughout the 1960s, its internal economy boomed; profits rose to record levels in 1966 and stayed there for several years, and unemployment dropped steadily toward the post-Korea low achieved in eary 1969. Only in the 1970s has the United States come to face simultaneously real international competition and an unsatisfactory internal economic situation.

This is why the United States pushed so hard for the Smithsonian exchange-rate realignment and, subsequently, an international monetary system that would maintain equilibrium exchange rates. The basic aim of its proposals for monetary reform is to improve greatly the balance-of-payments adjustment process, by placing major international pressure on both surplus and deficit countries to move promptly and in adequate magnitudes to rectify any imbalances they develop. The achievement of such a new monetary system, to help avoid any sizable or sustained disequilibrium in the exchange rate of the dollar in the future, is a necessary condition for the avoidance of further U.S. trade restrictions. The dramatic improvement of the U.S. trade balance (and overall balance-of-payments position) by late 1973, which resulted at least in large part from the series of exchange-rate changes of 1971 and 1973, appears to have demonstrated the effectiveness of the exchange-rate approach and suggests that the maintenance of adequate exchange-rate flexibility will provide a monetary framework within which it can again maintain a liberal trade policy.

The Trade Balance and the Level of Trade

The second key issue is whether U.S. trade policy should focus on the U.S. trade *balance* or on the *level* of U.S. trade.

One American point of view, which became widespread when the United States was in heavy trade and payments deficit in 1971-72, is that the other major countries should be willing to grant non-reciprocal trade concessions to the United States, to help the international adjustment process that finds them in surplus and the United States in deficit. Former Treasury Secretary Connally openly espoused this view, which confuses the appropriateness of minor trade concessions in the context of an overall effort to restore short-term payments equilibrium (as in the fall of 1971)—if countries choose to extend them rather than revalue their exchange rates further—with the inappropriateness of sizable non-reciprocal concessions in a negotiation over the long-term level of trade barriers that, as noted above, must proceed on the assumption that the monetary adjustment process will achieve balance-of-payments equilibrium.

Another school of thought reasons that the United States can afford to agree to a "reciprocal" reduction of trade barriers only when its trade balance is strong, for four reasons. First, "reciprocity" in tariff negotiations has traditionally been defined, very crudely, as equality in the products of the average percentage cuts in duties times the volume of trade affected.[9] For example, "reciprocity" is achieved between two countries if one reduces its duties on $1 billion by an average of 10 percent while one reduces duties on $500 million by an average of 20 percent.[10] This school feels that price elasticities of demand for imports are higher in the United

States than in other countries, so that equiproportionate tariff cuts from the relatively equal tariff levels that now exist in the major countries would have an adverse effect on the U.S. trade balance.[11]

Second, whatever the static effect of price elasticities, this school argues that the United States cannot afford "reciprocal" trade cuts because it is so uncompetitive in world markets that the dynamic effects of reducing trade barriers will be unfavorable to the U.S. trade balance. On this argument, the United States should avoid any new trade liberalization until it has first established a better underlying foundation of productivity growth and control of domestic inflation. This school of thought was promulgated by the Kennedy administration in the opposite direction, when it argued that the Kennedy Round would help solve the U.S. balance-of-payments problem by enabling the United States to capitalize on its highly competitive international position to increase further its trade surplus (and reduce unemployment at home in the process).

The third part of this argument is that the sharp rise in U.S. energy imports will make its trade position that much more difficult to balance. And the final strand is that "U.S. negotiators are always soft," because the United States always wants to bring negotiations to a successful conclusion for broad political reasons and hence are outdone in purely commercial terms by their foreign counterparts. The U.S. trade balance is thus bound to suffer from whatever is finally agreed.

In my view, there is some intellectual merit in each of these viewpoints. There is a place for non-reciprocal trade liberalization by countries running balance-of-payments surpluses, if they choose to adjust in that way. A much more sophisticated definition of "reciprocity" is clearly needed, as will be discussed below. The United States will certainly have to maintain a strong competitive position to assure avoidance of trade balance deterioration as a result of new trade liberalization, especially in light of pending increases in energy imports, and will be unable to do so if other countries hamstring U.S. exports in the two areas where they are strongest —agriculture, as Europe has been doing for some time, and high-technology goods, where the industrial policies that Japan, Europe, and Canada are in different stages of developing could have similar effects. And the United States did extend non-reciprocal trade concessions, at least in the early postwar period, due to broad political reasons that it (correctly) deemed of overriding importance at the time.

None of these considerations, however, should dominate U.S. trade policy. The objective of trade policy should continue to be the maximization of the welfare effects of international commodity flows. Such considerations are particularly important when inflation replaces unemployment as the primary concern of a country's economic policy, as the unilateral cuts in trade barriers by many countries—including the United States,

Japan, Canada, Australia, Germany, the United Kingdom—suggest has occurred in recent years. Welfare considerations may call for increasing or reducing the level of flows at any given time, however, for reasons we will come to shortly, but are related only indirectly to the trade balance.

The appropriate trade balance for a country can be determined only by the needs of its overall balance of payments, which may call for changes in the trade balance in either direction at any given time. Over time, the trade balance needed for payments equilibrium may change in response to structural changes in other parts of the balance of payments—such as the sharp and steady rise in U.S. income on its foreign direct investments.

In addition, the external payments positions of virtually all countries fluctuate between surplus and deficit several times within a decade. We often forget that Japan was in payments deficit as recently as 1966-67, and the United States was in payments surplus as recently as 1969. And the competitive position of an individual country can change very dramatically between the start of a trade negotiation and the completion of the liberalization resulting from it. The Kennedy Round, for example, spanned a full decade that started with the United States in a dominant competitive position and actively *seeking* new markets for Japanese exports and ended with a sharp reversal between those two countries. The latest turnaround in the American trade balance, from a deficit of over $6 billion in 1972 to a surplus of almost $2 billion in 1973, is the latest reminder of the rapidity of change; it should also lay to rest any notions that the objective of any new trade negotiation should be to help the U.S. trade balance.

Any major negotiation on trade barriers, in any event, sets the level of world trade restrictions for many years. It would be impossible even to tell which countries should benefit in trade balance terms from non-reciprocal concessions and which countries should extend them, let alone the magnitudes of such targets or even how the dynamic trade effects of liberalization would work out, so the trade balance could hardly be the focal point for trade negotiations. Indeed, most countries can only win internal political agreement to reduce their import barriers by pointing to the equivalent gains to their exporters that are inherent in a "reciprocal" negotiation. It is inconceivable that European governments would, to put it provocatively, "sacrifice their farmers so that American multinational firms could continue to buy up Europe." No country could be sufficiently confident of its future payments position to consciously negotiate a decline in its trade balance in such a context, particularly in light of the sharp increases in oil-import costs faced by virtually all industrial countries in 1974.

Nevertheless, there is a need to link the trade balance and trade policy in an operational way. Indeed, the monetary reform proposals of the United States do so by suggesting that countries have the option of adjusting payments surpluses by unilaterally reducing their trade barriers instead of revaluing their exchange rates. The problem with this idea is that such a step would reduce the bargaining position of any such country in the next round of international trade negotiations and might reduce the incentives of other countries to pursue additional trade negotiations in the future. The U.S. proposal thus needs to be amended in two ways: (1) countries would get credit in the next trade negotiation for trade liberalization undertaken earlier for purposes of payments adjustment[12] and (2) they could restore their previous barriers if they moved clearly into payments deficit before the next round of trade talks (in which case they would get credit only for the duration of the temporary liberalization). If there is any role for trade policy measures in the adjustment arsenals of deficit countries, it is for surcharges applied across-the-board to all imports for a temporary period of time; those who seek quota protection for particular commodities to help the balance of payments are still another school of thought, but one not worth serious discussion.[13]

Reciprocity

Two aspects of the problem of reciprocity require discussion. On the technical level, new concepts are needed to replace the crude techniques applied in the past to tariff reductions. Wholly new techniques will be needed to measure "reciprocity" in the reduction of non-tariff barriers, of which quantitative restrictions are the simplest but still raise difficult problems. The objective in all cases must be to quantify the changes in trade flows, which are likely to result from particular changes in trade restrictions, to give countries a much sounder gauge than they have had heretofore of whether the outcome of their bargaining over trade barriers will in fact be truly reciprocal expansion of trade flows in both directions. Such improvement may have to be limited to equalizing the static effects of changes in barriers, since the dynamic effects are so much more difficult to measure,[14] but that would still represent major progress.

A further technical problem is how to handle limits to import growth, such as the Burke-Hartke proposal for restricting imports to a fixed share of U.S. consumption. Retaliation in the past (as in the "chicken war" of 1962-63) has always related to actual rollbacks in trade, not limits to its growth. The problem could become particularly important in any new negotiation if new "safeguard" clauses are adopted along with cuts in tariffs and non-tariff barriers. The simplest approach would be to extend the practices of the past by letting country B place quantitative limits on a magnitude of its imports from country A similar in both regards to the limits placed on its exports by country A—emulation rather than retaliation in the conventional sense.

Such a search for better estimation techniques would further complicate a negotiation that already promises to be quite complicated. Countries could haggle endlessly over the accuracy of contending elasticities, and over formulas for converting non-tariff barriers to tariff equivalents. Improvement over past practices will almost certainly be needed, however, to achieve agreement on "reciprocal" liberalization among the major traders of today, all of whom are intensely concerned about their trade balances and may prove unwilling to liberalize at all unless they are assured of a "neutral" effect. And I indicated above that I see merit, not demerit, in extended (even constant) negotiation among the major trading countries.

This problem of adequately defining "reciprocity" was avoided in the past largely because the United States *was* willing—rightly, in my view—to accept liberalization that was not fully reciprocal from the standpoint of the U.S. trade balance in the short run.[15] The United States did so both because it was confident that its competitive ability would enable it to quickly offset any static economic losses with dynamic gains[16] and because it had a major foreign policy stake in seeing that each of the succeeding trade negotiations concluded successfully. As in the monetary case, however, both the economic and international political situations have changed markedly; the United States will now insist on full reciprocity in short-term trade balance terms.[17] U.S. trade policy, and the outlook for international economic cooperation, are thus again hampered by the legacies of a successful past. Because the traditional concept of "reciprocity" has been discredited in the United States, through its "misuse" in the past, a new concept will probably be needed if political support is to be generated for a new round of liberalization.

The more substantive aspect of reciprocity is whether the United States should offer concessions in the industrial sector in return for concessions in the farm sector. It has been estimated that net U.S. exports might rise by $3 billion if all agricultural trade barriers were removed, although this figure omits consideration of sugar (and a few commodities of minor trade importance) and thus may overstate the likely impact.[18] However "reciprocity" were defined, this would of course require reductions in barriers to industrial trade that would increase net U.S. imports of such products by similar amounts.[19]

First-round economic welfare considerations would of course support such intersectoral reciprocity. But there are offsets. Consider domestic job effects. Farm exports are highly capital-intensive, and even their sharp increase under free trade would produce relatively few jobs. The increased industrial imports, many of which would be in lower-skill industries, would by contrast be much more labor-intensive and eliminate far more jobs. To be sure, domestic macroeconomic and manpower policies could recoup the lost jobs, but the costs of doing so—including budgetary and other inflationary effects—have to be set against the welfare gains of the increased trade.

Long-term trade balance considerations might also be negative. On the one hand, there is a case for such a deal because the United States appears to have a clear comparative advantage in agriculture, which often goes unexploited because of foreign barriers, whereas it might well continue to lose ground on the relevant industrial items even without a further reduction of U.S. trade barriers. On the other hand, trade in most industrial items would tend to grow faster over time than trade in agricultural products. If the net result was to force future devaluations on the United States, there would be additional negative welfare effects to offset the original gains from improving the allocation of resources. These structural considerations suggest that the welfare effects of such a deal could be negative in the United States even if it achieved true reciprocity in static, trade balance terms.

Whether the United States should seek to trade industrial for agricultural concessions also turns on domestic political considerations. There are four political arguments that favor it: (1) further solidification of the support of the farm bloc for liberal trade, (2) the demonstration effect of tangible rewards for a community that has maintained a liberal trade stance, (3) the view of the farm community that the United States *gave* concessions on farm trade in return for industrial concessions in the Kennedy Round, and (4) the importance to overall U.S.-European relations (and hence to the world economic order) of getting meaningful European concessions on an issue that has been a focal point of the growing U.S. antagonism toward Europe.

There are two political drawbacks of making such a trade. One is the problems it would raise with the U.S. agricultural producers, now protected by import barriers (mainly in the dairy, sugar, and beef industries), whose short-term interests would have to be sacrificed to minimize the net concessions granted on industrial trade. The second is those industrial interests whose protection would be reduced further to compensate for the foreign concessions on agriculture—which is particularly important because none of the favorable job effects would accrue to the unions that would suffer most of the unfavorable job effects and because these very unions are the leaders of the whole protectionist push.

On balance, I would go for the trade on both economic and political grounds, because the welfare effects are probably close to neutral and because I place high priority on the political importance of breaking the U.S.-EC conflict over agricultural trade. However, I fear that neither the Europeans nor Japanese will give us the choice. Europe is not sufficiently interested in U.S. concessions on industrial trade to make the tough internal decisions that would be necessary to liberalize the CAP and does not seem to believe that new restrictions on such trade could result if forward progress is not made. Indeed, in joining the Community, Britain raised its duties on farm imports and lowered its duties on industrial imports—

thereby giving the United States reciprocity opposite to what is suggested here.

Internal Adjustment to External Disturbances

Another assumption underlying the policy conclusions of classical trade theory is full employment. In the United States, however, excessive unemployment has existed frequently throughout the postwar period and has thus added to the difficulties of pursuing a liberal trade policy.

But the problem is not just the aggregate rate of employment. The AFL-CIO supported the Trade Expansion Act in 1962 when the rate was 5.5 percent but became protectionist by 1969 when the rate had dropped to 3.5 percent. Its position on trade policy has thus correlated inversely with the rate of unemployment.

A major factor is changing value preferences. Most American workers have now entered the lower middle class and have achieved income levels that allow them to place much higher emphasis on job stability, relative to higher wages, than they could afford to do in the past. Reluctance to give up community, home, schools, and church may dominate the opportunity for marginally higher income, particularly in the absence of vesting of pensions and transferability of other fringe benefits from one job to another, for individual workers and for the labor force as a whole. American labor thus increasingly resists change—particularly change emanating from abroad, which is "different" in at least its susceptibility to successful resistance (and may also be substantively different due to the accelerating pace at which it is taking place). This attitude is greatly reinforced by the bureaucratic interests of the AFL-CIO, which knows that structural change of the U.S. economy means movement out of the highly organized, traditional manufacturing industries (such as steel and textiles) into the largely unorganized, modern high-technology and service industries.[20]

This increasing resistance to change clashes head-on with the increasing pace of change itself. A mix of two approaches will probably be needed to cope with this clash, if a complete restrictionist relapse is to be avoided. Of critical importance will be a vastly improved adjustment assistance program, especially for workers displaced by imports.[21] Adequate compensation and effective retraining and relocation programs will be necessary components of any such effort. Unfortunately, the record of manpower programs to date—not only in the United States, where they are now prime candidates for budget cuts, but in countries such as Sweden that have much longer and more comprehensive experience with them—is not encouraging.

The other approach is to slow the pace at which disturbances occur, by limiting the permitted growth of imports. It is quite likely that new mechanisms will in fact be required to "safeguard" against any massive dislocations at least from new trade liberalization that takes place. Agreement on how they might work was the major area of progress recorded in the recent Rey Report to the Secretary-General of the OECD [6, pp. 83-84]. They proposed inter alia that application of any such safeguards "should be accompanied by action to bring about domestic adjustment so that the use of the safeguard mechanism will in fact be temporary," which links the two approaches in order to avoid undue reliance on new controls.

The Foreign Reaction

The final ingredient needed to avoid a restrictionist trend in U.S. trade policy is a cooperative stance by other countries, in two senses. First, they will have to tolerate a much tougher U.S. trade policy than they have experienced in the past. The United States has already begun to administer its anti-dumping and countervailing duty laws with increased vigor and to bargain much harder over the level of particular concessions—not to mention the excesses of the fall of 1971—than it has in the past. This will be necessary to erase the legacy of the "soft positions" of the past, and establish sufficient credibility for any administration to win congressional and public confidence in its ability to negotiate major new trade liberalization without "selling out the United States interest." At a minimum, it is clear that other countries can no longer look to the United States to always take the lead in launching negotiations and in making concessions to break logjams so that the negotiations will succeed. Indeed, as both the largest world trader and the largest problem for world agricultural trade, Europe should exercise a special responsibility for launching new trade policies.

Second, other countries will have to be willing to make concessions on issues of real importance to the United States, such as the level of agricultural support prices in Europe and real market access in Japan. They may also have to be willing to renegotiate some of the basic GATT rules that govern both trade flows and trade relations in order to make them more relevant to present conditions. For example, the MFN rule may need to be modified to require compensation for trade diversion inherent in the new kinds of "free trade areas" represented in the EC's Mediterranean policy and to permit discrimination against countries that cause particularly severe trade and/or balance-of-payments problems. New rules are needed to cover issues not now treated in the GATT, or treated inadequately, but which have become sufficiently important to warrant some such international treatment (e.g., foreign direct investment and multinational corporations, environmental protection policies, regional and other industrial policies, and export subsidies).

To be sure, it will be intellectually and politically difficult for these countries to make the needed adjustment in their views. It is hard to reverse the momentum of a generation, and the signs that they will do so are not promising at present. Yet they must realize that the very foundations of the international economic system are at stake, that their actions will have major effects on U.S. internal politics, and act accordingly.

Fortunately, all countries have a common long-run interest in avoiding new trade wars, which would disrupt both their domestic economies and world politics, and in working together to construct a new international economic order and to deal with such joint problems as access to scarce supplies and multinational firms.[22] And the new situation of greater equality among the United States, the expanded European Community, and Japan provides them with plenty of scope for shifting coalitions in search of particular goals. The United States and Japan together oppose Europe's discriminatory restrictions against Japanese exports and its proliferating preferential arrangements. The United States and Europe together seek reductions in Japan's barriers to imports. Europe and Japan want to eliminate some present U.S. trade barriers, certainly wish to avoid new U.S. restrictions, and probably join in opposing the U.S. effort to free world agricultural trade. As long as these coalitions shift from issue to issue, they could form a stable basis for moving ahead on liberalization through a series of high-level policy trade-offs.[23]

Conclusion

It will obviously be difficult to achieve major progress on all the issues discussed in this chapter within even the next few years. If the conditions outlined do not overstate what is needed, and if concern with fighting inflation through all available means (including import liberalization) does not overwhelm all other factors, one must conclude that the outlook for avoiding a restrictionist U.S. (and world) trade policy is highly uncertain.

However, there are encouraging developments on several fronts. The dramatic improvement in the international monetary system, and through it in the U.S. trade and balance-of-payments positions, have been noted and are critical in removing a financial constraint from trade policy. The major countries have displayed an important degree of consensus in agreeing to launch new trade negotiations, the "Tokyo Round," and in pledging to avoid new trade restrictions despite the dramatic increases in the costs of their oil imports. In passing the Trade Act of 1974, the U.S. Congress decisively rejected all aspects of the Burke-Hartke bill, and significantly liberalized the trade bill originally submitted by the administration—an historical first.

At the same time, little has been done toward developing an effective adjustment assistance program or new concepts of reciprocity. The energy crisis has added new clouds of uncertainty to the future of trade policy. The onset of global recession has intensified traditional protectionist efforts. The continued failure of governments to deal with some of the problems raised by multinational corporations heightens these tensions. The proliferation of export controls has pushed the new issue of access to supplies, in which there is inadequate intellectual background and historical experience, toward the top of the agenda for international trade negotiations.[24] So the outlook for trade policy remains uncertain, both in the United States and for the world as a whole, although it appears far less likely to plummet into traditional protectionism than was true as recently as 1971-72.

Notes

An earlier version of this chapter was presented at the joint meeting of the American Economic Association and the American Agricultural Economics Association in December 1972 and was published in the *Journal of Agricultural Economics*, Vol. 55 (May 1973).

1. The bill also proposes severe new limitations on foreign direct investment by American firms. Though related to trade and contributing to the protectionist trade pressures because they accelerate the pace of change occasioned by trade flows, foreign investment raises a host of different issues and will not be dealt with in this chapter.

2. The Burke-Hartke formula would of course produce a greater reduction of world trade in absolute terms from the levels that would have been reached by the time of its enactment, and the percentage decline would be larger as well because *all* growth beyond the 1965-69 base period for items brought under quota would be rolled back.

3. For a complete analysis of the underlying economic and political changes that raise such a spectre, see Bergsten (1971). On "voluntary export restraints," see Chapter 15 of this volume.

4. Hence it is unfortunate that the EC, in the communique issued after its summit meeting in late 1972, called for the next round of trade negotiations to be concluded by 1975. Aside from the impossibility of moving that fast, in view of the wide range and complexity of the issues involved, it would be undesirable to do so because the shield against new restrictions would then again be quickly dropped.

5. By stimulating excessive allocation of resources to export- and import-competing industries in countries with undervalued rates, it also makes it harder for such countries ever to agree to revaluations—which would surrender their enhanced competitive positions.

6. For a theoretical explanation of the bias, see Bergsten (1970),

especially pp. 68-69. The dollar appreciation amounted to 1 to 5 percent, depending on the method of calculation and the precise time period chosen.

7. So perhaps the Treasury Department should at least share the blame usually leveled at the State Department for "selling out U.S. economic interests."

8. It must never be forgotten that it was the desire of the *United States* to adjust, not some Triffinesque collapse of the dollar overhang, which motivated the international aspects of President Nixon's New Economic Policy in August 1971. See Bergsten (1972), pp. 200-4.

9. Preeg (1970), especially p. 132 and note 20. He notes that additional considerations were often factored in on an ad hoc basis, but that the basic formula was as stated in the text.

10. "Reciprocity" has thus been defined in terms of changes in *absolute* trade levels. Some observers, including government officials, have however erroneously viewed "reciprocity" as meaning equal *percentage* rises in each country's exports and imports. This would increase the level of all existing trade surpluses and deficits and move away from, rather than toward, payments equilibrium. Thus it would certainly not be acceptable to deficit countries. Nevertheless, this view seems to be widely held in the United States, thereby strengthening the policy conclusion of some that trade liberalization is in the U.S. interest when the United States is running a trade surplus but is not when it is running a trade deficit.

11. Unfortunately, none of the economic analyses to date on price elasticities by country is sufficiently reliable to base policy on. One of the most elaborate efforts provides tentative support for this school of thought by concluding that an elimination of tariffs by all industrialized countries would hurt the U.S. trade balance by about $1 billion in 1975. Rita M. Rodriguez and Robert G. Hawkins, "The Effects of Trade Liberalization on International Trade Flows and the U.S. Payments Balance: An Estimate From a World-Trade Model," in Hawkins and Ingo Walter (eds.), *The United States and International Markets* (Lexington Books, D.C. Heath, 1973), pp. 229-54. A host of other issues, such as "disparities" between the dispersion of individual tariffs around the averages in the different countries, complicates the matter further.

12. See the proposal by Kiyoshi Kojima in Chapter 21 for achieving "reciprocity over time" in precisely this manner.

13. The United States has also proposed the use of import surcharges by the international community, or by individual countries, as sanctions against surplus countries that refuse to take steps to eliminate their surpluses. Such "sanctions" will always in fact be applied by someone; the U.S. import surcharge of August 1971 was such a step against Japan. The issue is whether they will be applied by individual countries outside any

international framework, or by the international community as a whole. I would strongly prefer the latter.

14. For example, no one negotiating the Kennedy Round, even at its conclusion, could have foreseen the deterioration of U.S. competitiveness due to its internal inflation in the immediately succeeding years.

15. Just as the willingness of the United States to eschew adjustment of its balance-of-payments position enabled other countries to achieve their trade (and payments) balance goals more easily. However, it is interesting to note the rejection in late 1972 of the Supplementary Chemicals Agreement to the Kennedy Round by the EC, on the grounds that the EC would lose from the deal in trade balance terms. In this case, at least, the U.S. negotiators apparently made a magnificant bargain for the United States, from a trade balance standpoint, since one must view the U.S. gain in this deal against the massive deterioration in the *overall* U.S. trade balance from 1967 through 1972.

16. This probably goes far to explain why U.S. labor supported free trade in the past, but does not now: they used to perceive that increased trade meant *more* jobs, whereas now they perceive that it means *fewer*.

17. Of course, the real gain to the United States from trade liberalization is the welfare benefit of reducing present restrictions plus, since trade policy is dynamically unstable, the avoidance of welfare (and international political) costs imposed by the new restrictions that would otherwise take place.

18. West (1973), pp. 19-20. Johnson (1973) estimates an increase of $5 billion in gross exports of U.S. *and Canadian* grains and oilseeds; he makes no net calculation for the United States, but his data confirm the broad magnitudes of the West estimate. These estimates were made before the onset of world food shortages in 1973 and hence may also overstate the effect on U.S. farm exports of foreign trade barriers by overestimating the availability of additional U.S. supply even if those markets were opened.

19. Most analysts agree that farm trade can be liberalized only through efforts to align domestic farm policies, rather than attacks on barriers to farm trade per se. I abstract here from the method by which farm trade is liberalized.

20. For a statistical analysis of the sharp differences between the composition of the AFL-CIO and the composition of the total U.S. labor force, which underlie the extreme protectionist stance of the federation, see C. Fred Bergsten, ''The Cost of Import Restrictions to American Consumers,'' in Robert A. Baldwin and J. David Richardson, eds., *International Trade and Finance* (Boston: Little, Brown, 1974).

21. As proposed in Chapter 17.

22. A further international political complication is that the less-

developed countries may oppose a new multilateral trade negotiation, even though they would not be required to extend reciprocal concessions, because it will erode the value of their newly won tariff preferences. This position is extremely short-sighted. On the one hand, the preferences are not very meaningful in economic terms (and the United States did not even extend any until 1975). On the other, the economic health of the LDCs rests fundamentally on healthy economic relations among the DCs. If a major new trade negotiation is needed to avoid continued slippage toward a world of trade restrictions, the LDCs—who need market access for their exports even more than do the DCs—would be among the major beneficiaries.

23. See Yalem (1972), pp. 1051-63, for an analysis of international political tripolarity that is broadly relevant to these considerations of international economic tripolarity.

24. For an analysis of that issue and proposals to deal with it, see C. Fred Bergsten, *Completing the GATT: Toward New International Rules to Govern Export Controls* (British-North American Committee, 1974).

References

Bergsten, C. Fred. 1971. "Crisis in U.S. Trade Policy," *Foreign Affairs*, Vol. 49 (July), pp. 619-35.

———, 1972. "The New Economics and U.S. Foreign Policy," *Foreign Affairs*, Vol. 50 (January), pp. 199-222.

———,1970. "The United States and Greater Flexibility of Exchange Rates," in George N. Halm (ed.), *Approaches to Greater Flexibility of Exchange Rates: The Bürgenstock Papers*. Princeton: Princeton University Press.

Houthakker, H. S. and Stephen P. Magee. 1969. "Income and Price Elasticities in World Trade," *Review of Economics and Statistics*, Vol. 51 (May), pp. 111-25.

Johnson, D. Gale. 1973. "The Impact of Freer Trade on American Agriculture," *American Journal of Agricultural Economics*, Vol. 55 (May).

Organization for Economic Cooperation and Development. 1972. *Policy Perspectives for International Trade and Economic Relations*. Paris: OECD.

Preeg, Ernest N. 1970. *Traders and Diplomats*. Washington: Brookings Institution.

Sorensen, V. L., and D. E. Hathaway. 1971. "The Competitive Position of U.S. Agriculture," in *United States International Economic Policy in an Interdependent World*. Washington: Government Printing Office.

West, Quentin M. 1973. "World Trade Prospects for U.S. Agriculture," *American Journal of Agricultural Economics*, Vol. 55.

Yalem, Ronald P. 1972. "Tripolarity and the International System," *Orbis*, Vol. 15 (Winter), pp. 1051-63.

Chapter 20 Commentary: Recent U.S. Foreign Economic Policy from a Japanese Point of View,

Ryutaro Komiya

On August 15, 1971, President Nixon announced that the United States would violate several of the basic rules of postwar international economic relations. The declaration to suspend the convertibility of the U.S. dollar, formally confirming its *de facto* inconvertibility since 1968, was a breach of the basic rules of the IMF system. The 10-percent import surcharge, DISC, and favorable tax treatment of capital expenditures on U.S.-made (but not foreign-made) capital equipment were violations of GATT. It is remarkable that, while violating the existing important international agreements unilaterally, President Nixon used the word "unfair" several times to implicitly blame other countries.

The U.S. Government and many Americans seem to think that the present economic difficulties of the U.S. are caused primarily by policies of other countries, and that other governments rather than the U.S. are responsible for the present international disorder. Therefore, in the minds of a majority of Americans, the U.S. is free to, or forced to, violate the existing international agreements. Nixon's speech of August 15 set the basic tone of present U.S. foreign economic policy. Various bills disregarding existing international agreements concluded by the U.S. in the past have been introduced in the U.S. Congress.

It is not the task of an economist as a social scientist to blame, or to judge who is morally or ethically responsible for a certain result. In the following, however, I wish to argue that:

1. The U.S. Government, or Americans in general, are wrong if they think that countries other than the U.S. are responsible for the present U.S. balance-of-payments deficits or unemployment.

2. U.S. tactics towards Japan—requesting Japan's unilateral trade liberalization in view of a large trade imbalance between the two countries—are not right in the long run and should be abandoned, although they may be effective to some extent in the short run.

U.S. International Monetary Actions

It is widely—but erroneously—believed that, under the IMF system, the measure of currency devaluation available to other member countries under certain conditions is not available to the U.S.

According to the IMF Agreement, the par value of each member country is tied either to gold or to the U.S. dollar with weights and fineness as of July 1, 1944. The U.S. tied the dollar to gold, and other member countries chose to tie their currencies to the "U.S. dollar with weights and fineness as of July 1, 1944." If the U.S. had proposed a depreciation of the dollar in view of a fundamental disequilibrium in its balance of payments, either in August 1971 or preferably much earlier, the IMF would have agreed and a multilateral exchange rate adjustment would have been properly effected. Certain countries would have devalued their currencies together with the U.S., and would have been allowed to do so, but surplus countries such as Japan and Germany could not lawfully devalue their currencies since their balance of payments was in fundamental disequilibrium only in the opposite direction, if at all. If Japan and Germany had depreciated their currencies following a lawful depreciation of the U.S. dollar, in order to keep the dollar exchange rates of their currencies as before, then it would have been not the U.S. but Japan and Germany who were to be blamed for violating the IMF agreement.

Thus multilateral currency adjustments such as the ones in December 1971 and February 1973 could have been effected in an orderly way much earlier, perhaps in the early 1960s had the U.S. been willing to do so. The two currency adjustments mentioned are about the only constructive measures taken since August 1971 to alleviate the U.S. balance-of-payment deficits. If the U.S. had acted lawfully, the situation would not have been any worse than it is now, and would possibly have been better.

The usual counterarguments to the above are as follows:

1. From an economic point of view, it is much better for surplus countries to appreciate their currencies rather than for the U.S. to depreciate the dollar, since dollar depreciation raises the value of gold and leads to expansion of wasteful gold-mining, among other things. In agreement with the economics contained in this argument, I deplore noncooperation of the governments of surplus countries. It is in Japan's own interests especially to have the yen appreciated rather than the dollar depreciated, since among major countries, Japan gains least from a higher dollar price of gold.

When opinions and judgment differ among governments, however, each government should choose policies allowed under international agreements, and should not force or threaten other governments to accept its view through means that violate international agreements. The surplus countries, such as Japan or Germany in recent years or the U.S. in the 1940s and 1950s, who did not propose currency appreciation in spite of "fundamental disequilibrium," are operating legitimately under the terms of the IMF agreement.

In international economic affairs, legal aspects are at least as important as economic ones. When opinions and judgment differ as to the solution for current difficulties, the government most eagerly wanting a change should act. And it should choose the policy measures allowed under international agreements. Otherwise the international agreement is of no use, and it is meaningless for governments to negotiate with each other.

2. The IMF system was not functioning, so one should not be sorry to see the IMF collapse. This is again an economic argument. I am in favor of flexible exchange rates or limited flexibility of a variety very near to flexible rates, but there are governments and persons who do not agree. U.S. citizens should realize that (1) the United States, and not other countries, is responsible for the collapse of the IMF (or at least for the suspension of the IMF's most basic rules); and (2) we have entered an age of power politics in currency affairs with no established rules—an age in which competitive depreciations such as those in the 1930s are possible.

3. Before August 1971, devaluation of the dollar was politically impossible or at least very difficult. Not only President Nixon, but also Presidents Johnson and Kennedy, repeatedly promised not to devalue the dollar. The U.S. legislative procedure for devaluation, which is very easy now, seemed very difficult then. The dollar-gold myth was then sacred.

But who is responsible for the dollar-gold myth? In other countries too, presidents and prime ministers often promised not to devalue or upvalue their currencies. Once having agreed on the basic rules of international economic relations, it is the responsibility of each government to take the necessary steps compatible with the international rules of the games. If, because of domestic political and legislative reasons, it was difficult for the U.S. to devalue the dollar before President Nixon's destructive action in August 1971, wasn't it the responsibility of the U.S. Government, and not of other governments, to change political conditions in the U.S. and to explode the dollar-gold myth, which had deprived the U.S. of a principal means of adjusting its balance of payments?

Since the U.S. has acted in a very destructive way, it would be natural for other countries to find it difficult to negotiate rationally and cooperatively with the U.S. If the U.S. unilaterally violates the fundamental international agreements when they become inconvenient for it, what is the use of international agreements with the U.S. for other countries?

U.S.-Japan Trade Relations

Trade negotiations between the U.S. and Japan in the last three or four years have been very unfortunate. In view of a huge trade imbalance, the U.S. asked Japan to lower its tariffs and other trade barriers unilaterally, while the U.S. was building up its own trade barriers.[1]

A sustained balance of payments disequilibrium is a macroeconomic phenomenon, and should not be considered as being caused by other countries' trade barriers, which have been in existence for many years. The failure of both the U.S. and Japanese Governments (especially the former, as discussed above) to adjust the dollar-yen exchange parity much earlier, in spite of shifts in basic factors determining the balance of payments, is primarily responsible for the imbalance. Its problems of faster inflation, stagnant productivity, overly high wages, and weak export efforts by American firms[2] should be the main focuses of U.S. policies to improve its balance of payments; the trade barriers of foreign countries should not be made the target of U.S. actions.

In any country, there always exist tariff and nontariff barriers which the government feels it difficult to remove suddenly, for both political and social reasons. There have been many such barriers erected by the U.S. Removing or reducing tariff and nontariff barriers is always a painful political process in a democratic society, even though it is clearly beneficial to the society as a whole. Since the nineteenth century, tariff reductions have thus taken bilateral form. The negotiating countries share not only the benefits from tariff reductions, but also the pains of the domestic political and social process in effectuating reductions in trade barriers. The government of each country can persuade its countrymen who are affected unfavorably by pointing out that the trade partner's government is taking similar steps.

In recent years, the U.S. and Japanese Governments have negotiated on trade liberalization, but the question has been on what items and how fast does Japan liberalize unilaterally. The U.S. has so far made no significant concessions in terms of tariff or nontariff barriers. This is not a negotiation in the usual sense of the term.

U.S. tactics to extract unilateral concessions from Japan may be, and have in fact been, effective in the short run, but are bound to arouse open and/or latent resentment among Japanese—among the public in general and among government officials concerned. Such a policy can be very costly in the long run, especially in terms of mutual friendly relations between the two countries. It should therefore be abandoned as soon as possible.

It might be argued that Japan's nontariff barriers are much more extensive than those of the U.S., so that unilateral concessions by Japan are in order. This argument is not true. While it is difficult to assess the trade-reducing effects of various trade barriers, the list of U.S. nontariff trade barriers looks quite formidable—for example, Buy American practices, voluntary export restraints forced upon other countries, ASP, and import quotas on textiles. I feel that by now U.S. NTBs have a larger trade-reducing effect than Japan's, though this is still an open question. At any rate, one cannot argue from the premise that Japan's NTBs are much more extensive than America's.

Those who do not see unreasonableness in the current U.S. trade policy towards Japan should look at the situation from another point of view. In the early postwar years, the U.S. had a huge trade surplus towards most countries. Other countries took various measures to reduce their deficits, including the U.K.'s devaluation of the pound in 1949. What would have been the U.S. reaction if the U.K., Japan, and other countries, instead of taking deficit-reducing measures available to them (including "lawful" devaluation), had requested that the U.S. reduce tariffs unilaterally, abolish its Buy American Act, stop supporting agricultural prices, and so on, without making any trade concessions in return?

It must not be thought from the above that I am against the lowering of NTBs. From an economic point of view, even a unilateral reduction of an NTB by a country is usually beneficial to it, if accompanied by proper actions for adjustments. But if political, social, and legal aspects are also taken into account, it is undesirable that one country press another hard to make unilateral concessions. Negotiation for freer trade among major trading countries should take at least the form of bilateral lowering of trade barriers. Multilateral concessions through GATT are still better.

Notes

1. For example, the U.S.-Japan Textile Agreement and more extensive use of antidumping measures than before.

2. Also, a lack of efforts on the part of American businessmen abroad to learn the language and customs of the countries in which they do business can be a serious obstacle to American exports to a country such as Japan where the customs are very much different.

21 Japan and the Future of World Trade Policy

Kiyoshi Kojima

The chapter by Sir Eric Wyndham-White is overwhelming, and I fully support his proposals for GATT renegotiation. However, it seems to me that nothing is new and dramatic in his chapter. Perhaps the present world needs to find brave new directions for GATT. I would therefore like to issue briefly my thoughts on world trade policies, mainly from Japan's point of view, with special reference to the coming GATT negotiation without due consideration of feasibility and legality.

A starting point of my observation is to ask whether the remaining tariffs and other non-tariff barriers are really large and still deter trade expansion. Legally, they do. Practically, it can be said that trade liberalization has been almost completed. Even free trade in the 1860s was never total. The tariffs and NTBs presently remaining appear to be largely for comparative cost differences in manufactured trade, and much narrower than those in the vertical trade of the nineteenth century. They are actually not large barriers and can be easily overcome by export efforts.

In the present situation, in which only the hard core of trade barriers is retained in each country, it should be asked whether it is right to push hard for further trade liberalization in the coming GATT negotiation or rather to stop the "liberalization war" and await the time when the effects of monetary realignment become more obvious. To attack a partner country's hard-core barriers in the present situation may simply invite antagonism and resentment. To eliminate hard-core barriers, the usual GATT negotiation is useless. Domestic structural adjustment in each country, and harmonization of domestic policies between them, are indispensable. Instead a complete reorganization of GATT into a new organization, à la the European Community, might be required—but this is unquestionably very difficult.

It is the time, instead, to expect unilateral reduction and elimination of trade barriers by each country that is ready to do so for its own interests and benefits (e.g., for achieving better re-allocation of resources, curbing inflationary pressures, and so forth). This is especially true in the case of non-tariff barriers. Non-tariff barriers can hardly become a subject of bargaining in accordance with the principle of reciprocity since they are not measurable in their effect, not comparable to each other, and differ from each other by country in the motivation and interest. However, such a rule

365

as "reciprocity over time" may be set up in order to facilitate this unilateral trade liberalization, as will be touched upon presently.

Instead of harshly attacking other countries' trade barriers, dynamic outlets for increasing world trade should be searched for and appropriate considerations for this purpose should be built into the GATT rules. Such outlets could include the creation of new products and new growth centers in world trade, structural adjustment to changing comparative advantages, agreed specialization in those products in which economies of scale dominate costs of production, better utilization of foreign direct investment, and so forth.

As an amendment of Article 19, the safeguard clause should include a precise obligation that "application of the safeguard measures should be accompanied by action to bring about domestic adjustment so that the use of the safeguard mechanism will in fact be temporary."[1] This is in the strong interest of Japan.

Although Japanese government and business circles stressed the difficulty of reducing tariffs during the Kennedy Round negotiation, we could do it without any difficulty and harm to our national economy. (Such a story applied not only to tariff reductions but also to the gradual elimination of quota restrictions and to the revaluation of the yen). On the contrary, Japan benefited very much from the Kennedy Round tariff reduction in the ratio 2.26: 1—that is, according to my estimation, which was done during the negotiation in order to inspire the government's decision,[2] Japan's exports would increase 10.4 percent and its imports only 4.6 percent due to the 50 percent tariff reduction in Japan and other advanced countries. I would guess that this "free ride" is one of the causes of the rapid increases in Japan's export surplus since 1968. In October 1972, the Japanese government reduced unilaterally by 20 percent its tariffs on almost all manufactured imports. We could do this; why not cut the duties by 100 percent? Also, the escalating tariff system will be revised very soon. The EEC and EFTA could eliminate intra-area tariffs. There is perhaps no reason why they cannot abolish external tariffs as well, in view of the deterioration in American competitiveness.

A renewed attempt to reduce by half the present low levels of tariffs (less than 10 percent on average) in advanced countries does not present an attractive target, when the time and labor required are compared with an expected result to be brought about. Rather, a complete and stage-wise elimination within, say, ten years of all tariffs on manufactured goods should be aimed at. If this were attained, many non-tariff barrier problems—such as customs valuation and procedure, tariff preferences of customs unions and to developing countries, and so forth—will automatically disappear. The Industrial Structure Council of MITI in the Japanese government, of which I was a member, recommended in May 1971 an entire elimination of tariffs on manufactured goods in the forthcoming GATT negotiation by saying that "as to tariffs, the abolition dates should be clarified not only for industrial products but for agricultural products, for which special efforts will have to be made."[3] Tariffs on manufactured imports were reduced unilaterally by 20 percent in October 1972, as already mentioned. Recently even business leaders have recommended the entire elimination of tariffs on manufactured products, temporarily, while our export surplus trend is strong.

Thus, Japan is ready to eliminate tariffs on almost all manufactured goods. But the government is still hesitating to propose this for the GATT negotiation. The reason is that Japanese competitiveness has become superior to other advanced countries and free trade is favorable to her; therefore, a Japanese proposal for total elimination of tariffs on a reciprocal basis might incur other countries' antagonism against Japan. Unilateral elimination by Japan remains possible, but some reciprocal arrangement is preferable for purposes of domestic persuasion.

I would like to propose to the GATT "a fair-weather rule of tariff reduction (or elimination)." A country should reduce tariffs while its balance of payments is favorable, but it should not be allowed to raise tariffs again even if its balance of payments turns difficult; at that time, other countries will have favorable balance-of-payments positions and will be expected to reduce tariffs. In this way "reciprocity over time" is assured, and tariffs of all advanced countries will be eliminated within, say, ten years. The fair-weather tariff-reduction rule may be implemented in more detailed fashion as a counterpart of the exchange-rate adjustment rule that is now under discussion for international monetary reform.

As regards non-tariff barriers, many Americans and Europeans accuse Japan of being most import-restriction minded and suggest that penetration of the Japanese market is almost impossible. This may have been true only a few years ago. Japan's trade liberalization first made rapid progress between 1960 to 1963 and again between 1969 to 1972 while, in the interim, the pace of liberalization was extremely slow and delayed because of the Kennedy Round of tariff negotiations.[4] Until a few years ago, Japanese imports were unter water-tight control through import quota (IQ), automatic import quota (AIQ) and automatic import approval (AA) systems, on the one hand, and exchange control of standard and non-standard methods of settlement, on the other. However, by the end of 1972, the AIQ system was abolished and the AA system was changed to mere import declarations. The number of items under the residual import quota restrictions was 120 in April 1969 but was rapidly reduced to 33 (24 agricultural, 1 mineral—coal, and 8 manufactured items, in terms of the BTN 4-digit classification) by April 1972. The problem of the residual import restrictions on manufactured goods might be said to have nearly come to an end with only eight items remaining unliberalized. Of these, four items are rawhide and leather (bovine cattle leather, equine leather, sheep and lambskin leather, and goat- and kidskin leather), and one is leather footwear. The liberalization of these items is said to be difficult because of the protection that will have to be accorded to subsistence producers in the so-called *dowa* districts where minority groups live on this work. The other four items consist of digital-type electronic computers, their machinery and parts, and integrated circuits. The government decided, and businessmen agreed, in March 1973 that those items are to be liberalized gradually within three years. In the agricultural field, however, in addition to the 24 items, several other items such as rice, wheat, butter, tobacco, and so forth are controlled under state trading.

Therefore, there are no big explicit non-tariff barriers to Japanese imports except in agriculture. What Japan might be blamed for is not the present level of restrictions, but the fact that her trade liberalization has been too cautious, too slow and undramatic. Because of this, Japan could not eradicate her bad image in foreign countries as a most restrictive country. Perhaps Americans and Europeans still complain about the difficulty of increasing imports to Japan due to more vague reasons like remoteness, the differences in customs, and even the Japanese language. However, there are counterpart difficulties that Japanese business encounters in American and European markets. They should not be called non-tariff barriers but mere inconveniences that should be overcome by keen export efforts.

Incidentally, Japan has decided on a plan to liberalize completely its investment controls from May 1973. Even foreign investment in computer industries will be liberalized by December 1975.

Foreign countries should now seek from Japan, instead of hasty further liberalization of non-tariff barriers, (1) monetary realignment up to an appropriate exchange rate for the yen, (2) domestic structural adjustment so as to increase imports of manufactured goods, and (3) diversification of tastes of consumption. The most effective argument for these steps, unilateral tariff reduction and further liberalization of non-tariff barriers, must be that they will help cure inflationary pressure in Japan.

All countries should abolish non-tariff barriers as soon as possible and shift to the tariff system. If it is possible to measure the tariff equivalent effect of non-tariff barriers, there is no reason why a shift to all-tariff systems is impossible. If it is not possible to measure such equivalents, it might be well to permit countries to levy or raise tariffs to the extent that they can be made to feel safe or secure by doing so, even if this might raise tariff barriers temporarily to some extent. However, after some time has elapsed, it will be proven and recognized through experience that high tariff rates are unnecessary. Then it might be well to set about a Kennedy Round type of tariff cutting negotiation, taking an appropriate occasion.[5] The "fair weather rule" could thus be made applicable to the elimination of non-tariff barriers as well.

Notes

1. Organization for Economic Cooperation and Development, *Policy Perspective for International Trade and Economic Relations* (Paris: OECD, 1972), p. 84.

2. Kiyoshi Kojima, *Japan and a Pacific Free Trade Area* (London: Macmillan, 1971), pp. 35-37.

3. *An External Economic Policy in the 1970s,* Report of the Industrial Structure Council, MITI Information Service, June 29, 1972, p. 31.

4. See, Kiyoshi Kojima, "Nontariff Barriers to Japan's Trade," *Hitotsubashi Journal of Economics* (June 1972), pp. 1-39.

5. See Gerard and Victoria Curzon, *Hidden Barriers to International Trade* (London: Trade Policy Research Center, 1970), p. 63; and Harold B. Malmgren, *Trade Wars or Trade Negotiation?* (Washington: The Atlantic Council of the United States, 1970), pp. 66 and 70.

Appendixes

Appendix A
The Maidenhead
Communique
April 12, 1973

Twenty businessmen, economists and labor union officials from Japan, North America, and Western Europe met in Maidenhead (near London) from April 7 through April 10, under the auspices of the Brookings Institution of Washington, to discuss trade policies among the industrialized countries. Most of the group had met in Bermuda last October to set an agenda for its work. A number of papers were prepared for the Maidenhead meeting on the basis of that agenda. The discussions were grouped under five headings:

1. The relevance of trade theory to international economic realities in the 1970s;
2. Multinational corporations and world trade;
3. The impact of government intervention on world trade;
4. National adjustment to economic disturbances caused by international trade and investment;
5. World trade policies for the future.

The group agreed that the steady liberalization of world trade after 1945 had played an integral role in the unparalleled growth of world production, employment and prosperity which virtually all nations have enjoyed since that time. It therefore noted with deep concern that much recent discussion, the trend in recent years toward a proliferation of new trade barriers and other distortions of trade, and the breakdown of international law as it bears on trading relationships among nations appear to overlook the enormous benefits which the high level of international trade has secured to national economies, the fragility of the system unless it is maintained and strengthened, and the high cost if it is seriously impaired under the pressure of temporary but remediable difficulties. The group concluded that there was serious risk that these trends might continue, and that it was urgent to stop them for several reasons.

First, rapid inflation is a global phenomenon of extremely serious consequences. It has not yielded sufficiently to national efforts to restrain demand within tolerable limits of unemployment, and calls for new policy responses. The group agreed that relaxation of barriers to international trade could be an important part of such a strategy. Imports raise the quantity and expand the choice of goods available within each country, and act to restrain domestic price rises. Recent actions by the United States Government to suspend import quotas on meat and oil to fight inflation

373

testify to this conclusion. So do the unilateral tariff reductions recently implemented by Japan and Canada, and the proposals for such cuts made by the Commission of the European Communities as part of a European anti-inflation program.

More important, particularly in industries characterized by a high degree of concentration, imports provide an essential competitive spur to improved productivity and reduction of costs. They can thus be an integral part of the new policy strategies needed to cope with global inflation. Indeed, the group concluded that there is a strong case for unilateral elimination of trade barriers by individual countries, for precisely this reason. The creation of new barriers to imports would undermine national efforts to fight inflation.

Second, a system of liberal trade may be expected to lead to higher employment. Governments today find themselves caught between the Scylla of inflation and the Charybdis of unemployment. In policy they often vacillate between accelerating and braking aggregate demand—stop-go policies that raise the average level of unemployment. Liberal trade, by introducing greater foreign competition into national economies, will moderate price and money wage increases and damp down any nationally generated price-wage spiral. It will thus permit a smoother growth of national output and employment.

This process of course requires a system for prompt adjustments of exchange rates in response to fundamental payments imbalances. At this time, the currencies of virtually all major trading countries are fluctuating in response to market forces, creating an environment that is conducive to reductions in trade barriers without jeopardizing domestic employment goals.

Third, a sharp reduction in national tariff and non-tariff barriers to international trade would remove an artificial incentive to multinational corporations to invest abroad. An important part of foreign investment appears motivated by these barriers. The group recognized the widespread and growing concern expressed about the role of multinational firms, and agreed that foreign investment motivated by trade barriers was a "second-best" response in terms of economic principles and policy. Hence a reduction of such barriers would serve world welfare both by expanding trade and by reducing such foreign investment as is not justified by comparative advantage.

Fourth, present trends suggest that the increasingly active role of national governments in pursuing the social and economic objectives of their people will generate conflicts among countries unless efforts are made shortly to deal with that prospect. In addition to the standard trade policy instruments, tariffs and quotas, government measures pursuing such policy ends as better income distribution and regional development can also affect trade flows, often unintentionally. Such policies are likely to grow increasingly important in the future, and thus warrant immediate attention in an international context so that their pursuit will not distort world trade and generate international recrimination and retaliation. Government procurement policies are one of the most important of these measures, and efforts to regulate their external effects should rank high on the agenda for action.

Historical experience suggests that trade barriers to protect special interests in individual countries tend to proliferate in the absence of active international efforts to reduce such barriers in the overall interest of all countries. The need to move forward is particularly urgent at this time because of an understandable turning inward that, for different reasons, can be observed in most of the world's leading trading areas. In view of the several reasons just cited to avoid new barriers to trade, the Maidenhead group thus concluded that new steps to assure the liberal direction of world trade are urgent.

The group also fully recognized that individuals within each country can be hurt as a result of trade flows. The group was encouraged by the strong evidence that the adjustments to completely free trade within the European Community and the European Free Trade Area (and in many other instances) had been quite smooth, and was confident that this problem would not in practice loom large. Nevertheless, complementary policies are needed to give those individuals who are displaced time to adjust to the new conditions and to help them do so. These policies should be of two types: temporary limitations on the rate of increase of imports which rise too rapidly to be readily absorbed, and government assistance to help affected individuals adjust comfortably to the new circumstances.

Temporary limits on the growth of imports should be available in cases where examination of all relevant facts shows clearly that injury to firms and workers, beyond their capacity to adjust with reasonable assistance, has been caused by imports. Such restrictions should be strictly limited in duration and degressive over time. In addition, an adjustment program which will enable the injured either to continue their present occupations or shift into new endeavors should accompany any such import limitations, to permit those limitations to expire on schedule. All these features of a new safeguard system should be subject to international surveillance. The new system should cover all policy instruments used to restrain trade, including the so-called "voluntary" export restraints, most of which have heretofore operated outside any international framework.

It is up to each country to decide precisely how to help its people adjust. Some countries may deal with trade-impacted firms and workers within the context of their overall national industrial and manpower policies. Other countries may need to devise special programs to provide such assistance.

But all countries should be responsible internationally for maintaining effective internal adjustment, to enable them to carry out their commitments to their trading partners.

In looking to the future, the group fully recognized that a wide variety of fundamental changes had occurred in the structure of the world economy since the late 1940s. For example, Europe and Japan had moved up alongside the United States as major economic powers. As a result of all these changes, many of the rules which were developed after World War II to govern international trade no longer provided an adequate basis for doing so. Without reaffirmation of those rules which remain valid, and the creation of new rules to deal adequately with present problems, it will probably prove impossible to sustain progress toward a more liberal world trading order.

The group concluded that the major countries should move immediately to begin a deliberate effort to head off the severe risks of further slippage toward protectionism. Such an effort should focus on reassessing and reforming the rules which govern international trade, to deal with the grievances now felt by a number of countries and to provide an orderly framework to deal with the grievances which will inevitably occur in the future. In addition, new reductions of trade barriers—carried out either through multilateral negotiations, such as those scheduled to begin later this year, or by individual countries in response to their own internal problems, such as inflation—would help counter the real risk of new restrictions. The group recognized that the European Community was preoccupied with internal concerns, including the adjustment to its recent expansion of membership and efforts to broaden its areas of unity, but agreed that Europe would suffer badly from a world retreat toward protectionism and must therefore play its full role in global trade policy.

The process of adapting the GATT to present circumstances will be complex and time consuming. No early deadline is possible or even desirable. But the present trade policy vacuum must be filled by new and vigorous constructive movement or it will certainly be filled by new trade barriers. The group urges the nations of the world to undertake the necessary political commitment, at the highest level, to begin such movement at once.

Appendix B
Conference Participants

Masao Aihara, Director, International Affairs Department, Japanese Confederation of Labour.

Carl E. Beigie, Executive Director, C. D. Howe Research Institute, Canada.

C. Fred Bergsten, Senior Fellow, Brookings Institution; formerly Assistant for International Economic Affairs, National Security Council, U.S. Government.

*Meyer Bernstein, United Mine Workers; formerly Director of International Affairs, United Steelworkers of America.

*Robert Best, Finance Committee Staff, U.S. Senate.

*W. Michael Blumenthal, Chairman and President, Bendix Corporation.

Michael Clapham, Deputy Chairman, Imperial Chemical Industries, Ltd.; President, Confederation of British Industry.

Richard N. Cooper, Provost and Professor of Economics, Yale University; formerly Deputy Assistant Secretary of State for International Monetary Affairs, U.S. Government.

*Louise Armand Devaux, Director, Societe Le Nickel.

William Diebold, Senior Research Fellow, Council on Foreign Relations, New York.

Albrecht Düren, formerly Executive Secretary, German Association of Chambers of Industry and Commerce, Bonn.

*Morihisa Emori, Vice President, Mitsubishi Corporation, Tokyo.

Herbert Giersch, Professor of Economics; Director, Institute of World Economics, Kiel, West Germany.

Sidney Golt, formerly Advisor on Commercial Policy, U.K. Board of Trade, Deputy Secretary of the Department of Trade and Industry, U.K.

George H. Hildebrand, Upson Professor of Economics and Industrial Relations, Cornell University; formerly Deputy Under Secretary of Labor for International Affairs, U.S. Government.

Harry G. Johnson, Professor of Economics, London School of Economics and University of Chicago.

Kiyoshi Kojima, Professor of International Economics, Hitotsubashi University, Tokyo.

Ryutaro Komiya, Professor of Economics, University of Tokyo.

377

David Lea, Secretary of the Economic Department, Trades Union Congress, London.

*Erik Lundberg, Professor of Economics, Stockholm School of Economics.

Göran Ohlin, Professor of Economics, University of Uppsala.

*Gardner Patterson, Deputy Director-General, GATT.

Aldo Romoli, Economist, Montedison S.p.A, Milano, Italy.

Anthony M. Solomon, formerly Assistant Secretary of State for Economic Affairs, U.S. Government.

Nat Weinberg, Director of Special Projects, United Auto Workers.

Eric Wyndham-White, formerly Director-General of GATT.

---

*Not present at Maidenhead meeting, or for other reasons did not sign Maidenhead Communique.

Index

Index

"Active industrial policy," 313
Adjustment assistance, 11, 280
  for communities, 299
  concept of, 287
  costs of, 302-305
  criteria for, 288
  delivery of, 289-291
  financing of, 308
  for firms, 298-299
  international, 307-313
  in Japan, 195
  OECD Fund for, 310-313
  task force on, 285-306
  workers and, 291, 293-298
Adjustment to liberal trade policy, 30, 181
  costs of, 30
  policies of, 174
  social aspect of, 226
  task force on, 285-306
Administration, of program of economic adjustment, 300-302
AFL-CIO, 237, 238, 350, 355
  interests of, 350
  protectionist measure of, 237
Agreements, "orderly marketing," 262n.
  See also Voluntary export restraint agreements
Agricultural Adjustment Act, 240
Agricultural Guidance and Guarantee Fund (FEOGA), 313
Agriculture
  British, 203
  and international trade, 331-332
  Japanese, 184-185, 194
  technology of, 91
  U.S. advantage in, 349
Aid, government, 205
Aihara, Masao, 8, 159-170, 377
Akamatsu, Kaname, 84, 97
Alcan, Ltd., 150
Allocation, multilateral, 150
American Agricultural Economics Association, 353
American Bridge Division, of U.S. Steel Corporation, 237
American Economic Association, 353
American Iron and Steel Institute, 230, 233
America Regional Conference, ILO, 164
Andean Pact, 152
Anti-Dumping Act, Canadian, 279
Anti-dumping laws, 351, 363
Anti-pollution campaign, in Japan, 192

Antitrust laws, 143, 274
  in Japan, 187
"Arbeitsfoerderungsgesetz," 221
Armco Steel, 237
"Arrangement Regarding International Trade in Textiles," 240, 241. *See also* Textiles
Article 1, of GATT, 322, 338, 339
Article 19, of GATT, 335
  amendment of, 366
  escape clause of, 279
  modification of, 283
Article 23, of GATT, 326, 336
Article 24, of GATT, 322, 323, 339
Article 25, of GATT, 329
Article 35, of GATT, 184, 196n, 324, 328, 339
Asian Advisory Committee, ILO, 164
Asian Trade Development Corporation, 78
"Assignment problem," 65
Atlas Chemical Industries, 107
Australia, secondary industry in, 108
Austria, GNP of, 213t
Automatic Import Approval (AA), 367
Automatic Import Quota (AIQ), 367
Automotive Products Trade Act, of 1965, 289, 303
Automotive Products Trade Agreement, of 1965, 262n
Auto workers, councils of, 165
  Japanese, 167

Balanced budget, 196n
Balance of payments
  and discriminatory QRs, 317
  disequilibrium of, 22, 362
  and GATT, 325
  Japan's, 192
  U.S., 125, 359
Baldwin, Robert E., 28, 31n, 202, 355n
Ball, George, 147, 151, 152
Bank of Japan, 186, 196n
Banks, Japanese, 189
Barber, Richard J., 145
Bargaining
  balance of power, 163
  oligopolistic, 97n
Barriers
  non-tariff (NTBs), 13, 45, 181, 199, 204, 225, 339, 347-350, 362, 365, 367, 368
  reduction in, 374
  tariff, 13
  trade, 33, 108, 123

Bauxite, 78
Beigie, Carl E., 377
Belgium, GNP of, 213t
Bendix Co.
  business objectives of, 118
  market opportunities for, 119
  overseas affiliates of, 124
  product fields of, 116
  research laboratories of, 123
Bergsten, C. Fred, 4, 10, 11, 12, 13, 15n, 30n,
    239-273, 317, 341-357, 377
Berle, Adolf, 138
Bernstein, Meyer, 10, 229-238, 273, 377
Best, Robert, 377
Blumenthal, W. Michael, 4, 7, 115-125, 377
Board of Trade (BOT), British, 279
Boom, 52
Bretton Woods, financial institutions of, 321
Britain. See Great Britain
British American Tobacco Company, 166
British Dyestuffs, 105
Brookings Institution, 4
Brunner Mond, 105
Brussels Commission, 210, 223
Buildings, and free trade, 26
Bureau of Budget, Japanese, 188
Bureaucracy, 124
Bürgenstock meetings, 4
Burke-Hartke bill, 258, 341, 347, 352, 353
Burke-Hartke import quotas, 305
Businessmen, American, 363
Buy American Act, of 1933, 202, 363

Canada
  Bendix Co. in, 122 (see also Bendix Co.)
  industrial policies of, 345
  ICs in, 147
  U.S. exports to, 262n
  U.S. relations with, 286
CAP. See Common Agricultural Policy
Capital
  domestic supply of, 41
  export of, 41, 43, 109
  and free trade, 26
  international investment of, 42
  and liberal trade, 30
  obsolete, 22
Capital inflow, controls on, 62
Cartelization, 271n
  of foreign textile industries, 248
Cartels, 65, 196n, 219
  export, 273
Center for Promoting Saving, of Bank of
    Japan, 196n
Central Intelligence Agency (CIA), 139
Chamber of Commerce, 285, 286

recommendations of, 305-306
  task force of, 11
Chemical industries, 80
Chile Conference, 99n
CIA. See Central Intelligence Agency
Clapham, Michael, 7, 9, 105-112, 199-206,
    377
Clayton, Will, 321
Clean float regime, 106, 109, 110
Clearing union, 8
Coal, 78, 202
Codes, international, 169
Collective bargaining
  absent, 63
  internationally coordinated, 166
  and multinational corporations, 170
Commerce, international, 13
Commission on International Trade and In-
    vestment Policy, 149
Common Agricultural Policy, 332, 333, 349
  liberalization of, 349
Common Market, 10, 209, 210
  competition in, 218
  external tariff of, 42
Commonwealth Preference, system of, 312
Communication, 26, 159
Communities, adjustment by, 299-300
  adjustment assistance for, 289
  and trade flows, 9
Companies, multinational, 107, 112, 115-118,
    159-170
  demerits of, 160-161
  merits of, 160
  and trade unions, 159-160, 162, 163-167.
    See also Multinational corpora-
    tions
Comparative advantage, 83, 85f
Compensation, 205, 317
Competition
  foreign, 61, 233
  import, 52, 312
  international, 69, 343
  from low-wage countries, 58
  "low-wage foreign," 230
  profit rates and, 55f
  and trade-oriented foreign direct invest-
    ment, 82
  U.S., 355
  Z-competition, 54
Computer industries, foreign investment in,
    368
Concessions
  from Japan, 362
  restrictions on, 150
  sought by ICs, 142
  tariff, 321, 327, 337

trade, 200
U.S. tariff, 287
Conferees, at Maidenhead Meeting, 377-378
Congestion, 23
Congress, U.S.
  and Article 19, 281
  VERs and, 258
Connally, John, 344
Constitution, U.S., 331
Consumer goods, 131
Consumers, 53
  Japanese, 134
  sovereignty of, 71
Consumers Union, 268n
Controls
  capital, 109, 121
  export, 353
  and foreign investment, 177-178
  price, 50
  trade, history of, 264n
  wage, 50
  wage-price, 285
Cooper, Richard N., 4, 14, 19-31, 78, 318, 377
Cooperation, economic, 348
Corporations, 155n
  international (ICs), 137-140, 154n
    abuses of, 149, 152
    and LDCs, 141
    power of, 147
    speculation by, 146
    U.S.-based, 145
  multinational (MNCs), 43, 75, 88, 89-90,
    154n. See also Enterprises
Cost-push theory, of inflation, 67
Costs
  comparative, 87t
  labor, 121-123
  zero opportunity, 49
Cotton textiles, VERs for, 242t. See also
  Textiles
Council of economic advisers, German, 226
Council of International Chamber of Com-
  merce (ICC), 140
Council on International Economic Policy,
  301
Council of Ministers, of EC, 219, 220, 222
  unanimity rule of, 223
Countervailing duty laws, 351
Countries
  Arab, 239
  capital-exporting, 164
  exporting, 259. See also Less developed
    countries (LDCs)
Credit, public procurement and, 178-179
Currency
  devaluation of, 61

Japanese, 194. See also specific currency
Customs Tariff Act, Canadian, 279
Customs Tariff Council, Japanese, 279
Cyclical model, of economic policy, 71
Czechoslovakia, and GATT, 337

Dairy products, VERs for, 242t
Debt, long-term, 23
Decision making, 118, 301
  in Bendix Co., 121. See also Policies
Decomposition, fallacy of, 39
Demand, expansion of, 49, 50, 69
Denmark, GNP of, 213t
Department of Defense, 300
Department of Labor, 303, 304
Depreciation, free, 200
Depression, Great, 49, 50
Deutschmark
  appreciation of, 61
  undervaluation of, 30
  upward floating of, 53, 55
Devaluation, 62
  overall, 50
Devaux, Louise Armand, 377
Developing countries, 330
  and American foreign manufacturing in-
    vestment, 82
  and GATT, 337
  industrial development in, 97n
  Japanese investment in, 77
  market imperfections in, 27
  multinational companies in, 309
  tariff preferences for, 260
  technology transfer to, 91. See also Less
    developed countries
Development, international, 309-310
Diebold, William, 4, 377
Diet, Japanese, 187, 188
Dillon Round, of trade negotiations, 253
Dirksen, Sen. Everett, 235
DISC, 7, 120
Discrimination, 321
  against foreign supplies, 206
Disequilibrium, of balance of payments, 22,
  362. See also Balance of payments
Disruption, market, 278
Distributional effects, of free trade, 20-21
D-Mark. See Deutschmark
Dollar
  depreciation of, 360
  devaluation of, 361
  exchange rate for, 343
  inconvertibility of, 359
  overvaluation of, 42
Dollar-gold myth, 361
Double-taxation, 41, 42

Dumping practices, 210, 279, 351, 363
Du Pont de Nemours, E.I., 105
Düren, Albrecht, 10, 31n, 209-227, 315, 377

EC. *See* European Community
Economic Planning Agency, Japanese, 188
Economics, welfare, 21, 45n
Economic system, international, 352, 359
Economies, of scale, 29
Economists, development, 309
Economy
  American, dualistic structure
    of, 81, 88, 90
  Common Market, 210
  competitive market, 20
  exchange, 19
  international, 159
  U.S., 350
ECOSOC. *See* United Nations, Economic
  and Social Council
Education, 35
EEC. *See* European Economic Community
EFTA. *See* European Free Trade Area
Eligibility, for trade adjustment assistance,
  287-289
Emori, Morihisa, 7, 127-135, 377
Employment
  change in structure of, 56
  and free trade, 49, 61
  full, 22, 62, 350
  non-union, 68
  and price stability, 6, 65
  and Z-competition, 57
Employment-protection argument, 49
Energy crisis, 352-353
Engineering, systems, 134
Enterprises, 155n
  government intervention in, 199 (*see also*
    Intervention)
  integration of, 133
  multinational, 3, 77, 80, 99n (*see also* Mul-
    tinational corporations)
  public, 179-180
  semi-public, 179-180
  Soviet-bloc, 151
Equilibrium, international monetary, 44
Equilibrium analysis, general, 49
Europe
  industrial policies of, 345
  as major economic power, 376
  U.S. relations with, 286
European Common Market, 29
  formation of, 53
European Community (EC), 12, 27, 181, 209
  adjustment aids of, 220
  adjustment in, 223-227

  Mediterranean policy of, 351
  tariff reductions within, 54
European Economic Community (EEC), 209
  agricultural policy of, 332
  Commission to the Council of Ministers,
    227n
  common commercial policy of, 337
  exports of, 211
  and less developed countries, 217t
  and policy of restraint, 176
  summit in Paris, 224
EEC Commission, 173
European Free Trade Area (EFTA), 176,
  209, 210, 375
  and EEC, 323
  exports of, 211
European Investment Bank, 221
Exchange rates, 23
  changes in, 108, 121
  equilibrium, 343
  flexibility of, 196n, 344
  meetings on, 4
Export-Import Permits Act, Canadian, 279
Exports
  of EEC countries, 211
  farm, 348
  foreign, 109-110
  German, 214
  interdiction of QRs on, 324, 325
  Japanese, 129, 130t
  job, 162
  less-developed-country, 39
  promotion of, 178
  restrained, 239
  steel, 230, 231, 249t. *See also* Voluntary
    export restraint agreements

Fair Labour Standards, 148
Fair Trade Commission, Japanese, 188
Families, 25
Farbenindustrie, I.G., 105, 106
Fertilizers, Japanese, 191
Financing, government, 190
Finland, GNP of, 213t
Firms
  adjustment by, 298-299
  adjustment assistance for, 288
  European, 90
  Japanese, 90
  and trade flows, 9
  unit labor costs of, 63
  and workers, 7-8
  and Z-competition, 55-56. *See also* Com-
    panies; Enterprises
Fiscal policy, and unemployment, 22
Flexibility, principles of, 226-227

Floating rates, policy of, 62
Ford, Henry, 142
Ford Foundation, 4
Ford Motor Co., 99n
Foreigners, taxing, 27
Foreign investments, rise in, 159
Foreign plants, production techniques in, 110
Foreign trade, 19. *See also* International
    trade; Trade
France
    business formation in, 216t-217t
    exports of, 219
    GNP of, 213t
    industrial policy of, 175
    manufacturing industries of, 214
Free trade, 5, 20, 33
    classical case for, 37
    distributional effects of, 20
    and Japan, 194
    orthodox theory of, 44, 47n
French Economic and Social Fund, 202
Friedman, Milton, 63
Fringe benefits, for workers, 292

Galbraith, John Kenneth, 54
Gas, 87
GATT. *See* General Agreement on Tariffs
    and Trade
General Agreement on Tariffs and Trade
    (GATT), 3, 153, 156n, 176, 316
    accession to, 327-328
    adapting, 376
    advantage of, 328
    and agriculture, 331-332
    Article 1 of, 322, 338, 339
    Article 19 of, 11, 254, 258, 275, 277, 279,
        280, 283, 335, 366
    Article 23 of, 326, 336
    Article 24 of, 322, 323, 339
    Article 25 of, 329
    Article 29 of, 148
    Article 35 of, 184, 196n, 324, 328, 339
    and balance of payments, 325
    concessions through, 363
    Director General of, 336
    and import restrictions, 11
    and Japan, 184
    membership in, 330-331
    modification of, 277-278
    renegotiation of, 339
    role of, 321
    and steel industry program, 135
    and VERs, 274
Generalized Tariff Preference Scheme,
    OECD, 309

General trading companies, Japan's,
    127-130t, 134, 166
Genkyoku, 187-188
Germany, 27
    business formation in, 215t
    distribution of income in, 28
    floating of the D-Mark, 53, 55
    GNP of, 213t
Giersch, Herbert, 6, 13, 49-59, 61, 62, 64, 65,
       66, 67, 69, 71, 377
    recommendations of, 68
GNP. *See* Gross National Product
Gold, 360
Golt, Sidney, 12, 315-318, 377
Good behavior, code of, 144
Goods, 19
Governments
    ad hoc measures of, 180
    ICs and, 146
    intervention of, 199
    Japanese, 183, 185
    and multinational corporations, 169-170
    national, 8
    pressure on, 199
    procurement policies of, 375
    purposes of, 37
Great Britain, 27
    in EC, 219
    GNP of, 59, 213t
Great Depression, 49, 50
Gresham's law, 142
Gross National Product (GNP)
    and competition, 55f
    of EEC, 212-213
    of EF TA, 212-213
    of Great Britain, 213t
    Italy's, 213t
    Japan's, 129, 131
    tendencies of, 59
"Group of Ten," 152
Growth
    and industrial reorganization, 214-217
    and stability, 277
Guidelines
    for controlling multinational companies,
       168
    for foreign investment, 169
    "for International Investment," 154
Gyokai, 189

Hamada, Koichi, 95n
Hartke, Sen. Vance, 232, 235
Havana Charter, 148, 156n, 322
Heckscher-Ohlin theorem, 80, 82, 83
Heckscher-Ohlin-Samuelson theorem, 89
Heckscher-Ohlin trade model, 41

Hildebrand, George, 6, 61-64, 377
Hodgson, James D., 297
Hoechst pharmaceutical co., 166
Home countries, regulation by, 143
Homeowners Assistance Program, 297
Hong Kong
    industrialization in, 79
    and VERs, 255, 284
Host countries, 139, 140, 145
Housing, 134
Housing and Urban Development, Depart-
    ment of, 297
HUD. See Housing and Urban Development
Hull, Cordell, 321
Human Relations Committee, 230
Hymer, Stephen, 80, 81, 89-90

ICFTU, 160, 163, 164
    affiliates of, 167
    and fair labor standards, 165
    MNCs Conference of, 167
ICI. See Imperial Chemical Industries
ICs. See International Corporations
IDI, in France, 203
IMF. See International Metalworkers' Fed-
    eration; International Monetary Fund
Immigration, 195, 196
Imperial chemical industries (ICI), 105-112
    foreign interests of, 113t
    in Indonesia, 108
    investment policy of, 107
    manufacturing development of, 106
    multinationality of, 11
Import Quotas (IQs), 367
    in Japan, 190
Imports, 10-11
    adjustment assistance, 11
    development assistance for, 77
    foreign, 109-110
    interdiction of QRs on, 324-325
    iron ore, 231
    Japanese, 130t, 185, 367
    steel, 230, 231, 249t
    temporary limits on, 375
    into United States, 125
    and VERs, 242t
    workers displaced by, 295-296
Incentives
    artificial, 13
    export, 120
    and multinational corporations, 124
Income, distribution of, 20
India
    exports to, 109
    ICI in, 109
Individualism, 45n
Indonesia, investing in, 108

Industrialization, Japanese, 128, 185-187
Industrial policy, 179
    "active," 313
    French, 175
    Japanese, 187-196
    reversibility of, 181
    rise of, 180
Industrial Reorganization Corporation,
    British, 203
Industry, 249t
    automobile, 117
    competitiveness of, 201
    computer, 368
    declining, 175, 176
    disadvantaged, 89
    European steel, 234
    foreign investment of, 81
    government intervention in, 199
    hit by imports, 237
    import-competing, 23, 28
    infant, 25, 26, 33, 38
    Japanese, 133, 191-192
    Japanese coal, 202
    machinery, 80
    monopsonistic, 265
    oil, 247, 248
    oligopolistic, 5, 75, 81, 82, 245
    price competitive, 75
    state-owned, 179
    steel, 229, 230
    "technological spearhead," 9
    textile, 247, 248 (see also Textiles)
    U.S., 325
Industry acts, in Japan, 190
Infant-industry argument for temporary pro-
    tection, 25, 26, 33, 38
Inflation, 13
    definition of, 50
    demand-pull, 67
    fighting, 352
    and monopoly, 63
    price, 51
    rapid, 373
    tariffs and, 341
    and unemployment, 285, 345
    in U.S., 64
Information
    on adjustment assistance, 290
    labor market, 64
Injury, determination of, 280
Insecurity, Japanese, 183-184
Intercontinental Hotels, 166
Interest rates, 64
Internal Revenue Code, U.S., 144
International Corporations (ICs), 137-140,
    154n
    abuses of, 149, 152

and LDCs, 141
power of, 147
speculation by, 146
U.S.-based, 145
International Fair Labor Standards, 148
International Federation of Chemical and
General Workers' Unions, 165-166
International Federation of Commercial,
Clerical and Technical Employees,
(FIET), 166
International Labor Organization (ILO), 148,
149, 152, 153
General Convention of, 164
on ICs, 154
International Metalworkers' Federation
(IMF), 153, 165, 229
Central Committee of, 234
Congress of, 152
International Monetary Fund, 150, 153, 361,
362
collapse of, 361
and GATT, 326
provisions of, 322
International payments, equilibrium in, 22-23
International Telephone and Telegraph
(ITT), 139
International trade, 34, 44, 322, 323, 333
classical theory of, 39
liberal regime of, 39
International Trade Organization, 148
International Transport Workers' Federation, 165
International Union of Feed and Allied
Workers' Associations, 166
Intervention, 37, 44
government, 63, 203-204
specific measures of, 201-203
of Japanese government, 190-191
regional, 205 (see also Regional policies)
state, 3, 9
Investment
American type of, 75
anti-trade-oriented, 91
direct, 83-86, 195
foreign, location for, 110
foreign direct, 75, 77
anti-trade-oriented, 87-88
Japanese, 77-82
oligopolistic, 77
trade-oriented, 76-82, 86
inward, 206
inward direct, 195-196
Japanese foreign, 102-104
Japanese type, 75
labor-oriented, 76
market-oriented, 76
natural-resource-oriented, 76

trade-barrier-induced, 77
trade-destroying, 6
Investment climate, 142
Iron ore, 78
imports of, 231
Isolationism, economic, 161
Italy
GNP of, 213t
public corporations in, 179
ITO Charter, 326
ITT. See International Telephone and Tele-
graph

Japan, 27, 352
antitrust laws of, 273
barriers to imports, 352
consumer markets of, 134
discrimination against, 257
distribution of income in, 28
foreign direct investment of, 77-82
foreign economic policy of, 193-194
foreign trade of, 7
and GATT, 318, 328
general trading companies in, 127, 130t,
134
genkyoku of, 187-188
GNP of, 59, 129, 131
gyokai in, 189
import restrictions on, 256
industrial policies of, 345
industry in, 133, 191-192
isolation policy of, 196n
"Japan, Inc.," 8
land reform in, 186
as major economic power, 376
manufacturing in, 78-79, 128
payment deficit of, 346
petroleum imports of, 185
postwar, 183-184, 187-192, 269n-270n
and private investment abroad, 102-104t
public opinion in, 192
restrictive policy of, 195
"technological spearhead" industries in,
194
trade outside, 134
and U.S., 286, 325, 359, 361
VERs in, 245, 247, 255, 262n
zaikai in, 189
Japan Development Bank, 190, 193
Japan Export Import Bank, 190
Jobs, loss of, 311. See also Unemployment
Johnson, Harry G., 5, 35-47, 67-69, 71, 95n,
318, 377
Johnson, Pres. Lyndon B., 236, 361
Joint ventures, 92
in Japan, 190
Jurong Industrial Estate, Singapore, 79

Justice, social, 163

Kaoshiung, Taiwan, 79
Kennedy, Pres. John F., 361
Kennedy Round, of tariff negotiations, 3, 13, 14, 45, 53, 253, 316, 321, 327, 333, 342, 345, 346, 349, 367
  and Japan, 366
  selling price in, 334
Keynesian economics, 49, 61, 63
Kissinger, Henry A., 3
Knowledge
  specialized, 134
  transfer of, 43. See also Information
Kojima, Kiyoshi, 13, 75-104, 354, 365-369, 377
Komiya, Ryutaro, 5, 6, 8, 11, 12, 33-34, 65-66, 273-275, 283-284, 316, 359-363, 377
Korea
  industrialization in, 79
  textile industry in, 251
  and VERs, 245, 255
Korean War, 229

Labor, 20
  cheap, 141, 149
  costs of, 121-123
  and creation of trade, 211
  and free trade, 26, 225
  good standards for, 144
  international, 89, 143
  international division of, 76, 94
  monopoly of, 51
  organized American, 28
  reliance on, 58
  scarcity value of, 43, 46n
  standard of living for, 59. See also Employment; Trade unions
Laborers, 75. See also Workers
Labor unions, multinational firms and, 7. See also Trade unions; United Steelworkers of America
Land reform, in Japan, 186
Law, international, 151, 169
  violation of, 139
Layoffs, and import increases, 302
LDCs. See Less developed countries
Lea, David, 11, 307-313, 378
League of Nations, 239
Leisure, 71
  alternative of, 68
Leontief Paradox, 28
Less developed countries (LDCs), 155n
  competition from, 58
  and EEC, 217
  economic health of, 356

  export incentive of, 120
  and international corporations, 141
  pressures on, 150
Lewis, Ben, 138
Liberalism, in prewar Japan, 186
Liberalization, trade, 5, 175
  in Europe, 29
  import, 352
  Japanese policy of, 192
  postwar, 14
  reciprocal, 348
  role of, 309-310
  world, 373
"Liberalization war," 365
Licensing, for foreign investment, 144
Location, for foreign investment, 110
Lockheed Tristar project, 203
Long-Term Arrangement (LTA), 251
  on cotton textiles, 240, 257
Lundberg, Erik, 378
Luxemburg, GNP of, 213t

Machinery, labor-saving, 58
Machinery industries, 80
Macroeconomic theory, 75
Magee, Stephen P., 250
"Maidenhead Communique," 4, 13, 373-376
Management, macroeconomic, 22
Manpower, 175, 286
Manufacturing, Japanese, 78-79, 128
Mark, appreciation of, 61
  floating of, 53, 55
  undervaluation of, 30
Market
  capital, 27
  distortions of, 23-24
  factor, 27, 51, 61, 62
  foreign exchange, 27
  goods, 51
  labor, 27
  oligopolistic, 66, 116, 218
  penetration of, 251
  product, monopoly in, 61, 62
  specific commodity, 27
  world, 160
Marketing
  internationalization of, 77, 93
  orderly, 341
Massey-Ferguson, Ltd., 147
Materialism, 45n
MCs. See Multinational corporations
Meat, VERs for, 242t, 243, 244, 255, 257
Meat Import Act, 258
Memorandum Industriepolitik, 221
Mercantilism, 37
Mergers, 65
Metal Trades Committee, ILO, 164

Mexico
  Bendix Co. in, 122
  export incentives of, 120
MFN. *See* Most-favored nations
Mill, John Stuart, 39
Mills bill, 238, 256, 258, 342
  Byrnes basket provision of, 269n
Miners, 232, 238
Ministry of Finance, Japanese, 188
Ministry of Industry and International Trade
    (MITI), Japanese, 187, 188, 190, 196n
  Industrial Structure Council of, 366
  report of, 95n
  and VERS, 247
Mintz, Ilse, 250
MITI. *See* Ministry of Industry and International Trade
MNCs. *See* Companies, multinational
Mobile homes, 117
Modernization, in Japan, 185-187
Monetary policy, and unemployment, 22
Monetary system
  dollar-centered, 343
  international, 151, 343, 352
Monopolies, 51
  control of, 94
  employment-reducing effects of, 71
  government ownership of, 201-203
  and inflation, 52
  labor, 68
  and monopsony, 67
Monopoly power, 38
  "international," 40
  and optimum tariff argument, 40
Monopsony power, 21, 51
Most-favored nations
  and Article 19, 283
  exception to, 322
  principle of, 253
  rule for, 351
Multinational corporations, 43, 75, 88, 89-90,
    154n
  oligopolistic nature of, 91
Myrdal, Gunnar, 156n

National action, 143
National industrial policies, 8. *See also* Industrial policy
Nationalism, 180
  economic, 178
Nation-states, and ICs, 147-148
Natural resources, 38
  development of, 92
  and international corporations, 141
Negotiations, 332-336
  international, 341
  reciprocal, 346

for tariff concessions, 321
  trade, 317. *See also* Dillon Round; Kennedy Round; Tokyo Round
NEP. *See* New Economic Policy
Netherlands, GNP of, 213
New Economic Policy, Pres. Nixon's, 132,
    354
New Zealand, ICI in, 109
Nixon, Pres. Richard M., 255, 258, 359, 361
  administration of, 146, 253, 342
  NEP of, 132, 354
  Nixon shocks, 256
Nobel Industries, 105
Nondiscrimination, rule of, 322
Non-tariff barriers (NTBs), 45
  and reciprocity, 347-350
  removal of, 225
Norway, GNP of, 213t
NTBs. *See* Non-tariff barriers

Objectives, national economic, 75
Oceanography, 134
OECD. *See* Organization for Economic
  Cooperation and Development
Office of Economic Assistance, DOD, 295,
    300
Office of Emergency Preparedness, 245
Ohlin, Göran, 8, 173-182, 378
Oil, 14, 78
Oil companies, 115
Oil crisis, 40
Oligopoly, 24, 65
  international, 145
  in steel industries, 249
  world, 8
OPEC. *See* Organization of Petroleum Exporting Countries
Organization for Economic Cooperation and
    Development (OECD), 11, 164, 173,
    181n
  adjustment assistance fund of, 310-313
  High Level Trade Group of, 307
  and Rey Report, 351
  Trade Union Advisory Committee
    (TUAC) to, 307
Organization of Petroleum Exporting Countries (OPEC), 28, 142, 239
Ottawa preferences, 322
Output, maximization of, 46n
Overspecialization, 25

Parity changes, 201
Patterson, Gardner, 378
Payments, international, 22-23, 44. *See also*
  Balance of payments
Petroleum, VERs for, 242t. *See also* Oil
Planification, 210

Policies
    "active industrial," 313
    adjustment, 174 (*see also* Adjustment assistance)
    anti-monopoly, 29
    anti-pollution, 29
    balance-of-payments, 313
    direct investment, 89-95
    expansionary, 71
    general credit, 200
    industrial, 173, 179, 180, 181, 187-196
    manpower, 286
    mercantilist, 45n
    national economic, 210
    protectionist, 283
    regional, 24, 29, 176
    trade, 35, 89, 95, 344, 365. *See also* Protectionism; Trade policy
Policy making, Japanese, 189
Pollution, 23, 134
    by-production of, 46n
Portugal, GNP of, 213t
Poverty, Japanese, 183
Power politics, 361
Prices
    agricultural, 363
    agricultural support, 351
    international, 90
    labor and, 63
    and social costs, 21-25
    stability of, 61
Privileges, special, 142
Procurement, public, 206
Production, 19
    evolution of, 35
    expansion of, 84
    and free trade, 58
    international, 81
    internationalization of, 77, 93
Product mix, 58
Products, new, 88
Profit, nature of, 66
Profitabilities
    comparative, 75
    comparative investment, 82-89
Profit rates, 85
    comparative, 87, 88
Profits, maximization of, 66
Profit sharing, 57
Projects, government intervention in, 199.
    See also Intervention
Prosperity, 52
Protection
    concept of, 44
    covert, 180
    infant-industry, 36, 39
    orthodox theory of, 36-40

    policy of, 26
    by tariffs, 33
Protectionism, 75, 321, 353, 376
    agricultural, 8
    Japanese, 191
    new, 173-174
    in U.S., 149
    of U.S. steel industry, 10
Protectionist pressures, 3, 14
Protocol of Provisional Application, for
    GATT, 331
Public opinion, in Japan, 192

QRs. *See* Quantitative import restrictions
Quantitative import restrictions (QRs), 184,
    211, 220, 239, 242
    discriminatory use of, 257
    economic effects of, 252f
    GATT prohibition of, 325
    interdiction of, 324-325
    relative effectiveness of, 241-245
    systematic use of, 324
    VERs and, 241, 253, 255-258
Quotas
    Burke-Hartke, 305
    discriminatory, 242
    steel, 235, 238
    U.S., 240
Quota systems, Japanese, 197n

Raw materials, Japan's imports of, 132
    and MNCs, 163
R&D. *See* Research and Development
Recession
    national, 21
    normal, 54
    steel, 235
Reciprocal Trade Agreements Act, 328
    extension of, 253
Reciprocity, 13, 206
    definition of, 354
    and NTBs, 365
    problem of, 347-350
    in tariff negotiations, 344
Refrigerator industry, French, 218
Regional policies, 176, 200, 205, 374
    for EC, 222
Regulation, international, 151
Reorganization, industrial, 214-217
Research and Development
    in Bendix Co., 123-124
    reliance on, 58
Resources, utilization of, 49, 51
Restraints, VER, 264n
Restrictionist trend, in U.S., 351
Restrictions, import, 253, 285
    economic effects of, 246f

import, discriminatory imposition of, 284
non-discriminatory, 326
U.S. trade, 344
Retaliation, 317, 347
Reuther, Victor, 234
Revenue, "tariff-equivalent," 251
Rey, M. Jean, 307
Rey report, 173, 260, 351
Ricardian theory, 83
Risks, social, 24, 25
Rolls Royce Co., 203
Rome Treaty, 209, 219, 220, 225, 335
safeguard clauses of, 218
Romoli, Aldo, 378
Rybczinski theorem, 82

Safeguard clause, 315, 335
Safeguards
adjustment programs, 280
import, 10
international, 277
in trade negotiations, 315
St. Gobain, strikes at, 166
Sanctions, 205, 329-330
Sato, Prime Min. Eisaku, 255
Savers' organizations, 53
Scientific instrument industries, 80
SDRs. See Special Drawing Rights
Secretariats, international trade, 164
Security, job, 162
Selective Employment Payments Act, 202
Selective Employment Tax, 202
Senate Finance Committee, 3, 235, 292
Services, 19
Sherman Antitrust Act, 249, 273
Shipbuilding, Japanese, 191-192
Shoes, 334
Small Business Administrations, 300
Smith, Adam, 137, 138
Smithsonian Agreement, 132, 343-344
and yen, 194
Social action, 25
Social costs, 20
of congestion, 23
market prices and, 21-25
of pollution, 23
Social Fund, of EC, 221, 224
Socialists-Communists, 152
Social Security system, 294, 304
Solomon, Anthony M., 10, 263n, 270n,
277-281, 283, 317, 378
Spain, and VERs, 255
Special drawing rights (SDRs), to LDCs, 150,
151
Specialization
international, 94
overspecialization, 25

trade and, 62
undue, 25
Stagflation, 51
model of, 6. See also Inflation
Standards
fair labor, 163, 165, 310
power of, 37
world, 112
Steel
international trade in, 249
prices of, 267n
protection of, 253
U.S., 240
VERs for, 242t, 255
Stockholm Convention, 323, 335
Stockpiling, by U.S. steel users, 248
Stoleru, Lionel G., 175
Strikes, steel, 229, 230
Studebaker Co., 295
Subsidies
government, 29
in Japan, 190
need for, 179
regional, 201
rules on, 327
Subsidization
of foreign investment, 41
policy of, 26, 33, 34
Subventions, government, 29
Sugar
QRs on, 250
VERs for, 242t
Sugar quotas, 46n
Supplementary Chemicals Agreement, to
Kennedy Round, 355
Surcharges, import, 354
Surpluses
agricultural, 46n
balance-of-payments, 37
Sweden
foreign investment of, 169
GNP of, 213t
and ICs, 155n
Switzerland, GNP of, 213t
Synthetic textiles, VERs for, 242t

Taiwan
Bendix Co. in, 122
textile industry in, 251
and VERs, 245, 255
Tariff Board Act, Canadian, 279
Tariff Commission, U.S., 174, 237, 279, 287
Tariffs, 44, 203, 239
EEC, 212
intra-area, 366
Japanese, 361
lowering of, 33

optimum, 5, 27, 38
reduction of, 367
as trade barrier, 315, 317
Task Force, of U.S. Chamber of Commerce,
11
Taxation, 119-121
indirect, 200
and ICs, 146
Tax incentives, in Japan, 190, 193
Tax policies, national, 110
Tax rate, 120
national, 7
Technological gap, 80
Technology, 35
changes in, 29
and foreign investment, 111
high, 176-177
Japanese, 194
software, 134
transfer of, 91, 92, 98
Techno-structure, 54
Terms-of-trade argument, 38
Textile Agreement, U.S.-Japan, 363
Textile industry, Japanese, 79
Textiles, 334
GATT agreement on, 325
LTA on, 240, 257
protection of, 253
VERs for, 242t, 243, 255
Textiles Arrangement, 240, 257, 325
Thailand, exports of, 78
Tickets, VER, 248
Tokugawa Shogunate, 186
Tokyo Round, of trade negotiations, 352
Trade
agricultural, 332, 349
barriers to, 123
enlarged, 174
farm, 355
free, 5, 6, 20, 33
classical case for, 37
distributional effects of, 20
and Japan, 194
orthodox theory of, 44, 47n (see also
Liberalization)
horizontal, 94
international, 34, 44, 322, 323, 333
interventions in, 37
liberal, 5, 20, 21, 30
non-tariff barriers to, 45
orthodox theory of, 36-40
power liberalization of, 53
restrictions on, 24 (see also Voluntary export restraint agreements)
world, 160
Trade balance, appropriate, 346
steel, 249t
U.S., 345

Trade Expansion Act, of 1962, 11, 174, 232,
237, 253, 287, 303, 350
Trade flows, 24
Trade laws, reciprocal, 229
Trade policy, 4
vs. direct investment policy, 89-95
international, 93, 177
for Japan, 192-196
problems of, 12
protectionist, 35
restrictive, 24, 35
U.S., 3, 64, 343, 348
and VERs, 252
Trade Reform Act, of 1973, 258, 341
Trade Reform Act, of 1974, 11, 258, 259, 260,
261, 263n
Trade theory, 4, 5
international, 89, 94
Trade unions, 63, 65
Asian, 166
cooperation among, 8
countermeasures of, 167
and liberal trade, 310
and MNCs, 159-160, 162, 163-167
Trade Union Advisory Committee (TUAC),
to OECD, 312
Trade Union Congress (TUC), British, 307
Trade wars, 161
Trading companies, Japanese, 127, 130t, 134,
166
Trading with Enemy Act, 143
Trading Firms' Presidents Club, 129
Training
industrial, 200
manpower, 286
Transfer, industry, 91
technology, 91, 92, 98
Transportation, 26, 159
Transportation industries, 80
Treaty of Rome, 55, 176, 323

UAW. See United Auto Workers
UNCTAD, 152, 153, 331, 337, 338, 340
Underemployment, 49
and inflation, 52
Unemployment, 50, 61, 63, 285, 374
and EEC, 220
and free trade, 65
insurance benefits for, 303
U.S., 359. See also Employment; Work-
ers
Unionization, 68
Unions, 143
multinational, 167-169, 170. See also
Trade unions
United Alkali, 105
United Auto Workers (UAW), 143, 149, 166,
235

United Nations, 152, 239, 321
  Economic and Social Council (ECOSOC)
    of, 152, 153
United States
  balance-of-payments difficulties of, 80
  foreign economic policy of, 93, 359
  GNP of, 59
  imports into, 125
  import restriction in, 253
  inflation in, 64
  internal politics of, 352
  international monetary actions of, 359-361
  Japanese trade relations with, 361
  market of, 27
  monopoly power of, 28, 40
  monopsony power of, 21
  negotiating position of, 334
  safeguard mechanism for, 281
  tax incentive of, 7
  trade policy of, 3, 64, 343, 348
  trade surplus of, 231
  unemployment in, 63-64
U.S. Steel Corporation, 232
United Steelworkers of America, 10, 229-238
Utility, maximization of, 46n
Utilization, resource, 49, 51

Vernon, Raymond, 80, 96n, 140, 154
VERs. *See* Voluntary export restraint
    agreements
Vietnam War, 343
Voluntary export restraint agreements
    (VERs), 10, 317, 325
  and antitrust laws, 273-274
  benefits of, 259, 262n
  dangerousness of, 318
  definition of, 273
  distributional effects of, 259
  economic effects of, 252f
  in Japan, 266n
  in Maidenhead Communique, 375
  meat, 255, 257
  origin of, 261n
  vs. QRs, 255-258, 263n
  relative effectiveness of, 241-245
  on sales to U.S., 240
  steel, 240, 249, 255, 269
  textile, 255, 271n
  trade policy effects of, 252-255
  types of, 241
Voluntary Restraint Agreement (VRA), 236,
    237
VRA. *See* Voluntary Restraint Agreement

Wages
  of American workers, 350
  Canadian, 166
  controls on, 50
  and import competition, 56
  liberal trade and, 29
  minimum, 64
  monopoly effects on, 69
  real, 56, 57
Wall Street Journal, 233
Walsh-Healy Act, 238
Washington Post, 233
Ways and Means Committee, House, 292
WCL, affiliates of, 167
Weiderhemmer, Robert, 233
Weinberg, Nat, 7, 8, 137-157, 378
Welfare economics, 21, 45n
Workers, 30
  adjustment by, 293-298
  American, 350
  choice of, 56
  compensation benefits for, 291-293
  and forms, 7-8
  fringe benefits for, 292
  imports and, 288
  laying off of, 291
  and multinational corporations, 161-163
  trade-dislocated, 296
  and trade flows, 9
  trade impacted, 293, 298
  world problems of, 167
World Automotive Conference, in Turin, 165
Wyndham-White, Eric, 11, 12, 13, 263n, 283,
    321-340, 365, 378

X-efficiency
  concept of, 36
  of market system, 51

Yen
  appreciation of, 360
  exchange rate for, 194
  underevaluation of, 30
Youth, unemployment of, 64

Zaibatsu, 128, 133, 186, 187
Zaikai, 189
Z-competition, 54, 55, 56, 57, 65

About the Editor and Contributors

C. Fred Bergsten is a Senior Fellow at the Brookings Institution, and was formerly Assistant for International Economic Affairs to the Assistant to the President for National Security Affairs.

Richard N. Cooper is Professor of Economics and former Provost at Yale University, and was formerly Deputy Assistant Secretary of State for International Monetary Affairs.

Harry G. Johnson is Professor of Economics at the University of Chicago.

Herbert Giersch is Professor of Economics and Director of the Institute for World Economics at the University of Kiel in West Germany.

Kiyoshi Kojima is Professor of Economics at Hitotsubashi University in Tokyo.

Michael Clapham is Vice Chairman of Imperial Chemical Industries and former President of the Confederation of British Industry.

W. Michael Blumenthal is Chairman of the Bendix Corporation and former Deputy Assistant Secretary of State for Economic Affairs.

Morihisa Emori was Vice President of the Mitsubishi Corporation in Tokyo.

Nat Weinberg was Director of Special Projects and Economic Analysis for the United Auto Workers

Masao Aihara is Director of the International Affairs Bureau of the Japanese Confederation of Labor (DOMEI).

Göran Ohlin is professor of Economics at the University of Uppsala in Sweden.

Ryutaro Komiya is Professor of Economics at the University of Tokyo.

Albrecht Düren was Chairman of the Institute of the German Federation of Industries.

Meyer Bernstein was Director of International Affairs for the United Steelworkers of America.

Anthony M. Solomon was President of the International Investment Corporation for Yugoslavia and Assistant Secretary of State for Economic Affairs.

David Lea is Secretary of the Economic Department of the British Trades Union Congress in London.

Eric Wyndham-White was Director-General of the GATT from 1947 to 1967.